TANGLED UP IN BLUE

TANGLED UP IN BLUE

THE RISE AND FALL OF
RANGERS FC

BY STEPHEN O'DONNELL

First published by Pitch Publishing, 2019

Pitch Publishing
A2 Yeoman Gate
Yeoman Way
Worthing
Sussex
BN13 3QZ
www.pitchpublishing.co.uk
info@pitchpublishing.co.uk

A CIP catalogue record is available for this book
from the British Library.

ISBN 978-1-78531-509-1

Typesetting and origination by Pitch Publishing

Printed and bound in the UK by TJ International Ltd

Contents

Acknowledgements

The author would like to thank the following people for their help in the writing of this book: Douglas Beattie, Alan Bissett, Dr Joe Bradley, Elizabeth Clark, Mark Daly, Gerry Dunbar, Alex Gordon, Sandy Jamieson, David Low, Joe McHugh, Pat McVey, Katherine Midgley, Professor Patrick Reilly RIP, Emily Rudge, Brendan Sweeney and Pat Woods.

PART ONE

RISE: RELIGIOUS BIGOTRY

Sine ira et studio, Tacitus

1

THE GLASGOW STRANGERS

T HIS is not a fairy story. Of the four teenagers who founded Rangers Football Club, following meetings and conversations in what is now Kelvingrove Park in the west end of Glasgow in March 1872, one was drowned, another declared insane, yet another was an accused fraudster, a bigamist and a 'certified imbecile', who lived out his days in a poorhouse, while the fourth was comparatively lucky – he died a lonely old man.

These boys, described with characteristic bombast by Bill Struth, the club's severe, authoritarian manager from 1920 until 1954, as 'The Gallant Pioneers', were looking to add the game of association football to their list of other vigorous pastimes, such as rowing, athletics and, since these lads were from the Gaelic stronghold of Argyll, shinty.

In many ways Peter Campbell, William McBeath and brothers Moses and Peter McNeil were just an ordinary group of young friends, recently arrived into the city of Glasgow from the area around the Gare Loch, an inlet in the Firth of Clyde, 30 miles up the coast from their adopted home. Living mostly in crammed households, with elder siblings rather than parents, they were from unexceptional, lower-middle-class backgrounds and held ordinary, white collar occupations. But, fired up with what youth imparts, they were also upwardly mobile and ambitious and, perhaps having had their eyes opened by the nearby ostentatious wealth of the leafy west end districts in the second city of what was then a flourishing British Empire, they had lofty ideas about their prospects and of making a name for themselves.

As an organised sport, football had burst out of the English public school system, following the codification of the game's laws in 1863, and taken the country by storm. Thrilling and uplifting, yet also earthy and rugged, the game was quickly adopted by the harassed working population, who, through a shared sense of identity and belonging, took to supporting their local teams over the course of the next few decades in increasingly remarkable numbers.

Inspired by the exploits of some of the other early Scottish sides such as Third Lanark and Vale of Leven, who were founded in the same year, and the dedicated amateurs of nearby Queen's Park, the Gare Loch boys showed tremendous dedication to their new pursuit, practising six nights a week and playing their games at Flesher's Haugh on the open spaces of Glasgow Green in the east end of the city. Often they would book their playing area hours in advance, with one of their group, usually Peter McNeil, given the task of guarding the field and planting the goal sticks in the morning, so that nobody would have moved on to their patch by the afternoon.

Like many of the other great urban centres of Britain, Glasgow had expanded exponentially over the course of the Industrial Revolution, as the rustic, agrarian lifestyles of the previous century based on the annual cycle of the harvest were replaced by a relentless, factory-orientated routine, unaffected by climate or season. Glasgow Green was built on land set aside by the enlightened city fathers, who wished to provide residents with some space for recreation, an idea which would be embraced even more fully by the working population following the introduction of half-day Saturdays in the second half of the 19th century. By law, all factory activity on a Saturday now had to end by 2pm, allowing skilled workers to enjoy an extended period away from the factory floor for the first time. Tagged on to the Sabbath, the day of rest, the idea of the weekend was born, and across Britain Saturday afternoon became the designated slot for watching and playing the popular new game of football.

Although the boys were probably still calling their new team 'Argyll' at the time, Rangers' first recorded match, with a side cobbled together from a collection of the friends, siblings and fellow clansmen of the teenagers, was a goalless draw against a team from the town of Callander in Perthshire, played in May 1872. Fifteen-year-old William McBeath, the only founder member not from the area around the Gare Loch, was in fact competing against his home town and probably helped to organise the fixture by securing the opposition for his club's inaugural match. Perhaps for that reason, young McBeath played out of his skin, was voted man of the match, and had to lie up in bed for a week following the bruising encounter in order to recover from his exertions.

Described as a 'terrible' spectacle by William Dunlop, an early Rangers player, future president and, later, club historian, the match would have borne only a passing resemblance to the familiar modern game, with most of the team not even properly stripped and playing in their day to day clothes. The only players to wear 'kit' were Harry McNeil, elder brother of Moses and Peter, and his mate, Willie McKinnon, both of whom were regulars with Queen's Park at the time, along with two other experienced players borrowed from a team called Eastern. Harry McNeil would go on to win ten caps for Scotland between 1874 and 1881. However, it seems unlikely that he would have been able to successfully introduce his amateur club's pioneering passing game to this team of novices.

Despite the tentative start, the young men persisted and it wasn't long before their club was up and running, with office bearers elected and training sessions formally organised. The enthusiastic youngsters even managed to secure the patronage of the future 9th Duke of Argyll for their new enterprise, Queen Victoria's son-in-law, the Marquis of Lorne, although the local aristocrat for the region of their familial homes left Britain in 1878 to become Governor General of Canada and never managed to attend any of their matches. They called their new team Rangers, as likely as not because they liked how it sounded, but it has also been suggested, perhaps rather implausibly, that the name might be a form of rhyming slang, as all these young men were still relative strangers to their adopted city at the time.

But the Rangers name is listed as belonging to a rugby club from Swindon in Charles Alcock's *English Football Annual* of 1870. Alcock was a founder member of the FA, and a veteran of the seminal 1863 meetings at the Freemasons' tavern in Lincoln Inn Fields in London, where the common set of rules for the game of football had been thrashed out and formally codified. He was also an important figure in establishing the first international fixture between Scotland and England, played at Hamilton Crescent in the Partick area of Glasgow in November 1872, just a few months on from Rangers' foundation. Moses McNeil, true sports fan that he was, had a copy of Alcock's annual and it was he who proposed the Rangers name, which was accepted unanimously. In 1877, the Rangers team were photographed, following their appearance against Vale of Leven in the Scottish Cup Final, in the same livery and colours as the Swindon club.

Rangers were not invited to take part in the Scottish Cup in its inaugural year of 1873/74, but having secured membership of the SFA in time for the following season, the club played its first competitive match in the new governing body's flagship competition in October 1874 and secured a 2-0 victory over Oxford, a team not from the English shires or the famous university, but from the east end of Glasgow. A year on from their formation, a childhood friend and contemporary of the founders, 16-year-old Tom Vallance, another aspiring young Victorian gentleman, had joined the club. Also from Garelochhead, he would go on to be one of the most significant figures in the club's early history, as captain and later president. A sturdy defender, Vallance was joined in the team against Oxford by Campbell and McBeath as well as by the McNeil brothers: Peter, who captained the side, Moses and their elder brother William. Dumbarton, one of the leading lights of Scottish Victorian football, would see Rangers off in the following round but an important first step had been taken.

Rangers had the advantage over the provincial sides of an enormous catchment area of prospective members and supporters, and their youthful energy and swashbuckling style of play quickly earned them a sizeable following. They were a nomadic club in the early years, and unlike teams such as Pollokshields Athletic, Govan and Partick Thistle, they were not tied to any particular area of the city, which, along with their continuing success, helped broaden their appeal as the years went by.

There was of course no league structure in place in these early days, so challenge matches against suitable opponents had to be organised by the committees and match secretaries of individual clubs. Queen's

Park initially offered to send their second team, known as the Strollers, to take on Rangers, not wanting to deliver a potentially demoralising defeat on the youthful new side, but the Rangers committee declined this proposal, and with the club winning 12 and drawing two of the 15 other matches which were arranged in season 1874/75, they were keen to gauge where they stood in the hierarchy of Scottish football by facing the very best that the country had to offer. Queen's eventually sent in their crack troops, and defeated Rangers by the comparatively narrow margin of 2-0 in November 1875.

By this time, Rangers had outgrown park football and the club soon moved to its first permanent home in the Burnbank enclosure, to the south of Kelvinbridge in the west end of the city, where their first game was a creditable 1-1 draw against the great Vale of Leven side, although the team from Alexandria in West Dunbartonshire played the entire match with only ten men. Still essentially a youth team centred on three families from Garelochhead, there were the three McNeil brothers, Moses, Peter and Willie (Harry was still playing for Queen's Park), Tom and his brother Alex Vallance, Peter Campbell, who was joined by his brothers James and John, alongside 18-year-old club president William McBeath.

Despite Burnbank being the most convenient location in terms of proximity to the founders' homes, the club only stayed in the West End for a year, moving south of the River Clyde to a ground at Kinning Park in time for the start of the 1876/77 season, after a cricket club called Clydesdale were unable to pay the rent and moved off the land. The new park, not far from the present Ibrox Stadium on a site which nowadays has the M8 motorway running through it, was opened on 2 September with a 2-1 defeat of old rivals Vale of Leven in front of 1,500 spectators. Rangers had added as many as half a dozen new players to their roster by this stage, including several from Sandyford, their former neighbours from the west end, who had recently disbanded, and the club seemed to be growing to maturity.

The same two teams, Rangers and Vale of Leven, then met again in the Scottish Cup Final, Rangers' first, which was played over three closely contested and controversial games in March and April 1877. By the time the Alexandrians eventually prevailed, winning 3-2 at the old Hampden Park in the second replay, Rangers' reputation and popularity had increased considerably at a point when growing numbers of people from across the communities of Britain, but especially in the great urban centres of Scotland and England, were catching the football bug. Vale would go on to retain the cup over the following two seasons, knocking out Rangers on each occasion, while the Kinning Park men would have to wait another 15 years before finally getting their hands on the famous old trophy.

It's around this time, however, that the four young founders, the so-called Gallant Pioneers, begin to drop out of the club's recorded history and their association with the team which they helped to establish begins to dissipate. Only recently has the full extent of their varied fortunes come to light, revealing the painful, unhappy story of what happened to the boys in later life. Moses McNeil was perhaps the least unfortunate of the four. He lived to the ripe old age of 82, making him easily the longest-surviving founder member of the club. A talented winger, Moses left Rangers briefly to join elder brother Harry at Queen's Park in October 1875 and, in his first game, helped his new team to a famous 5-0 win over the great English side Wanderers, captained by Charles Alcock, in front of 11,000 people at Hampden. He returned to Rangers though just four months later, where he continued to play until 1882, far beyond any of the other pioneers. In addition, he made two international appearances for Scotland, becoming Rangers' first capped player when he was selected to face Wales in 1876, and four years later he lined up against England at Hampden, in a game which finished 5-4 to the Scots.

After football, Moses was employed as a commercial traveller for a firm of hosiers in Glasgow, then as a brush and oils salesman for a paint company. In later life, he moved back to Argyll where his links with the club he founded remained tenuous; in 1898, he attended a 21st anniversary reunion dinner of the famous 1877 Scottish Cup Final with Vale of Leven, organised by restaurateur and former team-mate Tom Vallance, but he didn't manage to attend Vallance's funeral in 1935 and he declined several invitations to Rangers reunions, including the 50th anniversary dinner in April 1923. Childless and unmarried, Moses lived out his last years with his sister Isabella at their secluded home in the village of Rosneath on the Gare Loch.

After losing his place in the team he helped to found, Moses's brother Peter McNeil took up an administrative role at Rangers, serving as honorary match secretary from 1876, and he later became treasurer of the SFA as well, a job not without its challenges in the 1870s and 1880s. But he resigned from both positions in 1883, for reasons which were stated in the *Scottish Athletic Journal* as the 'pressure of business', in reference to his efforts to maintain a sports outfitters shop, which he owned and operated along with his brother Harry in Glasgow city centre.

The real reason for his departure from the football scene, however, seems to have had more to do with the declining condition of his mental health, although the full extent of his developing illness is unclear at this stage. But it says much for the regard in which he was held that, despite the appalling stigma often associated with such conditions in the Victorian age, his colleagues appear to have covered up his state of mind, offering sympathy and appreciation, and it was suggested that a testimonial should be organised for his benefit, although this never took place. Sadly the 'pressure of business' took its toll on Peter and his increasingly impoverished family. His outfitters shop had disappeared from the high street by 1896 and bankruptcy ensued, apparently after a quarrel or disagreement with his elder brother and business partner Harry. With his family now eligible for poverty relief payments from their local parish, it seems that financial failure was too heavy a burden to bear, and by the turn of the century Peter was considered a danger to himself and others. He was sectioned and admitted to an asylum in Paisley, where he died in March 1901 after suffering what his medical records describe as a 'growing mental paralysis for three years'.

The youngest member of the group, Peter Campbell, had just turned 15 when he helped to found Rangers Football Club in the spring of 1872. Born on 6 March 1857, his father was a steamboat captain and later something of an entrepreneur in the expanding steamship industry and the burgeoning field of tourism and local excursions on the Firth of Clyde. His mother was also from a family of reasonable means and the handsome sandstone villa of young Peter's childhood can still be seen today in Garelochhead, not far from the present site of the Faslane Naval Base.

Despite being from a more affluent background than his fellow pioneers, young Peter was put to work as an apprentice, then a journeyman, on the yards between 1872 and 1879 in a shipbuilding industry at it zenith on the Clyde. Along with his brothers James and

John, he played for Rangers in their very earliest years and his talents saw him earn two caps for Scotland, both against Wales, with Peter scoring twice on his debut at Hampden in 1878 in a convincing 9-0 victory, and then once more the following year in a 3-0 win in Wrexham.

A forward known for his pace and unselfish passing, Peter played his last match for Rangers in September 1879, a 5-1 defeat to Queen's Park in the Scottish Cup, before retiring from football following a brief spell at Blackburn Rovers. He then decided, perhaps following the family tradition, to take up the challenge of pursuing a career at sea and Campbell was appointed chief engineer on a steamer, the *St Columba*, which put to sea in January 1883 from the port of Penarth in South Wales, bound for the Indian colonies. However, a short time into its journey, the vessel was tragically lost in poor weather off the west coast of France. It wasn't until a month later that wreckage from the *St Columba* was washed up along the shore of the Bay of Biscay, confirming the loss of all on board. Peter Campbell was 25 years old when he died.

William McBeath was the only one of the Rangers founders not from the area around the Gare Loch in Argyll. Perhaps in recognition of his organisational skills, rather than his footballing prowess, McBeath was elected Rangers' first president in time for the 1874 season. However, his association with the club ended as early as 1876, after he was replaced in the team by George Gillespie, and his name fails to appear in any records thereafter. By 1884, he had completely dropped off the club's radar, when, at their half-yearly meeting in April, he was invited to dinner and presented with a gold badge by Tom Vallance in honour of his role in the club's foundation.

William's work as a commercial traveller had taken him away from Glasgow, where he apparently prospered in Bristol, but by 1897 he had lost his job, his relationship with his wife had broken down and his family had split up. He accepted a position as a commissioning agent, selling advertising space in a holiday newspaper but, along with his employer, he was charged with obtaining money under false pretences, a crime for which his boss was convicted and sentenced to 21 months of hard labour. Happily William, by now 40 years old and known as William McBeth, was acquitted of all charges. Later, he moved to Bradford and remarried, risking the wrath of the law once more by falsely claiming that he was a widower.

Perhaps to escape the charge of bigamy, he moved with his new bride to Lincoln, but the couple did not fare well. William spent time in prison, and was subsequently relocated to a poorhouse, from where his wife made numerous attempts to try and discharge him. She was unsuccessful and William frequently had to be escorted back to the residence by police officers acting as social workers. Like the amusing, but ultimately tragic half-man, Mr Dick, in Dickens's *David Copperfield*, McBeath's mental health seems to have irrevocably deteriorated and he was officially listed as a 'certified imbecile', an unforgiving diagnosis, although in modern medical parlance his condition may have been recognised as an advanced state of Alzheimer's disease. He died in the poorhouse infirmary in July 1917, aged 61, and was given a pauper's burial.

For William McBeath and Peter McNeil in particular, it might not be too facile to suggest that we can perhaps see an early, extreme example of the often devastating impact on the lives of young players who fail to make the grade as footballers. It must have been especially difficult in their cases, because they were founder members of a club which became hugely successful, once they were overlooked in favour of others. They had been put aside by their peers at Rangers and although they were both given administrative roles when they dropped out of the team, they missed out on all the glory, as over the course of their adult lives the game of football grew more popular than they could ever have foreseen. Coupled with failure in their personal and professional lives, they were sadly unable to recover from such a series of blows to their Victorian sense of self-esteem, with ultimately tragic consequences.

Rangers, meanwhile, the club which, back in the day, these star-crossed young boys had dreamt up and established, were continuing to grow on and off the field, although it seems that the club had a haughty, bad-tempered element associated with them, even from the earliest days. The young team had started to gain a bad reputation for themselves for persistently protesting results and decisions which had gone against them and there was growing indignation and criticism at the way their affairs were being conducted.

There had been controversy on the field as far back as 1875/76 during a second round Scottish Cup meeting with Glasgow rivals Third Lanark. Rangers won the initial game 1-0 at Cathkin Park, but they had apparently taken the kick-off at the start of both halves, a clear breach of the rules, so a replay was ordered which Rangers lost. Suitably miffed, this time it was Rangers' turn to complain to the SFA, on the grounds that Thirds' goalkeeper had not been properly stripped for the match and, wearing his everyday clothes, he couldn't be clearly distinguished from the other players. Rangers also claimed that Thirds' winning goal should have been disallowed for handball, a dubious appeal given that the referee's decision was final in these matters, and that the game had ended early after spectators encroached on to the field. Their protest was thrown out and Thirds progressed to the next round at Rangers' expense.

The following season saw the infamous, twice-replayed Scottish Cup Final of 1877, which pitched Rangers against a Vale of Leven side who, in an earlier round, had inflicted a first ever domestic defeat on Queen's Park in the ten years of the formative Hampden club's existence. After a 1-1 draw between the two finalists in the first game at Hamilton Crescent, the subsequent replay attracted a sizeable crowd, which estimates put at between 8,000 and 15,000, in all probability a British record at the time. Again the game finished tied at 1-1, but during the agreed period of extra time confusion reigned after Rangers claimed that, following a shot from Dunlop, the ball had passed between the goalposts and rebounded out again off a spectator. The Rangers players insisted that a legitimate goal should have been awarded, but the referee, after consulting his two umpires, who seemed to be divided on the matter, disagreed. The protests went on so long that a section of the huge crowd became restless and invaded the field and, amid chaotic scenes, the game had to be abandoned early when the Hamilton Crescent pitch could not be cleared. Vale of Leven subsequently won a second replay, 3-2 at the old Hampden Park, and took the cup.

An even more serious incident occurred two years later, again in the Scottish Cup Final and again featuring the same two teams, Rangers and Vale of Leven, on Saturday, 19 April 1879. Having defeated Queen's Park for the first time in torrential rain in the semi-final, Rangers were leading the final 1-0 when a second 'goal', a header from Struthers, was disallowed for offside. With Rangers holding on late in the game, and seemingly on the verge of collecting their first piece of silverware, Vale equalised when converted goalkeeper George Gillespie misjudged an angled shot from Ferguson at the near post. Almost as soon as the game had finished, Rangers let it be known that they were lodging an appeal, claiming that the earlier, disallowed goal should have stood. Quite rightly, the SFA again dismissed the protest on the grounds that the referee's decision is final and cannot later be overturned by any means.

Led by captain Tom Vallance, Rangers snootily refused to turn up for the replay, preferring a day out at Ayr races instead, and Vale were awarded the cup by default. Some measure of revenge was gained when Rangers defeated the same opponents 2-1 in the final of the Glasgow Charity Cup at Hampden later the same year, a notable achievement as the club collected its first ever trophy, but there was bad blood in that fixture as well, and several of the players were exchanging blows by the end.

Despite their growing popularity at the turnstiles, it's not hard to see how the still young club was starting to rub some people up the wrong way, as these protests became a feature of Rangers' fixtures over the course of the next few years. The game's administrators were appalled by their behaviour, as were certain newspapers and other sporting publications, with the *Scottish Athletic Journal* (*SAJ*) claiming that nobody outside of Kinning Park liked the club, and accusing them of bad sportsmanship, lack of humour and mean-spiritedness. In addition, the club's followers were starting to gain a bad reputation for their loutish and foul-mouthed behaviour and Kinning Park was considered one of the most notorious grounds in Scotland for unruly conduct among spectators.

If Rangers' popularity had risen in the 1870s among a relatively small but select group, who admired their youthful energy and captivating style of play, it was a different story by the mid-1880s as football's popularity continued to grow exponentially and the demographic make-up of the game's followers began to change. In September 1882, Rangers were drawn to play Queen's Park in the second round of the Scottish Cup at Hampden, a team that the *SAJ*, in April of the same year, had taken to task for their exclusivity and elitism: 'Social distinction in the matter of admitting members must be purged away,' the journal warned Queen's. 'It is true the men who upheld the name of the club so gloriously in days gone past had a class connection of a kind, but then they were of the few who played the game. Now everyone plays, and the commonest artisan has the same chance of becoming a great player as the youth who can command a certain social position.'

Despite being the home side, it was noted that Queen's had to endure stony silence when their three goals were scored, whereas Rangers' two strikes were greeted with enthusiastic cheering. By the time the sides met again three years later, again at Hampden in September 1885, the reputation of Rangers' followers had plummeted so low that the residents of Mount Florida were reluctant to let them anywhere near their respectable part of town.

Rangers' fans seemed to be at the opposite end of the social spectrum from the upper-crust Queen's Parkers, and they displayed their by now customary vulgarity during another bad-tempered 3-2 defeat for their team. The *Scottish Athletic Journal* called on Rangers to put their house in order, describing the atmosphere at Hampden as 'a perfect pandemonium'. In November 1888, former player John McCartney summed up the general mood when he observed that, 'the following of Rangers is the worst in Scotland', after he was heckled by the home crowd at the old Ibrox while playing for Cowlairs.

It wasn't just the fans, however, as ten years on from the club's foundation, Rangers' players by now were also acquiring a reputation for drunken and boorish behaviour. Most were not deemed to be gentlemen, according to the standards of the day, and many were often seen to be the worse for wear at club functions. In November 1883, following a Charity Cup match against Queen's Park, a rather sumptuous spread was set up in a nearby pub, the Athole Arms, for the players and officials of the two teams. Queen's, however, refused to attend the post-match bash, maintaining that it was an unnecessary expense for a fundraising game, so the Rangers camp, undaunted, tucked into the repast alone. In 1885, the club tried their hand at the FA Cup, the competition being open to all British teams at the time, although the cost of travel and accommodation meant that few Scottish sides chose to participate.

This changed, however, when the competition was regionalised and twice Queen's Park reached the final, in 1884 and 1885, losing on both occasions to Blackburn Rovers. Rangers were drawn against a Lancashire team called Rawtenstall, but the Glasgow club's participation in the competition got off to a false start when they refused to meet the Lancastrians, on the grounds that their team contained professional players. For their refusal to fulfil the fixture, Rangers were hit with a financial penalty of ten shillings, meaning that to this day the club retains the dubious honour of being the only Scottish side ever to be fined by the English FA.

Undaunted, Rangers tried again the following year when they were drawn to face Everton at their Anfield ground in Liverpool. Despite turning up late and causing the kick-off to be delayed by 15 minutes after being thrown out of their hotel for excessive drunken behaviour the night before, Rangers managed a 1-0 win with a goal from Charlie Heggie. The Glasgow club made further progress in the competition after successive home victories in the following rounds and were eventually drawn against Aston Villa in the semi-final. In a game played in front of 10,000 spectators in Crewe, Villa ran out 3-1 winners, thanks in no small part to a poor performance by the Rangers goalkeeper Willie Chalmers, who had overindulged himself at lunch on the day of the game. The *Scottish Umpire* reported, 'The weak points of the Rangers were in deficient combination and dash of the forwards, rather weak defence and downright poor goalkeeping.'

It would be the last game played by a Scottish team in the FA Cup, as at the end of the season, the SFA, fearing a dilution of its influence, banned its members from participation in any cup competition other than those organised under its own auspices.

Meanwhile, there was also trouble brewing behind the scenes at the Kinning Park club. On 11 November 1882, the team's match against St Bernard's in Edinburgh had to be cancelled at the last minute when club president Archie Harkness died suddenly from typhoid, aged 26. The untimely passing of Harkness had the unfortunate effect on Rangers of allowing the unscrupulous honorary secretary John Mackay to dominate the club and its business. Many clubs faced in-house difficulties around this time as the pressure to professionalise, in an increasingly competitive environment, clashed with the ideal of the amateur, Corinthian spirit, which was stridently cherished by some.

Professionalism was more or less allowed in England from the mid-1880s, but the amateur game held on in Scotland until the establishment of league football at the start of the following decade. Some clubs did not survive the transition, while others, such as Celtic, continued only after internal bloodletting. Famously, Queen's Park stood aloof from the societal changes in the game, even after the establishment of league football in Scotland, and they continue as an amateur club to this day, long after their counterparts in England, the military and the alumni teams from the boarding schools and universities who dominated football south of the border in the early years, have been consigned to the history books.

At Rangers, however, the in-fighting was particularly bitter, amid serious financial problems and chaotic maladministration. The tragic Harkness had been replaced as club president by the builder George Goudie, who immediately lent the struggling institution £30 in order to stay afloat. The early pioneers had long since departed the scene and even Tom Vallance had moved to India in February 1882, although he returned a year later after contracting a debilitating illness which effectively ended his playing career at the age of 26. As well as playing for Rangers for ten years and winning seven caps for Scotland, Vallance, handsome and imposing at 6ft 2in tall, also excelled at rowing and was an accomplished athlete. Like many Rangers players at that time, he was a member of the Clydesdale Harriers Athletics Club, who were associated with Rangers through their respective membership lists and their joint use of the playing fields at Kinning Park.

A socialite who liked to move in influential circles, Vallance diversified into the restaurant business and later became president of the restaurateurs' and hotelkeepers' association. Clearly something of a Renaissance Man, he was also a self-taught artist and his paintings were later exhibited at the Royal Glasgow Institute. On his return from India, Vallance assumed the role of the club's president in May 1883, with Goudie stepping down to vice-president, and immediately promised that the three major cups would all be won by Rangers in the new season. It turned out to be mere bravado however, and when Rangers were duly knocked out of the three competitions and no trophies were forthcoming, the *Scottish Athletic Journal* mischievously promised to provide Rangers with three tea cups instead.

Vallance's return failed to provide Rangers with the stability they required, as the scheming John Mackay assumed the role of match secretary following Peter McNeil's departure, increasing his stranglehold on power at the club as Rangers' tribulations continued. In 1883, the club agreed to play against Dumbarton in a benefit game, following the capsize of the steamer *Daphne* at its launch on the Clyde, which had resulted in the loss of 146 lives, to this day still the greatest disaster ever witnessed in the Glasgow shipbuilding industry. Dumbarton were shocked when the Rangers officials, despite the game being played at Kinning Park, drew their expenses from the relief fund, and after Rangers subsequently received criticism in the local press for their mean-spiritedness, Mackay fired off an angry response to the *SAJ*, complaining of a 'spiteful and baseless attack' against the club and effectively stating that it was okay for big clubs like Dumbarton to play for nothing, but Rangers couldn't afford it.

On several occasions during Mackay's troubled reign at the club, Rangers were also accused of fielding ineligible or professional players and, on at least one occasion, came close to having their membership of the SFA terminated as a result. In October 1884, the team faced Third Lanark in the Scottish Cup and selected former player Sam Thomson for the tie, a Scotland international forward who had previously joined Preston North End and was therefore no longer a registered member of the Kinning Park club. Thirds protested but the controversy could not be cleared up and, with the original game finishing 1-1, the replay went ahead the following week. Again the match finished in a draw and again Rangers had fielded a professional player, Archie Steel of Bolton Wanderers, although the matter was not investigated and, under the rules of the day, both clubs progressed to the next stage.

Perhaps inevitably, Rangers and Third Lanark were immediately drawn to face one another in the following round and once again the Kinning Park men were living dangerously. Mackay was suspected of doctoring documents, following the appearance of a T. Cook for Rangers, which Thirds were convinced represented another instance of Rangers fielding an ineligible player. The club had signed Tommy Cook in July, but it took until October before the player was properly registered with the SFA, although Rangers did have a J. Cook on their books at the time, who would have been authorised to play in the tie. The match card from the day subsequently turned up with the 'T' altered to look like a 'J', with Mackay implicated in the unauthorised amendment.

Not for the last time in their history, Rangers seemed to be flouting the rules and getting away with it, as a proven case of forged documentation would surely have seen the club expelled from the cup, and possibly even suspended from the SFA. The *SAJ*, outraged at the apparent injustice following Rangers' 3-0 win over their disgruntled opponents, described the affair as 'one of the biggest scandals that ever disgraced the annals of football', with the journal's editor apparently so vexed by the whole commotion that he was moved to suggest, 'I am certain the football world will agree with me that it is far better the Rangers should die than a noble pastime be dragged in the mire.'

Nevertheless, Rangers progressed to the next round where their opponents, Arbroath, defeated the Kinning Park men 4-3 at Gayfield. After the loss, Rangers complained that the pitch was too narrow, describing it, in a terse telegram sent back to Glasgow, as a mere 'back green'. Experienced protestors by now, club officials took a measuring tape out to the field to see if they could prove their case and when the pitch was found to be 11 inches short of the required width the inevitable appeal went in and a replay was ordered by the SFA, which Rangers won 8-1. The club then received a bye through to the quarter-final, but four days following their subsequent 5-3 defeat at the hands of eventual winners Renton, the *Scottish Athletic Journal* wryly observed, 'So far there has been no protest from Rangers.'

Even by the following year, the *SAJ* still hadn't let the matter drop when it stated in September 1885, 'Rangers last season protested their way from round to round and created in doing so a scandal which shocked the whole football world'. By the time Rangers moved to their new ground at Ibrox in 1887, however, the *SAJ* had clearly admitted to itself that it was fighting a losing battle in its campaign against the wayward club. Apparently realising that it was flowing against the tide in terms of Rangers' growing popularity, it replaced the chorus of disapproval with 'adoring approbation', as a rival publication, the *Scottish Umpire*, which had recently been established by, among others, John Mackay, noted with a degree of contempt. Rangers had effectively seen off their critics in the press, and within a year the *Scottish Athletic Journal* and the *Scottish Umpire* had merged to form the twice-weekly *Scottish Sport*, which would describe Rangers in the 1890s as 'Scotia's darling club'.

The days of youthful innocence at Rangers were well and truly over. President Tom Vallance, the only remaining link with the club's founders, was clearly exasperated at the direction the organisation was taking, and at some of John Mackay's antics in particular. Late in 1883, under Mackay's influence, the Rangers players refused to sanction the appointment of Vallance to umpire a game between their club and Dumbarton, just a few months after the incident over the *Daphne* disaster fundraising match, which had caused considerable bad blood between the two sides. Referees at the time were assisted by two umpires, one chosen from each team, but Mackay had persuaded his players that Vallance's honesty would undermine their efforts on the field, and was insisting instead that he should be nominated to stand referee himself. The club president immediately resigned in protest and was only persuaded to return after an apology was issued on behalf of the squad. Mackay himself continued to umpire, but was so incapable of impartial officiating that he would often provoke partisan interventions from his opposite number, the opponents' nominated man, with the result that games involving Rangers would frequently descend into bad-tempered chaos.

In October 1885, the *SAJ* had offered the view that, 'The social decadence of the Rangers may be dated from the day Mr Peter McNeil resigned the match secretaryship and J.W. Mackay took it up.' Perhaps as a result of such accusations, the tendency among the club's modern historians, in typical Rangers fashion, has been to scapegoat Mackay for these and other indiscretions and for the general condition of the club during this troubled period. It is a tactic which has often been repeated since, to blame an individual for his erroneous ways rather than contemplate the uncomfortable idea of a wider malaise at the club.

There was at this time a cultural failing at the heart of the institution, which allowed an individual of the calibre of Mackay to become such an influential administrator, a person who would not have been allowed anywhere near rival contemporary clubs such as Dumbarton, Renton, with its 'brotherhood of equality and fraternity' ethos, or Queen's Park, needless to say. Overall the impression is of a club borne out of the passion and youthful enthusiasm of a group of teenagers, but despite lofty Victorian notions about the civilising effect of manly, competitive sport, suffering from a lack of cohesive and moral leadership. With the departure of the youthful pioneers and the dwindling influence of Vallance, there was no older, father figure on the scene to nurture the club into maturity, to show concern for its future wellbeing, once it grew into something big, successful and ultimately unwieldy. The club had lost its way and grubby, boorish and uncharitable behaviour was the order of the day at Rangers.

The club's internal problems coincided with a terrible run of form on the field for the Rangers team. During a poor spell between 1881 and 1883, Rangers lost 16 of 29 matches, including five defeats in a row at one point, and the club was quarrelling with some of its best players, most notably George Gillespie and forward Charlie Heggie, a player who had the distinction of scoring four goals for Scotland on his international debut but never appearing for his country again, with both men eventually leaving the club. To make matters worse, by 1887 Rangers' lease on their Kinning Park ground had expired and the club was evicted. Still under the presidential stewardship of Tom Vallance, Rangers moved to the first Ibrox Park, built on derelict land at the Copland Road end of Paisley Road, a relatively remote area of Glasgow at the time.

Situated 100 or so yards to the north-east of the present stadium, the press helpfully printed maps and illustrations in order to help supporters find their way to the new location, which quickly sold out. An abortive attempt to relocate the club to the Strathbungo and Pollokshields area of the city had failed when local residents, wary of Rangers fans' poor reputation by this time, vetoed the idea and Vallance was concerned that the notoriety of their supporters would follow Rangers to their new home. The president tried to assuage such fears at a banquet for invited guests on the eve of the club's first match at Ibrox, when he announced, 'I have known very respectable people come to our matches and not renewing their visits but that has all gone and I am sanguine that in our new sphere we will be able to attract to our matches thousands of respectable spectators.'

Ibrox Park had opened in a blaze of publicity, but things didn't get off to a great start for the team at their new home. In a game played to mark the ground's inauguration, there were disturbances among spectators as well as a hefty defeat, as Rangers suffered an inauspicious 8-1 loss to Preston North End, the great Lancastrian side who would go on to win the first two titles of the newly established Football League in 1889 and 1890. By the closing stages, some of the capacity crowd of 20,000 spilled over on to the pitch, causing the game to be abandoned five minutes from full-time and following the match, at a reception dinner, the Preston chairman and manager, Billy Sudell, urged the Glasgow press to remind the Rangers fans about their manners, after the fixture came to an unruly and premature end.

Later the same year, a meeting was held at St Mary's Hall in the Calton area of Glasgow which would lead to the foundation of Celtic Football Club. If Rangers arrived early on the football scene, a young infant having to learn and grow gradually as the game evolved, Celtic by contrast were a team born late, like a foal, that had to spring up from the ground in an instant and start running around almost immediately, with its limbs in full working order, competing with its peers and rivals. The first meeting between Rangers and the new team from the east end of town took place in May 1888, as Celtic made their debut on the stage of Scottish football, and a 5-2 victory for the nascent club was followed by a convivial night's entertainment back at St Mary's Hall. The future success of both teams was toasted and initially there was great friendship and camaraderie between the two clubs; two of the Celtic players, brothers Tom and Willie Maley, were founding members of the Clydesdale Harriers Athletics Club, who functioned out of Kinning Park, and they knew many of the Rangers contingent well.

Celtic were founded by Brother Walfrid, a senior figure in the Catholic Marist religious order and the headmaster of St Andrew's school in the city centre, with the help of prominent members of the local Irish community, chiefly Doctor John Conway and the well-known and respected builder John Glass. Walfrid, Conway and Glass had been bouncing ideas around for some time about ways to help the children of the impoverished Irish immigrants in Glasgow's east end. There had been a sizeable Irish community in the Glasgow area for much of the 19th century; in 1840, it was estimated that the Irish, including many itinerant workers, made up around a quarter of the city's population and this only increased later in the decade with the disaster of 'An Gorta Mor', the Great Famine, caused by the blight on the potato crop, which led to the exodus from Ireland of over one million people. The Irish were generally unskilled and prepared to take on almost any form of employment and it was their labour on which much of the growth and industrialisation of Glasgow in the 19th century had been built. But despite the poverty and deprivation of so many, there were also prominent citizens, such as Conway and Glass, as well as the clergy, who were venerated in the Catholic community for their vocation.

The chief idea behind the new club's foundation was to raise funds in order to provide the needy children of the city's east end with 'penny meals' through the St Vincent de Paul Society, which was attached to the Sacred Heart mission in the four main Catholic parishes within the archdiocese of Glasgow. Many in the community had been badly affected by the collapse of the City of Glasgow bank a decade earlier, which had precipitated an economic slump with hundreds of labourers, from all backgrounds, being put out of work, including at the nearby Parkhead Forge ironworks which was forced into temporary closure. The Welfare State was still more than half a century away and there was no concept at the time of civil intervention on behalf of those who found themselves on the soft underbelly of society, but Walfrid and his colleagues were acutely aware of the plight of the less fortunate among their fellow countrymen and they had been active for some time in efforts to try and mitigate their circumstances.

In February 1887, the Scottish Cup was won in Glasgow by the Edinburgh side Hibernian, an exclusively Irish, Catholic team whose application to join the SFA in the 1870s had originally been refused, with their membership fee returned along with a terse letter explaining that the SFA was for 'Scotchmen, not Irishmen'. Walfrid, Conway and Glass witnessed the celebrations among the Irish in Glasgow at the success of the Edinburgh side, and before long steps were undertaken to establish a team which could similarly represent Glasgow's own community of Irishmen. Early in the new year, not long after the inaugural meeting at St Mary's Hall in November, the founders began soliciting for labour from a largely volunteer workforce to build a stadium for the proposed new club. The response was overwhelming, and by May Celtic were ready to take their first steps. Unlike their friends and neighbours Rangers, who had endured lengthy, nomadic years of development, often struggling to break even and wondering on occasion if they would have a ground to play on, Celtic simply had no time for such tribulations.

In order to accomplish their immediate goal of raising money for the needy, Celtic had to be fully functioning from the start and the club became an overnight success story, able to take players from other teams seemingly at will in order to get themselves off the ground, and a huge, almost instantaneous cultural phenomenon. In their first season, Celtic reached the Scottish Cup Final, before losing to Third Lanark, and by the second year of their existence, they were attracting crowds of 25,000 to their home in Parkhead. Celtic too had their blood on the carpet moment, caused by internal disagreements in the early days between the charitable arm of the club and the business faction, who saw professionalism as the inevitable way forward for football.

In the end, the pragmatists prevailed, just as professionalism had, as the argument was reflected in the wider game, and the Celtic Football and Athletic Company was incorporated in 1897. The idealists were swimming against the tide, as the game continued to grow in popularity, but the club retains a charitable tradition to this day, and the initiative and zeal of its modern-day supporters towards organising events and raising money for worthwhile causes remains impressive.

Despite the close early ties between the two Glasgow clubs and the spirit of sporting solidarity in evidence at St Mary's Hall in May 1888, the sudden appearance of a serious nearby rival seems to have had a galvanising effect on those associated with Rangers, with the Ibrox club's income quadrupling between 1889 and 1894. Over the course of the coming decades, the two clubs would find themselves locked in a seemingly endless *tête-à-tête*, each vying for supremacy over the other while leaving rivals floundering in their wake, as the Glasgow duopoly inevitably began to dominate the game in Scotland. Football, once the game of the patrician classes, now witnessed its most intense rivalry between Rangers, the grubbiest of the grubby, and Celtic, the poorest of the poor.

But with Rangers there would be a darker motivation, and it wasn't long before the club's whole identity and *raison d'être* would become intricately linked with their neighbours from the east end of the city. If Celtic were formed to support and represent an immigrant community, Rangers would go on to become the reactionary club, the sporting arm of a wider social movement to keep the Irish population in the west of Scotland firmly in its place, as the Ibrox club gradually assumed the mantle of the team to stop the Catholics.

2

'SCOTIA'S DARLING CLUB'

DOWN the decades, Rangers fans and others associated with the club have generally paid little attention to the club's history. The tradition of storytelling, of exploits recollected and hardships overcome, so common at other clubs, is not strong at Rangers, and the club has on the whole been poorly served by erstwhile historians. The relatively small market for books on the subject has, at least until recently, offered the discerning reader little beyond the established pattern of inane hagiographies of former players and managers, and uncritical, self-congratulatory chronicles of the team's achievements, usually written with the club's approval, which reflect on little beyond Rangers' seemingly unending association with sporting success.

Reading these books it is often difficult to get to the truth behind controversial issues and incidents involving the club, as rational analysis is sacrificed in favour of the more partisan perspective. There is also a predilection for the mundane and the jejune; when one writer, Robert McElroy, co-author of *Rangers: The Complete Record* was discussing his new book with a club director in the early 1990s the only significant question he was asked was, 'How many photographs are going to be in it?'

This general level of disinterest in discovering and enjoying the past has meant that the early period has often been overlooked, resulting in some particularly curious anomalies. By 1972, 100 years had elapsed since the club's foundation, but the centenary was allowed to pass without any acknowledgement or celebration, because the mistaken notion that the club was founded in 1873 had not been properly investigated and revealed. Victory in Barcelona in the European Cup Winners' Cup Final, achieved with a 3-2 win over Dynamo Moscow in May 1972 and arguably the high water mark of the club's on-field achievements, would have been a fitting way to salute such a historical landmark, but unfortunately, somewhere along the way, Rangers lost track of the fact that they were founded in 1872, and they wrongly marked their centenary the following year, in 1973, a season in which the club had been banned from Europe due to the behaviour of their fans in the Nou Camp.

It might seem strange that a famous football club should be unable to accurately pinpoint the date of its foundation, but then Rangers, at least until very recently, are a club with a fairly dismal record of producing historically reflective books. One early example was *The Story of the Rangers* by sports journalist John Allan, published in 1923. If traditional books about Rangers have offered little more than facile, obsequious eulogies, preaching to the already converted, then *The Story of the Rangers* is certainly no exception.

Allan at the time was an influential columnist with the *Daily Record*, who would later go on to edit the paper, and he was a fervent supporter of the Ibrox club and its interests. He was described by manager Bill Struth as having 'the clasp of a loyal Ranger', an early reference, no doubt, to dodgy handshakes and secret societies. Allan had almost unrestricted access to Struth's dressing room in the 1920s and he was on hand in the aftermath of the 1928 Scottish Cup Final, when Rangers finally ended their 25-year hoodoo in the competition with a 4-0 win over Celtic, to congratulate Davie Meiklejohn after he scored the opening goal from the penalty spot. 'You sunk that penalty like an icicle, man,' Allan told the stand-in Rangers skipper. 'Icicle?' 'Meek' promptly replied. 'I never felt so anxious in all my life. It was the most terrible minute of my football career.'

Allan, uncle of the malevolent 1960s club director and PR guru Willie Allison, was also editor of the official Rangers handbook, the annual chronicle of Rangers' sporting record. For season 1920/21, the annual

31

lists Rangers' foundation date as 1872, but in the following year's edition the date is omitted. It is also missing the season after that, but by 1924 the year of the club's establishment is once again included, but listed as 1873. Allan does not discuss any controversy surrounding the timing of the club's foundation in *The Story of the Rangers*, and, had he been in any doubt, a minimal amount of basic journalistic research would have confirmed to him the correct date of 1872, which had been universally accepted up to that point. It seems that Allan, in his determination to publish his history of the club in time for its 50th jubilee, perpetrated an Orwellian rewriting of events and simply altered the year to suit his own purposes. It is true that the office bearers of the club were first elected in 1873, and perhaps Allan used this as his pretext, but this is a relatively minor administrative matter in a club's history and not one used elsewhere to date a club's foundation.

By 1923, Allan was simply in a rush and misused his position as editor of the club's yearbook so that his deadline could be met. Incredibly, he altered the date just to give himself more time to write his book, and as a consequence of this historical vandalism, Rangers' Cup Winners' Cup victory in 1972 was allowed to pass without being properly celebrated as part of a centenary season success story. As late as 1996, Allan's date was still being used on club merchandise and retail outlets, and his gratuitous alteration is also the reason why visitors to Ibrox Park today can still see the year 1873 erroneously emblazoned on its listed building façade.

Much of this general historical apathy may have been due to a reluctance to peer under the bonnet, as it were, at the thorny issue of sectarianism, which has blighted the club for most of its history. It's an area which has often become a taboo subject for everyone concerned with Scottish football and certainly not a matter which is openly discussed in the club's approved literature. There is in fact no evidence that Rangers were an anti-Catholic team in their earliest guise, and although it is known that the young founders of the club were from Presbyterian stock, there is no record of their intentions or attitudes towards alternate branches of Christianity. While it's true that anti-Catholicism was rife in Glasgow in the mid-to-late 19th century, as it was across large sections of imperial age Britain, there are no early references to Rangers being associated with parochial Protestantism, and if there was any social prejudice around the team and the club in the early years, it would only have reflected wider Victorian attitudes, which were certainly not peculiar to Rangers.

Celtic, it seems, in spite of this broader malaise, were largely welcomed across the sporting community at their formation and there is little recorded evidence of initial hostility towards the team of Irishmen, even when they very rapidly became extremely successful. In fact the only significant early criticism of Celtic came from other Irish clubs, such as Hibernian and Carfin Shamrock, from whom the new Glasgow club, in the days before binding professional contracts, recruited some of their first players. Celtic also took two players from Renton FC, namely ex-Rangers man Neil McCallum, a scorer against his former side in his new club's first ever game in May 1888, and James Kelly, who would go on to make 139 appearances for Celtic, many of them as captain, before becoming a renowned director and establishing a dynasty at the Parkhead club which would last for over 100 years.

In terms of religious or ethnic prejudice, however, by and large sport was seen as a transcending force against such base dispositions and typically there was tremendous camaraderie among players of opposing teams. Celtic, for their part, took the decision very early on that the club would be open to all, and not, unlike Hibernian at the time, run as an exclusive institution for practising Catholics. When the 'Irishmen only' notion was briefly mooted by one of the competing factions in the run-up to the club's incorporation in 1897, the idea was dismissed by a columnist in the Irish-owned newspaper the *Glasgow Observer*, which noted, 'To raise the question of religion is singularly out of place when dealing with sporting matters, and I trust that the last has been heard of it in Celtic circles.' It was a message that would be heeded by Celtic, in all matters of recruitment, but sadly not by their great rivals, over the ensuing years.

This would be a great pity, not least because this civilising, essential fairness of football, a game of skill and guile as well as strength and speed, was one of the reasons the sport had such a captivating influence on the general population, the equality and fairness of its laws and principles standing in marked contrast to the harsh and grinding weekly routine of those earliest supporters and followers of the game, whose working lives at the sharp end of imperial age Britain would all too often have seemed less than fair. There was a close sporting bond between Celtic and Rangers in the very early days, which would seem to confirm the view that there was no significant prejudice or hostility at Ibrox even after the Irish team's formation, and the two clubs would often invite one another to their respective grounds whenever English opposition were in town.

In 1892, the *Scottish Sport* observed that 'the light blues are favourites with the Parkhead crowd', and the following year, when the two squads travelled together on the train to their matches in Edinburgh, the same publication noted, 'Both teams also returned together. They are getting very "pally". And why not?'

Soon, the neighbouring Glasgow clubs took to arranging numerous fixtures between themselves, convenient of course because of their shared locality, and on top of occasional player benefit matches they would often meet in the Glasgow Cup and the Glasgow Charity Cup as well as, from 1896, the Glasgow League, in addition to their fixtures in the Scottish League and the Scottish Cup. While it's true that, as time went on, there was the occasional ruction on the field in the heat of competition, behind the scenes the two clubs retained close ties, with Celtic generally taking the lead in challenging the vested interests of the conservative establishment which ran Scottish football at the time.

But if Celtic's stance overall tended to be bolder and more brash, they always included Rangers in their machinations because they needed a partner and ally, particularly after the Scottish League was established, which precipitated the era of professionalism. In these endeavours, the Parkhead club was actively supported by Rangers, as the two institutions started to flex their muscles in terms of their administrative power and their draw at the turnstiles. In 1894, both teams abandoned their customary trips to England over the festive season and instigated instead the first of the traditional Ne'erday matches against one another, a feature of the fixture card which has persisted down to the present day. The following year, the minutes of Rangers' committee meetings reveal what was referred to as the 'Celtic Agreement', an unofficial accord whereby neither club would rent out their ground without a healthy share of the takings being allocated to the host. With both grounds much in demand as neutral venues for cup ties, or for clubs who didn't have the luxury of a large-capacity stadium, this effective cartel established by the two clubs proved very lucrative.

By the time of Celtic's foundation and their establishment of a friendship with their near neighbours, Rangers had vacated their rented home at Kinning Park and moved to their new ground at Ibrox. The relocation was not accompanied by immediate success, however, either on or off the field. After an initial season treading water, which was notable yet again for complaints by opponents about Rangers fielding professional players, notably when striker Bob Brand appeared in a game against Cowlairs in the Glasgow Cup which resulted in Rangers' 2-1 victory being scratched and a replay ordered, the team's form slumped dramatically in season 1888/89. Of 39 games played, only 13 were won, with seven draws and 19 defeats, including a 6-1 thrashing at the hands of Celtic in the Glasgow Cup at Ibrox in the first competitive meeting between the pair. Off the field, the committee which ran the club was in uproar; the 1888 AGM was described by the *Scottish Umpire* as 'the most cantankerous ever in the history of the club... and that is saying a great deal', and amid further squabbling, the club's half-yearly meeting in November had to be adjourned for a week's cooling-off period to allow passions to thaw and tempers to subside.

By the end of that conference, Tom Vallance had announced his intention to sever his formal ties with the club and stand down as president at the end of the season, ending the final link between the club and its early founders. Despite all the publicity which had accompanied the initial move to Ibrox, crowds were now down as low as 500 and on at least two occasions the club couldn't find enough players to make up a full complement of 11. On New Year's Day 1889, Aston Villa arrived in Glasgow expecting to play Rangers, only to find that, due to an administrative error, their expected opponents were not even in the country, but had journeyed to England to fulfil a fixture instead, where they lost to Blackburn Rovers. In addition, the club was burdened with the debts incurred from the construction of the new ground and, with the accounts showing that annual turnover had dropped by £1,000, it's no exaggeration to say that Rangers were teetering on the brink of extinction at this time.

Things began to improve for the club, however, when, in May 1889, Rangers appointed 23-year-old William Wilton to the post of match secretary. Along with new president John Mellish, who had replaced Vallance, Wilton attended a meeting, at the invitation of the West

Dunbartonshire village side Renton, in Glasgow in March 1890, which would lead to the formation of a Scottish league. The league, based on the model which had been introduced in England two seasons earlier, would provide regular fixtures for the invited teams, as well as a trophy at the end of the campaign. Although it initially played second fiddle to the major cup competitions, the league quickly became a great success and a second division was introduced in 1893, which expanded to include teams from beyond the central belt.

The game, already hugely popular, would take further strides forward in the new decade as professionalism was finally and inevitably permitted in Scotland in 1893, in part to deal with the problem of Scottish footballers heading south to earn their living, where payments to players had been legitimised in 1885. The introduction of the league and regular fixtures led to a general improvement in the standard of play, but it also precipitated the decline of former giants of the game Queen's Park, the steadfastly amateur club having refused to join, which was perhaps most keenly felt following the heavy defeat inflicted by Celtic, the new kids on the block, in the Scottish Cup Final of 1892, 5-1 at Ibrox.

It was a warning that would go unheeded by the Mount Florida club. A new hierarchy was emerging in the Scottish game, based on the strength of the teams with the largest catchment area of supporters, at the expense of the smaller, more rural and amateur sides. In addition, after the emergence of Celtic, football fans from the outlying districts around Glasgow started to lose interest in the fortunes of their local teams, preferring instead to travel to Ibrox to support the only side that seemed capable of standing up to the Irish phenomenon. In the 1893/94 season, Celtic won the league but Rangers overcame their dreadful record against the Parkhead men up to that point by defeating them in four games out of six, a feat which no other team had previously achieved, and in the absence of any credible challenge from Queen's Park in the new set-up, the Ibrox side seemed to be the obvious candidate to restore wounded Scottish pride.

Two years later, in September 1896, the *Scottish Sport* were clearly indicating Rangers, whom they had started referring to without any obvious sense of irony as 'Scotia's darling club', when they appeared to issue a rallying cry for a native Scottish team to break the stranglehold of Celtic and the recently reformed Hibernian, who were leading the way in the race for the league championship after recent victories over Hearts and Rangers respectively. 'The two Irish teams are at the top of the table. Is this not a reflection on Scotland?' the paper lamented.

With the supporter base so polarised and the battle lines so clearly defined, the beginnings of religious and ethnic prejudice also began to appear in the press around this time. Cartoons were published in the pages of the sports journals with unflattering comparisons between the Irish Celt, generally depicted as rotund and ugly, and the true Scottish Ranger, which would unquestionably by today's standards, and perhaps even by the standards of the day, be considered racist. Commenting on sketches which appeared in the *Scottish Referee*, historian Bill Murray, who made a systematic study of these cartoons, noted that they 'depicted the Celtic player with the dumb look of a creature emerging from a peat bog, while the Rangers equivalent had the noble stature and intelligent eyes of the Aryan'.

Rangers were clearly being portrayed as the team of choice for the indigenous Scot, and the antidote to the phenomenon of the neighbouring Irish club, whose supporters, even in the lean years, seemed to follow their team with a quite astonishing degree of enthusiasm. The foundation of Celtic had an elevating effect on the impoverished section of the Glasgow Irish, but their emergence also coincided with the first tentative steps of prominent Catholics into the spheres of business, the professions and local politics, and the subsequent success of the club lifted spirits across the whole community. Rangers, on the other hand, such a controversial institution back in the 1880s, were now seen as the last great hope for the Scottish, Protestant establishment.

In the face of this polarisation, the fortunes of the provincial village sides must have seemed curiously irrelevant, even to many of the local residents, as the revolution in cheap and accessible public transport allowed fans to travel easily to Glasgow, where footballing passions were being aroused in great numbers, with attendances at Ibrox and Celtic Park regularly dwarfing the population of some entire rural communities. By the end of the decade, six of the original league invitees had been put out of business, including Victorian giants Vale of Leven, founding fathers Renton, whose belief in a 'brotherhood of equality and fraternity' had failed to survive the transition to professionalism, and Dumbarton, although within a few years the latter would re-emerge.

Dumbarton had won the inaugural league championship, jointly with Rangers, as the two teams completed their maiden campaigns with 29 points collected from their 18 fixtures. After a 2-2 draw in a play-off at Cathkin Park in a match which saw Dumbarton retrieve a two-goal deficit, the two clubs were declared joint champions. The following season, the Sons would march to the title and claim the championship outright for the first and last time in their history, but just five years later, after their 5-1 loss to Rangers in the Scottish Cup Final of 1897, Dumbarton, great stalwarts of the Victorian era, finished bottom of the Second Division and folded.

By contrast, following the appearance of Celtic and the introduction of the league, Rangers recovered quickly from their parlous off-field state at the start of the decade, with crowds of over 20,000 now being attracted to Ibrox for the big games. To secure the title outright, however, the club would have to wait until 1899, when Rangers completed the season by winning all 18 of their matches, a remarkable feat which has never been matched in world football, although they lost the Scottish Cup Final 2-0 to Celtic. By then, the Ibrox club had finally managed to capture the Scottish Cup for the first time, beating the same opponents 3-1 in the final in 1894 in a match which saw Celtic's attacks repelled repeatedly by the renowned Ibrox full-back pairing of Jock Drummond and Nicol Smith. Rangers then picked off their opponents, with the crucial third goal scored by talisman John McPherson, before Willie Maley's consolation.

After having to endure such a long wait before they could finally claim the old trophy, the Scottish Cup was won again by the Ibrox club in 1897 and retained in 1898, with victories in the Hampden finals over Dumbarton and Kilmarnock. Then, in 1899, the club took the step of forming a limited liability company, the Rangers Football Club Limited, and £12,000 was raised from new shareholders to help fund the construction of a revamped stadium on the site of the present Ibrox Park.

The incorporation of the football club meant the end of the old committee structure, which saw the club's business conducted openly, and the establishment in its place of a closed boardroom, where directors could now plot, scheme and ruminate behind the scenes in complete secrecy.

As part of the reorganisation at Ibrox, match secretary William Wilton was the first man to be appointed as the club's team manager, in May 1899. Wilton was born in Largs in 1865 and he paid his membership fees and joined up with Rangers in September 1883, although his talents seem to have been away from the football field, and he never played for the club's first team. He did, however, turn out for the 'Swifts', Rangers' reserve side, and after his appointment as match secretary in 1889 he found himself in charge of scheduling games for the 'Swifts' although, because he didn't understand football, he wasn't on the second string's selection committee. Gradually his influence on Rangers grew and he successfully argued for an expansion of the club's main selection committee following acrimonious in-fighting and a series of poor results in 1887. Later, he instigated the Ibrox Sports, a chiefly athletics event which put the stadium to use during the close season, and which continued to run during the summer up until the 1950s.

Bald, bespectacled and something of a busybody, Wilton had a ringside seat during some of the more glaring oversights and malpractices of the old committee, and he had seen the club at its administrative and financial nadir. Determined to improve matters, he oversaw the expansion of the first Ibrox stadium, including the construction of a new press box, for which he was fêted by the Fourth Estate, and he guided the club through the murky waters of professionalism and the arrival of the new league structure, combining his duties at Rangers with the role of the league's first secretary, in addition to a position within the SFA. After his appointment as the club's first manager following incorporation, he guided the team to new levels of success on the field, as the season of maximum points in 1899 was followed by three subsequent victorious campaigns, allowing Rangers to establish themselves as the undisputed best team in the land, with four titles in a row between 1899 and 1902.

Rangers were now looking at the prospect of a very bright future. With the incorporation of the club, a new stadium designed by renowned architect Archibald Leitch which was attracting an average of 13,000 fans for every league game (considerably more for the fixtures against the Irish teams, Celtic and Hibernian), and four consecutive league championships in the bag, all complemented by some heroically biased coverage in the Scottish press, everything seemed to be falling together nicely for Rangers by 1902. The 'New Ibrox' or 'Greater Ibrox' had, thanks to Wilton's solicitations, been selected as the venue for several cup finals as well as for the prestigious home international matches, the jewel in the crown of which was the annual Scotland versus England game. Prior to 1906, when the fixture was moved permanently to Hampden Park, clubs with suitable stadiums used to compete to host the big internationals and the 1902 match against England was to be held at Ibrox Park.

The fixture had been instigated as early as November 1872, thanks largely to Charles Alcock and his friends at the FA, at a time when competitive football was still dominated by alumni teams from the public schools and the universities. It was an era which, by the turn of the century, must have seemed curiously quaint after 30 years of almost uninterrupted growth and expansion in the game's popular appeal, and by 1902 the interest in the annual cross-border contest with England was huge. The crowd had been urged to arrive early and an hour before kick-off, on Saturday, 5 April, Ibrox was full, and as the marching bands provided their pre-match entertainment, latecomers continued to try to gain admittance to the stadium, resulting in an estimated attendance of 75,000, well in excess of what the new ground was designed to accommodate. The terracing was constructed from wood, supported and reinforced by a steel structure, which rose to 40 feet off the ground at the back of the stand. Iron railings divided each block of terracing, which were supposed to limit the capacity in specific areas and counteract the swaying effect of a large crowd.

Concerns were raised before the match that the structure might be unsafe but these were dismissed, with the press reporting that it had been tested by engineers and used safely in previous matches. However, the wet weather had degraded the strength and integrity of the wooden boards and around the tenth minute of the match, under intense pressure from the sheer weight of numbers in the crowd, who were probably stamping and swaying and grouping in a section towards the back of the West Stand, the structure collapsed and hundreds of people plunged through the yawning gap to the ground below. Twenty-five people were killed and more than 500 were injured in what would later become known as the first Ibrox disaster. The game was allowed to continue to a conclusion, but the result was eventually declared void, and the match was later replayed in Birmingham with proceeds going to the relief fund set up for the victims' families. At the time it was the worst accident in the history of British football, although sadly it wouldn't remain so.

Following the disaster, lattice stands constructed from steel and wood were gradually phased out across the country and replaced with terraces built on banks of earth and reinforced concrete, the kind of which were in use at football grounds throughout Britain for most of the 20th century. The accident reveals the extent to which football had developed by the turn of the century, beyond the capacity of the authorities to cope with its increased popularity, especially in west central Scotland where the game had been embraced with particular enthusiasm. At a subsequent trial, which effectively served as the inquiry into the disaster, the constructor of the affected section of terracing was acquitted of all charges, and while no blame was officially apportioned to Rangers, there was severe criticism in the press, including from the Catholic *Glasgow Observer*, who noted that Celtic Park was, 'a splendidly equipped ground, which has stood the test of previous record crowds', and which had been overlooked in favour of 'the Rangers wire-pullers'.

Celtic Park had in fact been selected to host the England fixture on all four of the previous occasions it was played in Scotland between 1894 and 1900, and seemed to be the preferred venue, but for some reason Ibrox was chosen in 1902. The finger of blame was being pointed at Wilton, who was stung by accusations that crowd safety had been jeopardised by the desire to pull in as many paying spectators as possible, and that, as a result of his behind-the-scenes machinations, the fixture had been moved to a less suitable ground. The manager responded by putting his entire squad of players up for sale in order to raise money for the improvements to Ibrox which were necessary to meet the new safety requirements. Over the next two years the club would spend £42,000 on Ibrox, including £15,000 on the outright purchase of the ground, but on the field they suffered as a result. Rangers would go on to win the Scottish Cup in 1903, but it would be a while before they would be able to field a team as strong as the four-in-a-row champions again.

The tussle in the awarding of the England fixture to Rangers and Ibrox in 1902 was indicative of the souring of relations between the two Glasgow clubs by this point. The friendly association between some of the early Celtic players and their counterparts at Rangers had long since melted away and been replaced, on the field at least, by a series of tousy incidents in numerous stormy clashes between the sides. As early as 1894, following a league game at Celtic Park, some Celtic players had complained to the *Glasgow Observer*'s columnist about the sectarian abuse they had been subjected to, with the paper subsequently reporting that, 'the language some of the Rangers players used was most disgraceful – "Fenian", "Papist", "Irish" all being hurled with, of course, the most vulgar accompaniments. This is not how it used to be; Rangers and Celts were always pretty friendly, and the change of front seems strange.' Clearly, the initial healthy rivalry between the two clubs was rapidly beginning to be disfigured by a religious and ethnic dimension, and it was now not uncommon for games between the teams to end in a brawl.

In 1896, following another heated encounter, the *Scottish Sport* laid the blame for the deteriorating on-field relationship at the door of both clubs, wondering if it was 'possible for the Celtic and Rangers to meet now, not even in a charity match, without the worst feelings and considerable amount of foulness creeping into the play'. The paper was moved to lament the 'bad blood' which had developed between the two clubs, and cautioned that the increasing antipathy 'would cool the public interest'. It was a warning which the broadcaster and historian Bob Crampsey would later describe as 'one of the most inaccurate prophecies of all time'.

This was the time of the emergence of the 'Old Firm', as they became known, a sarcastic reference coined by the Glasgow sporting journal *Scottish Referee* to describe not only the polarisation and extent of the rivalry between Rangers and Celtic by this point, but there was also the suggestion that this mutual animosity was proving financially beneficial to the two clubs at a time when the giants of Victorian football were going to the wall. The press had already noted a curious dichotomy in the affairs of both institutions which was becoming evident throughout the 1890s; on the field, the rivalry was growing increasingly bitter, with an attached religious and ethnic animosity becoming gradually more apparent, but at boardroom level there was still a tacit admission on the part of both clubs that their burgeoning rivalry was proving profitable at the turnstiles.

However, by the turn of the century, relations behind the scenes had also begun to cool, and even after the Ibrox disaster, the ill-feeling continued. Rangers had organised, as part of the victims' relief fund, a tournament involving the top two teams from Scotland and England, dubbed the British League Cup. The strength of the Glasgow sides at this time can be seen from the outcome of the two semi-finals, with an under-strength Rangers comfortably defeating Everton, the English league runners-up, while Celtic took apart champions Sunderland with a 5-1 rout of the Wearsiders' famous 'team of all the talents'. In the final between the two Glasgow clubs, Celtic came out on top and claimed the impressive Glasgow Exhibition Cup, which Rangers had offered to the winners.

Later, however, Rangers would ask for the trophy back, on the grounds that it was the property of their club, and that it had only been ceremonially presented to the winners. The cup had been won the previous year in an eight-team tournament to mark the Exhibition with a 3-1 defeat of Celtic in the final and was engraved with the inscription 'Won by Rangers FC'. Needless to say, Celtic refused all requests to return the trophy, maintaining that it was won fairly on the field of play in a properly organised competition.

Celtic and Rangers were by now establishing their dominance over the Scottish game by consistently annexing the league championship, including Rangers' four in a row between 1899 and 1902, which was surpassed by Celtic's six consecutive titles between 1905 and 1910. The changing of the guard seemed to take place at the end of the 1905 season when Rangers lost a play-off to Celtic for the league, 2-1 at Hampden, in a match which was noteworthy for the choice of referee.

Following more controversial incidents in games between the teams that season, including the enforced abandonment of a cup tie at Parkhead, the SFA took the unprecedented step of appointing an English official for such an important match, Mr F. Kirkham of Preston. It was not a happy end to the season for Rangers, who had also lost the Scottish Cup Final at Hampden after a replay, 3-1 to Third Lanark. Thirds, a former soldiers' team founded in 1872 as Third Lanarkshire Rifle Volunteers, who had only severed their links with the military the previous year, would go on to win the league the following season, but their 1904 success would be the only occasion the title would not be won by Rangers or Celtic until Motherwell's sole championship-winning season of 1931/32, which in itself was the only success outside of the Glasgow duopoly between the wars.

Increasingly during the Edwardian period, Rangers were attracting to Ibrox the kind of crowd which could match Celtic in terms of numbers and fervour, although, despite the clearly defined divisions in the supporter base, it seems that the rivalry had not yet had time to fester to the point of extremism in the wider society. The two sets of fans were still able to come together if they felt that the 'Old Firm' imperative was being used to exploit their allegiances, and in 1909 supporters of the two clubs were involved in an extraordinary event following the Scottish Cup Final replay between the two teams.

It was commonly believed at the time that Rangers and Celtic preferred to meet each other in the semi-finals of the cup competitions, so they wouldn't have to share the gate receipts with a third-party club, whose neutral ground would be in use for the final, but that year the two teams avoided each other until the showpiece, which ended in a 2-2 draw at Hampden in front of 70,000 spectators. Some newspapers had wrongly suggested that the subsequent replay would be played to a conclusion but, after another draw, it gradually became clear that there would be no extra time and that the final would have to proceed to a third match at a future date.

At this point the angry crowd, with the rival fans apparently acting in unison, started rioting, tearing down fences, setting fire to the pay-boxes and bombarding the police and the fire brigade, when they were eventually mobilised, with a shower of stones. The two clubs were embarrassed at the accusation that they had arranged a third payday for themselves, a claim which, although implausible, reflected the widespread view, chiefly emanating from the press, that the duopoly were still more partners than rivals at this time, especially when it came to the matter of exploiting the paying public for financial gain.

In the end, the clubs reached a mutual agreement with the SFA not to play a third match and the cup that year was withheld, depriving Celtic of the possibility of a third consecutive league and cup 'Double'. The riots, although shocking, suggested that an element within both groups of supporters still instinctively believed that they had more in common with each other than they did with the people who were running the game and those who were making so much money out of football's popularity. It seems conceivable that the rivalry in Glasgow might have developed along the same lines as in other cities along the west coast of Britain, particularly those who have benefited down the years from a strong Scottish and Irish influence, where evidence of a healthy relationship, in footballing cities such as Liverpool and Manchester, between Scottish migrants, Irish settlers and the local culture is readily apparent in the region's successful football teams. Big clubs in these and other cities in England had started to diverge along religious lines around the time of their formation, but the divisions were not allowed to persist.

In Glasgow, things were to take a different turn however, with Rangers adopting a strict no Catholics, exclusionary employment policy for most of the 20th century. To be fair, Rangers had attracted very few Catholic players to their ranks by the end of the Victorian era, but a few had turned out or guested for the team in the first 40 years since the club's foundation. In the first decade of the new century by contrast, Rangers seemed to have no compunction at all about signing Catholics, as the club agonised over their pursuit of Celtic, who were enjoying the most successful period in their history at the time, with a run of six consecutive titles between 1905 and 1910.

At least three Catholic players were signed by Rangers in the first decade of the century, although none made any impact at the club, with the possible lone exception of Willie Kivlichan, a Glasgow University medical student, who lasted the entire 1906/07 season at Ibrox, before switching to Celtic in a controversial swap deal with Alex Bennett. But the arrival on the Clyde in 1912 of the Belfast-based shipbuilders, Harland and Wolff, seems to have been a crucial turning point in the consolidation of a permanently divisive, sectarian element to the rivalry in Glasgow.

Harland and Wolff were not, it seems fair to say, an equal opportunities employer. Back in Ulster, they had allowed their Protestant workers to purge the company of Catholic colleagues at a time when the political situation across Ireland was becoming increasingly unstable, particularly after British Prime Minister William Gladstone's repeated attempts during the 1880s and '90s to introduce a Home Rule bill for Ireland. The proposed legislation had provoked a panicked, violent reaction from the Unionist community in the north of the country, which was stoked up by Lord Randolph Churchill for his own political purposes and later condemned by his son, Winston, who described the subsequent anti-

Catholic riots in Belfast over the summer of 1886 as 'savage, repeated and prolonged'.

Harland and Wolff were subsequently operating an exclusionary employment policy, which they had applied with impunity in Ireland and which they now brought with them to Scotland, along with thousands of workers over the ensuing years, whose skills were readily transferable to the Clydeside yards and who were far more zealous in their anti-Catholicism than their native colleagues. Soon after their arrival in Govan in 1912, the same year that the company's flagship vessel, the *Titanic*, foundered in the mid-Atlantic, Harland and Wolff loaned their neighbours Rangers £90,000, as the club continued to struggle with the costs associated with the construction and modernisation of Ibrox Park, as well as the ongoing fallout from the stadium disaster a decade earlier.

In his book *The Spirit of Ibrox*, Rangers historian Robert McElroy all but admits that as a condition of the loan, Harland and Wolff insisted that the Ibrox club should adopt the same employment practices as the shipbuilding firm and remain a Catholic-free zone. The exact details of the arrangement between Harland and Wolff and Rangers were not disclosed at the time, with the conditions of the loan agreement stating only that it was 'subject to those private agreements made between the parties but not subject herein'.

Some credence can be given to McElroy's claim, however, not least because it appears in an officially approved history of the club, although such an allegation is difficult to prove conclusively, both because of the veil of secrecy which had descended over Rangers' affairs in the years following the club's incorporation, but also on account of the tacit vow of silence in the face of controversy which surrounds the activities of Freemasons and other largely Protestant-only secret organisations, whose members would have included high-level officials in both institutions at the time. Also in the same year, 1912, the chairmanship of Rangers, following the death of the respected James Henderson, passed to Sir John Ure Primrose, a man who had previously split with the Liberal Party over his opposition to Gladstone's Home Rule bill in 1886 and who, as patron and honorary president of the club in 1890, had publicly established the enduring link between Rangers and the Masons when he recruited the Ibrox side to a fundraising event for the Grand Lodge of Scotland. In the absence of any formal arrangement between

Primrose's Rangers and Harland and Wolff, secret or otherwise, the club's deliberate failure to sign Catholic footballers from this point onwards can only be put down to coincidence and as a result, anti-Catholicism, and religious prejudice in general, would subsequently become a disease which would fester at the heart of Scottish football right down until recent times, a persistently chronic condition which has stubbornly resisted all attempts to eradicate it, returning spasmodically even when subjected to the most modern treatments. A failure to acknowledge and properly diagnose the problem, as it pertains to Scottish football, as primarily a Rangers matter from this moment on would ultimately only exacerbate the issue.

In the meantime, the Ibrox club were continuing to expand under diligent secretary-manager William Wilton. New turnstiles were ordered to accommodate an increased average attendance of over 20,000 for league games at Ibrox and the club finally ended Celtic's run of six consecutive titles by winning the league in 1911, then repeating the feat over the following two seasons. In 1914, Rangers recruited Bill Struth as the club's fitness trainer to replace James Wilson, who had died earlier in the year from pneumonia. Struth, then working for Clyde, had written to the club requesting consideration for the vacant position, which four years earlier he had turned down. As a former athlete, rather than a football player, Struth was perhaps the ideal man to oversee the training regime of an early-20th-century professional footballer, where the work consisted largely of strict fitness regimes involving running, shooting and long walks in heavy sweaters. Struth's regimented approach would give Rangers the edge over some of their less disciplined rivals, and he would later go on to succeed Wilton in the role of manager and lead the club to new levels of success and domination in the 1920s and '30s.

With the advent of war in Europe in 1914, Celtic restored their hegemony of Scottish football with four consecutive league titles, including a remarkable run of 62 games undefeated between November 1915 and April 1917, a record which stood for over 100 years, as league football continued to be played in Scotland during the conflict. It was thought that the game would inspire workers in the munitions factories and elsewhere by giving them something to look forward to at the weekend, but there was also a more cynical motivation behind the decision to maintain the league programme as, following a meeting between the football authorities and the War Office, clubs in Scotland were used as recruiting posts for the war effort.

With the country in the grip of a patriotic fervour at the perceived 'national danger', and with the war expected to be short and over by Christmas, many young men with an interest in football were enticed to join up and serve alongside their mates as part of a 'football battalion' attached to the Highland Light Infantry. Needless to say, most of these young men never came home. Back on the home front, Wilton's salary at Ibrox increased during World War One, as did his bonuses, and he arranged for himself a benefit match against Everton. In his correspondence with the Merseyside club, Wilton candidly explained, 'The proceeds go as complimentary to the writer after 30 years' service. I do not wish, however, to advertise it as a "benefit", so it will just be billed as an ordinary match.'

During the war, both Wilton and trainer Struth served with the Red Cross at Bellahouston Hospital in Glasgow, in addition to their duties with Rangers. Wilton himself was well beyond the age of conscription, but as the junior partner, Struth was given the choice in 1917 of either being recruited into the army or going full-time with the Red Cross. He chose the latter.

In season 1918, Celtic and Rangers were once again locked in a two-way tussle for the league championship, with both teams level on points going into the last game of the season. Rangers beat Clyde at Ibrox while Celtic were held at home by Motherwell, giving the Ibrox club their first championship success in five years. While criticism of Rangers was not often heard in the pages of the mainstream press at this time, the Irish-owned *Glasgow Observer* held no such reservations. Its football columnist, 'Man in the Know', described Rangers as 'the piebald champions', alleging that they had assembled a 'variety troupe' of footballers from other teams by taking advantage of the wartime rule that allowed players to move more freely between clubs on temporary loan arrangements.

The columnist also accused Rangers of buying their way to success rather than developing and nurturing young players, although the same writer displayed less chagrin the following year when the title was again won by a single point as, in a mirror image of the previous campaign,

Celtic captured the league on the last day of the season after a 2-0 win away to Ayr United.

On 28 April 1920, Rangers regained the title from their great rivals with a game to spare following a goalless draw at Dumbarton. A few days later, the fixture card was completed with a victory over Morton, after which a fatigued William Wilton embarked on a break with club director Joseph Buchanan. They were guests of James Marr, a former committee man with Rangers in the days before the club's incorporation, on his vessel the *Caltha* at Gourock on the Firth of Clyde. In the early hours of the morning, the boat was driven from its moorings by a storm and, as he tried to climb the mast and reach the safety of the quay, Wilton was swept overboard and lost, presumed drowned. It would be almost two months before the death of the Rangers manager could be officially confirmed, when his body was eventually found floating in the bay. Still aged only 55, it was a tragic end for a man who had looked after the interests of the club with diligence and dedication.

William Wilton was a manager in every sense of the word. One gets the impression that, had he been in charge of a bank, he would have managed that institution in much the same way that he had presided over the affairs of Rangers Football Club. Administrators such as Wilton are the reason the term 'manager' is still in common use today, to indicate the person in charge of the club's first team, rather than the more rarely heard, at least until modern times, continental terms such as 'coach' or 'trainer'. 'Trainer' in fact more usually referred to the fitness gurus, James Wilson and later Bill Struth, who had more day to day contact with the players, while the manager, an aloof authority, maintained his distance. Following the vacancy created by the untimely death of his boss, it was a role which would seem custom-made for Struth. If Wilton set the tone for Rangers' *modus operandi*, in the setting of standards and in his rigid, disciplinarian tendencies, his methods would be imitated, emulated and ultimately taken to a new level by his successor over the years to come.

3

THE GRAND OLD MAN
OF IBROX

O VER the course of the first 50 years of its history, Rangers
Football Club had come to be seen and defined in Scotland
as the team to face down the insurgents. Rivals Celtic had
been phenomenally successful in the early years of Scottish league
football, winning 16 of the titles contested between the inaugural
season of 1890/91 and 1922, exactly half. The competition between
the two Glasgow clubs had intensified on the field of play, but it was
becoming increasingly heated more broadly too, with Celtic able to draw
on the support of a huge, enthusiastic following from its Irish-extracted
community of fans.

As their local rivals, and with a big urban fanbase of their own,
Rangers, a wayward and widely vilified club in their earlier years, had
responded to the call from sections of the sporting press and elsewhere
for a team to stand up for the native Scottish interests and meet the
challenge posed by the foreign, Irish club. There is no date which can
be pinpointed as to when this process began or was complete, with the
nebulous world of Rangers' internal affairs being notoriously difficult
to penetrate, but what seems clear is that the Ibrox club were supremely
successful in this new capacity.

Between 1923 and the arrival of manager Jock Stein at Parkhead
in 1965, Rangers won the league title on 23 occasions compared to

Celtic's four. Other great teams flourished during the same period, notably Hibs in the late '40s and Hearts in the late '50s; both had great, multi-championship winning teams, but neither could maintain a sustained challenge to the relentless, trophy-gathering momentum of the Rangers juggernaut.

Of course, the gathering storm of the 'Old Firm' rivalry in Glasgow was not being played out in a social and cultural vacuum, but rather, in the early years of the inter-war period, against a febrile political environment across the British Isles. By 1922, Ireland had fought for and received a version of home rule, which allowed the newly created 'Free State' to be governed from Dublin, but the island would be partitioned and six of the nine counties of Ulster, what became known as Northern Ireland, an enclave with in-built Protestant majority, were to remain under British rule.

The fall-out from this agreement, obtained from Westminster by the Irish statesman Michael Collins, led to the bloody and internecine Irish Civil War of 1922–23, of which Collins himself was a casualty. Many of the Irish immigrants in Scotland were from the border counties of Donegal, Sligo and Cavan and, following the suppression of the Easter Rising in 1916 and the execution of its leaders, there was strong support among sections of the diaspora in Scotland for the cause of Irish nationalism. Irish Premier Éamon de Valera later thanked the Irish in Scotland for their support in the conflict, while on the other side of the divide, the bowler-hatted Orangemen of the north, many of them ethnic Scots, reacted with venom and fury to the concessions that had been made to the rebels, which they feared would threaten their protected status on the island of Ireland. Meanwhile, across the water, the backlash against the Irish community from the Scottish establishment was ferocious.

At a time when reactionary movements such as Nazism were germinating in mainland Europe, the Church of Scotland in 1923 commissioned a report on the malevolent influence of Irish immigration and the threat posed by the Education (Scotland) Act of 1918, which allowed for the provision of state-funded, Catholic education. While due acknowledgement must be given to any genuine concerns which existed at the time, it is fair to say the language of the report has dated badly over the ensuing decades and to the modern ear, more used as we are to the notion of multi-cultural, multi-faith societies, it is indeed a truly dreadful document. The report talks shamelessly and openly about the threat posed by 'the Irish intruders' to the native Scots and 'their racial supremacy in their native land'. According to the report, 'the time is rapidly approaching when... whole communities in parish, village and town will be predominantly Irish. It is, in fact, a sober and restrained prophecy to say that... the great plain of Scotland stretching from Glasgow in the west to Dundee and Edinburgh in the east will soon be dominated by the Irish race.' It urged the Scottish people in response to 'safeguard their heritage' and indeed to take 'whatever steps may be necessary to secure this just and patriotic end'.

Note that the report had no concerns about Scotland's tiny minority of native Catholics, 'who have a right to call Scotland their country, in common with their fellow-countrymen of the Protestant Faith', nor was there any complaint about the presence of what it referred to as an 'Orange population', immigrants from the partitioned six counties who were also moving across the water in increasing numbers at this time, for 'they are of the same race as ourselves and of the same Faith, and are readily assimilated to the Scottish population'. The sole target of the report's concern, the 'menace' as it describes them, was explicitly and specifically the Irish Catholic community who, it should go without saying, made up the vast majority of the Celtic support at the time. In an echo of the 'Judenfrage', the Jewish question, constructed by the Nazis in the years before the Holocaust, in Scotland the problem would come to be defined as an 'Irischefrage', the question of the Irish and what to do with them.

The report was submitted to the Church's General Assembly by the Committee on Church and Nation, whose members made up the rank and file of the Scottish establishment of the day: as well as the Moderator and the Procurator, the committee contained four Reverend Professors, eight Reverend Doctors, 17 Reverends, two MPs, three lawyers and two Lords. Despite the elite nature of the committee's panel, the report was never reluctant to flatter the native Scottish working-class chappie, dismissing any suggestion for example that he was being outbred by his more vigorous and fertile Irish counterpart – doubtless the kind of juvenile sentiment which would have played into the hands of football supporters of the day. To be fair to the Kirk, most of this gibberish was retracted in the 1950s, after World War Two revealed the full extent and brutality of the Nazi atrocities, but of course it subsequently proved far more difficult to erase such a mentality from a bunch of hard core football fans, especially when notions of Catholic bashing and Protestant superiority were already being effectively employed as a vehicle to sporting success.

Later in the decade, in March 1929, a series of articles published in the *Glasgow Herald* newspaper – a beacon of middle-class, Protestant respectability – poured scorn on the claim that the Irish were a menace to society, with the paper's forensic examination of crime, unemployment and other statistics effectively rubbishing almost every one of the report's allegations, claim by claim. With fantastically detailed research, the unknown author of the articles also ridiculed the idea, widely propagated at the time, that Scotland was being swamped by zealous Irishmen intent on converting the country to the Catholic faith, pointing out that, in contrast to the 'stream' of the previous century when Irish labour helped Scotland to become an industrialised nation, by the 1920s the levels of immigration from Ireland had been reduced to 'the veriest trickle', and came mostly from the partitioned six counties.

Nevertheless, set against the backdrop of the harsh economic conditions in Glasgow at the time, the razor gangs and the slums familiar to us from *No Mean City* and elsewhere, the report set the tone for a bitter and divisive segregation of Scottish society, which spilled over on to the stands and terraces of the day and exacerbated what was already one of the most virulent and sectarian rivalries anywhere in the football world.

For Celtic, trying to stand their ground and maintain their traditions, they found that the world was changing around them. As the report demonstrated, anti-Catholicism in Scotland had always been more of an issue among the establishment classes and the appointed elite, unlike in England for example, where the Stockport riots in the 1850s had seen Irishmen, fleeing the Famine, turned out of their homes and forced to live rough by the impromptu actions of an unruly mob. By the 1920s however, religious bigotry north of the border appeared to manifest itself most conspicuously in an unlikely, but growing alliance between the ruling and lower orders, which to a large extent bypassed the respectable, middle-class community – as the generally positive response to *The Herald*'s series of articles from its readers in that bracket of society later testified – while also flying in the face of such strong Scottish notions as working-class solidarity. This new, developing aspect to anti-Catholicism meant that the problem became particularly intransigent and harder to completely eradicate, and religious prejudice continued to tarnish sections of Scottish society long after the issue went out of fashion in the rest of mainland Britain.

In addition, Scotland in the 1920s was a country that seemed to have lost its sense of direction. An abortive attempt to introduce a bill for Scottish home rule had been put before Parliament in 1914 but, following the war, the issue did not resurface as the country preferred to see itself in terms of its role within the Empire. Culturally, it was a time of the emergence of familiar national stereotypes, of tight-fisted curmudgeons recognisable to readers of John Buchan's *The Thirty-Nine Steps* and, in Sir Harry Lauder's popular portrayals of Highlanders singing and dancing and 'roaming in the gloaming' the country's image of itself was reduced to little more than a music hall joke. With all the issues in Ireland spilling over on to the shores of her erstwhile Celtic cousin, including the movement back into the Glasgow area of a significant number of Ulster Scots, who brought their prejudices and discriminatory employment practices to traditional working-class occupations, most notably in the shipyards at organisations such as Harland and Wolff, anti-Catholicism in Scotland filtered down to the masses and became part of the *lingua franca* of everyday political discourse.

The role of Rangers in this process, with the club now openly practising an exclusionary employment policy and revelling in its self-appointed status as the nation's foremost Protestant sporting institution, cannot be underestimated. As Bill Murray observes of this period in his book *The Old Firm*, 'The directors, management and foremen of the heavy industries in Scotland were nearly all Protestants, often Freemasons, sometimes Orangemen: in each case their sympathies went to the native Scots; that is to say Scots by name and religion, for they would not have considered a Catholic a true Scot. This clannishness, looking after "one's own", was rife in the industrial sphere, and was reflected in the Rangers football club.'

Fellow historian Tom Campbell agrees, 'Rangers FC, which had not been totally exclusive in its recruiting policy prior to the First World War, closed ranks as their religious apartheid proved immensely profitable at the turnstiles, in an era of poisonous bigotry.'

Into this heady mix strode one William 'Bill' Struth, stepping with some poise over the unrecovered body of his former boss William Wilton to assume his role in the manager's office at Ibrox, in June 1920. Struth was a strict disciplinarian and possessed the kind of stern, authoritarian presence that would make Alex Ferguson look like Claudio Ranieri. Perfect for Rangers, he dominated the club for over three decades the way a sergeant-major dominates his regiment, although, like several other figures who have intervened in the club's history and helped to take Rangers in a radical new direction, Struth was not in fact a traditional Rangers man and had no traceable connection with the club before his appointment as fitness trainer at Ibrox in May 1914.

Born in 1876 in Leith, Struth grew up in Edinburgh, although his family home was in the mill town of Milnathort in Kinross-shire, where he frequently returned with his parents. He had been a middle distance runner in his youth, never a football player, and, in an era when the Corinthian spirit of the Olympic amateur was being revived, the young Struth was involved in the often murky world of professional athletics, racing for money, and on at least one occasion, he cheated in order to win the cash prize. At a meeting in Porthcawl, South Wales, around the turn of the century, Struth mingled with spectators at the start of the race, hiding the number on his shirt to disguise the fact that he was a competitor, and, when the starter pistol was fired, he darted out of the crowd and sprinted to the finish 20 yards ahead of the other athletes!

On crossing the line in first place, Struth made straight for the prize-winners' table, where he was handed a voucher for his winnings, before tearing off to the local bank to claim the cash while his bemused competitors were still arguing with the officials in protest. Despite the fact that he was a qualified and capable stonemason, he would travel around the country on public transport, often ducking and weaving to evade the ticket collectors, in order to compete for money. A working-class boy, who couldn't fit in, who cheated, he would take to his role as a figure of po-faced, establishment authority at Rangers like a duck to water.

When his running days came to an end, Struth joined Clyde FC in 1908 as the club's fitness trainer, and he moved to Rangers in the same capacity following the death of the incumbent James Wilson in 1914. Having worked closely with the players for six years, he was the natural successor to take over from Wilton after the secretary-manager was killed in a boating accident in May 1920, meaning that for the second time in six years Struth had benefited from the untimely death-in-office of his immediate predecessor at Ibrox. He displayed an initial reluctance, even a nervousness on his imminent appointment, telling the Ibrox directors that he wasn't up to the task of becoming the club's manager, but in fact he was the ideal candidate.

Struth's background in athletics had taught him the value of hard work, strict discipline and fierce determination, as well as a 'win at all costs' mentality, and he would emphasise the pride in playing for Rangers as the foremost club in the land. Under the new manager, players were expected to be properly turned out. The dress code for training was a collar and tie and, when the weather decreed, an overcoat of pure wool accompanied by, on matchdays or when representing the club in public, the *pièce de resistance*, a bowler hat. Everything had to be tip-top at the club; players would be pulled up or called into the manager's office if their hair was too long, their cravats weren't tied properly or if their collars were turned up, a working-class fashion statement of the day.

On one occasion, Struth offered to double youngster Willie Thornton's wages, after the striker arrived for training wearing immaculately shining, good-as-new boots, although young Thornton didn't have the gumption to admit that it was his mother who had polished them. A hierarchy existed within the changing room and the training staff would always seek out the senior players first to give them a rub down or towelling off when they stepped out of the huge bath in the home dressing room; less experienced players and youngsters would have to wait their turn or fend for themselves.

Perhaps more admirably, given the present day problem of 'simulation' in the game, Struth insisted that players who were injured during a match should play through their knock, rather than show their opponents a weakness by admitting that they were hurt. It was a mentality which the manager would often take to extremes, as reported injuries in general were treated with scepticism and stories abounded of players who were thought to be unfit being sent out on to the field and scoring the winning goal in games. Wing-half Tommy Muirhead, who captained the club for most of the 1920s, was only half-joking when he observed that Struth 'could persuade you to play with a broken ankle'. On one occasion the manager took matters into his own hands when, relying on skills he had picked up at Bellahouston Hospital during the war, but without any formal medical training, he carried out an operation on a player's troublesome soft corn using a sterilised penknife.

In return for their loyalty, the senior players at Ibrox in particular were treated like gods, and Struth's men could expect first-class travel on away trips and tours, as well as other privileges such as the best cinema seats in local theatres. In addition, at a time when footballers were generally seen as still belonging to the working-class communities from which they had emerged, Rangers players in the 1920s and '30s were among the best-paid sportsmen in Britain, with the senior pros earning a generous £8 per week, plus a £2 bonus for a win or £1 for a draw. In season 1929/30, that would have meant a total take-home pay of £442 for a Rangers regular, an unimaginable sum for the ordinary fan, as the Great Depression and the problems associated with poverty and deprivation in Glasgow blighted the outside, real world.

Struth made it his business to know everything that was going on in his players' lives and the manager would often surprise his charges by revealing that he was aware, through his network of spies and informants, of what pubs they were drinking in and even whether they had been to church on Sunday. He was unquestionably a shrewd operator and later admitted that he learnt the role of management, initially at least, by 'keeping his ears open and his mouth shut'.

The job, however, was almost unrecognisably different from the manager's, or head coach's, role today and at times it may seem difficult for the modern fan to comprehend the extent of Struth's responsibilities at Ibrox. There was no remit within his range of duties for coaching or improving players, and even the task of working with the squad on a daily basis and preparing the team for matches was left to the fitness trainer. The manager could have an influence over team selection, but the final say was always in the hands of the board, who rarely deviated from their preferred 11 every week, and the identification of potential signings was left to Struth's network of scouts, although the manager would always make the final decision on recruiting new players. There wasn't even much of an active role for Struth while a match was taking place, as tactical advice was non-existent and substitutions were not permitted, so the Rangers manager would often travel with his driver around the various grounds in Glasgow to look at players who had been brought to his attention while the game at Ibrox was still going on. He would then assess the ability of a potential signing on the basis of half an hour's viewing, claiming that he didn't require any more time to make up his mind. Once a target had been identified, as a necessary part of the vetting process, Struth would then enquire into the player's background and character, as these were considered at least as important as his technical ability, which he understood little about.

More usually during a match, when he wasn't gallivanting around Glasgow, the manager remained in the directors' box, and without the need for coaches lurking around dugouts, instructions and team talks were largely dispensed with or left to the captain and other senior players, who acted as the manager's on-field lieutenants, encouraging and instructing younger players in the style of play and what was expected of them. Former captain George Young told the club's centenary book *Growing with Glory*, 'The nearest he ever came to talking tactics was when he pointed out before an away game that it was a narrow pitch we would be playing on. Then he would suggest that instead of trying to squeeze five forwards across a narrow pitch, one should drop back and help create a bit more space. Then he left it to us to decide who that would be.'

From a modern perspective, it may seem difficult to imagine football players showing respect towards and taking instruction from someone who neither understood nor actively took part in the game, but this was an altogether more deferential age, when a man's position in society counted for more. Despite his humble background, Struth looked the part and acted the part, and that was considered more important at the time. The manager's vanity even extended to his fondness for the Ibrox UV tubes, meant for the treatment of injured players, but which Struth would regularly use to maintain his swarthy complexion over the winter, while the Rangers fanzine *Follow Follow* recorded an ex-player reminiscing about how Struth, when opening the Ibrox summer games, 'would take to the microphone in the centre circle... like a peacock strutting it's (sic) feathers'.

In addition, he kept a rack of suits inside Ibrox and would change at least once a day, while Struth also seemed to fancy himself as a bit of a singer, and he would often croon away over the Ibrox PA system on the day before a match. Another eccentricity was a fondness for his pet canary, which he kept in his office and which he would occasionally ply with whisky to encourage it to sing.

We might consider him something of a sociopath, but what Struth, this stonemason's son from Edinburgh, was carefully cultivating at the club was a superiority complex at a time when Rangers were becoming as much a part of the Protestant establishment as the Kirk itself. One of Struth's successors, Walter Smith, later referred to a 'Protestant superiority syndrome' at the club, which was still very much in evidence during Smith's first spell as manager at Ibrox in the 1990s. The requirement for players to wear a collar and tie to training persisted too, until the arrival of foreign mercenaries at Ibrox rendered the idea of a dress code obsolete, an inexplicable anachronism. Back in the day, however, Struth wasn't just satisfied with training and matchday smartness, he also wanted his players to look sharp on the field, and to this end in the dressing room before a game Rangers players were obliged to sit around in their underwear until moments before kick-off, for fear of creasing their immaculately pressed kit. At half-time, the entire team would customarily change their shorts and jerseys and have the mud scraped from their knees and boots, while the opposition took to the field for the second half with their outfits still smeared with the dirt and grime of their first-half toils. Disobedience or indiscipline was punishable by instant removal from the club. Anyone with a grudge or a grievance wouldn't last long either, while any player who was looking a bit 'peeky', unfit or not quite up to coping with Struth's rigorous training regime was dropped.

The grandness of Rangers was also reflected in the architecture of the stadium, as Struth commissioned a reconstruction of the Main Stand at Ibrox with an impressive exterior façade, modelled on Aston Villa, which was officially opened on New Year's Day 1929 by Glasgow's Lord Provost Sir David Mason before the traditional game against Celtic. The match was notable because the result, a convincing 3-0 win for the home team, meant that for the first time Rangers had edged ahead of the Parkhead side in the head-to-head tally of league encounters between the clubs, with the Ibrox men having now recorded 26 victories in the fixture compared to their rivals' 25, with 27 games drawn, an advantage which, in the decades to come, Rangers would only extend over their floundering neighbours.

The whole attitude at Struth's Rangers meant that the club expected to get their way, on the field and off it, and for the most part they did. There was very little, if any, criticism in the press of the club's antediluvian policies or of their rugged style of play, and players and officials at Ibrox were considered untouchable. All in all, it was a successful formula; Rangers romped to the title in Struth's first season in charge, losing only one game and finishing ten points clear of second-placed Celtic. The tone had been set for the years to come, as the Ibrox club went on to accumulate a remarkable 14 titles between 1921 and 1939, adding the Scottish Cup on a further six occasions, including a noted double in 1928, which culminated in the famous 4-0 cup final win over Celtic at Hampden, blasting away the club's 25-year hoodoo in the competition. As biographer David Leggat remarks, after Struth's appointment, 'For the following 34 years he ruled Rangers with a rod of iron, while Rangers, in turn, ruled Scottish football.'

Celtic were generous in their praise after that 4-0 Scottish Cup Final defeat of 1928, the first such occasion to feature the two teams since the infamous replayed final of 1909, which was abandoned due to rioting. The record crowd of over 118,000 saw Celtic enjoy the better of the first half but fail to take the lead, and the Parkhead men were subsequently punished when Rangers won a penalty shortly after the interval, which was fired home by stand-in skipper Davie Meiklejohn after regular taker Bob McPhail, aware of the significance of the moment, declined the responsibility. The release of tension subsequently precipitated a rout, as McPhail soon added a second, before a brace from Archibald confirmed the result. Celtic could only offer their congratulations and on the whole, despite the depressing religious polarisation and increased antipathy between supporters in the wider community, relations between the two clubs, at an official level at least, remained cordial.

Inside-forward McPhail later recalled that after the game, 'Celtic couldn't have been more gracious in defeat. There were ready handshakes and smiles for all of us. I recall the Celtic chairman, Tom White, [saying] to our chairman, Bailie Joseph Buchanan, "I was very glad to have lived long enough to see you lift the Scottish Cup. We at Parkhead are delighted that Rangers have won. It is their turn."'

Buchanan himself observed, 'The cup is fuller because we have beaten the Celtic. It was a grand game and a determined struggle between giants... These Rangers/Celtic encounters do much to popularise the game – long may the friendly rivalry continue.'

Relations deteriorated, however, after a tragic incident at Ibrox on 5 September 1931. Celtic goalkeeper John Thomson was fatally injured when he collided with on-rushing forward Sam English, his head striking the left, standing knee of the Rangers player as he dived forward, resulting in a depressed fracture of the skull. Thomson was treated at the scene by Celtic club doctor Willie Kivlichan, before being transferred to the Victoria Infirmary, where he died around 9pm, minutes after his parents, summoned from the family home in Fife, had arrived at his bedside.

Even after so many years, the briefly glimpsed footage of the incident on YouTube still has the capacity to shock, English hobbling back to check his prone and unconscious opponent, while Rangers captain Meiklejohn, aware of the seriousness of the situation, tries to calm the baying Ibrox crowd.

In the wake of Thomson's death, at the age of just 22, Rangers sent Celtic a terse note of sympathy, abrupt even by the deferential standards of the day, which can still be seen in a cabinet at Celtic Park today. English was exonerated of all blame at a subsequent inquiry, but controversy later surrounded the remarks of Celtic manager Willie Maley, who told the inquiry, 'I hope it was an accident, but I did not see enough to enable me to form an opinion.'

Maley, when questioned under oath, had provided a forensic, dispassionate reply; the incident happened in the blink of an eye and the judge, Sheriff George Wilton KC, was trying to ascertain exactly what occurred, with Maley clearly unable to definitively enlighten him. His response provoked anger in some quarters however, and subsequently a tragic incident, both for Thomson and indeed for English, who felt the need to leave Scotland and whose career never fully recovered, became a situation in which, in the eyes of Rangers, it was Celtic who were culpable.

Celtic, meanwhile, whose previous approach to Rangers' gathering dominance seems to have been to try and smother them with kindness, brooded on their anger at their rivals' response, at the general course that the Ibrox club seemed to be adopting and at their own increasingly marginalised status within Scottish football and society.

* * * *

Struth's early Rangers teams were built around a number of key players, including eventual club captain Davie Meiklejohn, winger Alan Morton, pacy inside-left Bob McPhail and strikers such as Jimmy Smith, whom the club's fans dubbed 'the biggest centre-forward in the world'.

Meiklejohn was the leader, Struth's first lieutenant on the field and an inspirational skipper once he had taken over the role on a permanent basis from Tommy Muirhead. He played centre-half when centre-half was still a midfield position, protecting the defence and instigating attacks with his range of passing. Later, after the change in the offside law from 'fewer than three' attacking players between the ball and the goal line, to 'fewer than two', and the subsequent universal adoption of the WM formation to replace the old 2-3-5, Meiklejohn became the nominated right-half to allow out-and-out defender Jimmy Simpson, father of Celtic's European Cup-winning goalkeeper Ronnie, to step up from the reserves and play as the third back.

Meiklejohn captained Rangers for eight seasons and his leadership qualities were all the more remarkable because, as part of the role, he had to analyse the strengths and weaknesses of the club's opponents. The manager himself was incapable of thinking tactically, so Meiklejohn was effectively the footballing brains behind the whole on-field operation, and it became part of his routine to meet with Struth on a Sunday to debrief the manager and take him through everything that had happened at the game the previous day.

Struth made Alan Morton his first signing when he took the winger from Queen's Park in June 1920. Queen's had retained their status as an amateur team and Morton was a qualified mining engineer, a trade which he continued to practise when he moved to Ibrox. A professional man, he was known as 'Pinkie' because of his short stature among the land of giants that was the Rangers team at the time, who were all rugged, strong, tall and fast. He is best remembered for his role in the match between Scotland and England at Wembley in 1928, the Scots winning 5-1 and giving rise to the legend of the 'Wembley Wizards', although in reality the fixture that season was effectively a play-off for the wooden spoon in the Home International Championships. Morton played for Rangers until 1933 by which time he was almost 40 years old, and immediately on retirement, he became a director of the club, a position he held until his death in 1971.

Sandy Archibald was another quick winger who, according to Bob McPhail, once challenged Eric Liddell to a race and won. Liddell had earned a gold medal at the 1924 Olympics, memorably recounted in the film *Chariots of Fire*, and although he was an athlete and a rugby player, Struth liked to associate Rangers with the most high-profile and successful Presbyterian people of the day, and Liddell would occasionally be seen at Ibrox. It was during a training session that Archibald reportedly issued his challenge to an apparently reluctant Liddell, who didn't even bother to change into his shorts, and lost. When Archibald retired in 1934, after serving the club for 17 years, Celtic manager Willie Maley acknowledged his contribution to the club by declaring that he never felt confident of beating any Rangers team which had Sandy Archibald in the line-up.

Bob McPhail, the source of the Archibald/Liddell story, completes his anecdote by claiming that he himself then challenged Archibald to a race and emerged the victor. McPhail certainly injected a bit of pace and dynamism into the Rangers team when he joined them from Airdrie for the considerable sum of £5,000 in the summer of 1927. An attacking inside-left, he scored 230 goals for the club, a record which stood until 1997, when it was surpassed by Ally McCoist. These stalwarts of Struth's side in the 1920s were supplemented by inside-forwards like Andy Cunningham and Tommy Cairns, William Wilton's last captain and a hardman among hardmen, and tough-tackling half-backs such as Jock Buchanan and former Celtic man Thomas 'Tully' Craig.

The inter-war period saw Rangers achieve unparalleled levels of success on the field; after finally lifting the Scottish Cup in 1928, the club banished the hoodoo once and for all by winning the trophy again, after replayed finals in 1930 and 1932, with victories over Partick Thistle and Kilmarnock respectively, the latter avenging the 1929 final between the same two teams which Kilmarnock had won 2-0. Rangers then went on to capture the trophy for three years in a row from 1934, beating St Mirren, Hamilton and Third Lanark at Hampden, meaning that, after a 25-year stretch without winning the cup, notwithstanding a five-year period when the competition wasn't contested during World War One, Rangers had taken the old trophy six times in nine seasons.

In addition, they racked up championship after championship, with Celtic's win in 1926 and Motherwell's acclaimed triumph of 1932 the only interruptions to Rangers' title successes between 1923 and 1935. At times the club's dominance seemed all-encompassing; the league and cup Double was achieved on no fewer than four occasions between these years and by the end of the 1930 season, Rangers had won every competition they entered, capturing the league as well as all three domestic cups, although the Charity Cup had to be awarded on the toss of a coin, after a 2-2 draw with Celtic in the final at Hampden. In 1934, the club repeated the feat, winning all four of the major titles they contested, and this time no coins were required.

Sweeping all before them domestically, Rangers began to see themselves as the foremost and best club not just in Scotland, but in the whole of Britain, and in the early 1930s Struth began to associate the club with Arsenal, the grandest and most successful team in England, as the Gunners captured the First Division championship three years running under legendary manager Herbert Chapman between 1933 and 1935. Struth instigated an annual 'Battle of Britain' style challenge match between the sides, and Rangers showed their overall strength by winning home and away against the English champions in September 1933, although despite their popularity with both sets of fans, these games held little or no interest to the wider public.

To capture the imagination of the country, it would take a more formally organised cross-border tournament, and in 1938 the Empire Exhibition was held in Glasgow, which included a cup competition to be held at Ibrox, involving the best sides of the day from Scotland and England.

The exhibition was opened by King George VI, whose stuttering address to the Ibrox dignitaries apparently so struck actor Colin Firth that the leading man was moved to tears when he viewed the Pathé News footage as part of his research for his role in *The King's Speech*. It was set up perfectly for the Ibrox club, but Rangers failed to make an impression on the tournament, losing to Everton in the first round, and to make matters worse, the competition was won by Celtic, who beat the Merseysiders 1-0 in the final.

The Parkhead club fought back strongly in the late '30s, winning the title in 1936 and again in 1938 with a gifted team led by the legendary forward Jimmy McGrory, to this day the record goalscorer in the history of British football. Rangers, however, recaptured the championship in 1939 and they had started the following season strongly, in first place with nine points from five games, when war broke out with Germany and league football was formally suspended across Britain. Struth, however, was not about to allow the conflict to break up the team which he had spent nearly 20 years presiding over, and during World War Two, through his network of contacts, the manager kept the majority of his players back from front-line service by securing them jobs on the Clyde, mostly in the workshops, shipyards and munitions factories in what were known at the time as 'reserved occupations'.

Football continued during the conflict, although not in an official capacity, but if anything Rangers, with the majority of their best players held beyond the draft, were even more dominant during the period of wartime football, winning 25 of the 34 regionalised cups and mini-leagues which they entered. With the cancellation of all contracts, players were allowed to make guest appearances, and the great English winger Stanley Matthews turned out a couple of times for Rangers alongside the local boys, such as youngster Willie Waddell, a future Rangers manager, who spent much of the war working as an electrician with Harland and Wolff. It was football, but not quite as we knew it, as some bizarre scorelines were registered, including Rangers' 8-1 defeat by Hibs in September 1941, and a victory over Celtic by the same margin in front of 30,000 at Ibrox on New Year's Day, 1943.

Old Firm tribulations continued during the war years, on and off the field; the 1943 game had seen two Celtic players sent off, while two years earlier, the authorities had threatened to discontinue the fixture for the war's duration after Celtic fans rioted during a game at Ibrox. Celtic, it seems, were not entirely committed to their part as wartime cheerleaders and made only a lacklustre effort to stay competitive during the conflict, while Struth by contrast saw it as Rangers' role to keep up morale at home while others were overseas, fighting for king and country. This was his pretext for keeping back so many players from active service, a stance which was wholly justified in his eyes. 'We on the home front, charged with a duty to maintain the morale of the workers in the factories, shipyards and other branches of industry, can claim to have played our part in the victorious end of the German war,' he had the brass neck to maintain after the defeat of Hitler and Nazi Germany.

After the end of the war, the resumption of league football in Scotland and England for the 1946/47 season was taken as a sign that things were getting back to normal in austerity-ravaged Britain. Huge crowds flocked back to football grounds the length and breadth of the country, revealing that, if anything, the game had acquired an even greater role in the weekly routine of working people in the immediate post-war period. 'Normal' by this time in Glasgow of course meant that football was polarised along a marked religious division, and for those hoping that the spirit of solidarity and the post-war consensus would lead to a realignment of attitudes in Scotland, there would, sadly, only be disappointment, as the country continued to seethe with bigotry, which had become entrenched in the culture of the west of the country by this time.

The Kirk had pulled back from some of its more controversial language of the 1920s, after the Nuremberg trials laid bare the Nazi ideology in all its hideousness, but by then the damage had been done. Rangers, still revelling in their role as the sporting wing of the Protestant establishment, led the way with their policy of exclusivity, but they were by no means the only institution at the time to be implementing, overtly or otherwise, such discriminatory employment practices. The media and the banks as well as certain law firms and industries all largely continued to be Catholic-free zones after the war, while Sir George Graham, secretary of the SFA since 1928, felt complacent enough not to bother hiding some of his extra-curricular activities from the general public, openly listing a parallel career as 'Past Grandmaster, Grand Lodge of Scotland' on his 'Who's Who' page in 1956.

A prominent Freemason and an Orangeman, Graham had clearly been climbing the greasy pole to the top of more than just the governing body. Scotland has a long and dispiriting association with Freemasonry, and Graham hadn't even bothered to disguise his links to the organisation, despite the Masons supposedly being a secret society. In his role as SFA secretary, Sir George was responsible for all appointments and advancements within the governing body; 'No Irish need apply' was a common attachment to advertised vacancies at the time, and needless to say, members of that community did not feature prominently in the SFA's role of employees during this period.

Also in the 1950s, the 'Orange vote' ensured that the Conservative Party held the kind of electoral majority in Scotland which in subsequent years it struggled to maintain in the English shires and Home Counties. The Conservatives won over 50 per cent of the popular vote north of the border at the 1955 general election, a feat which their Labour opponents have never been able to match, even in the landslide victories of 1945 and, more recently, 1997 when Tory MPs were wiped off the political map in Scotland. Indeed, the modern decline in acceptability of voting along religious lines is one of the main reasons Tory grandee Sir Malcolm Rifkind has cited to explain his party's lack of popular support in contemporary Scotland.

The old clichés and excuses about football being a microcosm of society didn't apply here however; Rangers by now were part of an establishment network that was Protestant, Unionist and virulently anti-Catholic, and indeed as a sporting institution, they were in many ways the avant-garde of the whole movement, the means by which ordinary, working-class Protestants were given a stake in and allowed to revel in the institutionalised bigotry of the period. There is, unfortunately, no getting away from the fact that, over the course of the ensuing decades, Rangers supporters embraced and relished their role in this process to a truly appalling extent.

Of course, in order to reinforce this elevated sense of their own status within society, Rangers had to win. The club began the post-war period by helping themselves to the league title in 1947 and then the Scottish Cup the following year, before in 1949, following the introduction of the League Cup after the resumption to compensate for the reduced number of league fixtures per season to just 30 from the pre-war 38, Rangers achieved a noted success when they collected all three of the available domestic trophies to win a first Treble, or the 'Triple Crown' as the press dubbed it at the time.

Rangers were captained at this time by Jock 'Tiger' Shaw, whom the manager had rescued from the Lanarkshire coal mines and part-time footballing obscurity when he signed him from Airdrie for £2,000 in 1936. A no-nonsense full-back who rarely ventured forward, Shaw epitomised Rangers' uncompromising style of play with his tough tackling and his rugged defensive discipline. Still led by the indomitable Struth, now into his 70s, Rangers were evolving into an even more stridently defensive side, with hardman Shaw having replaced the altogether more cultured Meiklejohn as the on-field leader.

Just as the deposed Prime Minister, Sir Winston Churchill, was touring the world, making speeches and warning that in Europe, 'an Iron Curtain has descended across the continent', in reference to the emerging Communist bloc, so a similar 'Iron Curtain' had latterly been drawn across Scottish football, in the form of the Rangers defence, as the wartime leader's mantra was immediately adopted by the press to describe Rangers' back-five formation of Young, Shaw, McColl, Woodburn and Cox. This defensive solidity was supplemented by long diagonal passes or balls up the line to the wingers, with particular reliance placed on the skill and speed of outside-right Willie 'Deedle' Waddell and the iron forehead of centre-forward Willie Thornton.

The success of the Iron Curtain defence was not down to astute tactical organisation or any kind of strategic solidity in the ranks. Rangers attacked as much as they could, they were just an unexceptional offensive unit and by way of compensation, they had five hatchet men at the back – imposing, tough-tackling figures in an era which was more indulgent of the physical side of the game, men who would argue it out among themselves in the dressing room afterwards if they so much as conceded a goal.

The club's hegemony within the domestic game was challenged during this period from an unlikely source; Hibernian produced an extraordinarily gifted team, containing, in noted contrast to the Iron Curtain defence operating at Ibrox, the 'Famous Five' forward line of Turnbull, Reilly, Ormond, Smith and Johnstone. The Easter Road men captured the league title on three occasions, in 1948, 1951 and 1952, yet Rangers, only an average team by comparison, lacking the flair of their capital rivals but still as remorselessly solid and consistent as ever, collected the championship four times over the same period, in 1947, 1949 when they overtook Dundee on the final day of the season after the Taysiders succumbed 4-1 against Falkirk, 1950 and, in 1953, holding off Hibernian only on goal average after another tense finale. Using the modern system of goal difference, Hibs were ahead and would have won by one goal, but the older, more complicated classification method was still in place and, with Waddell scoring a crucial equaliser against Queen of the South to earn a 1-1 draw in their final fixture, the players and staff in the Rangers dressing room had to wait until the permutations were properly calculated before they could be confirmed and acknowledged as champions.

Domestically at least, Rangers were still the team to beat, but once again, just as in the Empire Exhibition Cup of 1938, the club passed up a rare opportunity to make an impact before a wider audience, as in 1953 another cross-border knockout tournament was organised, this time to celebrate the accession to the throne of George VI's daughter, the young Queen Elizabeth. The top four teams from north and south of the border were invited to take part in the Coronation Cup, with Rangers falling at the first hurdle in a defeat to Manchester United. Mortifyingly, Celtic, who were such a mediocre and ineffective team domestically at the time that their original inclusion in the competition was called into question in some quarters, beat Arsenal then Manchester United and lastly Hibernian, conquerors of Spurs and Newcastle and arguably the greatest side in Britain at the time, with a 2-0 scoreline in the Hampden final.

Without wishing to read too much into a limited set of results, the impression is nevertheless unavoidable that while Rangers were happy to rule the roost in Scotland, outside of their domestic comfort zone they struggled to cope with the challenge of opponents who were perhaps less impressed by the self-styled notion of their own supremacy. Celtic by contrast, along with many other clubs whose momentary *aristeia* flared up all too briefly during these decades, seem to have been stifled by the environment of Scottish football at this time and yearned for the opportunity to show what they were capable of on a broader stage. It was a mentality which would reach its apex in the European Cup win in 1967, the Parkhead club's first attempt on the competition after repeated failures by Rangers.

The Coronation Cup win inspired Celtic to a league and cup Double the following year, but in the 20 years following the war, until Jock Stein arrived at the club in the mid-'60s and led them to European success, 1954 was their only year of championship glory. In truth, for whatever reason, Celtic did themselves no favours during this period of nepotistic navel-gazing under the complacent and stubborn chairmanships of Tom

White and Sir Robert Kelly, as the club were for the most part reduced to the role of happy-go-lucky but feckless also-rans.

By now, Bill Struth was ailing badly and questions were starting to be asked, covertly and discreetly at first, about his position as Rangers' manager. As early as April 1947, club chairman Jimmy Bowie had hinted that the veteran boss, then aged 71, might consider a move upstairs to become a director. Struth baulked at the suggestion, however, and within a short space of time it was the chairman's own seat which had been vacated, rather than the manager's. Struth went to war on Bowie, mustering the club's major shareholders against the chairman, who had made the mistake of upsetting Struth just two months before he was due for re-election.

Once the manager moved against him, it became clear that Bowie's position as chairman was deceptively weak, and at the club's AGM in the summer of 1947, he was eventually forced out and replaced on an enlarged Rangers board by, among others, Struth himself. Instead of becoming an unwaged director, as Bowie had initially hoped, Struth had maintained his position as manager and joined the board on his own terms, after successfully suing, in partnership with club secretary William Rogers Simpson, to have the club's constitution amended to allow paid employees at Ibrox to become directors. A Rangers man his entire life, first supporter, then player, followed by director and finally chairman, Jimmy Bowie never set foot in Ibrox again.

By contrast Struth, now a widower following the suicide of his wife Kate in 1941, was starting to spend almost his entire waking life within the confines of Ibrox Park. The stadium wasn't just his spiritual home, it was his real and actual abode as the manager effectively set up residence within the ground, only returning to his flat around the corner on Copland Road to sleep. Struth's position appeared to be strengthened considerably going into the 1950s, having ousted Bowie and become a director himself, although by this time he was afflicted with significant health problems. Increasingly frail in appearance and condition, Struth was suffering from pain on his lower left side and he eventually developed a gangrene infection in his left foot, which, in the autumn of 1950, had to be amputated. But still he soldiered on, putting on a brave face and stoically hiding his ailments as best he could behind his otherwise still immaculate deportment, which, following his leg operation, was augmented by the addition of a modish cane. At least now he had a handy instrument with which to beat his errant players!

His power seemed to be waning, however, and Rangers failed to win a trophy in 1951, losing the league to Hibs and exiting the Scottish Cup at the hands of the same opponents. The following year, the club repeated the feat, the first time that Rangers had endured two consecutive trophy-less seasons since Struth took charge at Ibrox. The team rallied in 1953, capturing the title from their Edinburgh rivals by a whisker on the last day of the season, and winning the Scottish Cup as well, but they missed out on the prized Coronation Cup and when Celtic took their first title since the war the following season, the game was finally up for the Grand Old Man of Ibrox. Chairman John Wilson had been reluctant to move to replace Struth, understandably given what had happened to Jimmy Bowie, and during 1953/54 the manager's health continued to deteriorate. He had to be carried up and down the marble staircase to his office and was continuously in and out of hospital. Barely able to stay on his feet, Struth suffered repeated falls, most seriously when climbing the stairs to the directors' box at Ibrox, and then again at Celtic Park during the Ne'erday game, after which he found himself back in hospital again. He was absent from Ibrox as often as not, and captain George Young was repeatedly left in charge of team affairs due to the manager's constant non-attendance. It was a disaster and Celtic romped to the Double.

Struth finally bowed to the inevitable and was cajoled into stepping down in the summer of 1954 at the age of 78, after 34 years in the job; the builder John Lawrence had joined the Rangers board in March, and he was able to accelerate the process of the manager's eventual retirement. Two years later Struth was dead. At Celtic Park the flags, including the detested Irish Tricolour, flew at half-mast and half a minute's silence was impeccably observed within the ground. Struth had died on the eve of an Old Firm game, which was won, fittingly, 2-0 by Rangers.

To modern sensibilities he would be considered, perhaps quite rightly, a dastardly old blimp, a pompous old windbag, far too concerned with the projection of his own inflated self-image. He was distinctly old school, implementing and propagating 19th-century values well beyond their expiry date, and on the issue of religious prejudice, the legacy of bigotry which infested the game in Scotland during the period of his stewardship at Ibrox remained an issue for all those who watch and enjoy Scottish football right down to the present day. Perhaps *Herald* columnist Hugh MacDonald summed it up best when he described Struth as 'naïve and full of what a skittish bull can leave behind'.

At the unveiling of a portrait in oils on 15 May 1953, Struth was described by Thomas Kerr, the Lord Provost of Glasgow and a Rangers partisan of long standing, as 'a Napoleon who had never met his Waterloo'. In reply the manager, by now in his late 70s but still not yet retired, declaimed as follows, 'I have been lucky – lucky in those who were around me from the boardroom to the dressing room. In time of stress their unstinted support, unbroken devotion to our club and calmness in adversity eased the task of making Rangers FC the premier club in this country.

'To be a Ranger is to sense the sacred trust of upholding all that such a name means in this shrine of football. They must be true in their conception of what the Ibrox tradition seeks from them. No true Ranger has ever failed in the tradition set him. Our very success, gained you will agree by skill, will draw more people than ever to see it. And that will benefit many more clubs than Rangers. Let others come after us. We welcome the chase. It is healthy for all of us. We will never hide from it. Never fear, inevitably we shall have our years of failure, and when they arrive, we must reveal tolerance and sanity. No matter the days of anxiety that come our way, we shall emerge stronger because of the trials to be overcome. That has been the philosophy of the Rangers since the days of the gallant pioneers.'

The portrait in oils hangs today in the trophy room at Ibrox.

4

THE THIRD MAN

STRUTH'S successor as Rangers manager was the former East Fife and current Preston North End boss James Scotland 'Scot' Symon. Proper, formal, somewhat aloof and certainly difficult to get close to, even within the camaraderie of a dressing room, Symon had made few, if any, close friends during his time as a player at Ibrox in the 1940s. He seems to have been much of a muchness as a footballer, in and out of the first team, with a solitary international cap to his name, but his single-mindedness and professionalism ensured that by the end of his playing days he had amassed over 250 appearances for the Light Blues. The record books, however, would reduce that total to just 37, as Rangers continued their domestic dominance during the unofficial fixtures of the war years.

He was a tough-tackling half-back in an era of tough tacklers; team-mate Willie Waddell noted that when he hit an opponent, they 'stayed hit'. Symon was something of a surprise choice to become only the third manager in the Ibrox club's history; the favourite at the time was former captain and current manager of Partick Thistle, Davie Meiklejohn, but by this stage 'Meek' was known to be fond of a drink and this had counted against him in the eyes of the ever-influential Struth. With the tacit approval of his predecessor, Symon assumed his seat in the Ibrox manager's office in the summer of 1954.

It was tricky for him at first. There were still members of his squad whom he had played alongside, and although Symon was not the type to go in for dressing-room fraternisation, it was always going to be a difficult transition for a former team-mate to replace such an über-authoritarian figure as Struth. In truth, Symon inherited a mess from his predecessor; the 'Iron Curtain' defence was past its peak, and hadn't been replaced. More generally though, things had been allowed to wither on the vine at Ibrox, as Struth's health inexorably deteriorated and his grip on power at the club waned.

A somewhat pathetic figure by the time he was finally ushered towards the exit door, the manner of Struth's decline had been dispiriting for everyone to behold and morale in the dressing room was low at the time of Symon's appointment. Celtic had just captured a rare league and cup Double, their first since 1908, winning the championship by five points from Hearts and defeating Aberdeen 2-1 in the final of the Scottish Cup, a team who in turn had put six past Rangers without reply in the semi-final, in what was perhaps the most traumatic in a series of poor results for the Ibrox club at this time.

In addition, 35-year-old centre-half Willie Woodburn, the pivot of Rangers' renowned defence, whom Symon had asked to carry on in the short term to help him reshape and rebuild the team, was given a life ban from the game for head-butting Stirling Albion's Alec Paterson in a League Cup game at Ibrox in only the new manager's fourth game in charge. Woodburn, a dominant and destructive figure at the heart of the Iron Curtain, had a track record of violent indiscipline; he had previously been suspended for 14 days in 1948 following a clash with Motherwell's Dave Mathie, for 21 days in 1953 for punching Clyde's Billy McPhail, and latterly for six weeks after a sending-off, also against Stirling, the previous season. Having warned the defender that 'a very serious view would be taken of any subsequent action', the SFA, no doubt emboldened by the departure of the obdurate Struth, threw the book at Woodburn, imposing the harshest possible sanction, suspending the player *sine die* after a committee meeting which lasted all of four minutes. Rangers finished the 1955 season without a trophy.

Things might have been worse for Symon if the championship that season had been retained by Celtic. That would have seen the Ibrox club's great rivals winning back-to-back league titles, something which had never happened under Struth, but instead the trophy headed north to Aberdeen, Celtic finishing three points off the pace, with Rangers a further five behind in third. Celtic, who in 1949 had rejected an offer to manage the team from Matt Busby, a man steeped in the club's traditions, remained an infuriatingly inconsistent side in the 1950s, sometimes spectacular, more usually awful. After winning the Double in 1954, the club failed to consolidate and build on their success, and this bought Symon some time. In the early post-war years, the Parkhead club had entered a period of purgatory that endured for 20 years, during which time they often contrived to lose more games than they won over the course of a season and, on at least one occasion, flirted with relegation.

In the period following the post-war resumption, Celtic had been more noted for their brushes with authority than their achievements on the football field, and on a couple of occasions they were asked to post notices in the stadium warning fans about their behaviour, following incidents of crowd trouble on the back of perceived injustices in matches against Rangers. Then in 1952, following another troublesome Old Firm game on New Year's Day, in a series of recommendations the investigating Glasgow magistrates requested that the SFA consider whether 'the two clubs should avoid displaying flags or emblems which might incite hostile feelings among the spectators'.

Within the committee rooms and the corridors of power at the perennially blinkered SFA, this suggestion crystallised as an instruction to Celtic to remove from Parkhead the Irish flag, various versions of which, along with the flag of the Union, had flown over the stadium since it was built. Chairman Robert Kelly was appalled at the notion, but there were many, it seemed, for whom the Tricolour was indeed an inflammatory and provocative emblem, and these apparently included SFA acting president Harry Swan of Hibernian and secretary Sir George Graham, who had instigated the directive. The irony of Hibernian, a club with such demonstrably Irish roots, leading a campaign of this type against Celtic, with their similar tradition, seems to have been lost on no one, and at one point during the ensuing crisis, with Kelly and his team of lawyers stubbornly refusing to accede to the SFA's demands, there was a chance that Celtic could have been thrown out of the league.

The matter came to a head at an SFA council meeting in April when Swan gave Celtic three days to comply, but his proposal was eventually defeated by a single vote. Calmer heads had prevailed and the situation died down, largely because Rangers, despite their nominal involvement, had remained suitably aloof and nonplussed by the whole affair, and eventually voted with their rivals when it came to the crunch. It has since been claimed that Rangers sided with Celtic because of the 'Old Firm' financial imperative, the idea which went back to the days of the previous century that the two clubs, despite their great rivalry, fed off one another commercially. While the potential pecuniary impact of an expulsion of their Glasgow cousins cannot be ignored, Rangers were canny, and knew that, in a sporting sense, they had Celtic where they wanted them; a big club, yes, but an outsider, an underachiever, the black sheep of Scottish football.

The last thing Rangers wanted was for Celtic to take down the flag, abandon their Irish heritage and potentially be rehabilitated into mainstream Scottish footballing orthodoxy. This was more or less exactly what had happened with Hibernian, and the Easter Road club were now arguably the most potent force in British football. Celtic had stood their ground and survived – just – without being humiliated, although the whole episode serves as an indicator of how the establishment in Scottish football was aligned during this period. As Celtic historian Tom Campbell pointed out of the affair, 'Whatever the outcome intended – and humiliation [rather than expulsion] was the more likely – the motivation behind it lay in bigotry.'

By 1956, Scot Symon well and truly had his feet under the table at Ibrox. He bought Bobby Shearer from Hamilton, another uncompromising full-back who would go on to captain the club, and teenager Alex Scott emerged, a pacy outside-right, to replace the veteran Willie Waddell, who had opted for retirement in the face of persistent knee and hamstring problems. Symon further added to his squad with the signing of striker Don Kichenbrand, who arrived from South Africa to play alongside his compatriot, the ever-present winger Johnny Hubbard. Known as 'The Rhino', Kichenbrand was a physical centre-forward who became associated with a series of outrageous misses, although he scored plenty as well in a free-scoring age.

Unsuspected by anyone at Ibrox at the time, Kichenbrand had been brought up as a Catholic back home in South Africa, and in Scotland he went to extraordinary lengths to disguise his faith, even joining the local Masonic Lodge in Lanarkshire. The Rangers scout had forgotten to do his homework on the striker and only learned of the player's background when the pair were on the point of departure to Glasgow, as Kichenbrand later confided to the *Daily Record*, 'The only time anyone asked about my religion was a few minutes before I boarded the plane at Johannesburg for the flight to Scotland. Charlie Watkins, the man who had convinced Glasgow Rangers they should sign me, suddenly said, "By the way, you're not Catholic, are you?" When I told him "yes", he nearly collapsed. Then he growled, "Don't mention that again – to anyone!" I never did. My team-mates and bosses at the club just assumed that I had been vetted before I was signed. Every player was.'

Symon was also allowed to appoint his own backroom staff, a relatively modern development at the time, and he replaced former centre-forward and ex-team-mate Jimmy Smith with a new trainer in close confidant Davie Kinnear, although the manager was still obliged to submit his team selections on a Thursday night for approval by the board. Rangers won the league in 1956 and they won it well, taking the title on the back of an undefeated run of 23 games. The following season Symon made the important transitional move of replacing his ageing skipper, the giant George Young, by returning to his former club East Fife to sign Harold Davis, a war veteran who had sustained injuries while serving with the Black Watch in Korea and still had shrapnel embedded in his chest.

Rangers successfully defended the title in 1957 and in the same season the club ventured into European football for the first time, when, after initially receiving a bye, they were drawn to play French champions OGC Nice in the second round of the European Cup. Symon's side won 2-1 at Ibrox in a game which was remarkable for English referee Arthur Ellis's mistake of blowing the full-time whistle after only 85 minutes, before the Halifax-based official was obliged, after realising his error, to recall the players from the dressing room so that the match could be completed. In the second leg, despite taking the lead through a Johnny Hubbard penalty, Rangers were defeated by the same scoreline, as right-half Willie Logie became the first British player to be ordered off in a European tie following a confrontation with Nice's Bravo, who was also dismissed. Unfortunately for Rangers, Nice won the subsequent play-off 3-1 in Paris to ensure that the Ibrox men exited European competition at their first attempt.

By now it seemed clear that normality was being restored in domestic Scottish football, with Symon steering his side back to their accustomed position at the forefront of the national game. The only serious aberration at this time was an astonishing 7-1 defeat to Celtic in the League Cup Final in October 1957, a scoreline which remains a record margin of victory in any British cup final. But once again it proved to be a one-off for the Parkhead side, as Rangers embarked on a run of consistent success over the next several years. The 1950s overall had seen other teams challenge the Ibrox club, initially and most notably Hibernian, in a more evenly contested era than previous years. Celtic and Aberdeen had won titles too, and towards the end of the decade, Hearts assembled a formidably gifted team, led by the legendary Dave Mackay and with an attack spearheaded by the so-called 'terrible trio' of Wardhaugh, Bauld and Conn.

The Tynecastle side won the league in 1958, scoring an astonishing 132 goals in the process, and then repeated the feat in 1960 after agonisingly losing out to Rangers in their defence of the title the previous year. Hearts had beaten Symon's side 2-0 at Tynecastle in the penultimate match of the season, leaving Rangers just two points clear going into the final round of fixtures. The Ibrox men, needing only a point to secure the championship at home against a relegation-threatened Aberdeen team, lost 2-1, but they were rescued by Celtic, who completed a joyless campaign by defeating Hearts by the same scoreline at Celtic Park and in the process handing the title to their rivals.

Heading into the new decade, however, Rangers seemed capable of sweeping all before them once more. Dundee, managed by Bob Shankly, challenged successfully for the league in 1962 with an attack built around the brilliant Alan Gilzean and former Hibs and Hearts winger Gordon Smith, who became the only player in Scottish football to win the title with three different clubs, none of them in Glasgow. On the back of that triumph, the Taysiders reached the semi-final of the European Cup the following season, where they were eventually defeated only by the great AC Milan team of Maldini, Trapattoni, Rivera and co.

But Rangers were the team who were knitting together all the gaps in these other clubs' elusive glimpses of the limelight. Still the most consistently successful team in the country, the Ibrox side appeared in the 1950s and early 1960s to have won the affection of the nation, and it was estimated that the club could now claim roughly half the watching public in Scotland among its supporters. Rangers, it seemed, had become almost the default team of choice for vast sections of mainstream Scottish society, while still maintaining a hard-core following who were ferociously loyal to the Ibrox cause. Jock Stein's father, when his son was a Celtic player in the early '50s, used to wish his boy good luck before a game at the weekend with the words 'I hope you manage to draw', as he himself preferred to head off to Ibrox to watch Rangers.

But the club's popularity among the football-supporting public at this time is perhaps best illustrated by the scenes which greeted the team after they returned undefeated from a three-match tour of the USSR in June 1962. Against Soviet club sides depleted by the absence of key players, who were competing for their country at the World Cup in Chile, Rangers had earned narrow but worthy victories over Lokomotiv Moscow and Dynamo Tbilisi, before ending the tour with a creditable draw against national champions Dynamo Kiev. On arriving home in Glasgow, the Rangers squad were welcomed back on to Scottish soil like conquering Cold War heroes by an army of supporters responding to a call from the Rangers Supporters' Association for 'every available fan' to turn out and acclaim the team at the airport. Even the Glasgow Lord Provost, Mrs Jean Roberts, weighed in when she told the *Scottish Daily Express*, 'My husband is a keen Rangers fan. They have been jolly good ambassadors for Glasgow and Scotland. I would like to say to them, "Well done boys and welcome home."'

The estimated crowd of between 10,000-15,000, which congregated at Renfrew airport on the evening of Monday, 11 June, caused chaos by breaking through steel barriers and flocking on to the runway apron as the Rangers team plane was about to land. With the police undermanned and unable to intervene, fans crowded around the plane in jubilation, unaware of the risk to their own and to the public safety, as the airport tower set off flares warning away incoming aircraft, whose pilots were obliged to execute a go-around manoeuvre. On the ground, the crew of the Rangers plane refused to open the doors to allow the players and other passengers to disembark, causing delays to several other flights which were unable to depart, while an earlier arrival, a BEA flight from Manchester, had to make an emergency stop on the runway and cut its engines with supporters perilously close to its whirling propeller blades, after it was wrongly identified as the Rangers plane. All the local newspapers subsequently described the unprecedented chaos and disruption at the airport, which resulted in a report being sent to the Minister of Aviation, Peter Thorneycroft MP, but overall the hacks, many of whom had travelled on the Rangers plane, were almost as enthusiastic as the fans in their reporting of the incident and of the team's success on foreign soil, with some of the coverage apparently suggesting that Rangers, by remaining unbeaten on their tour of Soviet Russia, had successfully defended the honour not only of Scotland, or Britain, but of the whole of western civilisation.

Under the headline, 'Hail, the conquering heroes', Gair Henderson, writing in the *Evening Times*, decried the scenes at Moscow airport, when cosmonaut Yuri Gagarin successfully returned to earth after becoming the first man in space, which could only have seemed low-key in comparison to the welcome that had attended the Rangers party, while in the *Scottish Daily Express*, youngster Willie Henderson, who had been used mainly as a substitute on the tour, noted, 'I thought we'd done well in Russia, but you'd think we'd won the World Cup.'

Only the *Glasgow Herald*, a publication which only condescended to cover football fleetingly alongside such minority sports as cricket, yachting and bowls, offered a dose of reality, suggesting that the enthusiasm of the reception was out of all proportion with the team's accomplishments, with the paper's editorial making the salient point that it had been, 'A good successful tour. But it was not, say, the European Cup', before adding in parentheses, 'A British team has yet to win that, and it may be time enough for unprecedented welcomes when one does.'

Perhaps aware of his club's increasing favour among the Scottish public, Symon moved to add a touch of sparkle to his squad in June 1960 when he signed the talented youngster Jim Baxter from Raith Rovers for £17,500. The transfer was a gamble not only because of the fee, a Scottish record at the time, but also because Baxter, with his idiosyncratic swagger, was not a typical Rangers signing. In Scottish parlance, Baxter was 'gallus', an elusive quality somewhere between confident and arrogant, a kind of man-of-the-people's version of egotism, perhaps best illustrated by the cocky way the midfielder taunted England by juggling the ball during Scotland's 3-2 victory over the 'Auld Enemy' at Wembley in April 1967.

Most divisively of all though, as far as the Rangers dressing room was concerned, Baxter was a rebel, an anti-authoritarian maverick. Happy-go-lucky, ready to take on the world, a bit of a joker on the pitch, his attitude seemed to set him on a collision course with many of his more strait-laced team-mates, who inhabited a Rangers dressing room which was still at the time, in the words of David Leggat, Symon's biographer, 'a bastion of tradition, conservatism and respect for authority'. In another break with the standards of the day, Baxter had at least as many friends in the Celtic squad as he had in his own, and he associated freely with rivals Pat Crerand, Billy McNeill and Mike Jackson, often running up huge bar tabs, which he would then bill to his employer. He never allowed these friendships to affect his performances on the field, however, and for the big 'Old Firm' derbies, Baxter would always have his game head on, and he produced many of his best Rangers performances in the fixture. During his first five years at the club, Rangers lost only two of 17 games against Celtic, and he also gave the team an extra dimension in the new arena of European football.

Ever since he had taken over at the club, Symon had strived to continue in the Struth tradition, with much of the old methodology at Ibrox during his tenure harking back to the distant 1920s. Symon, like Struth, refrained from offering any tactical advice to his players beyond the perfunctory: work hard, win the tackles and give the ball to Jim Baxter. On matchdays, again following the ancient custom, Symon would sit in the directors' box, suited and booted, maintaining an apparent emotional distance from the events unfolding on the pitch, but it is tempting to see the signing of Baxter as an effort by the manager to adapt to the modern, changing world of the early 1960s, as well as adding a touch of genuine class to his functional team.

When Symon started to indulge Baxter and his errant ways, however, the rest of the dressing room reacted against it. Players such as Eric Caldow, 'captain cutlass' Bobby Shearer and ex-soldier Harold Davis couldn't stomach Baxter's non-conformity and lack of discipline, but their contempt was reserved in particular for the manager, who in their eyes failed to get a grip on the situation by forcibly bringing Baxter into line, the way he would with any other player. Things became worse when Baxter broke his leg in December 1964, after which he started drinking heavily during a four-month period of recuperation, and he was eventually transferred to Sunderland in the summer of 1965. The Rangers board had refused to break their wage structure for the player, and when the Wearsiders offered to double his salary, from £45 to £90 per week, Baxter was off, without Symon even being consulted. It is said that, when he learned the news of his most gifted player's unexpected departure, Scot Symon had a tear in his eye.

Regardless of any disharmony brought about by Scot Symon's indulgence of his favourite player, the Rangers side of the early 1960s was one of the best and most successful in the club's history, playing a style of football that was much easier on the eye and beyond the capacity of the team of bruisers which the manager had inherited. Orchestrated chiefly by Baxter at left-half and with winger Willie Henderson, so often the maverick's partner in crime off the field, supplying the effective strike partnership of Ralph Brand and Jimmy Millar, by 1964 Rangers were masters of all they surveyed domestically. Unfortunately, Symon's side often struggled to replicate their form on the European stage and there were some painful humiliations along the way for the Ibrox men, most notably a 12-4 aggregate trouncing by Eintracht Frankfurt in the semi-final of the European Cup, a team who were subsequently beaten 7-3 by Real Madrid in the famous Hampden final of 1960. For those who wondered about the scale of the potential disaster which might have unfolded had Rangers made the final, their answer came three years later when the Ibrox club suffered a 6-0 defeat in the Bernabeu against a Real Madrid team which was well past its best by then, on the back of a 1-0 home loss at Ibrox in the first leg.

Rangers were also outclassed by the great Spurs team of the early '60s, beaten home and away in the European Cup Winners' Cup in 1962, but there were some successes too, notably when the club reached the final of the same competition in 1961, only to lose both legs to the Italians of Fiorentina. Baxter's signing had made a difference, and after their humbling by Eintracht Frankfurt in 1960, Rangers once again met German opposition the following season in the Cup Winners' Cup. With 'Slim Jim' now orchestrating the midfield alongside the studious Ian McMillan, Rangers disposed of Borussia Mönchengladbach 8-0 at Ibrox. Overall though, their efforts in Europe in the '60s could at best only be described as a qualified success, as many felt that two appearances in the final of the tertiary Cup Winners' Cup, where they lost on both occasions, represented an underwhelming effort for the best team in the country. Scottish teams at the time expected to do well in

Europe: Dundee reached the semi-final of the European Cup in 1963; their neighbours, Dundee United, beat Barcelona home and away in the Inter-Cities Fairs Cup in 1966/67 (then repeated the feat in 1987, leaving them with a current record of four wins out of four against the Catalans); even Celtic reached the semi-final of the Cup Winners' Cup in 1964, and, as everyone knew, the Parkhead men were a shambles of a team at the time.

Despite the occasional European misadventure, however, by 1964 Symon must have seemed almost untouchable in his role as Rangers manager as the Ibrox club collected a second domestic Treble. With a smattering of young players being added to the squad in cousins Jim Forrest and Alex Willoughby, as well as eventual club legends John Greig and Willie Henderson, the Ibrox men met their hapless rivals Celtic on five occasions over the course of the season, and won all five. The League Cup was secured with a 5-0 victory over plucky Morton of the second division in the final and the more prestigious Scottish Cup was added when Dundee were defeated 3-1 at Hampden. In the league, Rangers were chased all the way by Kilmarnock, then managed by former Ibrox winger, the gruff Willie Waddell, but the Ibrox side eventually triumphed by six points to complete the historic Treble as Symon celebrated ten years in the job.

The following year, however, was not a happy one for the Ibrox club. The season began well enough with a 2-1 win over Celtic in the final of the League Cup, with Baxter, now captain, reprising his role as the Parkhead side's tormentor-in-chief. There followed a 3-1 victory over Red Star Belgrade in a play-off at Highbury in the first round of the European Cup after the sides finished 5-5 on aggregate in the days before away goals and penalty shoot-outs, with Baxter again a key influence. But the talisman suffered a broken leg against the club's next opponents, the victim of a cynical challenge from Rapid Vienna's Walter Skocik, whom Baxter had tormented with a series of nutmegs. The injury occurred in the final minutes of the tie, with Rangers' passage into the next round already assured with home and away victories, and although the quarter-final wasn't until the following spring, Baxter hadn't recovered in time and Rangers lost narrowly, 3-2 on aggregate, to Inter Milan, the dominant force in European football in the mid-'60s. It was perhaps the closest Rangers would come to winning the European Cup.

Nevertheless, the run in Europe, completed without Baxter, had shown what a formidable side Symon had put together by this point. The strength in depth of Scottish football overall was clear from a glance at the league tables, which showed that, by mid-October, this great Rangers team had managed to accumulate a mere seven points from eight games. The club eventually finished the season in a lowly fifth position, as the title that year was won by Kilmarnock, a team that had finished runners-up in four of the previous five campaigns. Needing a two-goal victory over league leaders Hearts on the last day of the season, the Ayrshire side finally managed to get their hands on the championship trophy, recording a famous victory over the Tynecastle men by exactly the margin required.

And that was really that for Scot Symon's Rangers. The manager was helpless to prevent Baxter being sold to Sunderland that summer and the club never again won the league under his stewardship. On 30 January 1965, Rangers visited Easter Road and lost 1-0 to Jock Stein's Hibernian. Just a few days later, Stein was named the new manager of Celtic, although he agreed to stay on at Hibs until his replacement could be found. It wasn't until early March that Bob Shankly, brother of Bill, who had managed Dundee since 1959, took over at Easter Road and Stein was free to assume his fated position as manager of the Parkhead club.

Stein's impact at Celtic was immediate and extraordinary; in January 1965, the *Daily Mail* had proclaimed that the Parkhead men were, 'being left so far behind by Rangers that it is no longer a race'. Within a few weeks of the new manager's arrival, however, Celtic had collected the Scottish Cup after a 3-2 victory in the Hampden final over Dunfermline Athletic, a team who finished well above the Glasgow side in the league that season and only missed out on the championship by a single point. The following season, Celtic won their first league title since Stein had captained the club to the Double in 1954, and the season after that they won everything, including of course the European Cup.

It's hard to overstate the transformative effect that Stein's arrival had on Celtic. For the previous 20 years, the club had been managed by former player James McGrory; not a particularly well-known figure beyond the club's fanbase, McGrory is, quite simply, the greatest goalscorer in the history of British football. Between 1923 and 1937, he amassed a total of 468 goals for Celtic from 445 appearances, including a remarkable 55 hat-tricks, a record eight goals in one game against Dunfermline in 1928, and another record in his total of 59 league and cup goals scored in 1926/27.

In charge of the dressing room, however, McGrory seemed to epitomise the old cliché about being too nice to be a manager. In contrast to the regimented authoritarianism being successfully implemented by his counterparts at Ibrox, in the words of Pat Crerand, a former player who left Celtic for Manchester United in 1964 fed up at chairman Robert Kelly's over-involvement in the running of the club, 'Jimmy didn't do discipline.'

On one occasion, when McGrory was obliged to inform goalkeeper Frank Haffey that his wages were being cut, the manager burst into tears when Haffey complained, admitting that it was the chairman's idea. Too compliant towards the boardroom, McGrory was not in charge of team affairs and this led to some ridiculous scenarios, such as on the occasion when the Celtic players, travelling on the team bus to Airdrie, spotted third-choice goalkeeper Willie Goldie making his way to the game in the club's colours as a spectator. Chairman Robert Kelly immediately stopped the bus and invited the player on board.

Kelly was so impressed with Goldie's apparent dedication to the cause that by the time the bus arrived in Airdrie, he was in the team! The chairman was presumably anticipating the fairytale scenario of a fan-turned-player ending up as the hero of the hour, but what Kelly had failed to appreciate was that Goldie had been out drinking and dancing until 3am in the not unreasonable expectation that he would be having Saturday afternoon off. Needless to say, the rookie goalkeeper threw in a couple of goals, Airdrie won 2-0 and Goldie never played for his beloved Celtic again.

The image of the happy-go-lucky, cheeky chappy Celts, playing the game with freedom and enjoyment, in contrast to the stern disciplinarians from across the city, was wearing thin. For the 11 years that McGrory and Symon were in direct opposition, Celtic didn't win the league once, with the Celtic manager's only title triumph in 20 years coming against a debilitated Struth in 1954. Stein's arrival changed all that, however, as the new manager at Parkhead, tracksuited and now in sole charge of team selection, was able to get the best out of his squad by making relatively slight adjustments, such as asking them to play in their best positions.

When they won the European Cup in 1967, only one of the 11 players who defeated Inter Milan in the Lisbon final had been brought to the club by Stein; the rest were either already there, or, as in the case of midfielder Bertie Auld, on their way back to the club when he arrived. Contrary to popular perception, however, Symon's initial joustings with Stein were relatively even. In the new Parkhead manager's first full season in charge, Rangers and Celtic played each other five times, with two wins each and one draw, as Celtic took the title and the League Cup, Rangers the Scottish Cup. The following season, however, Celtic completed their remarkable grand slam, winning every competition they entered, and Symon's position was further weakened by a Scottish Cup defeat to lowly Berwick Rangers in January 1967, then under the stewardship of future Ibrox boss Jock Wallace. The 'wee Rangers' claimed a noted scalp in defeating their more celebrated Glasgow namesakes when inside-forward Sammy Reid, who had been Bill Shankly's first signing as Liverpool manager in 1960, scored the only goal of the game after half an hour. In the aftermath, Scot Symon seemed almost paralysed with shame and embarrassment, describing the result as 'the darkest day in Rangers' history'.

Initially the manager received the support of his chairman, John Lawrence, who was quick to point out those who were culpable for the debacle in his eyes, 'The only people who can be blamed for the defeat are the players. The play of some of them made me sick,' he fulminated. At most other big clubs, even the most successful, being the unfortunate victim of an act of giant-killing in the cup is considered an occupational hazard; it's humiliating and embarrassing, but most teams eventually manage to put the defeat out of their system and move on. But at a club like Rangers, still with such an elevated sense of its own importance, there had to be consequences and by the following week the scapegoats had been identified and sanctioned, as strikers George McLean and Jim Forrest were dropped for the visit of Hearts to Ibrox. Neither man would play for Rangers again, and within weeks the pair had been shipped out the door, to Dundee and Preston North End respectively.

Regardless of the circumstances, the treatment of both players by the club seems harsh to say the least. McLean had scored a commendable

82 goals in 117 games for Rangers, while Forrest, at the age of just 22, had already netted 145 times in just 165 appearances for the Ibrox side. Forrest, a forward of extraordinary potential, had already been a Rangers regular for three and a half years and in season 1964/65 scored a total of 57 goals in all competitions for the club – a post-war British record which still stands to this day – yet the youngster, in a team full of experienced internationals, was made to carry the can. It was a ludicrous, panicky decision by the Rangers hierarchy which, by the end of the season, they would have good cause to regret.

Speaking years later, Forrest admitted that the treatment he received from the club still rankled with him, 'We should all have taken equal responsibility when we lost… I was never given the opportunity to sit down and talk with the manager, or any of the directors, as to why I was being booted out. I still feel to this day that Symon owed me an explanation, but he took the coward's way out and he simply wouldn't discuss it with me.'

The decision to dispense with two such valuable strikers came back to haunt the club when, on 31 May 1967, Rangers lost the European Cup Winners' Cup Final to rising force Bayern Munich in Nuremberg. It was an achievement in itself just to reach the final, but Rangers went into the match in the Städtisches Stadion with the shadow of Celtic looming over them, after the Parkhead men had won the European Cup just six days previously, a result which seemed to be preying on the mind of everyone concerned with the Ibrox club in the build-up to the game in Bavaria. Celtic were being lauded all around Europe after their victory over Inter Milan, which had ended the Latin axis of domination of the tournament stretching back to the great Real Madrid team of the previous decade, and the manner of Celtic's win, achieved with fluent, attacking football was seen as a defeat of the defensive *catenaccio* system favoured by Inter, whose pre-eminence on the stage of European football was effectively ended by Stein's side that day. By contrast Rangers, in an inferior competition, couldn't hope to match Celtic's achievement even with victory, and this seemed to have had a negative effect on their preparation. It's still astonishing to consider that a club would take to the field in a European final mentally encumbered by the success of a team from the same city just the previous week, yet the Rangers players of the day freely admit that this was the case.

The Ibrox men were also hindered by the absence of any recognised forwards in their side, having dispensed too hastily with Forrest and McLean after the trauma of Berwick. With free-scoring Alex Willoughby, Forrest's cousin, overlooked for unexplained reasons, Symon decided to draft in no-nonsense defender Roger Hynd as an auxiliary striker. The tactic backfired when Hynd, shortly before half-time, wasted Rangers' best chance of the game, missing poorly from six yards when it looked easier to score, before the Germans, having survived such a scare, subsequently went on to net the only goal of the game in extra time. Rangers chairman John Lawrence later lamented that the converted defender's shocking first-half miss had, in all probability, cost him a knighthood.

The Ibrox club looked to put a traumatic 12 months behind them as the 1967/68 season opened with the sectional rounds of the League Cup. In a group that included Celtic, Aberdeen and Dundee United, qualification came down to the second Old Firm meeting at Parkhead. Rangers were winning 1-0 after an early goal from Willie Henderson and, with less than 15 minutes remaining, the Ibrox men were awarded a penalty. Kai Johansen's spot kick rebounded down off the crossbar, however, and with new signing Alex Ferguson stretching to head in the rebound, the Danish defender stupidly charged in and put the ball into the empty net himself. The effort was correctly disallowed under the rule that prevents the same player from striking the ball twice, and to make matters worse, Celtic then scored three late goals to run away with the game and secure their progress to the quarter-final. Jock Stein later described the win as Celtic's greatest ever Old Firm victory.

In the league, the season progressed with the two clubs matching each other blow for blow until, in late October, Dunfermline Athletic came to Ibrox and inflicted a crucial setback to Rangers' title credentials. The ambitious Fifers, who had beaten the Ibrox men home and away the previous season, left Glasgow with a point after a goalless draw, a result which immediately provoked a chorus of boos from unhappy Rangers fans as their team left the field at the final whistle. The ill-feeling, however, wasn't restricted to the players as, sitting in the directors' box, the manager and members of the board also found themselves the target of the fans' venom.

It proved to be a definitive moment as a few days later, on 1 November, chairman John Lawrence dispatched an accountant, a man with no formal connection to Rangers, to negotiate the terms of the manager's release from his contract. A bemused Symon subsequently told the press, 'I was informed by a Glasgow businessman at his home that at a meeting of the directors of Rangers Football Club it was decided to terminate my appointment as manager forthwith. I am awaiting confirmation of this.'

Arguably it wasn't the best way to relieve a man of 13 years' service to the club from his position as team manager. Alex Ferguson, Symon's last major signing, was so enraged by the decision that he had to be talked out of demanding a transfer by coach Bobby Seith, who promptly resigned in disgust himself. 'I no longer want to be part of an organisation which can treat a loyal servant so badly,' the manager's assistant harrumphed. Lawrence explained the decision in a statement to the press, 'We spent considerable sums of money buying players, at Mr Symon's request, but the results were not forthcoming and it could not go on indefinitely. The board were not satisfied with the results, which can be seen in the league tables.' Rangers at the time were undefeated and sitting top of the First Division.

Lawrence and his fellow directors at Ibrox were, however, correct to point out the amount of money which had been spent on player transfers. Rangers had always been a buying club, and the strategy was accelerated as Celtic continued their rise, with each expensive new signing trumpeted as the man who was going to restore the club's fortunes. Unfortunately, most of the best Scottish players were either doing quite nicely in England or were already in Stein's Celtic squad, which, especially after the European Cup win, continued to be augmented by an exceptionally talented batch of youngsters. Rangers therefore found themselves in the impossibly frustrating position of not being able either to buy or to nurture the players they required. The limitations of the spending strategy had been cruelly exposed, but of course the responsibility for its implementation lay principally with the men who held the purse strings, namely the directors, rather than the manager, who in the end was made to pay as much for Celtic's extraordinary renaissance as for his own team's failures.

If the chief role of Rangers in the early decades of the 20th century was to stop Celtic at all costs, then by the late 1960s it was clear that they had been utterly unsuccessful in their aim. Symon, in the end, found himself caught up in something of a time warp, his methods outdated and increasingly discredited, while the Rangers board, as can be seen by some of their more panicky reactions to adversity, appeared overtaken by events. Chairman John Lawrence, who had helped to usher Bill Struth into eventual retirement the previous decade, was himself well into his dotage by this stage and he had trouble remembering people's names in public, including the club's players, and in vice-chairman Matt Taylor, and loathsome PR man Willie Allison, nephew of the false Rangers historian John Allan, he had deputies who were not exactly up to speed with the 1960s zeitgeist.

Symon himself continues to divide opinion; he seems to have been an upstanding, respectable man, a far more sympathetic figure certainly than his predecessor Struth, and there have been recent attempts to try and rehabilitate him in the eyes of the Rangers public, who have on the whole in the intervening years paid scant regard to his achievements at the club. Rangers' hegemony within the domestic game was lost on his watch and to many that has seemed unforgivable. To this day Alex Ferguson reportedly remains an admirer, praising him in particular for his strength of character and for never criticising his players in public, which, given that he very rarely spoke in public, seems a slightly odd tribute. But he was also cold and inflexible, and his treatment of George McLean and in particular Jim Forrest after the debacle of Berwick, a result which he himself, as manager, carried the ultimate responsibility for, was inexcusable. Eric Caldow, who lost the captaincy of the club under Symon, is another former player who describes the manager as 'rude and unapproachable', and in many ways he might be considered a fairly unimpressive figure; taciturn, diffident, unable to socialise freely with his peers, including of course the 'gentlemen' of the press, whom he preferred to keep at arm's length. It was another era of course, and football had a very different relationship with the mass media in the 1950s and early '60s compared to the access-all-areas world of today, but it says a great deal about his reticence that by the time he left his post as Rangers manager, very few people, including most Rangers fans, knew what Scot Symon's voice sounded like.

In a more deferential age of course none of this mattered, but by the mid-to-late '60s, Symon, like Struth before him, was a man who was out of his time. He had remained true to the Struth tradition in his appearance, in his disciplinarian tendencies and his presence, but as the nominated heir, Symon harked back to a Victorian methodology that was antiquated even in Struth's day, never mind the changed world of the late 1960s. The training had not evolved since the days of athlete Struth's reliance on track work and physical exercise, which Alex Ferguson describes as 'uninspired'. There had on occasion been an improvement in the team's style and overall play since the time of the 'iron curtain' bruisers, and Rangers had at times, despite the odd harsh lesson, learned to adapt reasonably well to the new challenge of European football; but they had been overtaken on both fronts, domestic and international, by the detested Celtic and nobody at the club seemed to know how to cope with this development.

Perhaps most damningly of all to a modern observer, Symon had led the club into a more liberal age while utterly failing to deal with, or even address, the perennial Rangers issue of anti-Catholicism. The febrile and institutionalised bigotry which had been rife at the club since the heyday of his predecessor was allowed to fester unchecked during his time in charge, both within the club and among its supporters, and that left Symon guilty by association. It was of course ironic that the man who would ultimately prove to be his nemesis, Stein, was himself a Lanarkshire Protestant, who had played for and captained Celtic in the troubled era of the early '50s, and taken the club to his heart. Stein seemed to be Symon's antithesis; ebullient and outgoing, with a sophisticated understanding of the tactics of football, he was a track-suited manager with experience of coaching Celtic's reserves as well as improving players at Dunfermline and Hibs.

Scot Symon, suited and booted, with his ubiquitous waistcoat and soft hat, the symbols of his aloof authority, never improved a player in his life. Stein would eventually get the better of his publicity-shy rival by outsmarting and defeating him on the field, and outmanoeuvring him off it in the important area of public relations, where the Celtic man actually engaged with, used and even manipulated the press, to their mutual advantage.

The demise of Symon and the story of Rangers at this time serve as a salutary warning that in sport if you're merely standing still, you're in fact going backwards. Rangers had many fine players during the period in question and, even without the peerless Baxter, they had maintained their level; but Celtic had raised theirs, a sleeping giant had awoken and it would be a long time before the Ibrox club enjoyed such supremacy in the domestic game again.

* * * *

A few days after the controversial sacking of Scot Symon, the Rangers directors met with the former boss's assistant, 34-year-old Davie White, who had been taken on at Ibrox only that summer as a training ground coach, and appointed him as the club's new manager. The previous year, White had led Clyde to a creditable third-place finish in the league, behind their two Glasgow cousins, and his team had also reached the semi-final of the Scottish Cup, where they took all-conquering Celtic to a replay. The Shawfield side were unlucky not to qualify for the Inter-Cities Fairs Cup, with UEFA rules stipulating that only one team from any given city in Europe could play in the tournament and Clyde, the third best team in Scotland that season, were also the third best team in Glasgow. Instead, White would get the chance to lead Rangers in the competition, while his former team's European spot was taken by sixth-placed Dundee. Both Scottish sides would ultimately be eliminated from the tournament by the same opponent, with Don Revie's Leeds United accounting first for White's Rangers in the quarter-finals and then for Dundee in the semis, before going on to defeat Ferencvaros in the two-legged final.

White was one of the first ex-players to go through the SFA's new coaching courses and, in attempting to improve his knowledge of the game, he had attended both Rangers' and Celtic's European finals in Nuremberg and Lisbon respectively in May 1967. He had then been invited to join the Rangers backroom staff by a club hoping to add some youthful vitality and know-how to its set-up in response to the criticism of Symon's old-fashioned approach, and after Bobby Seith resigned, following the manager's dismissal, White was practically the last man standing. After meeting with the board in early November, he agreed to become the club's new manager on the condition that he would be in sole control of team affairs. White was aware that this was a privilege not afforded to his predecessor, with Symon having to submit his provisional selections for the directors' approval every Thursday night before a match. But given what was going on with Stein at Celtic and the fact that he was intended to be a tracksuited manager, working more closely with the players in training every day, the board accepted this provision and White's promotion was confirmed.

At the time of the new manager's appointment, Rangers were sitting three points clear at the top of the league, although closest rivals Celtic still had a game in hand due to their involvement in the Intercontinental Cup in South America. With things going well on the field, White was understandably reluctant to implement wholesale changes at the club, but he was determined to morph Rangers into a more attacking unit, especially when it became clear that, with the two Glasgow sides dropping very few points, the title might well have to be decided on goal average. He instructed his players, in games where victory was already secured, to try to score as many goals as possible, and on various occasions Rangers put six past St Johnstone, netted five each against Partick Thistle and Stirling Albion, and hit hapless Raith Rovers for ten.

The Ibrox men were in the middle of an extraordinary run of 19 wins from 20 games, a sequence interrupted only by a 2-2 Ne'erday draw at Celtic Park, a result which itself felt more like a victory after Kai Johansen scored a late equaliser in a match which Celtic had twice led, prompting Jock Stein to declare that the title was now Rangers' to lose. This was mind games of course, perhaps calculated to unsettle the new manager, and with White's side dropping points in the run-in, with drawn matches against Morton and Dundee United, Celtic eventually made up the ground.

By late April, the two teams were level on points with only one fixture each remaining, but the Parkhead men held the advantage because, despite the goal splurge, Rangers had been unable to match their rivals' average of over three goals per game. Just as in 1959, Rangers lost their final game of the season at home to Aberdeen, their only defeat of the entire campaign, meaning that Celtic, who had won every league game since the New Year draw, were confirmed as three-in-a-row champions when they beat Dunfermline 2-1 the following midweek at East End Park, in a match postponed by the Fifers' involvement in the cup final. After the Aberdeen defeat, angry supporters protested outside Ibrox and smashed in the windows of the home dressing room, where the Rangers players were in lockdown, unable to venture out into the street.

When striker Alex Ferguson finally made a dash for it two hours after the game, he was attacked by a fan who gave him a hefty kick in the calf as he tried to escape in a friend's car. White's Rangers had come close, but not close enough.

In August 1968, at the start of what would prove to be White's only full season in charge, Rangers lost home and away to Celtic in the sectional round of fixtures in the League Cup and were eliminated from the competition. The original intention on White's appointment to the position of team manager was for Symon to stay on at Ibrox in an executive capacity and become the club's general manager, but he had refused the post and it was now quickly becoming clear that, without an overseer, White, who Rangers were apparently still hoping would become their version of Jock Stein, was in need of some assistance. To this end, legendary centre-forward Willie Thornton, then managing Partick Thistle, was appointed White's assistant in September 1968, while the managerial vacancy created in Maryhill was in turn filled by none other than Scot Symon.

Sadly the changes didn't work out for either Rangers or Thistle, as Celtic took another title, this time by an increased margin of five points, despite losing home and away to White's Rangers in the league. The Parkhead side then went on to secure a second Treble in three years following a 6-2 defeat of Hibs in the League Cup Final and an equally emphatic 4-0 win over the Ibrox men in the Scottish Cup Final in front of almost 133,000 at Hampden, as Rangers suffered their first defeat in the final of the old competition since the 1920s and completed their third full season without a trophy.

Symon, meanwhile, fared little better at Thistle, as his team finished bottom of the league in 1970 and were relegated, having won only five games all year. He seemed to have lost his confidence and his modus operandi was no less antiquated in Maryhill than it had been at Ibrox. After he was replaced as manager following his club's relegation, Thistle bounced straight back up as champions of the Second Division, but it says a great deal about the regard in which he was held at his new club that, despite relegation and his dismissal as team manager, Symon was now operating in the role of general manager at Firhill, a post to which he seemed much more suited, and where he remained until 1984, a few months before his death.

Meanwhile, shortly after the loss of the league and the cup final embarrassment against Celtic, Davie White's Rangers travelled to Newcastle for the second leg of the Inter-Cities Fairs Cup semi-final. It was perhaps no surprise that the fixture attracted a great amount of publicity, given the relative proximity of the two cities, the Anglo-Scottish rivalry and the presence of exiled Scottish players in the Newcastle team. In addition, somewhat unusually, there was a considerable amount of verbal jousting prior to the tie from both sides, but Rangers remained confident of progress against a Newcastle team which they considered vastly inferior to the Leeds United side which had eliminated them from the same competition the previous year. After the first leg at Ibrox, which ended in a goalless draw thanks to Andy Penman's missed penalty for the home team, a large contingent of Rangers fans made the short journey across the border for the return, where goals from 'Anglo-Scots' Jim Scott, brother of former Rangers winger Alex, and Jackie Sinclair gave the Tynesiders a second-half lead.

At this point, empty bottles of Newcastle Brown Ale began to rain down on the pitch from the Gallowgate End, as Rangers fans, not used to being goaded by an opponent and then beaten, and apparently angered by refereeing decisions, invaded the field in an attempt to get the game called off. This was just the start of the disorder, which escalated after the game in Newcastle city centre and continued late into the night, causing a great deal of vexation in the Scottish press. Ex-Rangers player and future manager Willie Waddell, then working as a journalist covering the game for the *Scottish Daily Express*, described the Rangers supporters as 'uncontrollable savages' who had disgraced the name of the club. 'I felt like crawling stealthily back over the border under cover of darkness, stunned and shocked that I had been connected with this club and its fans for more than 30 years,' Waddell admitted. Newcastle United, who had finished tenth in the First Division the previous year and only qualified for the Fairs Cup because of the 'one team per city' rule, went on to beat Ujpest Dozsa of Hungary in the final to collect their, to date, last major trophy.

It seemed that by now the writing was on the wall for Rangers' young manager. At the start of the new campaign, White's team were once again eliminated from the League Cup in the early season group stages by Celtic, and their patchy form in the race for the title included defeats to Ayr United as well as the Parkhead men, who secured their first league win at Ibrox for 12 years in what turned out to be Jock Stein's only league victory over White. In Europe, despite that crushing cup final defeat, Rangers had entered the new season as Scotland's representative in the Cup Winners' Cup, where they overcame Steaua Bucharest in the first round. But when they then lost home and away to Polish outfit Górnik Zabrze, White was relieved of his duties the following morning, on 27 November 1969, a little over two years after his appointment. The sacking was made considerably easier for the Rangers board given that, during initial negotiations, White had refused the offer of a five-year contract, insisting instead that full control of team affairs was his only prerequisite for accepting the post.

Until Frenchman Paul Le Guen's ill-fated spell in charge of the club in the mid-2000s, White remained the only Rangers manager never to have won a major trophy. Like Le Guen, White had tried, unsuccessfully, to introduce a more progressive approach and move Rangers on from what was seen at the time as the burden of their own traditions. To an extent he can be seen as an unlucky manager, running a tremendous Celtic team extremely close in his first season, despite the Parkhead club being able to concentrate solely on the league after early elimination from both the Scottish Cup and in their defence of the European Cup. But Celtic managed to claim five of the six domestic trophies that were available during White's two years at the helm and Rangers simply weren't used to this level of failure.

The manager also spent considerable sums of money on his squad, including the purchase of Scotland's first £100,000 player, Colin Stein, who was signed from Hibernian as an intended replacement for the discarded Alex Ferguson. He also failed in a bid to revive Jim Baxter's career when he brought the former talisman back to Ibrox on a free transfer from Nottingham Forest, but the magic had gone, Baxter's lifestyle had caught up with him and he was a shadow of his former self. White was not reluctant to give youth its chance, in the form of Alex MacDonald, signed from St Johnstone, and he played an important role in the development of Derek Johnstone, Colin Jackson and Alfie Conn Jnr – all four of whom, along with Stein, would play an important role in Barcelona a few years later, when Rangers finally got their hands on a major European trophy.

A talented, forward-thinking coach, who had been recommended by Jock Stein for several posts prior to his appointment as Rangers manager, White enjoyed some success at Dundee after leaving Ibrox, leading the Taysiders to three consecutive Scottish Cup semi-finals, where they were defeated on each occasion by Celtic. However, he finally managed to get the better of his nemesis, Stein, when Dundee, with a team containing ex-Celt Tommy Gemmell, one of the heroes of Lisbon, defeated the Parkhead men in the final of the League Cup in December 1973.

By then, however, White's name was already fading from the memories of those who follow Rangers. While his contribution to the club in the end was modest, at times it almost seems as if White has been airbrushed out of the Ibrox side's history, with *The Official Biography of Rangers*, by Ronnie Esplin and Graham Walker, listing his date of birth only as ??/??/1933, while his place of birth is left blank in the book. For the record, David Wilson White was born on 23 August 1933 in Motherwell, North Lanarkshire. He died on 17 July 2013, aged 79, in nearby Wishaw General Hospital.

Intriguingly, former Rangers captain John Greig claims that, during his spell at Ibrox, White may have been let down by certain players, who failed to show the manager the respect he was due. One player whom White certainly never saw eye to eye with was Scot Symon's last signing for the club, Alex Ferguson, who considered himself a stronger, harder man than the manager, and the pair never got on. Greig, who played with and against Ferguson, describes his former team-mate's style of play, 'He was always a handful, a pest. He bustled about with his elbows parallel to the ground – and he was all skin and bone so that, when he got you, it was like being stabbed.'

Ferguson, who cost Rangers a record £65,000 from Dunfermline in the summer of 1967, endured a short and unhappy spell at Ibrox, as, in the end, the club ganged up on him and the striker became the ultimate stooge during his time at the club. The manager didn't rate him, the directors had their own reason to be suspicious of him, and the boyhood Rangers fan became a victim of the club's increasing tendency to look for scapegoats for their fluctuating fortunes at this period in their history. McLean and Forrest were made to take the blame for the Berwick episode, Symon carried the can for Celtic's resurgence and by 1969 Ferguson would be held responsible for the 4-0 defeat to Celtic in the Scottish Cup Final. Drafted into the team due to the absence of his intended replacement at the club, the temperamental Colin Stein who was serving a five-week suspension, Ferguson failed to pick up Billy McNeill at a corner as the Celtic captain headed his team into an early lead, from which Rangers were unable to recover.

However, this wasn't Ferguson's only offence in the eyes of the Rangers board, and in particular the club's PR guru, Willie Allison. Ferguson describes Allison, one of the chief plotters who moved against Symon, as 'a diseased zealot' and 'a religious bigot of the deepest dye', and of course Ferguson's wife Cathy was a Catholic. When he arrived at Ibrox, another director, Ian McLaren, had asked Ferguson where he had been married and when the player replied that the ceremony had taken place in a registry office, rather than in a Catholic church, it seemed that the club's new striker had got away with his strange choice of wife. But he was never fully accepted; Symon had been sacked only weeks after Ferguson joined the club and the player had a strained relationship with White, who didn't seem to appreciate his rugged style of play.

After the cup final defeat, Ferguson was made to train with the Rangers third team and play against amateur sides, until he was eventually transferred to Falkirk. Having grown up in Govan as a Rangers supporter, Ferguson subsequently lamented in his autobiography, 'No other experience in nearly 40 years as a professional player and manager has created a scar comparable with that left by the treatment I received at Ibrox.' He pinpointed Allison as the main cause of his distress and when the arch-manipulator approached the striker towards the end of his time at Rangers to reveal that he had cancer, Ferguson admits that he didn't have an iota of sympathy for the man.

The whole episode with Ferguson presented Rangers in a very poor light, revealing a nasty streak at the heart of the club in moving against one of their own in this way, as the Ibrox institution failed to honourably face up to a range of unforeseen challenges at this time. It wasn't just on the football field that the club found itself floundering; the shifting sands of social reform seemed to have left the whole Rangers edifice on shaky ground, as the traditions which the club represented came to be questioned by the changing attitudes and the reinvigorated social climate of the 1960s.

Throughout the Depression era of the inter-war period, the Catholic community in the west of Scotland had found itself at the sharp end of the poverty and deprivation which blighted the region, but by the time of the rise of Jock Stein's Celtic, Glasgow had benefited from widespread improvements in living and working conditions. The provision of affordable housing, which had begun in the 1930s with the slum clearances, expanded after the war under both Tory and Labour governments, with a surplus of modern council houses ensuring that for the first time working-class people had access to such basic amenities as electricity, hot water and indoor sanitation.

At the same time, the post-war economic expansion across Britain ensured high levels of employment, rendering the nepotism and parochialism of the 1920s and '30s, when Catholics had been excluded from much of Scotland's workforce, a redundant and inefficient anachronism. The modern welfare state, introduced by the post-war Labour government, had helped to lift the standards of health, education and social security among the community as a whole, but these new public services also opened up an undiscovered land of career opportunities for Catholics in sectors with no previous history of discrimination against them. In this new era of a more liberal, egalitarian outlook, it wasn't long before Catholics, now with a more tangible stake in society, began to enter the business and professional classes in considerable numbers, and as the process of integration continued, many of the old fears and myths about Scotland being swamped by zealots and succumbing to radical Popery were revealed as the lies and prejudices which they had always been.

Politically, it was a time of the rise of the Labour Party, still with an unashamedly Socialist agenda and a bastion of Catholic support in pre-war times, which now came to replace the Tories as the default party of choice among the broader Scottish electorate. By the late 1960s, changes in society allowed even the concept of celebrity, unlike today, to feel like a refreshing new breakthrough in an era when for the first time people from ordinary backgrounds could become rich and famous, especially if they had a talent for music or sport. This new cultural narrative, accompanied by a widespread challenge to the age of deference and all the other old certainties which had long been cherished by the Scottish establishment, meant that for the first time Rangers' exclusionary employment policies came under serious scrutiny, in the media and elsewhere, and throughout the 1970s the club was repeatedly left squirming by its inability to shrug off the unwelcome accusation, which was at last being uttered against it – the best-kept secret in Scottish football – that Rangers were a sectarian club.

It's notoriously difficult to equate the fluctuating fortunes of particular football teams with cultural changes in the wider society, but it's impossible not to conclude that during the iconoclastic 1960s the times just caught up with Rangers. The modern world gatecrashed their party, leaving them isolated and confused, out of time and out of place, the sly Willie Allison still trying to manage the club's hidden agendas. Rangers fans, uncomprehending, looked back to the all-conquering side of 1964 and wondered where it all went wrong, as Stein's Celtic, a team which hadn't won back-to-back league titles since the days of World War One, went on to collect nine consecutive championships between 1966 and 1974.

The Ibrox side weren't about to go quietly into the night, however, and Celtic, the erstwhile European champions, were chased every step of the way for the first few years of the Jock Stein era, but ultimately they couldn't be caught, and in the early '70s the challenge from Ibrox was starting to wilt. By then, however, football, even in Glasgow, would be placed in its proper perspective by the full force of tragedy.

5

DISASTER AND
TRIUMPH

D AVIE White had been dogged throughout his spell in charge
of Rangers by the club's former player Willie Waddell, who
had won the title as manager of Kilmarnock in 1965, but who
was now working as a football writer for the *Scottish Daily Express*.
An assassin with a typewriter, Waddell had mockingly dubbed White
'the boy David' in his influential column, a reference to White's youth
and perceived lack of managerial experience. More than just a clash of
personalities, the two men had an obvious history of antipathy towards
one another, possibly because, as a one-club man in his playing days and
now a successful manager in his own right, Waddell himself expected
to be offered the Rangers job when Symon was dismissed, or he may
have resented the fact that White, as a player with Clyde, had spurned
his advances when he tried to sign him for Kilmarnock, White later
admitting that he turned down the proposed move because he 'didny
fancy' Waddell. Whatever the reason, Waddell won out in the end
when Rangers turned to their former player in the autumn of 1969 and
appointed him only the fifth manager in the club's history.

Waddell's appointment, like White's, was, in part at least, a reactive
move, designed to counter the apparent advantage which Celtic had
recently been exploiting in their dealings with the media. Rangers were
being outflanked on the public relations front by Jock Stein, who knew

how to use the press to his advantage, and he was on amicable terms with many journalists; Waddell, having worked for two tabloid newspapers since his retirement as a player in the mid-'50s, was considered an industry insider and it was hoped that he would be able to manipulate the news agenda back in Rangers' favour. He was a gruff, abrasive character, not fussed about winning popularity contests or gaining the approval of others. Club legend Sandy Jardine described him as 'in many ways a bully, goading players into a response through his strong personality'.

In terms of discipline and authority, Waddell was very much an acolyte of former manager Bill Struth, whom he had played almost his entire career under since making his debut for the Ibrox club as a 17-year-old in 1938. Rangers were reverting to type and it was hoped that Waddell would whip them back into shape in the traditional manner, after White's more laid-back approach. To this end one of the first casualties of the new regime was Jim Baxter, back at the club for a second spell after being re-signed by White on a free transfer from Nottingham Forest. Deemed unfit by Waddell, he was considered surplus to requirements and Baxter, ever the drama queen, promptly retired in disgust.

The new manager seemed to have a positive initial impact on the Rangers team. Winger Willie Johnston remembers that he made a strong first impression, marching into the dressing room on his first day in the job and announcing, 'My name's Waddell, some of you already know me and those of you who don't soon will.' Rangers won eight of their first nine games under the new regime, a run of results which put them back in contention for the title, with the only interruption coming against Celtic at a freezing Parkhead in January, when the Ibrox men secured a creditable goalless draw. But after being knocked out of the Scottish Cup at the same venue in February, their form slumped badly over the spring and Rangers finished the season with only two wins from their last ten matches. In May, Celtic reached another European Cup Final, where, despite being considered favourites, they were defeated, 2-1 after extra time, by the underrated Dutch side Feyenoord. The setback, however, had no impact on the Parkhead club's continuing dominance of the Scottish domestic scene, as the championship headed to the east end of Glasgow for the fifth season in succession, this time by the comfortable margin of 12 points.

Nevertheless, the encouraging start made under Waddell continued into the following season when the League Cup was won by Rangers in October 1970. The only goal of the final against Celtic came just before half-time, when 16-year-old Derek Johnstone beat Billy McNeill in the air to head home the winner and become the youngest player ever to score in a British cup final. It was the Ibrox club's first major trophy in four and a half years, since winning the Scottish Cup in 1966, and Johnstone's goal prevented the trophy from heading to the east end of Glasgow for the sixth successive season.

Rangers fans must have felt that the Parkhead club were on the point of extracting a measure of revenge for that loss at Hampden, when just a few weeks later, on 2 January 1971, in the final minute of the game, Celtic opened the scoring at Ibrox through a Jimmy Johnstone header after a shot from Bobby Lennox had bounced down off the crossbar. It looked like the champions would finally end their 50-year run without an away victory in the traditional Ne'erday fixture but, with almost the last kick of the game, Colin Stein equalised for the home side from a Dave Smith free kick and the match finished 1-1.

What happened next is still the cause of some controversy. At first it was believed that supporters, who had turned to leave the ground in despair at the prospect of seeing Celtic celebrate victory, tried to return when they heard the roar of the crowd after Rangers equalised and, in the ensuing melée, disaster struck. The alternative, widely accepted view of more recent times, however, is that stairway 13, in the north-east corner of the ground, was simply too steep and too narrow to safely accommodate the departure of almost one third of the over 80,000 people who were in attendance that day. Regardless of the cause, 66 people, remarkably few of them over the age of 30, were crushed to death. A further 145 were injured.

Exactly what triggered the calamitous events has never been definitively pinpointed, but it doesn't seem credible to preclude the late drama in the game as a possible contributory factor at least, in the late jubilation and swirl of spectators, particularly given the sudden and diametrically contrasting mood swings among the heaving crowd following the late goals for either side. Rangers fans had developed a sense of fatalism when it came to Old Firm games at this time, and during the match they had started singing 'The Northern Lights of

Old Aberdeen', in quaint recognition that the only realistic challenge to Celtic's title hopes that season was likely to come from the Pittodrie club.

Journalist Graham Walker, a 14-year-old spectator in attendance on the day, writes how he saw one man head-butting a fellow supporter in sheer frustration at Celtic's late goal; but, when the equaliser was scored, 'the relief and joy were overwhelming. I have never been part of such an intense goal celebration, even when the goals were match and trophy winners.' Strathclyde Police's chief superintendent concurred when he described the scenes at the subsequent Fatal Accident Inquiry in February 1971, 'The excitement was tremendous, jubilation, they were singing, shouting, they were jumping up and down, waving their arms, hugging their friends, the terracing was in uproar. I would say it was football mania at its highest.' Also at the FAI, local residents testified that they saw people stop on the stairway to join in the celebrations, and that the late Rangers equaliser complicated the situation with the crowd.

Recent attempts to play down the late, dramatic action in the match as a factor in what followed seem to be a well-meaning attempt to exonerate both goalscorer Colin Stein, who many years later was still lamenting his role in what happened, and the fans themselves, particularly in relation to their conduct on the day. Rangers supporters, and the club itself, have in modern times developed an over-sensitivity to criticism regarding their reputation for sectarianism and other, more general forms of anti-social behaviour, and this perhaps explains some of the revisionism.

But there can be no question of the conduct of the crowd being to blame for what happened; there was no uncontained hooliganism, no frenzied whirlpool of departing spectators rushing to return and colliding with other fans. It's likely that at least one person stumbled and fell forward, perhaps carrying a friend on his shoulders in celebration, and then, as one witness described, 'The crowd caved in like a pack of cards, as if all of them were falling into a huge hole.' The steel barriers, which divided the stairway into seven lanes, buckled and gave way, and, as the FAI more prosaically concluded, 'The downward pressure of the crowd above, forced other persons to fall or collapse on those who had fallen first and as the downward pressure continued, more and more persons were heaped upon those who had fallen or were pressed hard against them.'

For all the uncertainties in the detail, the primary, root causes of the disaster remain clear: the unsafe, 'waterfall' design of passageway, or stairway, 13, which had been the location of several previous incidents in the preceding ten years, after one of which, a fatal crush in September 1961, it had been poorly redesigned and was now arguably an accident waiting to happen; a huge, teeming crowd in full celebration of an unexpected result, with many people already on the stairway who, not having witnessed Rangers' equalising goal, added to the numbers by not continuing their departure in the usual fashion towards the coach parks and the nearby underground station on Copland Road, which stairway 13 was the closest exit to; someone falling forward, perhaps losing his balance with a friend or a child on his shoulders.

Witnesses at the FAI testified that it was not uncommon to leave the stadium via stairway 13 without your feet touching the ground. To that extent, the finger of blame should, if anywhere, be pointed at the elderly, out of touch and aloof Ibrox board of directors, whose grasp on reality was limited at the best of times, and whose inaction and incompetence resulted in a failure to heed the warnings from three previous incidents in the same stairway. These earlier accidents had caused a total of 85 injuries, including the fatal crush in September 1961, again following a late equalising goal against Celtic, which left two people dead.

Had these warnings been properly addressed by the time of the 1971 match, many lives could have been saved. Meetings were arranged and advice was sought from the police, but in 1971 the role of the police at football matches was very much directed towards targeting hooliganism, with spectator comfort and safety not featuring prominently on their list of priorities. As Graham Walker acknowledges, 'The events of 1971 demonstrated that neither Rangers, nor the police, had absorbed the lessons of the 1961 tragedy, even after the further warnings of 1967 and 1969. The two parties evidently did not purposefully combine to address this specific problem, although relations between them were mutually acknowledged to be excellent.'

The original inquiry, completed by the end of February, criticised Rangers for their oversight and maladministration, but ultimately exonerated the Ibrox club of all blame for the disaster. It's a conclusion which still shocks to this day. How could Rangers and its directors have escaped the charge of negligence, when the warnings of so many repeated incidents in the same location had not been heeded or acted upon?

The minutes of board meetings, which were produced at the inquiry, confirmed that no effective action had been taken after the 1961 tragedy, and instead, the half-hearted adjustments, including the installation of high perimeter fences either side of the stairway, had only made things worse ten years later by preventing people from escaping. In addition, by the early 1970s, spectator safety at football grounds was a live issue across Britain following the publication of a series of reports into the relationship between the game and its public; the Chester inquiry, commissioned in 1966, looked at every aspect of football administration and how 'the game may be developed for the public good'; the Harrington report of 1968 advised all clubs to pay more concern to public safety and comfort within stadiums; and the following year, on the back of Harrington, a working party chaired by Sir John Lang made 23 recommendations designed to improve spectator safety and comfort at football grounds. It's not clear to what extent the Rangers directors had taken on board, or were even aware of these reports' recommendations, but it's not as if they hadn't been warned.

However, in a private prosecution brought against Rangers in October 1974, Margaret Dougan, a disaster widow who lost her husband Charles, a boilermaker from Clydebank, on stairway 13, was awarded damages of £26,261 by Sheriff James Irvine Smith. In reaching his verdict, the judge was scathing of the board's failure to act on the previous incidents in the same location, and in a note attached to his findings which ran to 27 pages, Sheriff Irvine Smith effectively accused former director David Hope and former manager Davie White of lying under oath during cross-examination at the civil suit. He also berated the other board members for trying to pass the buck on to another former director, Ian McLaren, who had since died and was therefore unable to defend himself.

Among many other criticisms, Sheriff Irvine Smith concluded that the accident was caused by 'the fault and negligence of the defenders', and he condemned a Rangers board which had apparently 'proceeded on the view that if the problem was ignored long enough, it would eventually disappear... Certain of their actions can only be interpreted as a deliberate and apparently successful attempt to deceive others that they were doing something when in fact they were doing nothing.'

The findings of the civil suit judge were reported in *Foul*, an early football fanzine put together by budding journalists and writers from Cambridge University. Inspired by *Private Eye*, the aim of *Foul*, which ran to 34 issues between 1972 and 1976, was to produce more in-depth coverage of the game as well as lengthier pieces focused on stories often ignored by the mainstream media, and, as *Foul* noted in an article on the disaster published in October 1976, 'The ruling of Sheriff Irvine Smith and its staggering implications were relegated to page five of the *Daily Record* and page eight of *The Scotsman*. This sycophancy [towards Rangers] has even spread to the BBC, who had to send a man up from London on the day of the disaster, because they could not trust their man on the spot to ask the right questions.'

Under the heading 'Falling Masonry', the article by contributing editor Alan Stewart, later a TV producer, went on to effectively claim that the original FAI was a Masonic cover-up and that Sheriff Irvine Smith's conclusions were a far more reliable and accurate account of the disaster's causes. 'Freemasonry is a strand that is woven so deeply into the history of Rangers that the two are inseparable,' wrote Stewart. 'The club celebrates the Masonic ideal and a brotherhood whose secrets are too precious for public knowledge.'

Stewart also accounted for the testimony to the civil case of former manager Davie White, who was accused of perjuring himself on behalf of a club which had ruthlessly sacked him a few years earlier, by alleging, 'The secret society had reached out and put the finger of loyalty on his lips.' If true, the implications are stunning: Rangers, through backdoor deals conducted beyond the reach of public scrutiny, escaped almost all responsibility for the unprecedented disaster, which, according to a later judge, had been caused by the club's own failings, and at which 66 of their own fans had perished. It certainly wouldn't be the last time in Rangers' history that a court had initially looked favourably on their case, only for the original decision to be later called into question when scrutinised again by a different set of judicial eyes.

In the immediate aftermath of the tragedy messages of condolence and support flooded into Glasgow from across the world, including from President Nixon's office in America, and from Sir Keith Holyoake, Prime Minister of New Zealand. In Rome, Pope Paul VI lamented, 'We have in our hearts the dead and injured in the terrible disaster in Glasgow,' and from across the football world there were offers of assistance and availability of players for victim support matches.

Within Glasgow itself, from every side of the community, there was a tremendous amount of sympathy and generosity extended towards Rangers, and, as the city came together in grief, manager Willie Waddell acknowledged, 'The show of goodwill has broken all barriers of nationality and creeds.' On 5 January, at St Andrew's Catholic Cathedral in Glasgow, Archbishop James Scanlon said Mass before a congregation of 1,200 who had come to pay their respects. In his sermon he stated, 'In offering this Mass today, we of the Catholic community are paying the highest tribute in our power to the victims of Saturday's appalling disaster.' Folk singer Matt McGinn, himself a member of the Catholic community, composed a song in tribute to the victims which spoke of Scotland coming together in grief and of the Old Firm united in prayer.

By the end of the month, a tribute match between a Rangers/Celtic select XI and a Scotland XI had been organised, with guest appearances made by Peter Bonetti, George Best and Bobby Charlton. The match was played at Hampden on 27 January and refereed by the same officials as on the fateful day, with proceeds going towards the Lord Provost of Glasgow's disaster relief fund, which both Rangers and Celtic had already given generously to.

Ultimately, over the years ahead, Rangers would squander much of the sympathy and goodwill that was being expressed towards them at this time, and in particular, the problems associated with the exclusionary signing policy and the club's sectarian stance could have been dealt with at this opportune moment, but instead they were left unresolved, with the manager and directors refusing even to address the issue. As journalist Graham Walker noted, 'Waddell could have used the latitude his powerful personality afforded him to bring the club truly into a new era... The times could not have been more propitious in view of the impact of the tragedy. However, Waddell chose to behave as defiantly over the issue as the Rangers directors then and before. He denied that sectarianism was practised by the club and concentrated instead on eradicating the problem of hooliganism which he regarded as a separate matter. In this he failed. The hooligan behaviour actually worsened.'

Nevertheless, the disaster would leave a lasting legacy on Rangers Football Club. Manager Waddell, standing in as spokesman for the elderly and confused directors, who seemed paralysed by events, initially claimed that Ibrox Park was one of the best-maintained stadiums in Britain. This was clearly far from the truth, and Waddell knew it. There had been multiple recent incidents on the same stairway, and as recently as December 1970, club physiotherapist Tommy Craig had described the stadium to Waddell as a 'death-trap', although after the accident, Waddell and Craig agreed never to mention publicly that they had ever discussed the condition of the ground. In addition, according to veteran sports journalist Rodger Baillie, who was working at the match on the day of the disaster, the old Ibrox press box, accessible only via a spiral staircase, was a fire hazard.

Bill Struth's stadium development of the 1920s might have afforded Ibrox the appearance of grandeur, but by the 1970s it was clear that the old stadium was beginning to show its age. The initial adjustments and improvements to the terracing following the disaster, as with the incident in September 1961, were largely superficial. After that first fatal accident ten years earlier, a central wooden barrier, which had shattered in the crush, was removed and replaced with steel tubes which divided the steep stairway into seven narrow lanes, and the wooden stairs were concreted over. On either side of the exit, reinforced high wooden perimeter fences were also installed, which safety officers had vainly urged the directors to remove after the incident at the Ne'erday game in 1969, and which tragically, exactly two years later, many people had been crushed against. Too late, they were taken down after the disaster and replaced with handrails, and a sign was placed over the precipitous stairway 13 which read, 'Caution. First step down'.

Waddell soon came to accept, however, that wholesale changes were required at the ground and he appointed himself as the man to take charge of the new stadium project. In June 1972, he resigned as team manager and moved into the position of general manager, where he could concentrate his efforts on the task of rebuilding Ibrox. Setting out on a tour of the modern arenas of European football, Waddell eventually selected Borussia Dortmund's Westfalen Stadium, one of the venues for the 1974 World Cup in West Germany, as the blueprint for Rangers' new ground. The plans were announced in 1977, which would see only Struth's grandstand remain from the original stadium, and two years later, in August 1979, before the first 'Old Firm' fixture of the season, the new Copland Road Stand was opened, replacing the old east terracing where stairway 13 had been located. An identikit stand at the opposite end of the ground, the Broomloan Road, which housed away supporters, was unveiled the following summer, and in December 1981, three days before Christmas, the Govan Stand, renamed in 2014 as the Sandy Jardine Stand following the death from cancer of the legendary full-back, was opened before a friendly against Liverpool.

Later additions and improvements were added over time, such as seating in the corners of the Govan, which brought the capacity up to 50,500, and with undersoil heating and computerised ticketing, the new Ibrox was later awarded five-star status by UEFA. Along with Pittodrie Stadium in Aberdeen, Rangers' rebuilt home became one of the first 'all-seater' grounds in Britain, so that when another, equally appalling disaster struck British football, at Hillsborough in April 1989, and the requirement for all-seater stadia was set out in the subsequent Taylor Report, which the SFA agreed to adopt, Ibrox Park was already in place to meet all of the new criteria.

* * *

During Willie Waddell's two and a half years in charge of Rangers, rivals Celtic had continued to dominate domestically, including a remarkable sequence when the Parkhead men secured three victories at Ibrox in the space of four weeks at the start of the 1971/72 season. In the first game, a sectional League Cup tie moved to Ibrox due to renovations at Celtic Park, a young Kenny Dalglish played in his first Old Firm derby and showed great calmness under pressure to score from the penalty spot.

In the wake of their Lisbon success, Celtic at this time were nurturing an extraordinary batch of talented youngsters, known affectionately as the 'Quality Street Kids', some of whom, including the jewel in the crown, Dalglish himself, had grown up supporting Rangers. Over at Ibrox, of course, they were still unable to reciprocate in kind and bring to the club young players who had grown up in a Celtic-supporting environment, as Rangers' ongoing refusal to sign footballers from a Catholic background, a policy which director Matt Taylor had recently claimed was a source of strength to the club, continued into the new decade.

Rangers' poor form at the start of the season carried over into the championship campaign, as the club lost four of their opening five league games in 1971/72, effectively putting themselves out of the title race by the beginning of October. Waddell seemed to have lost the magic touch that he had displayed previously in his spell in charge of Kilmarnock, but there were other factors affecting the team too by this stage, less tangible social and cultural influences, which were adding to Rangers' troubles at this time. Quite simply, Celtic, so long considered the black sheep of Scottish football, were by the early 1970s very much seen as the cool club, the place to be, the team that had dazzled Europe with their scintillating attacking football in Lisbon and which Rod Stewart would sing about, memorably, in his ballad 'You're In My Heart'. The idea of a glamorous rock star being moved to compare Rangers, a club still seen as representing the vested interests of a dour establishment, to a beautiful woman at this time was a risible, absurd notion.

Out of touch from the boardroom down, with the reputation of their fans plummeting in Britain, and eventually across Europe too, and clinging to an out-of-date, sectarian signing policy that was insular and regressive even when it was implemented in the early part of the century, Rangers were now being viewed with growing suspicion and even hostility by sections of a newly emboldened and critical media, who for so long had considered the club untouchable. The Ibrox institution was increasingly being forced towards the fringes of polite society, an embarrassment even to the Protestant middle classes, their diminished status in the national consciousness reflected painfully in dwindling success on the field.

The club eventually ended the season by winning only two of their final seven matches and finished third with a total of 11 defeats, their most since the war, a distant ten points behind runners-up Aberdeen and fully 16 points off Celtic. It was a difficult time for everyone associated with Rangers, with midfielder Alex MacDonald, who had grown up supporting the club, later reflecting on this period, 'When you are not doing well as a Rangers player, the postman tells you, the grocer tells you, the street-sweeper tells you, your granny tells you. Half of Glasgow is angry with you, the other half is laughing at you. It can be painful and we were coming near the end of our tether.'

With his last act as team manager, however, Waddell secured a notable success with victory over Dynamo Moscow in the final of the European Cup Winners' Cup in Barcelona in May 1972. Rangers had only qualified for the tournament as lucky losers after defeat to Celtic in the Scottish Cup Final the previous year, the third time in successive seasons that the club had been beaten in the competition by their old rivals.

Despite an equalising goal in the final from youngster Derek Johnstone, who repeated his heroics of the 1970/71 League Cup Final when he came off the bench to tie up the game at 1-1, Rangers lost the subsequent replay 2-1, but nevertheless qualified for the Cup Winners' Cup due to Celtic's involvement in the European Cup.

The club's passage through to the Nou Camp final was tortuous and eventful; in the first round, Rangers were paired with the French side Rennes, whose main threat Waddell identified as coming from their quick and technical forwards. The manager instructed his full-backs to man-mark the wingers, and with MacDonald taking care of the number ten, Waddell used his own strikers to close down the spaces and harry Rennes' ball-playing defenders. With Johnston providing the only outlet on the counter attack, the match served as a good early indication of how dogged Rangers were prepared to be in pursuit of European success, perhaps as an antidote to their domestic tribulations, but Rennes manager Jean Prouff was not impressed. 'That was not football, it was anti-football,' he complained after the 1-1 draw. 'They came here only to stop us playing football.' Maybe Prouff was being naïve, maybe Waddell's cynicism was ahead of its time, because the tactic worked and the draw in France was followed by a 1-0 win at Ibrox, which allowed Rangers to progress.

The second round provided the Ibrox club with a more demanding fixture against Sporting Lisbon, one of the favourites for the competition. Rangers edged ahead of the Portuguese with a 3-2 win at Ibrox in the first leg, but two weeks later the scoreline was mirrored in Lisbon, when the match initially finished 3-2 in the home team's favour. Both sides then scored again in the subsequent period of extra time to produce a 4-3 result, 6-6 on aggregate, but the Dutch referee, seemingly unaware that the recently introduced away goals rule also applied to goals scored in extra time, a ruling which would have put the Scots through, insisted that the tie should be settled on penalties. Sporting won the shoot-out with ease, Rangers missing from the spot with every one of their kicks, and the players trooped off amid the commotion of 60,000 celebrating

Portuguese fans, who left the stadium believing their team had advanced to the next round.

It was only after the game that reporter John Fairgrieve, an old mate of Waddell's from his days as a journalist and the author of *The Rangers: Scotland's greatest football club*, banged on the dressing room door waving a copy of the UEFA rulebook. Winger Willie Henderson, who scored in both legs of the tie, explains what happened next, 'The manager opened it and one of the Scottish pressmen was standing there. He and the manager went away and were in some kind of conversation. We didn't know what was going on but after what seemed like an eternity the manager came back in and said we were through. We just went wild.'

Rangers had progressed to a quarter-final meeting with Torino the following spring, where they survived an onslaught in the away leg, after being gifted an early goal by a goalkeeping blunder, to draw 1-1. The meticulous Waddell used to provide his players with comprehensive dossiers on their European rivals, which included photographs and information outlining their opponents' strengths and weaknesses. Prior to the match at the Stadio Comunale, the manager identified the Italians' danger man as attacking midfielder Claudio Sala and instructed his captain, John Greig, to nullify the threat from the playmaker, as Greig reveals in his autobiography: 'The boss held up a photograph of one of the Torino players and said to me, "John, this is their number one player, Claudio Sala. He is just 19 and he is the new Italian wonder boy. I want you to put him out of the game."' Greig, naturally, warmed to the task, but what the Rangers captain failed to realise was that Waddell had deceived him; Sala was no teenager. He was 24 years old and had already been around for some seven years in Italian football by the time of the tie with Rangers.

But Greig took the bait, as his account of the game reveals, 'When I received the ball [straight from the kick-off] I deliberately knocked it a yard in front of me, knowing that Sala's inexperience would almost certainly result in him making an immediate challenge. I was correct, but when Sala committed himself to the challenge I hit him with all my force and knocked him six feet in the air. I immediately bent over Sala with my back to the referee, making out as if I was apologising for the tackle, but instead I grabbed the startled youngster by the throat and said, "Figlio di puttana", which translated means, "Son of a whore!" I also drew my forefinger across my throat and growled "Glasgow".'

Waddell's neat trick had clearly worked; his misinformed skipper had scared the shit out of Sala, regardless of his age, and it was no surprise when the Italians' most creative player was so ineffective against Greig in Turin that he didn't even make the team for the second leg. Afterwards, Torino coach Gustavo Giagnoni admitted that Rangers had beaten the Italians at their own game, 'Rangers came here and played the Italian game. It was too defensive but it is the kind of game that Italian teams have used often when they are away from home in a European tie and we can have no complaints.'

Just as against Rennes, the away draw in Italy was followed by a 1-0 victory at home, meaning that in the semi-final Rangers would face Bayern Munich for the third time in five years. Bayern had won the previous two encounters, including the 1967 Cup Winners' Cup Final, and if anything, by 1972 they were an even stronger side, who would go on to dominate European football in the middle years of the decade, as well as providing the bulk of the West Germany squad who won the European Championship in 1972 and the World Cup on home soil in 1974.

In the first leg, played at Bayern's Grünwalder Stadium, in the last European tie to be staged at the old ground before the club moved into the Olympic Stadium, Rangers were subjected to an all-out attack as Bayern threw everything at them in the opening stages. Full-back Sandy Jardine describes the Germans' relentless assault as the biggest hammering he had been on the end of in his entire career, while John Greig admits that the opening 20 minutes were 'the most sustained onslaught I have ever experienced'.

By half-time, every Bayern outfield player had managed an effort on the Rangers goal, but only Paul Breitner's strike divided the teams. Rangers' good fortune continued when, early in the second half, home defender Rainer Zobel headed a cross from Colin Stein into his own net and the match finished in a 1-1 draw. Two weeks later, for the second leg in Glasgow, 80,000 fans packed inside Ibrox to witness Sandy Jardine give Rangers the lead after just two minutes. The tone was set for the game, during which such luminaries as Franz Beckenbauer and Sepp Maier were seen arguing among themselves in frustration, as the

Germans' game totally fell apart on an Ibrox pitch that was so uneven as to be almost unplayable. In the 24th minute, Derek Parlane scored from a corner and Rangers never looked back; they had arrived in the final and would be heading to Barcelona.

Rangers' opponents in the final would be old friends Dynamo Moscow, who, in November 1945, had graced Ibrox with their presence for a glamorous friendly to mark the Allies' victory over Nazi Germany and the end of World War Two. In the Nou Camp, Rangers rushed into a three-goal lead with goals from Stein and a double from Johnston, but the Russians hit back through substitute Eschtrekov, and when Makivikov made it 3-2 with only minutes remaining, captain John Greig was pleading with the Spanish referee to end the match. Greig had played the final with an undiagnosed stress fracture of his foot and, by his own admission, he was wilting badly and would not have lasted through extra time. He had even declared himself unfit before the biggest match of his career, but Waddell had insisted that he play.

After each of the three goals for their team, the travelling Rangers fans invaded the field and had to be cleared from the pitch. Then, with a minute of the match remaining, the Spanish referee blew his whistle for an offside decision, which prompted yet another pitch invasion by supporters who believed that they had heard the final whistle. Franco's authoritarian Spanish state police were not impressed, and when Rangers held out for the remaining minutes, and took the trophy, a full-scale riot broke out. Amid the ensuing mayhem, Greig had to be called out into a corridor by a Barcelona official and ushered into a Nou Camp committee room, where he received the trophy from the UEFA dignitaries.

It has been debated ever since, whether Spain being a largely Catholic population had any influence on the trouble, as outside Rangers fans, who were celebrating arguably their club's greatest ever achievement, indulged in a running battle with the police. Perpetrated in victory rather than defeat, with no opposing fans in the stadium due to Soviet travel restrictions, the disturbances in Barcelona were illustrative of why Rangers fans had acquired such a poor reputation by this time, unable to enjoy themselves without spreading mayhem. They had been determined to match, or perhaps even outdo, the celebrations in Lisbon five years earlier, but instead the fans had disgraced the name of their club with their drunken, riotous behaviour.

However, the role played by the militaristic local law enforcement cannot be underestimated either and the mixture of Franco's authoritarian state police, combined with the Catholic-hating drunkards within the Rangers support, was always going to produce a particularly strange brew, with witnesses subsequently blaming both sides for what happened. Jim Blair of the *Evening Times* reported, 'It was a night to remember – but, sadly, for all the wrong reasons. Rangers' 3-2 win... was virtually overshadowed by a running riot at the end of the game.' Describing the worst scenes of unrest at a football match that he had ever seen, Blair also blamed the police, 'To put the matter in its proper perspective, however, the Spanish police were far from blameless. Their actions to "charge" the fans and wield batons came, quite significantly, when television coverage stopped.'

Barcelona's Reuters correspondent, attending the match, pointed out the political dimension, telling match commentator Archie Macpherson, '[This] is the fascist police in action. That is the only way they can handle any disturbance. They are experts in ruthless suppression. They are not even local police. They are not Catalans. That is why they are so hated in this city. They are Franco's men. They are recruited from Castile or Murcia. Anywhere but Catalonia. They are in this area to maintain a dictatorship... These supporters simply do not understand their lives could now be at risk.'

But ultimately the Rangers supporters could not escape blame for their role in the night's events. Alex Cameron in the *Daily Record* observed, 'I can honestly say I have never seen anything as unruly or stupid anywhere', while Allan Herron, given a few days to reflect before his piece was published in the *Sunday Mail*, noted that the hooliganism had not merely been restricted to the stadium on the night, but that the fans had left their mark elsewhere on the Catalan capital, 'Let there be no excuse: the fans were to blame for what happened in Barcelona... What provoked the fans into wrecking hotels, throwing bottles from hotel balconies, smashing cars, tearing restaurants and floral displays apart?'

As a result of the crowd trouble, Greig was prevented from raising the trophy aloft against the Nou Camp backdrop in the traditional manner, and the iconic image from the night is of the captain and his team-mates celebrating their success with the trophy in the bath instead. Nevertheless, the triumph was a notable boost in morale for everyone associated with the club; the whole campaign had been a welcome diversion from their domestic woes and Rangers had beaten some great sides along the way. Waddell had successfully developed a new, ultra-cagey strategy for European football which allowed Rangers to play a more defensive game, even at home, against arguably superior sides, in contrast of course to the Scottish league where they were expected to take the game to their opponents.

Following the crowd trouble, Dynamo refused to accept the result, arguing that the game had been interrupted by the numerous pitch invasions, particularly the last, and their demand for a replay was supported by UEFA president Gustav Wiederkehr, who described the behaviour of the Rangers fans as 'shocking and ugly'. For a while there were genuine fears within Ibrox that the cup could be taken away from the club, but the Russian protest was ultimately in vain. Instead of a void result, Rangers were banned from European competition for two years, later reduced on appeal to one. Despite his condemnation of the fans' behaviour three years earlier in Newcastle, when he was working as a tabloid journalist, Waddell threatened to resign if the club's directors refused to appeal the two-year ban handed down to the club. The reduction in the length of the suspension was a success for Waddell, but it meant that Rangers would be unable to defend the trophy the following season.

However, the club magazine, *Rangers News*, set up at the start of the season, had boasted after the final that Rangers were now 'Kings of Europe', and, at Waddell's instigation, a challenge match was arranged with the European Cup winners Ajax to decide who could unofficially lay claim to this title. A Dutch newspaper suggested that the contest should be played over two legs and called the European Super Cup, and, in January 1973, the classy Dutchmen, led by Johan Cruyff, eased to a 6-3 aggregate success over Rangers, after victories in both Glasgow and Amsterdam.

The games were a great sporting and financial success and the following season, this time under the official auspices of UEFA, the European Super Cup was formally inaugurated, with Ajax again, this time without Cruyff, who had left Holland to join Barcelona, romping to a 6-1 win over AC Milan.

6

THE OTHER 'BIG JOCK'

IN June 1972, just two weeks on from the triumph of Barcelona, Willie Waddell surprised everyone, outside of his Ibrox clique at least, by announcing that he was stepping down as Rangers manager. Or, more precisely, what Waddell had engineered for himself was a step up, away from team affairs, effectively promoting himself into the newly created position of general manager at the club.

With no inkling of his intentions, the unsuspecting press were summoned to Ibrox, where he informed them, 'I have never made any secret of the fact that in my opinion team management is a young man's game and it becomes more and more difficult these days for one man… to handle all the details involved in league and European football. That is the reason behind the change… I become general manager and more or less still in the number one position.'

Too crafty, too worldly-wise to spend his entire non-playing career slaving away on the training field, Waddell was leaving football management on his own terms, just as he had done seven years earlier after winning the title with Kilmarnock. Still very much the boss, and with such a feckless and ineffectual group of directors in the boardroom, Waddell would now take charge of almost every aspect of the club's administrative affairs. As well as the matter of the new stadium, which initially consumed much of his time and energy, he looked after the club's finances with a miserly diligence, becoming notoriously difficult to deal with over the issue of players' contracts and bonuses. He retained control over the buying and selling of players, and he continued to represent and stand up for the club's interests off the field in a difficult era for Rangers.

Waddell's association with the club stretched back to 1938 when he made his debut as a 17-year-old, scoring the only goal of the game in a friendly against Arsenal. By the time of his resignation as a director and consultant in 1984, when he effectively severed his last remaining ties with the club, on top of his 17 years as a player, he had spent a further 15 years in a variety of roles, including team manager, general manager, and subsequently vice-chairman and managing director, leaving Waddell as one of the most celebrated and influential figures in the club's modern history.

He was not without his critics however, including those who maintained that, having secured his status among the club's pantheon of legends with victory in the Cup Winners' Cup Final, Waddell was now simply stepping out of the firing line. With no obvious strategy available to halt the Celtic juggernaut, he left his assistant in charge while he absconded to the relative safety of the boardroom, still very much the boss. But it was his increasingly cantankerous personality which left him largely unloved, even within the walls of Ibrox, and once he was elevated to the boardroom, Waddell tended to behave like a king among his ministers.

At board meetings, the other directors were afraid to even open their mouths until Waddell permitted them to speak, while his treatment of his successor in the manager's office was often that of a subservient underling. Even close confidant Tommy Craig, nominally the club's physiotherapist, but in effect Waddell's henchman, describes his boss as 'an out-and-out bully'. On one occasion, the general manager threw the BBC's Martyn Lewis down the marble staircase at Ibrox after he tried to sneak into a press conference from which television journalists had been explicitly excluded at Waddell's instruction. Broadcaster Archie Macpherson summed it up neatly, 'While I pay due credit to Waddell as the only leader who could have guided Rangers through their horrendous crises, I pay much less to him for generally spurning the milk of human kindness.'

Waddell's replacement as team manager was his unheralded assistant, Jock Wallace Junior. A former soldier with the King's Own Scottish

Borderers, Wallace had seen action during the Malay Emergency as a teenager in the 1950s, earning him the nickname the 'Jungle Fighter', but as a goalkeeper with West Brom and Airdrie his career had been less celebrated. The undoubted highlight came when, as player/manager of Berwick Rangers, he oversaw the borderers' famous 'giant-killing' cup victory over their more renowned Glasgow namesakes in January 1967, after which he reportedly flattened one of his players with a punch, or 'tanned him in the jaw' to use the local vernacular, for having the temerity to address him as 'Jock'.

A larger-than-life character and an imposing physical presence, Wallace had made a positive impression at Berwick and as John Harvey's assistant at Hearts, before he joined the Rangers backroom team in April 1970, at a time when Waddell was looking to step back from involvement in training with the players on a daily basis. The manager's attempt to become a tracksuited coach at Rangers had turned out to be a short-lived experiment, and Waddell quickly realised that he needed to add an additional coach to his staff. Now, just over two years later, after his resignation as team manager and subsequent self-promotion, the departing manager was keen to stress from the start that Wallace would be in sole charge of team affairs.

'The partnership between myself and Jock is terrific and I am sure he will do a good job… Jock is in complete charge of training, tactics and team selection and though we will be working closely I know that he will never be a puppet on a string. He is his own man and I respect him for that,' Waddell announced as he handed over the reins to his successor. Despite these reassurances, however, the working relationship between the pair would come under increasing strain over the years ahead, until it finally reached breaking point at the very height of their success.

Like so many others who have played a key role in Rangers' history, Wallace was not a west of Scotland man, hailing instead from the village of Wallyford, to the east of Edinburgh. As a coach, he placed a great deal of emphasis on physical fitness, training his players to the point of sickness and exhaustion in pre-season on the sand dunes of Gullane Beach, a few miles further up the East Lothian coast from his home. The brawn behind Waddell's brain, his strengths were considered to be on the motivational, rather than the tactical, side of the game and he was very much a traditional Rangers type, who loved the club and bought into the culture fully over the course of his association, and he emphasised the values of discipline and strength in the traditional Rangers manner.

The new season opened with defeat to Hibs at Easter Road in the semi-final of the Drybrough Cup, a short-lived pre-season tournament between the four top-scoring teams in the first and second divisions. The game witnessed further ugly scenes involving Rangers supporters and, coming so soon after the disgrace of Barcelona, Waddell, in his new role as the club's general manager, didn't mince his words when he addressed the 'tykes, hooligans, louts and drunkards who have no respect for society'. For a club which in more recent years has so often been on the defensive over their fans' behaviour, Waddell deserves credit for the unequivocal tone of his condemnation, 'The name of Rangers has been smeared all over the world by an unruly mob who spread destruction and terror. Unfortunately the stain sticks to every decent Rangers fan. We want no part of those who cause destruction to public property, throw bottles, fight and spread viciousness with party songs and foul and obscene language. It is because of your gutter rat behaviour that we are being publicly tarred and feathered.'

On the field, the club's fortunes took a while to improve in the early days of Wallace's reign. Perhaps trying too hard to assert his authority after his unexpected promotion, the new manager fell out with several important players, including Willie Johnston and Alfie Conn, although in the case of Conn, manager and player were eventually reconciled. There were embarrassing defeats to Second Division sides St Mirren, 4-1, and Stenhousemuir, 2-1, both at Ibrox in the League Cup, although the latter came on the back of a 5-0 win at Ochilview in the first leg, and Rangers eventually progressed to the semi-final of the competition.

In the league too, they struggled initially, and there were early losses to Ayr United, Celtic and Kilmarnock, all by the end of September. Results slowly began to improve, however, as Wallace gradually began to grow into his new role. The turning point came when the languid Dave Smith was injured just before Christmas and the manager decided to move the tough-tackling midfielder Tom Forsyth, later nicknamed 'Jaws', whom he had signed from Motherwell in October, into central defence alongside the still teenage Derek Johnstone. Smith, a gambling addict who was jailed in 1983 for embezzlement, was not a particularly physical defender, relying more on his ability to read the game, and in fact he had never been booked and was prone to congratulating opponents who got the better of him. He eventually left Rangers for Arbroath in November 1974, fed up with Wallace's persistent instruction that he should leather opponents.

The Barcelona squad was starting to break up, as Wallace began to shape the team which he had inherited. Jackson and Smith were no longer first picks and the temperamental strike partnership of Colin Stein and the pacy Willie Johnston, who had recently been banned for nine matches, was dismantled with both players transferred south, to Coventry and West Brom respectively. Wallace dismissed the departing pair as 'prima donnas' and they were later followed by Alfie Conn, who moved to Spurs, before returning to Glasgow after a short spell in north London to play for Jock Stein's Celtic. Wallace's team finally discovered their form around the turn of the year, and in the second half of the season Rangers embarked on a 29-match unbeaten run all the way to the cup final, including in January their first win over Celtic since the 1970 League Cup Final.

It was a relentless, but ultimately vain pursuit of the champions, who collected their eighth consecutive title by the margin of a single point. However, the Parkhead men were overcome in the 1973 Scottish Cup Final, the centenary of the old competition and one of the great Old Firm occasions, when Forsyth scored the winner in a five-goal thriller, squeezing the ball home from all of six inches to give Wallace his first trophy since taking charge of the club on a memorable day at Hampden. After the match, with the victorious manager being interviewed on *Grandstand*, Wallace appeared increasingly distracted during the course of the live broadcast. His boss Willie Waddell was gesticulating furiously at him, and when Wallace was finally prised away from the cameras, the general manager issued him with a very public dressing down before they left the field. Waddell had been a boyhood hero to Wallace as a young Rangers fan, but already it was becoming clear that the professional relationship between the pair was growing fractious, with the irritable Waddell apparently unwilling to see his manager taking the credit for the team's achievements.

The expected momentum evaporated early the following season, as Wallace's side contrived to lose three of their opening five matches in the championship and, by the end of September, found themselves sitting just a point off the foot of the table. A few weeks later, after they were beaten 1-0 at home by lowly East Fife, Rangers still hadn't managed to score a single goal at Ibrox in any of their four league games and the team were jeered from the field by their supporters. To make matters worse, they then lost the League Cup semi-final to Celtic and were eliminated from Europe by Borussia Mönchengladbach, a 5-3 aggregate defeat putting paid to the prospect of another run in the Cup Winners' Cup and a repeat of the heroics of two seasons previous.

The club didn't have their troubles to seek and, after losing to lowly Arbroath for the first time, 3-2 at Ibrox in February, Derek Johnstone was stripped of the captaincy. Off the field, there was more crowd trouble at a friendly against Manchester United in March, after which a local senior policeman stated, 'It's about time Glasgow Rangers fans were kept in Scotland.' In the *Sunday Mail*, correspondent 'Judge' wrote, 'Rangers supporters lived up to their hooligan reputation in Manchester, confirming beyond reasonable doubt that they remain the most anti-social element in modern day European football.' Bob Patience in the *Daily Record* put the problem down to religious bigotry, 'For me, that's the driving force which incites these fanatics to the extremes, and which has made them the scourge of Europe.' Jock Wallace though was having none of it; he used to send his players out on to the field with the loyalist battle-cry 'No Surrender!' ringing in their ears and there was no appetite within the dressing room for the club to end its Protestants-only employment policy.

Rangers' form eventually recovered towards the turn of the year, as the Ibrox men climbed the league to second place, but at Celtic Park a Bobby Lennox goal settled the Ne'erday derby and Celtic's ninth title in a row was all but confirmed. The club's fans by now were voting with their feet, and by the last home game of the season there were only an estimated 6,000 hardy supporters at Ibrox to witness a 3-1 win over Dumbarton.

In the end, Rangers were beaten to second place by Hibs on the final day of the season and, having missed out on the Scottish Cup with a 3-0 home defeat to Dundee in February, then managed by former Ibrox boss Davie White, they failed to qualify for Europe for the first time since 1965.

Wallace, however, about to enter the final year of his three-year contract, was determined to remain positive. 'The atmosphere is right and we now have the men who are playing for each other, and playing for Rangers,' he announced. 'We will be a better team next season. We were winning games this season but things just weren't right. I'm not afraid of the new season – I feel no pressure. I have neither fear for the future of this club nor my own future. The feeling is right – and the music is good!'

The upbeat approach clearly worked because, in 1975, Rangers finally won their first championship since Scott Symon's Baxter-inspired Treble winners of 1964 and in the process they put paid to Celtic's aspirations of claiming a tenth consecutive title. Caldow and Shearer, grainy black and white footage, Jimmy McGrory still plodding on manfully with his dismal Celtic side; in reality little more than a decade had passed, but to those who had followed Rangers over the intervening years, 1964 must have seemed like the remote and distant past in comparison with the changed world of the mid-1970s.

The season started positively when, in September, Rangers came from behind to win 2-1 at Parkhead, their first league victory over Celtic in the east end of Glasgow for six years. This precipitated a surge in confidence, which was reflected in subsequent results, capped by six-goal splurges against weaker opponents Kilmarnock and Dunfermline. By the turn of the year Celtic were again leading the way, but they were comprehensively defeated at Ibrox, 3-0, meaning that Rangers had completed the double over Celtic in the final season of the old 18-team First Division. The ten-team Premier League, in which sides would face each other four times a year, would be introduced for the following campaign, meaning that there were very few meaningless fixtures in the run-in, with mid-table teams fighting to remain in the newly formatted top flight.

The title was eventually claimed with a draw at Easter Road, after nine-in-a-row champions Celtic faded badly towards the end, losing three games in succession over late February and early March and eventually finishing behind Hibs in third position, 11 points off the pace. Rangers' all-important equalising goal against Hibs had come from Colin Stein, the first in his second spell with the club, after Wallace had re-signed the striker from Coventry City only weeks earlier, with the explicit purpose of propelling an understandably nervous Rangers over the line in the title race. In the end, the Ibrox men were comfortable winners, taking their first title in 11 years with four games to spare.

More was to come from Wallace's Rangers, as the following season the manager led the club to a remarkable Treble. With the new streamlined ten-team league in place, Celtic were determined to regain the title, but the Parkhead club suffered a traumatic setback when manager Jock Stein was involved in a serious car crash and spent almost the entire season recovering in hospital. Under caretaker Sean Fallon, Celtic were leading the way in the championship as late as March, but once again they finished the season poorly and allowed their rivals to claim the honours. Having already defeated the Parkhead side 1-0 in the League Cup Final, Rangers completed a clean sweep by beating Hearts 3-0 in the Scottish Cup Final.

It was a remarkable achievement, given that, by the standards of previous years, this was not a great Rangers team. They had struggled badly at times during the season, at one point slipping into the bottom half of the table after only one win in seven games during the early autumn. In addition, Wallace's side exited the European Cup with barely a whimper, losing home and away to classy French outfit St Etienne in the second round. The overall strength of Scottish football seemed to have dipped, certainly in regard to Rangers' domestic opponents, with Celtic falling well below the standards they had set during the early Stein years and the previously strong challenge of Hibernian was also fading, while Aberdeen and Dundee United were not yet the forces which they would become. But Rangers had shown the necessary staying power and the Treble was a noted success, especially as the club had not collected more than one trophy in a season since 1964.

Celtic, with a fit-again Jock Stein restored at the helm, regained the title and won the Double in 1977 in a poor season for Rangers, during which it took the Ibrox side four games to see off First Division Clydebank in the League Cup. Having eventually managed to reach the semi-final, they were promptly thrashed 5-1 by Aberdeen. In Europe, Wallace's men were eliminated at the first hurdle by unexceptional Swiss outfit FC Zurich, after which one commentator noted, 'The Rangers players – Tommy McLean apart – lacked class. We just don't have it in Scotland any more. In our desperation to find new idols to replace immortals like Morton, Baxter and Meiklejohn, we glorify players who wouldn't have been allowed to carry a hamper into Ibrox 20 years ago.'

Rangers then found themselves in further trouble off the field when Wallace took his team down to Birmingham for a friendly against Aston Villa in October. After the home team took a two-goal lead, the match had to be abandoned early in the second half when rioting broke out among the travelling fans and, in one of the worst and most sustained outbreaks of hooliganism ever seen at that point, dozens of people, including several policemen, were subsequently left seriously injured. Willie Waddell seemed at a total loss, stating, 'These louts are killing us, it's a bloody disgrace. The best thing for clubs to do is not to ask us to face them in a challenge match, which is a tragedy. We are crucified within Britain.'

Curiously, however, when the SFA threatened to intervene, after more trouble at a match against Motherwell in February 1978, Waddell bristled. He took to the field at Ibrox during the next home game to declare, 'No way will we accept that they [the SFA] will crucify the club for the actions of five per cent or less of our support.'

It seemed that there was a curious dichotomy in the reaction from Rangers, under Waddell, to their troubles at this time; in the face of mounting criticism, the general manager was happy to issue conciliatory, apparently heartfelt statements of regret in order to try and pacify the media, but at the same time he wouldn't tolerate a word of condemnation towards the club from the footballing authorities. If his remorseful announcements were an attempt to mollify the press however, he appeared to have failed when, after the incident in Birmingham, decorated journalist Ian Archer, a Scot who had grown up in England and therefore perhaps had a broader perspective and a less indulgent attitude towards the whole Rangers phenomenon, appeared to arrive at the apex of media criticism towards the Ibrox club at this time when he wrote in *The Herald*, 'As a Scottish football club, they are a permanent embarrassment and an occasional disgrace. This country would be a better place if Rangers did not exist.'

By the end of the season, after Rangers lost the Scottish Cup Final to Celtic in a game settled by an Andy Lynch penalty, awarded following a handball on the goal line by Derek Johnstone, it seemed that the Ibrox club was in turmoil. Sandy Jardine, a stalwart of the side for much of the decade and the only Rangers player to have been selected by Scotland manager Willie Ormond for his 1974 World Cup squad, refused the offer of a new contract and was left behind as the club embarked on an end-of-season tour of Sweden. Meanwhile, veteran skipper John Greig was contemplating retirement, telling the club that if he was dropped from the team the following season, he wouldn't hang around on the sidelines and accept charity.

The pressure began to ease once the new season was under way however, as the underperforming team of 1976/77 was strengthened by the addition of striker Gordon Smith from Kilmarnock, the emergence of promising youngster Bobby Russell, who was brought to the club from Junior side Shettleston, and the acquisition of legendary winger Davie Cooper, who was signed from Clydebank. The campaign started slowly, and when an opening day defeat at Pittodrie was followed by a 2-0 home loss to Hibernian, there were fans outside Ibrox calling for Wallace's head. Celtic also made a stuttering start to the season, however, following the departure of star player Kenny Dalglish, who had left Glasgow to join Liverpool over the summer. After defeat at Ibrox in the first Old Firm game of the season, when Rangers retrieved a 2-0 half-time deficit to win 3-2, the rudderless Parkhead side found themselves at the foot of the table with only one point from four matches.

Rangers' own sluggish opening to the season was compounded by an early exit from the Cup Winners' Cup at the hands of the unheralded Dutch outfit Twente Enschede, who bamboozled the Ibrox side with the intelligence and fluidity of their movement and passing, marshalled by Frans Thijssen and Arnold Mühren in midfield, resulting in a thoroughly merited 3-0 aggregate win. Domestically, however, Rangers recovered to win the newly formatted League Cup, now a straight knockout competition with the final in March, after a 2-1 extra-time win over Celtic at Hampden; the Scottish Cup, defeating Aberdeen in the final by the same scoreline; and the league, completing a second, this time far more convincing Treble in the space of three years. The mood music at Ibrox had totally changed over the course of the season, as evidenced by the decision of John Greig, who had been threatening to pack it all in only 12 months earlier, to sign a new contact at the club, with the captain declaring, 'I'll be back at Ibrox next season looking for more medals.'

Wallace himself reflected that he considered this Treble to be the sweetest of them all and his achievement is highlighted by the fact that no Rangers manager, before or since, has won two domestic clean sweeps. Celtic could only finish fifth, losing as many games as they won in 1978, a season which brought to an end the remarkable tenure of Jock Stein at Parkhead. But just as one 'Big Jock' was stepping down in Glasgow, so the other was doing the same. Just 17 days after the cup final, Wallace announced that he was quitting Rangers following a terminal breakdown in the relationship with his nominal boss Willie Waddell.

Seven and a half years on from the Ibrox disaster, the club had acquired the funds, chiefly through the popular Rangers Pools, to begin work on the reconstruction of Ibrox Park. The meticulous Waddell, who had been named vice-chairman in September 1975 after the death of Matt Taylor, had done the sums and he knew that Rangers would have to run a tight ship over the next few years if the renovations were to be completed both on schedule and without the club going into debt, something he was determined to avoid at all costs. Wallace, however, wanted money to be spent on the team; he knew that the earlier Treble, of 1976, had been followed by a barren season and to avoid a repeat he was insisting that the club should break its wage structure in order to compete with sides from England to acquire the best Scottish talent.

The manager wanted Rangers to be able to attract to Ibrox names such as Dundee United's Andy Gray, recently acquired by Aston Villa, and Alan Hansen, who had left Partick to join Liverpool, instead of allowing these home-grown players to head south for financial reasons. Crucially, however, Wallace also demanded a hefty pay rise. Striker Derek Johnstone later recounted the manager's explanation for his departure from Rangers, 'When I saw him that Thursday he just said to me, "Deedle [Waddell] won't pay me any more money. He just refuses an increase, and I know many managers in the game down south are getting much more than me, so I'm getting out and that's where I'm heading."'

Wallace and Waddell had in fact been engaged in a running dispute over money for a considerable period of time. The relationship between the pair had for several years now been fractious, and the situation could not have been helped by Waddell's erratic state of mind at this time, as the lifelong Rangers man began to succumb to the disease of alcoholism from about the middle of the decade onwards. He would often be half-cut by early afternoon, provoking drunken tirades, usually directed towards Wallace, with the testimony of many contemporary journalists revealing the heated arguments and fraught exchanges between the pair, often filled with expletives, which could be heard as they attended their duties at Ibrox. Club physio Tommy Craig remembers, 'Even at the time of winning Trebles under Jock Wallace, he would come into the dressing room and shake hands with everybody and ignore Jock completely before walking out again.'

Waddell later described Wallace, back in Scotland a few years later and managing Motherwell, as 'a fucking clown' in front of the Fir Park directors, an insult for which he was subsequently forced to apologise, although not to Wallace, but to the Motherwell chairman. The Ibrox supremo's health and state of mind appeared to be deteriorating, his dependency on alcohol exacerbated by a stubborn refusal to seek help for his worsening addiction, and as he fell victim to the disease, Waddell, never much of a Pollyanna even at the best of times, became ever more difficult to deal with and relate to, an increasingly cantankerous drunk.

Despite his heavy drinking, however, Waddell remained the club's vice-chairman and managing director, whereas Wallace was middle management, so in the end there was only going to be one winner. Wallace quit his beloved Rangers at the end of May to take up the challenge of steering Leicester City out of the English second division, although it wasn't long before he was followed out the door at Ibrox by his former boss and erstwhile nemesis at the club. Clearly feeling the strain, Waddell also resigned just over a year later, although he remained a director until 1984 and oversaw the completion of the new stadium in 1981, at which point the board terminated his £15,000-a-year consultancy. After resigning his directorship, he retained the title of honorary director until his death in 1992.

* * * *

In the wake of Jock Wallace's unexpected resignation, Rangers looked to their captain of the last 13 years, John Greig, who was appointed the club's seventh manager on 24 May 1978, just a day after Wallace's departure. With the two Jocks leaving their posts within a few weeks of each other, Greig would renew his rivalry with Scotland colleague and his counterpart at Parkhead for many years, Billy McNeill, who took over at

Celtic as Stein's replacement just four days later. An imposing defender, Greig had acquired near legendary status during his playing days at the club, a reputation which would later be confirmed when he was voted Rangers' greatest ever player in a poll of the club's supporters, and he appeared to be the obvious, ideal candidate to take over from Wallace.

Greig's time in charge at Ibrox began promisingly with a famous win over Giovanni Trapattoni's Juventus in the European Cup, a team which would provide nine of Italy's World Cup-winning squad in Spain a few years later. Switching to a sweeper system with Sandy Jardine deployed behind a back four, Rangers escaped from Turin with a 1-0 defeat, but scored goals in each half through Alex MacDonald and Gordon Smith in the return leg at Ibrox to progress to a second-round match against PSV Eindhoven. The Dutch champions were defending a 25-year unbeaten home record in Europe, so when a 0-0 draw was secured at Ibrox followed by a first-minute goal for the home team in Holland, the Dutchmen became overwhelming favourites to progress. Rangers were fearful of another harsh lesson, similar to the one dished out to them in the same country only a year earlier by Twente, but they managed to turn the tie around late in the game, with a terrific final goal from youngster Bobby Russell securing a 3-2 aggregate win.

The signs of progress under Greig were indisputable and the manager had raised hopes of a potentially memorable European campaign with his detailed and thorough preparation, learned from Waddell, and his intelligent analysis of the strengths and weaknesses of continental opponents. However, after a narrow 2-1 defeat in the following round to the German side Cologne, who progressed to a semi-final meeting with eventual winners Nottingham Forest, many senior players wore the look of men who knew that their last chance of winning a European trophy had gone. The side was ageing and Greig was now determined to put in place a youth programme, something which had been conspicuously lacking at Rangers under his predecessor, and he managed to persuade the club's best young player, Derek Johnstone, who had been agitating for a move, to remain at Ibrox. The new manager handed the versatile and experienced 25-year-old the Rangers captaincy and switched him to his preferred position in central defence, but ultimately, over the next few years, Greig struggled to implement the changes which he felt were necessary at the club.

The championship that season came down to a final 'Old Firm' encounter on 21 May 1979 in a game held over from the freezing winter. Earlier in the month, Rangers had beaten Celtic 1-0 at Hampden, where the game was moved to accommodate the largest possible crowd, with work already under way on the reconstruction of Ibrox. Rangers knew that even a draw at Parkhead would suit them, as the club still had two fixtures remaining in the league due to a twice replayed Scottish Cup Final with Hibernian, which the Ibrox men eventually won 3-2.

With the League Cup already secured as well, another Treble was in the club's sights when Rangers took the lead through Alex MacDonald after only nine minutes and the visitors' chances improved even further when Celtic's Doyle was red-carded early in the second half. It proved to be a topsy-turvy game, however, as Celtic fought back, with the ten men edging ahead following goals from Aitken and McCluskey. The title was heading to Ibrox once again when Bobby Russell equalised to make the score 2-2 late in the game, but an own goal from Jackson allowed Celtic to regain the lead and Murdo MacLeod made it 4-2 with an effort from distance, with what was almost the last kick of the game, on a famous night for the Parkhead men. It was the closest John Greig would come to winning the league as Rangers manager.

Sadly for the Ibrox men, over the next few years, they never seemed to fully recover from the traumatic setback of losing the league to Celtic in such a fashion, after being a goal up and a man up in the second half of a decisive game from which only a draw was required. The following year, Greig's side finished the season without a trophy, trailing in a distant fifth in the Premier Division behind Alex Ferguson's victorious Aberdeen team, who claimed the championship for only the second time in the club's history with a flourish after a 5-0 trouncing of Hibernian at Easter Road. The Pittodrie side finished a point ahead of Celtic, who were held to a goalless draw by St Mirren on the same day, and in the process delivered Ferguson the first trophy of his career in management. Aberdeen had earlier inflicted further disappointment on Rangers by eliminating them from the League Cup at the third round stage, and frustratingly, after a decent draw in Spain against eventual winners Valencia, Greig's side were knocked out of the Cup Winners' Cup following a 3-1 defeat in the Ibrox return, a result inspired by the legendary Argentinian forward, Mario Kempes.

The Scottish Cup offered the prospect of respite after Rangers made it to the final, but they eventually lost to Celtic, with the only goal of the game coming in extra time when McGrain's shot from distance was deftly turned into the net by McCluskey. It turned out to be a memorable final, although sadly not for the match itself, decent spectacle though it was, played out in glorious sunshine, but for the shocking scenes of alcohol-induced hooliganism which succeeded it. The sight of Celtic supporters, some already on the pitch after the game and celebrating with the Parkhead players at the traditional Celtic, or King's Park end of the ground, was too much for some to bear, as hundreds of Rangers fans, in their indignation at the result, swarmed down from the terraces on to the field in an attempt to confront their rivals.

The Hampden match commander, Chief Superintendent Hamish MacBean, described the unfolding scene, 'It was kids who came on at first from the Celtic end, over the safety fence. Now, when you get one side winning an Old Firm final, the supporters of the losing side normally head for the exits as quickly as they can, leaving the stadium to the victors. But I will never forget what I saw at the other end. The Rangers supporters were heading out and most of them were halfway up the terracing. But I always remember the sudden change of direction. For when they saw what was happening at the other end, with bodies coming over the fence, they suddenly stopped, turned en masse, headed downwards again and swept on to the pitch. They were then joined by reinforcements and in no time the field was covered.'

Unfortunately, MacBean had stationed most of his troops outside the ground, where the worst trouble was anticipated, instead of deploying a cordon of officers around the track at the end of the game, and with both sets of supporters enjoying almost unfettered access to the Hampden pitch, a full-scale riot ensued. As the Rangers fans swarmed towards the opposite end of the stadium, police, other officials, anyone in fact who was unlucky enough to be in the way of the rampaging Bears was subject to the same treatment. A photographer, who was dealt a hefty kick in the shin by a light blue warrior, retaliated by smacking his assailant over the head with his camera, leaving the unfortunate victim to be carried off the field on a stretcher. Unpoliced, both sets of fans had now invaded the field in considerable numbers and there were charges in both directions, accompanied by a hailstorm of glass bottles being hurled hither and thither.

All of this was played out live on television, with BBC commentator Archie Macpherson, by his own admission lapsing into war correspondent mode, observing on air, 'It does seem to me pathetic, scandalous and disgraceful that this should have been allowed to happen. Hampden Park meets all the requirements for curtailing spectators from coming across and yet I am astonished that there didn't seem to be a cordon of police down that end of the ground. That's where it started. These supporters didn't come on belligerently, they came on to congratulate their team but that was enough to signal a counter-charge from the other end.'

Eventually the cavalry arrived, mounted police charging into the midst of the drunken combatants and dispersing them, but not before 100 people had been injured in the disturbance. The final tally of casualties could have been far higher, but it seemed that, in their drunkenness, the rampaging fans were largely incapable of any serious fighting and the entire incident had lasted no more than a few crazy and eventful minutes. Just 160 people were eventually arrested inside the ground, a small percentage of those who had participated in the disorder.

Afterwards the SFA, through president Willie Harkness, blamed the Celtic players for celebrating in front of their fans, wearing hats and collecting scarfs, and Celtic supporters for their over-exuberance. The lap of honour celebrations had been banned in Scotland after similar scenes at the League Cup Final back in October 1965, when disgruntled Rangers fans invaded the Hampden pitch following Celtic's 2-1 win. By 1980, it seemed, lessons still hadn't been learnt. The police, on the defensive and refusing to accept any blame themselves for stationing the majority of duty officers outside the ground, and leaving those inside Hampden under-resourced and outnumbered when trouble erupted, seemed to agree with Harkness that it was all the fault of the Celtic players and supporters, despite what the match commander had witnessed. Even the Secretary of State for Scotland, George Younger MP, reiterated the SFA's view in the House of Commons that it was 'drink and the actions of some Celtic fans' that was responsible.

The Rangers board, wary of the club's dreadful reputation by this stage and anticipating an avalanche of condemnation in the press as well as the inevitable questions once more over the signing policy, issued a terse and wholly inadequate statement saying that they concurred with the views of Harkness and Younger. Celtic chairman Desmond White, perhaps just as predictably, immediately suspected a conspiracy among the blazered community. 'They blame us,' he stated in reference to the reactions from the SFA, the police and Rangers. 'It annoys me. In fact it appals me,' White added, pointing out that the only people who had entered the field with the intent of causing trouble were the Rangers fans, and he claimed that the Celtic players had in fact received permission to approach their supporters.

In the end, both clubs were fined £20,000 and ordered to a meeting where they were asked to renounce all forms of sectarianism. Celtic complied, but Rangers responded with defiance, maintaining that the club's policy on the matter was already in accordance with the governing body's wishes, a reply which was not to the SFA's satisfaction. However, the matter was soon dropped and another opportunity to address the perennial issue affecting football in the west of Scotland was missed. There were, though, other repercussions for the game over the longer term, as a blanket prohibition on alcohol at all football grounds in Scotland, and on trains and coaches carrying spectators to matches, was introduced after the final, a ban which remains in place to this day.

With no European distractions to concern them after a dismal, trophy-less campaign, an ageing Rangers team managed to remain unbeaten in their first 15 games of the new season, a run which included home and away wins over Celtic, with the 3-0 victory at Ibrox in November inspired by Willie Johnston, one of the heroes of Barcelona. Approaching his 34th birthday and back at the club on a short-term deal, Johnston had in the meantime enjoyed a seven-year spell at West Brom and been sent home in disgrace from the 1978 World Cup after failing a drugs test. Since his return to Ibrox, he had already been sanctioned for stamping on Aberdeen's John McMaster, with the forward claiming in his honest, if somewhat flimsy defence, that he had mistaken his victim for Willie Miller.

Rangers' season fell apart, however, after elimination from the League Cup by Aberdeen was followed by an ignominious exit from the Anglo-Scottish Cup at the hands of Chesterfield. Respite once again came in the Scottish Cup, where after a replay in the Hampden final, Dundee United were beaten 4-1, and later in the year, in November 1981, the League Cup was also won, with Ian Redford's last-minute chip from the edge of the box giving Greig's side a 2-1 win in the final, again over the Tannadice men, but overall the sense was one of stagnation and decline. The club was struggling to attract players, as Ally McCoist, later an Ibrox hero, rejected Greig's advances to sign for Sunderland, and the team were well off the pace in the league. Aberdeen took Rangers' scalp in the 1982 Scottish Cup Final, 4-1 after extra time and the European adventure had lasted only one round, after an early exit in the Cup Winners' Cup to Dukla Prague.

Despite the capture of two cups in the space of six months, the emergence of the 'New Firm' was bad news for Greig and Rangers, for although Celtic managed to keep up with the 'Dandy Dons' of Aberdeen and the 'Tangerine Terrors' of Dundee United, capturing the league in 1981 and '82, Rangers could not. In 1982/83, Greig's team reached two cup finals but lost both, 2-1 to Celtic in the League Cup and 1-0 to Aberdeen in the Scottish Cup, while Dundee United took the league title for the first and only time in the club's history. The Tannadice men had claimed the championship by a single point from Aberdeen and Celtic, but Greig's Rangers were nowhere to be seen in the title race, eventually finishing fully 17 points off the pace.

In Europe, spirits were raised by a 2-0 aggregate win over Borussia Dortmund, but against Cologne in the following round, after a 2-1 win at Ibrox, Rangers were thrashed 5-0 in Germany. One of the main problems for Greig was in replacing his ageing squad with reliable youngsters who shared the same hunger and ambition as the old stalwarts. Colin Jackson, another veteran from the successful Cup Winners' Cup campaign of 1972, stated his belief, 'Many of the younger lads were unprofessional… They didn't have the same kind of respect for the manager or Rangers and that is probably why none of them went on to make a real name for themselves in the game, despite their ability.'

While there was undoubtedly some truth in Jackson's observations, the manager also came up short in terms of the qualities and attributes required to be a successful coach at the highest level. Despite his undoubted inspirational qualities on the field, Greig, to the surprise of many observers, turned out to be a poor man manager, unable to relate to the needs and difficulties of his players in ways which might have been expected of a former captain of the club, as former team-mate Alex MacDonald remembered: 'He lost the dressing room. He had absolutely no man management skills, absolutely zero. You wanted Greigy on the park beside you. When he wasn't there, you missed him. Off the park his influence wasn't the same.'

Striker Gordon Smith, he of 'Smith must score' fame, after his agonising late miss in the 1983 FA Cup Final against Manchester United, returning to Ibrox on a short-term loan deal from Brighton and Hove Albion, agreed, 'As soon as I went back into the dressing room I felt, right away, that the place was a disaster. It was the worst atmosphere ever. When I had been there in my first spell the team spirit was great, the dressing room was bubbly. It was nothing like that on my return.'

Confronting the manager, Smith found that Greig was aware of the problem but incapable of rectifying the situation. Smith admitted, 'He said, "I know, there's a terrible atmosphere down there in the dressing room." I couldn't avoid saying, "Well, whose fault is that then?" He just said, "I know," as if acknowledging his own failure. For although he was a good coach and tactician, he knew nothing about man management.'

Of course Greig wasn't helped by the fact that he was faced with two geniuses, Ferguson and McLean, in the opposing dugouts of the 'New Firm', with both men, in their own inimitable fashion, determined to take the fight to the Glasgow duopoly, as Aberdeen and Dundee United enjoyed the greatest periods in their respective histories, while over at Celtic, according to winger Davie Provan, manager Billy McNeill, in contrast to Greig, 'had the dressing-room in the palm of his hand and we would have gone through brick walls for him'.

The 1983/84 season started badly for Rangers and the stress of managing the club was starting to make John Greig physically ill. Once Willie Waddell had stepped down from his day-to-day involvement behind the scenes at Ibrox in September 1979, Greig was on his own and effectively in charge of every aspect of running the club. As well as his often mundane administrative and logistical duties, there was also the problem of trying to put a winning team on the park, not an easy task in these troubled times for the Ibrox club. After a draw with St Mirren in the opening fixture, Rangers were defeated by Celtic, Hearts and latterly by Aberdeen at Ibrox, a game which witnessed an impromptu mass exodus of Rangers fans from the new Copland Road Stand, after Mark McGhee scored two late goals to leave Greig's side sitting on just one point from four games. The club was in crisis and the manager admitted to being a prisoner in his own home, while the board remained as feckless and ineffectual as ever, prone to squabbling among themselves.

In Europe, after the fun and games of an 18-0 aggregate win over whipping boys Valletta of Malta in the Cup Winners' Cup, Rangers were drawn against Porto in the second round. At Ibrox, the home side were enjoying a comfortable first leg lead, 2-0 up and seemingly cruising, but an error from goalkeeper Peter McCloy gave the Portuguese a late, vital away goal.

Greig would not be around for the return match in Portugal, however, as he quit the Ibrox hot seat a week later. His last league match in charge was a 2-1 home loss to Jock Wallace's struggling Motherwell, although a few days later Greig managed to secure the club's progress to the League Cup semi-final with victory over Hearts, before he resigned. With nine games of the season gone, Rangers were languishing seven points behind champions and league leaders Dundee United, who still had a game in hand, and after Greig left, apparently so scarred by his experiences in charge of the club that he quit football altogether, the manager-less Ibrox side, now under the caretaker stewardship of Tommy McLean, lost 3-0 to St Mirren at Love Street and found themselves sitting just one place above the league's bottom position. The following week, they were knocked out of the Cup Winners' Cup on away goals by Porto after a 1-0 defeat in Portugal, and as if matters couldn't get any worse, Celtic then travelled across Glasgow and won 2-1, inflicting a fourth league defeat in a row on the once proud Ibrox club.

In their search for Greig's replacement, the Rangers board had drawn up a shortlist of two candidates, namely the New Firm double act of Jim McLean and Alex Ferguson. Ferguson had just won the Cup Winners' Cup with Aberdeen and was the preferred choice, but after talks with the directors he turned Rangers down, perhaps still harbouring a grudge over his mistreatment by the club as a player back in the late 1960s. Ferguson also consulted with his former manager Scot Symon, who informed him that the boardroom at Ibrox was hideously split, but the Aberdeen boss later revealed the main reason behind his thought process, confiding to Archie Macpherson, 'How could I go back and not sign Catholics? What would I tell my friends who are Catholics? "You lot aren't good enough for us?" I just couldn't do that.' After rejecting Rangers, Ferguson signed a lucrative new five-year contract at Pittodrie and his side would go on to win the league in both 1984 and 1985, before he eventually moved south to join Manchester United in November 1986.

Jim McLean, manager and by now also a director of Dundee United and brother of Rangers' caretaker Tommy, was next to be offered the job and he was reportedly assured by the board that there would be no restrictions on which players he could sign, irrespective of religious background. Clearly tempted, McLean sought the advice of Scotland boss Jock Stein, whom he had an almost reverential respect for after serving as his assistant with the national squad for two years. Stein believed that the move would be good for McLean personally and urged him to accept the offer from Ibrox, as did his assistant at Tannadice, Walter Smith, but evidently tortured with indecision, McLean too eventually spurned Rangers' advances, apparently changing his mind at the last minute and deciding to stay with the Tayside club 'for family reasons'.

By now the club's directors were panicking; although Ibrox grandee Willie Waddell remained associated with Rangers as a director and consultant, the club was being run by chairman Rae Simpson and his deputy, John Paton, who appeared to be out of their depth. Desperately short of options, they seemed reluctant to turn to a man who had walked out on the club five years previously, despite the relative success of his previous tenure at Ibrox. The following week, however, Motherwell were approached about the availability of their manager and a deal was thrashed out to allow Jock Wallace to return to Rangers.

Wallace, and his impish agent Bill McMurdo, had played hard to get, demanding the same financial package that had been offered to Ferguson and McLean. The feeling was, certainly on Wallace's part, that he had collected two Trebles in the space of three years and in the period of time since his departure, by contrast, the club had won very little, so he believed that he was still very much the man for the job. Clearly his affection for Rangers was undiminished, despite the somewhat rancorous nature of his previous exit from the club. 'Managing Rangers is my dream job, the one thing in my life I have always wanted more than any other,' Wallace told reporters shortly after his reappointment. 'I know this will bring the obvious question that if I'm so Rangers-daft then why did I leave in 1978, but I'm not prepared to rake over the ashes of that decision. I did what I thought was right at the time and have no regrets.'

In the end though, overall, Wallace's second spell at Ibrox turned out to be an extended period of disappointment for the club. He seemed to be living out his childhood fantasy in a Rangers wonderland and the appointment proved to be a retrograde step at a time when those running the club would have preferred to have put a more forward-thinking man in charge. Their options were growing thin, however, after rejection from the New Firm duo and West Ham's John Lyall, who had also turned Rangers down, and Wallace, struggling badly with his limited Motherwell side, was very much last chance saloon.

The new manager's first act after being reappointed team manager was to endure a gruelling 3-0 loss to Aberdeen at Pittodrie, their fifth league defeat in a row, after which Wallace moved to appoint Alex Totten, boss of part-time Falkirk, as his new assistant, replacing Tommy McLean. Wallace's preference had been to take Frank Connor, his deputy at Motherwell and a former Celtic goalkeeper, to Ibrox but inevitably Connor's religion was an issue and he was advised against it, principally by McMurdo, his fanatical Rangers-supporting agent. Wallace told his players that they would be given six weeks' leeway, after which it would be down to them to prove that they were capable of turning the club's fortunes around, and gradually things started to improve.

With his last game in charge, Greig's team had secured their passage through the group to reach the League Cup semi-final, and Wallace finished the job. After a 3-1 aggregate win over Dundee United in the last four, a hat-trick in the final from Ally McCoist, who had clearly bucked up his ideas after Wallace threatened to ship the striker out to Cardiff City on loan, sent Celtic to a 3-2 extra-time defeat, handing the club its first trophy in two years and Wallace's first since returning as manager.

Results were encouraging in the league too, and a lengthy unbeaten run included a much improved performance in the New Year against champions-elect Aberdeen, after which Ferguson declared himself happy with a point following a hard-fought draw at Ibrox. But the gap between the teams could not be surmounted and the unbeaten run inevitably came to an end with a 3-0 defeat at Celtic Park on 2 April. Rangers eventually trailed in fourth once again, behind the New Firm and Celtic, meaning that the club had now gone six years without winning the league.

The following season, Wallace's side continued their fondness for the League Cup, retaining the trophy after a 1-0 win over Dundee United in the final, but there was more mediocre fare in the league. In early December, Rangers had slipped seven points behind Aberdeen on the back of a 2-1 loss to the Dons at Ibrox, and in the return match against Ferguson's side in January, their flickering title hopes were extinguished, as Wallace's side were beaten 5-1 at Pittodrie, the club's heaviest league defeat for 20 years.

Europe too was a painful experience, as Rangers managed to progress past Irish side Bohemians in the UEFA Cup, but only following a 3-2 defeat in Dublin in a match that was marred by crowd trouble. After some Rangers fans tried to scale a wire fence and invade the pitch, Wallace took to the field to try and calm the situation, but he was berated by a section of his own fans, some of whom, by calling him a 'Fenian bastard', suggested that they didn't seem to know who he was. 'They don't know how to behave,' Wallace lamented. 'They can sing, shout and bawl all they want but they are not entitled to throw coins and break fences. I was scared of these guys. They behaved like crazy men. I was more worried about them than the game.'

Inter Milan eliminated Rangers in the following round and their season was effectively over when Dundee inflicted a home defeat in the Scottish Cup, after which mounted police had to disperse a few hundred supporters who were protesting outside the ground. The new Ibrox, almost all-seater, with only the bear pit of the old East Enclosure offering space for standing fans, lacked the atmosphere of the old ground and poor performances were increasingly being reflected in dwindling attendance figures, as Rangers, under Wallace, continued to drift along on a tide of apathy and mediocrity. Only 8,424 hardly souls turned up for the club's next league game, a 3-1 win over Dumbarton, after which Wallace, presumably in exasperation, took his team off on a tour of Iraq, where they lost 4-1 to a Baghdad Select XI.

Rangers eventually finished fourth for the third year in a row, 21 points behind Aberdeen in a league still operating on a two-points-for-a-win system. At the end of what had turned out to be another disappointing season, chairman John Paton, in a prescient indication of a change of strategy at the club, promised that Rangers were prepared to go deep into debt in order to back Wallace's ambitions, something which would never have been countenanced when the puritanical Waddell was still running the show.

The 1985/86 season started brightly as Rangers won their first three games and found themselves top of the league, a position they retained after a 1-1 draw at Celtic Park. But the form soon collapsed, as they exited the UEFA Cup at the hands of Spanish low-flyers Osasuna, the League Cup with a semi-final defeat to Hibs and they were soon knocked off their perch in the league after successive defeats at Ibrox, including a 3-0 mauling at the hands of Aberdeen. Celtic were dispatched 3-0 at Ibrox in November, but once again Rangers couldn't capitalise, losing their next two games, to Hearts and Dundee, and soon finding themselves back in fifth position. In the new year, Celtic gained a measure of revenge with a 2-0 win at Celtic Park on New Year's Day, and when Hearts knocked Wallace's men out of the Scottish Cup later in January, once again Rangers were left floundering, with months of the season still remaining and little to play for.

Around this time there was a significant change in the club's boardroom when, after years of infighting behind the scenes, Lawrence Marlborough, grandson of former chairman John Lawrence, acquired enough shares in Rangers to allow him to take a controlling interest in the club. A tax exile based in Nevada, USA, Marlborough then appointed David Holmes, a former joiner from Falkirk, as the club's new chief executive officer with instructions to run the Ibrox operation from Glasgow, while at the same time there was a boardroom cull, with directors Jim Robinson, Tom Dawson and Rae Simpson all leaving the club. It appeared that Wallace might be the next casualty of the new regime, and the manager was duly sacked on 7 April after a friendly defeat to Spurs at Ibrox and replaced by Graeme Souness, who only had a few games left in the season to run the rule over his squad of players. It would be the start of a new era for Rangers, one that was far more in tune with what was happening in Thatcher's Britain of the day.

Jock Wallace, who died of a heart attack in 1996, aged 60, after a long struggle with Parkinson's disease, is a man who still divides opinion to this day. Many have been quick to dismiss him as a one-dimensional dinosaur, who played ugly, physical football, claiming that his outdated methods ultimately led to his downfall, because he failed to rescue a stuttering Rangers side. Others, including many who played under him, maintain that Wallace was an inspirational figure and a great motivator, a man who was shrewd enough to know what to say to players in order to get the best out of them.

Perhaps there is a degree of truth in both points of view. Some at least were prepared to indulge his ostentatious affection for Rangers and forgive the way he appeared to embrace some of the more unwholesome aspects of the club's history, including veteran broadcaster Archie Macpherson, who opined, 'Wallace's trumpeting of his Protestantism always seemed to me to have a strong element of theatricality to it... Wallace was in fact a warm-hearted, genuinely kindly man, lumbered by the traditions he adhered to without a shred of bitterness as a result of the intense bigotry which he supposedly espoused.'

That's fine, but it's doubtful whether Macpherson would have been quite so sanguine if it was racist, rather than sectarian values, which Wallace seemed to spend much of his life wallowing in so ironically.

The last word on Wallace goes to Robert Prytz, the 50-times capped Swedish international midfielder who played for Rangers between 1982 and 1985, appearing in 77 matches for the Ibrox club. 'My style of football was always the sort that is played on the ground, and that wasn't always the case in my time at Rangers,' Prytz admitted, while maintaining a certain admiration for Wallace. 'Jock was a tremendous manager: tough and strict and honest. I think he quite liked me because he used to punch me in the stomach every morning when I came in for training.'

7

BIGOTRY IN THE MODERN ERA

F OR half a century or more, following the clandestine, sealed agreement between Rangers and the Belfast-based shipbuilding firm Harland and Wolff in the early part of the 20th century, the Ibrox club's exclusionary employment practices had gone largely uncommented upon in polite society. Gradually, however, over the course of several decades or more and despite the lack of appetite within the club itself for things to change, isolated murmurings of disapproval and occasionally even outright criticism of Rangers' stance had begun to appear in the popular press and elsewhere, usually in association with rioting fans in Birmingham, Manchester, Barcelona and various other locations.

It was implicit at first; matchday programmes, when introducing Rangers as the visiting team would hint at issues peripheral to the club, which everyone with a stake in Scottish football already seemed to know about but few were prepared to openly acknowledge. A Kilmarnock programme from 3 September 1966, announcing Rangers as the home team's opponents for a sectional League Cup tie, mentions the controversy over two recent expensive signings who had failed to settle at Ibrox, as well as the negative headlines surrounding the club's outdated training methods. More enigmatically, the programme editorial then states, 'But controversy and Rangers have walked hand in hand for a long time now.' It may not sound like much, but in terms of Scottish football's attitude towards Rangers and the club's continuing policies at the time, here at last was the suggestion at least that the worm was beginning to turn.

An early voice of disapproval was the journalist Cyril Horne, who worked for *The Herald* for many years and was the paper's chief football correspondent through to the early 1960s. Somewhat ironically, given *The Herald*'s own rigid no-Catholics stance, Horne was an early critic of the exclusionary policy and of Rangers' physical style of play. Often writing anonymously, but fearless and persistent nonetheless, he aimed his barbs in particular at the perennial ineptitude and complacency of the Rangers directors, who continued to oversee and maintain the club's policies and traditions. As academic Tom Gallagher notes in his book *Glasgow, The Uneasy Peace*, 'It was middle-class businessmen with masonic loyalties who (as directors and shareholders) ensured that Rangers football club still retained an all-protestant image.'

In 1965, former Rangers striker Ralph Brand criticised the club in a polemic series of interviews published in the *News of the World* under the by-line 'The lid off Ibrox'. Brand, by then playing in England for Manchester City, had used the Scottish edition of the newspaper to voice his invective, lamenting the outdated training methods and selection policies at Ibrox as well as, briefly, censuring the club over its exclusionary signing policy. Scottish sports journalism had never seen anything like it, week after week the criticisms of the Ibrox regime kept coming, with Brand not fazed in any way by the inevitably ferocious backlash which his articles provoked from the fans, the press and the club itself. But while the Ibrox hierarchy, for the most part, fumed in silence at the outrage committed by one of the club's former players, their friends in the media were not so reticent. In an excoriating riposte for the *Sunday Mail*, Allan Herron lambasted Brand for, 'castigating the very heritage of Rangers F.C. in a manner no other player in the history of this great club has ever done before.' As well as his own personal relationship with the player having effectively ended as a result of his transgression, Herron also maintained that, 'the doors of Ibrox have now been slammed for all time on Brand.'

In fact, many years later, Brand, who had joined Rangers as a teenager and played for the club for twelve years, did return to Ibrox as a matchday host for corporate clients in the club's latterday hospitality suites. Nevertheless, Scot Symon's biographer, David Leggat, maintained that even after such a long interval many fans of a certain age were still angry at Brand's alleged 'bitter betrayal' of the Ibrox code of conduct, and while Leggat himself was prepared to be magnanimous and accept the former idol's rehabilitation into the Ibrox fold, interestingly this forgiveness did not come because Leggat believed, after all this time and with the benefit of hindsight, that Brand had done the right thing in calling out Rangers over the club's anti-Catholicism and other arcane practices, but rather because, 'When he said what he did, Ralph Brand was just having a bad day.' A bad month more like, as Brand's excruciating series of articles, much to Rangers' embarrassment, extended over six editions of the newspaper, from late September through until the end of October 1965.

A few years later, in 1968, Ibrox vice-chairman Matt Taylor was asked about the club's Protestants-only policy while Rangers were on a tour of North America. 'It is part of our tradition. We were founded in 1873 as a Presbyterian Boys' Club,' Taylor stated, inaccurately on both counts. 'To change now would lose us considerable support.'

The candour of this reply is revealing, with the directors clearly seeing the need to maintain the club's sectarian image in order to keep the fans coming through the turnstiles. But while Taylor seemed happy to ascribe the anti-Catholicism at Rangers to the club's supporters, any suggestion that the problem was limited merely to the stands at Ibrox was called into question when, in May 1973, chairman John Lawrence, who in one of his first acts as a director nearly 20 years earlier had helped to coax the ailing manager Bill Struth into belated retirement, was himself finally standing down from the club's board, amid his own health problems.

Lawrence's successor was to be David Hope, who had built up the Rangers Pools, founded in 1964, and the Rangers Social Club, both of which had grown into extremely successful commercial operations. These ventures contributed millions of pounds over the years to the Rangers Development Fund, money that was later put to use in the rebuilding of Ibrox Park as a modern all-seater arena. But Hope had married a Catholic some 43 years earlier, and although his wife had died 15 years previously, he lasted only 17 minutes in the chairman's seat and two years later he was no longer on the board at all. Amid scurrilous rumours put about by Taylor, the club's resentful vice-chairman, that Hope himself had converted to the Roman faith, Lawrence blinked and was immediately reinstated as chairman at a hastily reconvened meeting. Rangers Football Club was still riddled with religious bigotry all the way from the fans right through to the boardroom by the 1970s.

For the most part, however, there seemed to exist a cosy conspiracy of silence between the club, the football authorities and the press, which had allowed the problem to fester and continue to the point where the situation became almost universally accepted as the norm. As so often with taboo subjects, when the first, occasional mentions begin to filter down into popular culture, comedy is usually the vehicle used to tiptoe on to such difficult terrain. Consider the following exchange between a security guard and one of the main protagonists from the iconic 70s TV show *The Likely Lads*: 'Careful how you go tonight, there's been a match.' 'Aye, I know. A friendly with Rangers.' 'There's no such thing as a friendly with Rangers, they'll be on the rampage.' 'Aye, hooligans.'

This was a gratuitous reference to the plummeting image of the Glasgow club and its supporters thrown into the script of a popular programme and broadcast UK-wide without any dramatic justification in terms of plot or characterisation. Even in an era becoming increasingly notorious for football hooliganism, Rangers, after a succession of high-profile and shocking incidents, were acquiring a particularly poor reputation, which the club was constantly at pains to try and redeem.

Similarly in *Porridge*, another sitcom scripted by the successful comedy writing partnership of Dick Clement and Ian La Frenais, Ronnie Barker's Fletcher tries to bait his adversary, Scottish prison officer Mr MacKay, in the following way, 'He's a strict Glasgow Presbyterian, you know. Sex is only allowed up there when Rangers beat Celtic.' Later, within Scotland, the comedy sketch show *Scotch and Wry* ventured into similar territory with a scene starring Rikki Fulton and a young Gerard Kelly, in which the Rangers manager (Fulton) unwittingly signs a terrific young talent, a player called Brendan O'Malley, who, the audience are told, scored seven goals for his team in the first half, but missed the second half because he 'had to go to Mass'. Few viewers will forget Fulton's stunned reaction to this revelation only seconds after the boy has signed a five-year contract!

In 1982, a play called *The Bigot*, by James Barclay, was produced at the Pavilion Theatre in Glasgow. Fanatical Rangers man Andra Thomson is stunned when his daughter's fiancé turns up at his house in full Celtic regalia to meet his future father-in-law. Things become even worse for the self-styled eponymous bigot when his son enters the priesthood! There are numerous other examples of the twin issues of hooliganism and bigotry at Ibrox entering popular culture: an exchange from an episode of the 70s police drama *The Sweeney*. 'GBH, assault with a deadly weapon, attempted murder,' whereupon Dennis Waterman's Detective Sergeant George Carter wonders, 'What are they, Rangers supporters?' In a more recent reference, in the BBC satirical comedy *The Thick Of It*, Rangers fans are compared to a baying mob of journalists, who are 'about to eat their own cocks'.

Back in the real world, the Rangers directors, misinformed about the club's early history and with a vigilant eye on the takings at the gate, were still persisting with the 'Presbyterian Boys' Club' approach. As Celtic stepped out of the shadows and began to dominate Scottish football in the late '60s, the growing sense of disapproval of their Ibrox neighbours started to creep into the national coverage of the game, particularly after the disgraceful scenes witnessed at the Fairs Cup defeat in Newcastle, in May 1969. In reference to the continuing absence of Catholics in the Rangers playing squad, veteran tabloid journalist Alex Cameron, writing in the *Daily Record*, called for 'a vigorous clean-out of inbred bigotry which coincidence no longer begins to explain or excuse'.

Yet the club continued to deny that any such policy even existed. A few years later, after more trouble at the friendly against Aston Villa in Birmingham, general manager Willie Waddell, in response to a nationwide wave of indignation, announced, 'We are determined to end Rangers' image as a sectarian club... no religious barriers will be put up by this club regarding the signing of players.' It was one of the first public references to a 'sectarian' agenda at Ibrox and there was widespread jubilation and hope among the wider community that Rangers might eventually, in the not too distant future, sign a Catholic football player.

But as the years went by and no Catholic player appeared in light blue, perhaps as a result of the lack of leadership and continued in-fighting in the Ibrox boardroom, these hopes were dashed. In his book *Glasgow's Giants*, Bill Murray seemed to hit the nail on the head when he observed of Rangers' habitually empty promises, 'To the media and the public at large these statements were taken with large spoonfuls of scepticism. They had heard it all before: they were a necessary disclaimer to keep any investigators from FIFA at bay. A sop to the media and a wink to their fans who knew that everything would continue to be as it should be at Ibrox.' Even Walker and Esplin concede of Waddell's statement in *The Official Biography of Rangers*, 'In retrospect, this appears to have been a stalling tactic to alleviate the intense pressure the club was then under.'

In 1978, the Church of Scotland decided that it would attempt to intervene in the ongoing situation at Ibrox. *The Bush*, a pamphlet produced by the Kirk's Glasgow Presbytery, published a strong editorial under the heading 'The Blue Barrier', which called for an end to the exclusionary policy. It read, '"Are you a Catholic?" That's the big disqualifying question to an applicant for any job at Ibrox. Four years ago this Presbytery condemned that sectarianism. Rangers said it didn't exist. Two years later they changed their non-existent policy. "We'll sign a Catholic," said their general manager. Two weeks ago, they still hadn't. Nor are they likely to. Blind prejudice is no respecter of football skills alone.

'Over the summer we investigated the Ibrox situation. We unearthed stories of people applying for advertised jobs who were asked their religion as almost the first question. We have a quote from a director that boldly states why Catholics should not play for Rangers. We looked at the careers of some players who were unfortunate enough to fall in love with Catholic girls… And we conclude that far from changing anything with a new policy, Rangers Football Club is more anti-Catholic than it ever was.'

This was as bold a step as it sounds from the Kirk, which had clearly indulged in a fair amount of soul-searching since the days of the infamous 'Report' back in the early 1920s. Reverend Donald MacDonald, one of the ministers responsible for the editorial, later explained that he hoped the Church's intervention would have a positive, ameliorating effect on the wider social problem, and in particular on the issue of segregated sport at Ibrox. Sadly though, it didn't end well for *The Bush*. There was no wider support in the community and successive parishes cancelled their bulk orders of the pamphlet. Circulation plummeted, it became uneconomic and before long *The Bush* ceased publication.

One such player at Ibrox around this time who was 'unfortunate enough to fall in love' with a Catholic girl was forward Graham Fyfe, who claimed that, despite his wife effectively renouncing her faith and their marriage taking place in the Church of Scotland, he nevertheless felt the need to leave Ibrox in 1980, after being questioned by the club's management about his wedding arrangements and his private life in general. Fyfe's allegation was contested by other players at the time who had also married Catholic women, such as Bobby Russell and Derek Johnstone, both of whom remained at the club into the 1980s.

By 1982, the situation with unsuitable brides at Ibrox appeared to have been cleared up once and for all, when Rangers player Gordon Dalziel announced his engagement to a Catholic girl. The player, who left Rangers a year later for footballing reasons (he wasn't very good), told the press at the time, 'I have already had the all-clear at Ibrox. It will not make any difference. I'm not going to get married in the chapel or anything like that... There should be no trouble at Ibrox. I don't see how there can be. Bobby Russell is already married to a Catholic and his career has not been affected.' Manager John Greig added to the general tone of reassurance, when he informed the media, 'It doesn't matter who he is marrying. It doesn't matter to me and it doesn't matter to Rangers. Bobby Russell's been married to a Catholic for years. Gordon Dalziel has a right to marry who he wants.'

Despite such worthy assurances however, the stench of religious bigotry continued to pervade Ibrox and following their unsuccessful intervention a few years earlier, the Church of Scotland returned to the issue again in 1980 after the violent scenes witnessed around the world following Celtic's 1-0 victory over Rangers in the Scottish Cup Final. The Kirk's General Assembly proposed a motion calling on Rangers to end their exclusionary employment practices and publicly distance themselves from such discrimination, which was passed by a majority of 200. But of the 1,250 commissioners, 400 had held their noses and abstained, so the result was seen as ambiguous and the expected impact failed to materialise. Nevertheless, the General Assembly report of the same year noted, 'Tensions would be eased if all clubs, and Rangers FC in particular, would publicly disclaim sectarian bias in management and team structure, and through integrated team selection, publicly prove that sectarianism has no place in Scottish sport.'

The Church's willingness to take such a risk in alienating itself from a section of its own flock shows what an embarrassment Rangers had become to the Presbyterian middle classes by this time and what a bad advert for Scottish Protestantism they were now considered to be. Even the Orange Order felt the need to weigh in with its own condemnation of fans' behaviour and to disassociate themselves from Rangers supporters. 'The same examples of low animal life who force their support on Glasgow Rangers are one and the same with the foul-mouthed drunks who cause us great embarrassment every July when they turn up to "support" our annual rallies,' the Order harrumphed, following the Birmingham riot in 1976.

Meanwhile Celtic, as a result of a decision taken by the club's directors back in the 19th century and following a policy seemingly pursued by every other known sporting institution in the world, continued to select players irrespective of their religious background. Non-Catholics at the Parkhead club in the 1970s included right-back Danny McGrain and forward Kenny Dalglish, whose father had been a regular at Ibrox while Dalglish was growing up. The striker describes his father's reaction to his son joining Celtic, 'Although he was a Rangers supporter, he wasn't bigoted in any way. Celtic had just won the European Cup and he told me, if you want to learn how to play football, then that's the place to go.'

McGrain, ludicrously, was overlooked by a Rangers scout, who, upon inquiring about the player, incorrectly assumed that a boy named Daniel Fergus McGrain had to be from a Catholic background, and lost interest. It was a costly mistake; McGrain went on to play 663 times for Celtic between 1970 and 1987, and he remains at the club to this day in a coaching capacity. McGrain also made 62 appearances for Scotland, including captaining the national side at the 1982 World Cup, and in 2004 he was one of the original inductees into the Scottish Football Hall of Fame.

Celtic's assistant manager at the time, Sean Fallon, rather impishly suggested that they would sometimes use Rangers' policy to their advantage, noting that if the club was looking at two youngsters of equal ability, one from a Catholic background, another Protestant, Celtic would often take the non-Catholic player, because they knew that the other lad would not end up at Rangers. 'So we win 2-0,' Fallon concluded smugly. The reality was rather more prosaic, but Jock Stein later admitted to Graeme Souness that Rangers' policy at least allowed Celtic to deliberate longer over the Catholic youngsters, whereas they were in a rush to tie up the likes of Dalglish and McGrain in order to prevent them from escaping to Ibrox. Souness, who played under Stein for Scotland over several years, made a mental note of his former boss's confession and stored it away for future use.

By the time that Jock Wallace returned to manage Rangers for a second time in November 1983, it was clear that the growing controversy surrounding the exclusionary employment policy, unofficial or otherwise, was not going to go away. On the day of his reappointment, Wallace emerged from the stadium on to Copland Road and told the waiting media, 'I have been told by the board that I have complete control over who I select, and I will sign players on ability. Religion will not come into it.' He then turned on his heels and departed without taking further questions.

A few days later, when he was asked explicitly about the signing policy, Wallace replied, 'To listen to some people you'd think all the problems of Rangers could be solved at a stroke – by signing a player who is Catholic. But for me, that's not a priority... I have signed many Roman Catholics – and released a few. When I was with Leicester I also signed several coloured players – and freed some of them too. It's ironic that in my last spell with Rangers, when we were winning the occasional Treble the subject of signing Catholics seldom came up, but now that the club is going through a difficult spell, everyone is jumping on that particular bandwagon. It has been turned into a campaign and exploited by people who should know better.'

Wallace, it seemed, having returned to his 'dream job', was still living out his schoolboy fantasy as manager of his favourite team. 'I've always been a Rangers fan,' he announced after the first game of his second spell in charge at Ibrox, a 3-0 defeat to Aberdeen at Pittodrie, 'ever since I was a lad of nine and they came through to play near my home on the east coast. The team that made me a Rangers fan for life still trips off the tongue: Brown, Young, Shaw, McColl, Woodburn, Cox, Waddell, Gillick, Thornton, Duncanson and Caskie,' he said, rattling off Struth's team from the immediate post-war period. On that first trip up to Pittodrie, Wallace invited his agent Bill McMurdo, whom he had dubbed 'Agent Orange' because of his Rangers allegiances and his political views, on to the team bus. A founder member of the Scottish Unionist Party and an acknowledged Orangeman and Freemason, McMurdo had turned his Uddingston home into a Rangers shrine, naming it 'Ibrox' and decking it out in the club's colours of red, white and blue.

On the journey north, McMurdo provided Wallace with a cassette so that he could play Rangers songs over the speaker system and the manager encouraged his players to join in the singing of 'No Surrender'. McMurdo later confided, 'Jock acted as compere and… those who didn't know the words were urged to learn them for the next away game. [Ulsterman] Jimmy Nicholl knew the words inside out and Jock said to him, "Brilliant Jimmy, you know all the words, you're the captain today!"'

It's an apocryphal story; Nicholl had only just arrived at the club, having been signed by John Greig in his final days in charge at Ibrox, and the Irishman didn't in fact captain the side that day. But nevertheless, it's easy to see how a Catholic player might have struggled to flourish in such an environment and, needless to say, by the time Wallace was sacked in April 1986, there was still scant sign of a Catholic football player at Rangers, with only youngster John Spencer having made a handful of first team appearances for the Ibrox club.

Wallace's subsequent replacement as team manager was the former Liverpool and Sampdoria player, Graeme Souness, who arrived at Rangers just as the old guard in the boardroom were being swept aside by Lawrence Marlborough's Ibrox *coup d'état*. Immediately on his appointment, Souness was quizzed about the signing policy. 'I was asked the question the very first day I went to Rangers, would you sign a Catholic?' he later recalled. 'And my answer then was quite simple. I said, look, my wife is a Catholic, I've got two kids who've been christened Catholic, so you're saying to me I can't come to work with a Catholic, but I can go home to a Catholic? I said of course I would sign a Catholic.'

Once again, hope sprang eternal that this more genuine sounding claim would lead to the longed-for breakthrough. Souness seemed determined to end the policy and privately, behind the scenes, he was making enquiries about the potential impact of such a signing, almost from the moment he arrived. The sheer iconoclasm of the idea appealed to Souness's maverick personality and, as well as the backing of the new

Rangers board, Souness also found that there was tentative support from the wider community for the potentially seminal change, with one young Rangers-supporting journalist telling the new manager that he thought such a signing would be accepted, 'As long as it wasn't Peter Grant or Maurice Johnston!' Publicly however, as time went on, the old issue kept reappearing, with the situation not helped by the fact that Souness was a provocatively confrontational figure who seemed to be always looking for an enemy, and who now found himself at the centre of one of the most heated and intense rivalries anywhere in world football.

Initially, rather than Catholics, it was the strange sight of Englishmen turning out at Ibrox, many of them internationals, which attracted widespread attention during the early years of Souness's tenure. A number of the manager's new recruits had moved north to play their football in Scotland, in the process reversing the trend, which stretched back to the Victorian era, of Scottish players heading the other way for mainly financial reasons.

Ever since the Heysel Stadium disaster in Brussels in 1985, when 39 Italian fans lost their lives following clashes before the European Cup Final between Liverpool and Juventus, English clubs had been banned indefinitely from UEFA competitions. The players were attracted to Rangers by the prospect of high wages, European football and competing for trophies as well as the challenge of working under a charismatic and respected figure such as Souness, a man who had experience of mixed English and Scottish dressing rooms from his time at Liverpool. Terry Butcher, much like Souness himself, freely admits that he didn't know what he was letting himself in for when he signed for Rangers, but it was the Scottish triumvirate of Cooper, Durrant and McCoist who quickly schooled the England captain and his fellow countrymen in the Rangers 'traditions'.

Butcher explains how, when the players came in for training, in the required dress code, Davie Cooper would inspect every inch of their outfits 'with a magnifying glass to ensure there was no fleck of green'. If any was present, Cooper and his team-mates would rip the clothes off their backs. According to Butcher, the banter was 'fierce', Cooper referred to the big defender as 'Lurch' and would announce 'You rang, my lord', whenever he entered his presence.

Inevitably there were high-profile incidents, most notably on 17 October 1987, when Rangers met Celtic at Ibrox in the second Old Firm encounter of the season. The final scoreline of 2-2 suited the Parkhead side, who had a four-point lead in the title race at the time, after winning the first fixture between the teams in August, a match in which Souness had been ordered off and defender Graham Roberts had caused controversy by refusing to shake hands with his opponents at the end of the game. But the result of the October rematch felt more like a victory for Rangers, who recovered from two goals down while playing with nine men to Celtic's ten. It was, however, in the words of the *Sunday Mail*'s Allan Herron, 'a game destroyed by nastiness'.

Rangers, the champions, were determined to send out a message that they would not surrender the title lightly and Souness, suspended for this match after his red card in the August encounter, had heightened tensions before kick-off by refusing to allow his players to take the field side by side with their opposite numbers. As early as the 17th minute, Celtic's McAvennie and Rangers' goalkeeper Woods were dismissed by referee Jim Duncan following a clash which also involved Butcher and Roberts, who appeared to flatten McAvennie with a punch. Butcher was booked for his part in the incident and his afternoon went from bad to worse when he later scored an own goal, Celtic's second of the match following a strike from Walker, and the England captain was then sent off himself in the second half after a shove on Celtic's prone goalkeeper Allen McKnight.

Rangers subsequently scored through McCoist and, in the final minute, Gough, after which Roberts, who had taken over from Woods in goal, was seen to 'conduct' the jubilant singing of the Rangers fans in the Copland Road Stand behind his goal, as he prepared to take a goal kick with the clock winding down. Englishman Roberts later offered a defence of complete ignorance as to the nature of the sectarian singing, 'The Billy Boys' being a song about William of Orange and murdering Catholics. All four players involved in the original incident later appeared in court, charged by the procurator fiscal with 'conduct likely to provoke a breach of the peace'. The four men all denied the charges at their trial the following April, when Woods and Butcher were found guilty and fined £500 and £250 respectively. The case against Roberts was found not proven, that uniquely Scottish verdict, while McAvennie was acquitted.

An article in *The Herald* 25 years later in October 2012, recalling the game, fails to mention Roberts and the sectarian singing, but refers to the day when 'the Old Firm clashes almost died of shame'. Assistant Chief Constable of Strathclyde Police, John Dickson, describing the atmosphere at the match, considered it to be 'as bad as anything I have experienced in 33 years with the police'.

The English players in the Rangers team in particular seemed to have been caught up in the rivalry, and *The Herald* reporter of the day was moved to consider, 'I wonder if these players, especially those who have come from England, fully understand the powder-keg situation they are in every time they take part in an Old Firm game. If not, then it is time for someone with a sense of responsibility to spell it out in full.'

It is perhaps ironic then that in their autobiographies and elsewhere, Butcher and another English recruit, Ray Wilkins, later condemned the sectarianism at Ibrox, Wilkins admitting that he found it 'ridiculous', while Butcher, the first Rangers captain to admit publicly that he *wasn't* a Mason, acknowledged that he allowed himself to become too caught up in the religious issues at the club, going too far in order to try and ingratiate himself with the Ibrox crowd, until his wife gave him a private dressing down about his behaviour. 'I remember when I moved to Coventry it was as if a huge weight had been taken off my shoulders,' he confessed. 'I swore I would leave it all behind and not bother with religion in football again.' Neither man said anything against it at the time, however, and no such febrile bigotry was noted by players joining Celtic or any other club in Scotland during this period.

Incredibly, this wasn't even the first contentious Old Firm encounter since Souness arrived at Ibrox. As early as November 1986, Celtic's Maurice Johnston was involved in a particularly notorious incident at the end of the Skol (League) Cup Final against Rangers at Hampden, which would turn out to be Souness's first trophy as Ibrox manager. After being ordered off late in the game, in the face of gleeful abuse from the Rangers supporters, Johnston blessed himself as he left the field. This was considered provocative firstly because, although he was brought up in the faith, Johnston was not, unlike some of his Celtic team-mates, a practising Catholic and it was later pointed out by an indignant press that the striker was the only member of Celtic's Catholic contingent who had not attended Mass on the morning of the game. In addition, the custom of making the sign of the cross, common among football players around the globe, was unofficially outlawed in Scotland at this time and Johnston's actions became the precursor to a series of controversial incidents in Scottish football involving the sign of the cross, or blessing oneself. In December 1994, Rangers chairman David Murray warned his newest signing, the French defender Basile Boli, not to make the sign of the cross publicly in case it 'infuriated Rangers fans'.

Such fury was in evidence in February 1996, when Partick Thistle's Rod MacDonald blessed himself after scoring an equalising goal against Rangers, which provoked a number of the Ibrox club's fans to complain to the police. Match referee Jim McGilvray subsequently called the player into his office at half-time and issued him with a yellow card, but the Maryhill club resolved to stand by their man, after McDonald was later ordered off in the second half following a second, in Scotland at least, bookable offence. Thistle chairman Jim Oliver hinted at the reason behind the apparent taboo, 'because we have the Rangers situation here, it seems a different set of rules are invoked', while manager Murdo MacLeod reflected, 'As far as Rod is concerned it is normal practice for him. It's at times like this you know which city you are in.'

Some time later, when it became apparent to the Scottish football authorities that players being cautioned for blessing themselves was not something which was likely to go unnoticed in the global village of world football, particularly in an era of mass communication and satellite television coverage, the indignation continued nevertheless. In 1999, after Celtic's Mark Viduka was allegedly spotted blessing himself during a match against Rangers, an angry letter to the *Daily Record* in response suggested, 'There is a time and a place for that kind of thing. It is in the Chapel on a Sunday and certainly not on the football pitch during an Old Firm match.'

Between 2005 and 2010, Celtic's Polish goalkeeper, Artur Boruc, incited numerous scornful headlines in the popular press for his habitual practice of blessing himself. The *Sunday Mail*, in June 2006, lamented the consequential damage to Scotland's reputation: 'Each time the story is retold, it is explained how sectarian hatred is a scar on Scottish society. The image of Scotland being beamed around the world is not one we can take any pride in.' Curiously, however, the finger of blame seemed to be pointed more at Boruc himself, rather than those who were apparently upset by his gesture. The player's actions were denounced as a provocative, 'sectarian' act, with *The Scotsman* reporting, 'Last night a Rangers fan spokesman accused the Celtic goalkeeper of trying to incite the crowd by blessing himself during yesterday's game.'

The same paper, an otherwise respectable Edinburgh-based broadsheet, was later the subject of a complaint from the Catholic Church in Scotland after it featured an image of Boruc blessing himself on its front page, with a tagline which noted, 'For the second time in a year during yesterday's Old Firm match, the Celtic goalkeeper Artur Boruc provoked Rangers fans by making the sign of the cross.' Unsurprisingly, although Boruc continued the practice, no such complaints were reported in Italy or England, where the goalkeeper played out his career.

Back in 1986, Johnston's actions sparked outrage. The idea that he might one day sign for Rangers seemed utterly unthinkable. Yet little over two and a half years later, in the summer of 1989, Rangers rocked the world of Scottish football when they signed the player from under the noses of his former club Celtic, as the national game in Scotland collectively fell of its chair in astonishment. Johnston had spent the previous two seasons in France with Nantes, scoring a respectable 22 goals, but he had apparently grown restless with the slow pace of life and the relatively low profile of football in France.

After initially vowing that he would never go back to Scottish football as a result of the sectarian abuse and press scrutiny which he was subjected to following the Skol Cup Final incident, Johnston announced publicly, in May 1989, that he was indeed on the verge of returning to his boyhood heroes Celtic. The Parkhead side were then managed by club legend Billy McNeill, who had been made aware of the striker's willingness to return home by his captain Roy Aitken, whom Johnston had been entreating while the players were together on international duty with Scotland. Johnston was subsequently paraded at a press conference wearing a Celtic shirt, where he professed, amid a lengthy roll call of footballing platitudes and truisms, his undying love for the club.

With the benefit of hindsight, some of Johnston's quotes from this period expose just how meaningless and trite the kind of carefully contrived soundbites we're typically used to hearing from sportsmen on these set-piece occasions really are. It's difficult to think of a better example of a footballer talking in carefully coached media-speak and telling people what he thinks they want to hear, which in this instance was particularly egregious, given the complete volte-face that Johnston was about to perform. 'When I joined Celtic in 1984 it was like an answer to prayers, and I don't say that lightly,' the striker assured readers of the *Celtic View*. 'At that time I fully intended to see out my career at Celtic, if the club would have me,' he continued. 'I never fell out of love with Celtic... when I joined Nantes it had always been my intention to return to Celtic one day. No one can accuse me of being two-faced... I didn't intend to leave Celtic then and I don't intend to now', Johnston maintained, while rumours of a desire to join Manchester United were fabricated, chiefly because, 'there is no other British club I could play for apart from Celtic'.

The son of a Protestant father and Catholic mother, Johnston attended St Roch's secondary school in the Royston area of Glasgow and supported Celtic as a boy. He played for Partick Thistle, then Watford, before Parkhead manager Davie Hay signed him as an intended replacement for Charlie Nicholas, who had left Celtic for Arsenal the previous year. He went on to form a prolific partnership with the intelligent Brian McClair, scoring 52 goals in 100 appearances for the Parkhead side, and even at this time Johnston already had something of a history of hyperbolic statement when it came to his feelings for Celtic. Back in 1984, he told Radio Clyde that he would walk from Watford to Glasgow in order to play for the club he loved, while earlier in the same year, after he had appeared for Graham Taylor's team in the FA Cup Final and suffered the disappointment of a 2-0 defeat to Everton, Johnston later declared that he was equally upset over Celtic's loss to Aberdeen on the same day, 2-1 after extra time, in the Scottish Cup Final. 'I suppose it was round about then that I was reminded of where my heart really lay,' he later wrote.

After handing in a transfer request, as rumours of Celtic's interest grew, he finally signed for the Parkhead side in October 1984, with the club spending £400,000 on the player, a record Scottish fee at the time. Manager Davie Hay's previous six signings had cost a combined total of £375,000, so this was a considerable outlay from a parsimonious

Celtic board and evidence of their commitment and belief in the striker, who was still only 21 years old at the time. A few years later in his autobiography, Johnston spoke of the reception he received from the fans on his debut against Hibs, 'I'll never forget that ovation until I breathe my last. It was so emotional I just couldn't speak... Put it this way, by comparison making love is like watching paint dry.'

After Johnston's infamous Celtic press conference in May 1989, the player travelled with his proposed new colleagues on the team bus to the club's final league fixture of the season against St Mirren in Paisley, where Joe Miller scored the only goal of the match to give Celtic a 1-0 win. The following week, Miller repeated the feat, lighting up the showpiece Scottish Cup Final with the game's solitary strike against Rangers, leaving Ibrox manager Graeme Souness furious at being denied a potential Treble.

Souness was reported to have told his players in the dressing room after the defeat that he had something up his sleeve which would rock Celtic, and that the Parkhead club had a shock coming. Something had evidently changed during the week between Miller's two winning goals and over the summer rumours continued to circulate that the proposed deal on Johnston's return to Celtic might not be as cut and dried as everyone assumed. The fly in the ointment seemed to be the player's agent Bill McMurdo, Agent Orange himself, the same man who had represented Jock Wallace and whose Rangers allegiances and political views were a matter of public record. McNeill had informed Johnston that he would not deal with McMurdo and the striker appeared to accept this condition when he signed a 'letter of agreement' to join Celtic, which, although not a contract, was later ratified by FIFA as being legally binding, the equivalent of a modern-day pre-contract agreement. It was on this basis that Celtic decided to go ahead with the May press briefing and photo shoot, but the jilted McMurdo sent a letter to the club informing them that it was his company, rather than Nantes, who owned the player's registration and that the agent could not therefore be bypassed in any transaction. While Celtic were pondering the implications of all this, McMurdo was offering the player to Souness on the other side of the city.

The Rangers manager soon became aware of the contractual difficulties over Johnston's proposed move to Celtic, and he immediately expressed an interest in the striker. Souness admired the player and he persuaded owner David Murray that with one swoop they could secure the services of a talented forward who had apparently been destined for Celtic, gazumping their old rivals in the process as an added bonus, and at the same time end the exclusionary signing policy, which with every passing year was becoming more of a black mark on the club's reputation, with potentially serious implications in the increasingly important world of business and finance in football.

At the time FIFA were investigating racist and religious prejudice in the game and Rangers' arcane practices were sure to come under the microscope at some point, with the world governing body holding the power to impose the ultimate sanction of withdrawing licences and shutting errant football clubs down.

Johnston and McMurdo subsequently met Souness at the manager's Edinburgh home, where a deal to bring the player to Rangers was agreed in principle.

Meanwhile Celtic, who had been unable to contact Johnston over the close season, were becoming increasingly aware that their putative deal for the striker was unlikely ever to be completed. Souness and McMurdo had turned the player and it wasn't long before Johnston was privately threatening to quit football altogether if he was compelled to honour his previous commitment to his boyhood club. Despite the FIFA-endorsed agreement and with Nantes waiting expectantly for receipt of the £800,000 balance which would conclude the transfer, the Parkhead club, faced with the prospect of having an unhappy player on their hands, announced publicly that they were pulling out of the deal.

At the time McNeill was still on holiday in Florida and he received his employers' statement down the telephone, read out to him by a journalist. Had Celtic dug their heels in, they could have controlled Johnston's future – even if he would never go on to play for the Parkhead club, they could have had a hand in his ultimate destination. As late as 2 July, McMurdo was still describing the rumours of a link with Rangers to the *Sunday Mail* as, 'a complete fabrication – you can run that story for ten years and it still wouldn't be true'. When the paper's chief sports writer Don Morrison called Ibrox to try and get to the bottom of the matter, he was told by assistant manager Walter Smith, 'Remember the

The 'Gallant Pioneers'; the Rangers team which reached the Scottish Cup Final in 1877. Tom Vallance (centre) is wearing a lion rampant badge to indicate his status as an international. Peter Campbell (on one knee) is to his left with Moses McNeil (arms folded) next along. Other founders Peter McNeil and William McBeath were no longer playing for the club.

THE RANGERS NEW GROUND (LOOKING TOWARDS COPELAND ROAD).
Fred. Braby & Co., Ltd., Glasgow, Contractors.

The original Ibrox Park, 1887; the row of houses in the background (behind the goal) still stand and give a good indication of the position of the old ground relative to the modern stadium.

The Glasgow Exhibition Cup, won by Rangers in 1901 but presented to Celtic as the winners of the British League Cup in 1902. Celtic have since refused all requests to return the trophy to Ibrox.

The first Ibrox disaster, April 1902; hundreds fell through the gap, 70 foot long and 10 foot wide which opened up in the western terrace during the Scotland vs England international match. Twenty-five were killed.

Rangers 2 Celtic 2, Scottish Cup Final replay, 17 April 1909: Using cheap whisky as fuel, rioting Old Firm fans set fire to pay boxes at Hampden in the belief that the result had been arranged to ensure another lucrative replay. The cup that year was withheld.

Illustration of Rangers player Jimmy Bowie, October 1922; later a director and chairman, Bowie was ousted in a boardroom coup by the club's all-powerful manager Bill Struth in 1947.

The Rangers team pose with directors after beating Celtic 4 -0 in the Scottish Cup Final of 1928, ending a 25-year run without winning the trophy. Penalty taker and stand-in skipper Davie Meiklejohn is standing, second from the left.

Fatal collision; Celtic goalkeeper John Thomson dives at the feet of Rangers forward Sam English, Ibrox Park 5 September 1931. Thomson suffered a depressed fracture of the skull and later died.

Portrait in oils of Bill Struth, Rangers manager from 1920–54, in the Trophy Room at Ibrox.

Old-fashioned Rangers; European Cup semi-final first leg, April 1960, Eintracht Frankfurt 6 Rangers 1. Manager Scot Symon was later criticised by some of his players for failing to offer any tactical or motivational advice at half-time with the score at 1-1.

Rangers left-half Jim Baxter arrives at the Victoria Infirmary with his leg in plaster, alongside Davie Wilson, December 1964. With Baxter's injury went any hope Rangers had of winning the European Cup.

Action from the Cup Winners' Cup Final May 1967, Bayern Munich 1 Rangers 0 aet: Rangers players later admitted that Celtic's European Cup win in Lisbon less than a week earlier had a negative effect on their performance.

St James' Park, May 1969, Rangers' Ronnie MacKinnon beats Newcastle's Wyn Davies to the header. Newcastle won the match 2-0 precipitating the first in a series of outbreaks of hooliganism, linked to religious bigotry, by Rangers fans at this time.

Stairway to hell: Sixty-six people died at the second Ibrox disaster, 2 January 1971. The 'waterfall' design of Stairway 13 was later found to have been unsafe. Rangers escaped blame for the disaster at the subsequent Fatal Accident Inquiry, leading to accusations of a cover-up.

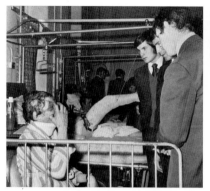

Rangers players Derek Johnstone, Colin Jackson and Dave Smith visit injured spectators at the Victoria Infirmary following the Ibrox disaster.

John Greig, captain of the Rangers/Celtic Select XI, introduces the Lord Provost of Glasgow, Sir Donald Liddle, to team-mates including Billy McNeill, George Best and Bobby Charlton.

The Rangers players receive the trophy in their dressing room after victory over Dynamo Moscow in the final of the Cup Winners' Cup, May 1972. There was no trophy presentation in front of the fans.

The Rangers team which won the Treble in 1976. They later repeated the feat in 1978, before manager Jock Wallace (front row left) quit the club in acrimonious circumstances.

May 1989: Now you see him...

July 1989: Now you don't... Maurice Johnston became the first known Catholic to sign for Rangers since the Edwardian era.

'The Three Amigos': Souness reversed the flow, stretching back decades, of Scottish talent heading south by bringing high profile English players to Ibrox. Here, Chris Woods, Terry Butcher and Graham Roberts make their way to Glasgow Sheriff Court, after being charged with 'conduct likely to cause a breach of the peace' during a match against Celtic in October 1987.

Graeme Souness conducts the Prime Minister on a tour of Ibrox Park, March 1990. Rangers' spending at this time was described as a Thatcherite bubble, which never seemed to burst.

The spending at Rangers continued under the new partnership of manager Walter Smith (left) and chairman David Murray (right) with the club bringing in talented foreign players such as the Danish winger Brian Laudrup.

The apex of Rangers' unsustainable spending came during the extravagant Dick Advocaat years: The Dutch trainer shares a word with his £12m signing Tore André Flo.

DJO/sh

THE RANGERS FOOTBALL CLUB plc
— Founded 1873 —

23 November 2000

Mr Tore Andre Flo
Richmond House

Dear Tore,

Further to discussions, I confirm that Rangers Football Club will arrange net payments into a fund under the Club's Employee Benefit Trust for your benefit as follows:-

30 November 2000	£450,000
30 November 2001	£700,000
30 November 2002	£700,000
30 November 2003	£500,000
30 November 2004	£500,000

Each of these amounts will paid into the Trust on the due dates on condition that you have been registered with the Club on the due dates, except that £200,000 of the sums due in each of 2001 and 2002 are unconditional. The total funds including investment returns will become payable to you immediately after 31 May 2005 or earlier date of termination of your contract.

The Club is taking appropriate professional/legal advice in relation to the documentation concerning these payments. However, I can confirm that the payments are not contractual being not related to your proposed contract of employment with the Club nor represent an inducement to enter a new contract with the Club

The Club indemnifies you against any liability including the UK and Norway to income tax on amounts receivable by you under the arrangement subject to you advising any movement of funds to enable the Club to offer appropriate advice to limit any exposure under this indemnity, such advice not to be unreasonably rejected.

The terms of this letter are and must remain strictly confidential

Yours sincerely,

D. J. ODAM
FINANCE DIRECTOR

TELEPHONE: Customer Services 0870 600 1972 Tickets 0870 600 1993 Hospitality 0870 600 1964 Commercial 0600 670 1800 Retail/Mail Order 0990 99 1993
FACSIMILE: 0141 580 8690 WEBSITE: www.rangers.co.uk
REGISTERED OFFICE: IBROX STADIUM 150 EDMISTON DRIVE GLASGOW G51 2XD

A copy of the side-letter used to top up the remuneration of Tore André Flo. These letters were kept hidden from both the SFA and HMRC, which led to an investigation by both bodies.

Rangers captain Barry Ferguson lifts the CIS Insurance Cup after a 2-1 defeat of Celtic, the first part of a domestic Treble in 2003. It was later revealed that Rangers were employing the unlawful EBT tax avoidance scheme throughout these years, which allowed them to retain and pay players they would otherwise have been unable to afford.

Frenchman Paul Le Guen's short-lived spell as Rangers manager was characterised by a strange recruitment policy, including the purchase of Slovakian striker Filip Sebo from Austria Vienna.

May 2011; Craig Whyte is congratulated by Rangers fans after completing his purchase of the club, for £1, from Sir David Murray.

'Preferred bidder' Charles Green (right) with David Whitehouse from administrators Duff and Phelps. After the club's liquidation, Green acquired the business and assets of Rangers from former owner Craig Whyte. The colour-coded irony of the transaction was lost on no one.

How the media originally covered the liquidation of Rangers in June 2012; they would soon change their tune.

The Rangers crest on the Bill Struth main stand at Ibrox. The inscription bears the wrong date of the club's foundation, which caused confusion to club historians for many years. (courtesy of football-stadiums.co.uk) traditions of this club and, if we were going to break them, it wouldn't be for that cunt.'

But with Celtic now officially out of the way, things moved forward quickly and the deal to bring Johnston to Rangers was finally concluded in a Paris café. It seemed inevitable that news would leak, despite all the mendacity and espionage, and by 9 July the *Scottish Sun* appeared to have the story, thanks to a 16-year-old trainee reporter who had noticed that Johnston's name had mysteriously appeared on Rangers' insurance documents, which were being handled by his girlfriend's father. The young lad, having apparently unearthed the biggest story in the history of Scottish football, presumably with the help of his intended father-in-law, dutifully conveyed his information to the paper's editor, Jack Irvine, who had just stepped off a plane after holidaying with Souness in Majorca. 'Print it,' the Rangers manager said to Irvine, who went ahead and devoted 16 pages of Monday's paper to their scoop.

Still nobody could quite believe it, with the other papers, clearly paralysed with incredulity, refusing to run the story, even after early editions of the *Sun* hit the stands. It wasn't until Johnston was unveiled as a Rangers player at a press conference, on the morning of Monday, 10 July that the rumours were finally confirmed. The striker, looking particularly sheepish and wearing a Rangers blazer that was at least two sizes too big for him, was ushered into the Blue Room at Ibrox alongside Souness, where he spoke, in more guarded terms this time, to his astonished audience of his 'huge admiration' for the Ibrox club, something he'd clearly managed to keep to himself up to that point.

After Johnston's signing some Rangers fans burned scarves, cancelled season tickets, and even laid wreathes at the gates of Ibrox, while others who had perhaps seen a move of this nature coming for some time were heard to observe, 'It's not that I object to us signing Catholics, I just didn't want us signing *that* Catholic.' Fan spokesman David Miller summed up the general mood when he told *The Herald*, 'It's a sad day for Rangers. There will be a lot of people handing in their season tickets. I don't want to see a Roman Catholic at Ibrox. It really sticks in my throat.'

Miller then went on to claim that signing a Catholic from the continent would have been easier to stomach. Within the club itself, opinion on Johnston's arrival appeared to be divided; the English squad members, largely bewildered by all the fuss, agreed to attend a press conference, welcoming the new player to the club, but their Scottish counterparts declined the same request, and refused to be photographed with Johnston, while Ibrox kitman and bus driver, Jimmy Bell, snubbed the club's new acquisition, preferring not to provide him with his playing gear and withholding chocolate bars from the striker.

Over on the other side of the city, the Celtic fans reacted to Johnston's perceived treachery with predictable fury. They might not have believed every word of the striker's regurgitated platitudes, but the last thing they could have expected was that he was about to join their greatest rivals. The Celtic fanzine *Not the View*, perhaps reflecting Johnston's penchant for hyperbole, captured the widespread sense of revulsion when they described the player as 'the human incarnation of the contents of Beelzebub's dustbin'. Others dubbed their former idol 'Judas', 'le petit merde' and during Old Firm games sang songs aimed at the forward, such as 'Who's the Catholic in the Blue?' and 'What's it like to sign a Tim?' At least they did for most of the game, until in November 1989 Johnston scored an injury time winner at Ibrox against his former club, silencing the Hoops faithful and precipitating something of a turning point in his acceptance at Ibrox.

In the aftermath of the signing, the press lavished Murray and Souness with praise for finally allowing Rangers to employ a prominent Catholic footballer, often with far greater enthusiasm than they had criticised the club's now former, unofficial policy, which, given that it had just been so spectacularly done away with, was now able to be openly acknowledged.

The Johnston signing seemed to have a gradual, but nonetheless remarkable, transformative effect on the public discourse of questions surrounding religion and bigotry and how these issues pertained to Scottish football. The evolving issue of 'sectarianism', so long considered a taboo subject, was now well and truly up for discussion. A survey, conducted by Dr Joe Bradley of Stirling University, of the use of the term 'sectarian' in Scottish newspapers reveals the gradual change which occurred over the 1990s:

Year	Number of mentions
1992	93
1993	229
1994	481
1995	714
1996	1,021
1997	>3,000, and the same for each subsequent year

A similar pattern emerges with the cognate term 'sectarianism':

Year	Number of mentions
1992	20
1993	63
1994	207
1995	325
1996	428
2000	1,308
2001	>3,000, and the same for each subsequent year

In retrospect, however, the signing of Maurice Johnston can be seen as something of a missed opportunity in the fight against sectarianism in Scottish football; if anything it only seemed to exacerbate the issue. While it would not have been timely or appropriate, in the wake of Johnston's arrival at Ibrox, to lambast Rangers for the policy which the club had only just dispensed with, the new era of openness which followed might have provided an opportune moment to reassess the decades of institutionalised bigotry at Ibrox and the fans' continued airing of songs such as 'No Pope of Rome' and 'The Billy Boys'. Instead, there appeared to ensue a period of equivocation, appeasement and 'whataboutery', where Rangers fans and their apologists in the press seemed more inclined to try to deflect the problem on to other clubs, rather than acknowledge or attempt to deal with the ongoing issue at Ibrox. Some even claimed that, with the Johnston signing, Rangers now occupied the moral high ground, and the label of sectarianism could no longer be applied to the club.

From a purely footballing point of view of course, it was unarguable that Rangers had pulled off a terrific coup: the club had signed a valued striker, who had seemed destined to re-join their great rivals and, over the course of the next two years, before Johnston was transferred to Everton in November 1991, they would field the player against his former team and win trophies with him in their side. Souness was entirely candid about his belief that it would take the Parkhead club ten years to recover from the loss of Johnston to Rangers, as he later admitted to the *Daily Record*, 'There was an element of mischief. I believed we were hurting Celtic by signing him.'

This was all perfectly fair and above board; Rangers at the time had gained the upper hand in the club's unending rivalry with the Parkhead side, and the Ibrox boss was understandably keen to press home and extend his team's advantage. However, there was more to this story than just football, and in terms of reducing sectarian tensions within the Scottish game and wider society, certainly in the immediate aftermath of the Johnston signing, it was as if petrol had been poured on the flames. Souness's car was attacked even as he drove away from Ibrox after the press conference at which Johnston was unveiled and both the manager and the club's controversial new striker had to be accompanied by bodyguards for the next six months.

In the end, sadly, there was no cathartic moment, no admission of guilt, no humility or contrition, not even any acknowledgement of previous wrongdoing by Rangers after the Johnston signing. It was almost as if a switch had been flicked: the club weren't employing Catholics before, but now they've bought one and they did it while managing to stick two fingers up at their rivals at the same time. If there was any hope of reconciliation with the Catholic community, Rangers could hardly be considered, by signing Maurice Johnston from under the noses of Celtic, to have extended the olive branch. Any notion of an apology, or even a statement of regret from the Ibrox club, either to Scotland's Catholic community, whom Rangers had been discriminating against for decades, or to Scottish football as a whole, remains to this day no more than a pipe dream, and the club has at no point been held accountable for its policies down the years. Perhaps as a result of the insensitive way in which the Johnston signing was handled, Rangers continued to be dogged over the ensuing years by the issue of sectarianism, which has refused, even in more recent times when the club has been regularly fielding Catholic footballers, to disassociate itself from the Ibrox institution. In May 1999, after victory over Celtic in the Scottish Cup Final handed Rangers a rare Treble, the club's then vice-chairman, Donald Findlay, was caught on camera going through the club's sectarian repertoire, singing songs including 'The Billy Boys' and the loyalist battle anthem 'The Sash' at the Rangers Social Club later that evening. Findlay, an advocate known for his distinctive appearance – mutton-chop sideburns, pocket watch and pipe, like something out of a Sherlock Holmes novel – was forced to resign his directorship at Ibrox after footage of the ten-minute impromptu karaoke session was obtained by the *Daily Record*.

Under the headline 'Findlay's songs of hate', the paper subsequently reported, 'Donald Findlay was secretly filmed bellowing songs full of bigotry and hate at the weekend... Flushed and sweating, the QC grabbed the microphone to launch into a poisonous musical medley... Findlay is seen punching the air as he sings and struts in front of hundreds of cheering supporters.'

The lawyer, whom the paper alleged does not celebrate his birthday because it falls on St Patrick's Day, was clearly no stranger to the dangers of sectarianism, as he had already in his career represented several serious offenders, including in 1996 one Jason Campbell, who despite Findlay's undoubtedly capable defence was jailed for life for the unprovoked murder of a young Celtic fan, whose throat Campbell had slashed in a Glasgow street. Findlay subsequently had to face up to the loss of his position as Lord Rector of St Andrew's University and he was also fined £3,000 by the Faculty of Advocates in the wake of his indiscretion, which later the same year prompted the composer Sir James MacMillan to observe in a famous speech to the Edinburgh festival on anti-Catholicism in Scotland, 'The sanctimonious Scottish myth that all bigots are uneducated loutish morons from the lowest level of society was undermined at a stroke.'

Findlay later admitted that he felt so ashamed of his actions that he contemplated suicide, telling BBC Scotland's *The Kirsty Wark Show*, 'I'll never be free of it because the one thing that I know is that come the day when somebody writes my obituary, it will be there somewhere, large or small, and that is an appalling thought.'

From the boardroom down to the fans, any notion that the signing of Maurice Johnston, and Rangers' subsequent recruitment of other Catholic players and even coaches, might have brought about an end to the wider problems associated with the club has proved to be misguided. Rangers supporters in recent years have continued to sing sectarian songs from the stands at Ibrox, even inventing new ones, such as 'The Famine Song', which was first aired in 2008 and has been subsequently proscribed, and the particularly unpleasant chant 'Big Jock Knew', a reference to a child abuse case at Celtic Boys' Club in the 1960s, which was weaponised by Rangers fans and used as a stick to beat the Parkhead club and its supporters.

As journalist Graham Spiers noted in *The Times* when the slogan was first heard at Ibrox, 'I have to admit I never thought I'd ever see the day when Scottish football supporters sang a song about a child sex abuse case, yet Rangers have duly delivered. Even more amazing is Rangers FC's on-going silence on the matter, as this cretinous chant builds up its head of steam among supporters.' Spiers was correct about the increasingly frequent usage of the slogan and 'Big Jock Knew' or 'BJK' later migrated from the Ibrox stands to become a ubiquitous acronym graffitied around Glasgow as well as a salutation used by Rangers fans when they greeted one another in the street.

In the end, rather than any domestic authority, it was the European governing body UEFA who took exception to Rangers' sectarian songbook and sanctioned the club after a number of high-profile cases in the 2000s, including, in May 2006, a fine accompanied by a warning over any future misconduct after incidents of hooliganism and bigotry surrounding the club's Champions League tie earlier in the year with Villarreal. Privately, UEFA were disturbed and appalled when they uncovered what was still going on at Ibrox in the 21st century, with one official telling Spiers, 'Yes we have racism today in football and many other problems. But it is still shocking to us that, in the year 2006, we still have supporters in Glasgow shouting "Fuck the Pope" and such things. We thought the world had moved on from this.'

Perhaps the clearest indication that anti-Catholicism continued to be a problem for sections of the Ibrox support came with the treatment received by the former Celtic captain Neil Lennon, who was signed by the Parkhead club in December 2000. Lennon is a Catholic from the Armagh town of Lurgan in Northern Ireland, who enjoyed a relatively unmolested career in England with Crewe and Leicester, during which time he appeared more than 30 times for his country, but his move north to join Celtic, the club he supported as a boy, precipitated a change in how the player was viewed and received in his religiously divided home province.

After he was named captain of his country for a friendly game against Cyprus at Windsor Park, Belfast in August 2002, Lennon was forced to pull out of the squad on police advice and subsequently retired from international football having received death threats from loyalist paramilitaries. In Scotland, as if fans were taking their cue from the extremists, Lennon was the frequent object of abuse and, more seriously, the target of several attacks, which usually took place well away from the often hostile and partisan environment of the football field.

In May 2003, Lennon was confronted and assaulted while driving home in his car by two students in Glasgow's prosperous west end, suggesting once again that the ill-feeling towards Catholics in general and Lennon in particular wasn't merely confined to the soft underbelly of society, but had penetrated the aspirational classes as well. The following February, a motorist swerved in front of Lennon on the M8 motorway near Charing Cross in Glasgow and subjected the player, who had a young child in his car at the time, to a series of obscenities and vulgar gestures. Lennon immediately pulled off the motorway and called the police, leading to the culprit later being convicted and fined £500, after admitting, 'I did it because I'm a Rangers fan and he is a Celtic player, but I'm not a bigot.'

This revealing attitude is often displayed by Lennon's assailants, who, because they saw the player as an enemy of Rangers, seemed to be convinced that they had done nothing wrong in challenging or even attacking the footballer. It's the 'We are the people' mentality, the mistaken, yet intractable idea, born of a sense of entitlement and standing, that an enemy of Rangers, an inappropriate description of Lennon in any case, is also somehow an enemy of the established order of things and therefore fair game.

In May 2004, sectarian abuse and the words 'you're a dead man Lennon' were daubed on the road near the player's home in the west end of Glasgow. The fact that the perpetrators knew where he lived was clearly meant to intimidate Lennon, who nevertheless vowed to remain at Celtic for the rest of his career. Later, on the night of 31 August 2008, following a 4-2 win for Rangers at Celtic Park, Lennon, by now on the Parkhead club's coaching staff, was attacked by two men in the west end of Glasgow near his home. He was assaulted and left lying on the ground unconscious, after his head hit the cobblestoned road in the fashionable west end drinking spot of Ashton Lane.

At their trial the following January, two men in their 40s, who admitted to being Rangers fans, were found guilty of assault, although the words 'aggravated by religious prejudice' were deleted from the charge sheet by the jury. Sentencing the men to two years in prison, the judge remarked, 'He [Lennon] was curled up, trying to protect himself and offering no resistance. The complainer was fortunate that he did not receive more serious injuries given the ferocity of the assault.'

In 2011, post office workers intercepted a 'viable explosive device' which had been sent to Lennon through the mail. Other similar devices were also sent separately to Lennon's lawyer, Paul McBride QC, and retired Labour MSP Trish Godman, who had worn a Celtic shirt to Holyrood on her last day in Parliament, as well as to the Glasgow-based Irish institution Cairde na hEireann (Friends of Ireland). Suspicion soon fell on two Ayrshire-based Rangers fans in their 40s, who, in March 2012, were found guilty on almost all the charges against them in relation to the devices, although the charge of 'conspiracy to murder' was reduced to 'conspiracy to assault'. One of the men admitted that he was terrified of the other, telling police, 'I know he's got pure hatred and it seems to be aimed at Neil Lennon and anything to do with Celtic Football Club.'

These persistent and increasingly malignant attacks on Lennon and the continuing issues with religious bigotry surrounding Rangers and the club's fans have recently led some to consider whether Scotland's and Scottish football's general widespread concern over 'sectarianism' should be rebranded and addressed in terms of the more specific problem of anti-Catholicism. Such a reclassification would of course immediately cast new light on the perennial debate about the 'Old Firm', the tag associated with Rangers and Celtic since the turn of the 20th century, with its inherent implications of how both sides are as bad as each other when it comes to these issues, effectively the two faces of the same coin, an argument which has been stridently propagated in certain quarters for many years.

Needless to say, the suggestion that there may be an imbalance of blame and responsibility within Glasgow's footballing duopoly has proved a particularly difficult nettle for some people to grasp, yet any putative notions of the reverse consideration, anti-Protestantism, existing as a malign force within Scottish society are not held to be widely credible. Accordingly the debate, led mainly by Catholic writers and academics, has recently begun to shift towards the particular problem of anti-Catholicism. In 2000, Patrick Reilly, the first Catholic to be named Head of English Literature at Glasgow University since the Reformation, wrote, 'To ask if there is anti-Catholicism in Scotland is like asking if there are Frenchmen in Paris.' The novelist Andrew O'Hagan agrees, 'Scotland is a divisive, bigoted society.' Reminiscing about his Catholic upbringing in Ayrshire, O'Hagan recalled, 'The birds on the trees sang sectarian songs. The Catholics seemed out on their own somehow: a happy group for the most part, an irrational group sometimes, but a group nonetheless.'

In a more subtle criticism, speaking of his childhood love of books, particularly Scottish novelists such as Stevenson, Scott and Gray, O'Hagan nevertheless lamented, 'The truth is I never read a single scene in any of those books exactly like a scene from my own life... And though I knew it was nothing to do with discrimination – more like disadvantage – it added to my sense of Catholics being not altogether present in Scotland. It made me feel like we were outsiders, even to ourselves.'

Similarly Joseph Bradley, head of the school of sport at the University of Stirling, has argued extensively in numerous academic papers about anti-Catholicism, particularly within the environs of Scottish football including fans, certain clubs and sections of the media, having a disruptive and deleterious effect on Scotland's conduct of its public affairs. Perhaps the most celebrated intervention of recent years, however, came from the composer Sir James MacMillan, who, in a speech to the Edinburgh Festival in 1999, traduced the recent coverage of the incident with Donald Findlay earlier in the summer, highlighting the vociferous apologists of Findlay's actions, particularly in notionally respectable media outlets such as *The Herald*, and spoke of the widespread nature of the problem of anti-Catholicism in modern Scotland, which he referred to as 'Scotland's shame'. 'In many walks of life,' MacMillan argued, 'in the workplace, in the professions, in academia, in the media, in politics and in sport, anti-Catholicism, even when it is not particularly malign, is as endemic as it is second nature.'

There are alternative views of course and other academics disagree, with some arguing that anti-Catholicism is a historical problem and not one that affects modern Scotland in any meaningful way, although even at the highbrow level, the splits tend to be along religious lines. Often the papers and articles of various scholars and writers are published together in anthologies and the reader, if he can decipher all the academic rhetoric, is left to make up his own mind. The issue will continue to be debated, but it undoubtedly remains the case that there is a significant body of opinion from within the Catholic community in Scotland which continues to feel the presence of an unwelcome threat to their identity and their culture, and, as has happened with other ethnic groups in the UK, it seems only right that their concerns should be acknowledged and treated as genuine.

After all, we're not talking about the grievances of the Green Brigade here or other youthful, radical groups, but professors and authors, knighted composers. If the most senior and respected figures within a community, the intellectual elite, continue to feel the need to articulate their concerns over perceived discrimination, even if it is only within the context of progress to a more pluralist society, then surely they deserve to be listened to and have their concerns taken seriously. Perhaps then, in this new light, the most persistent and objectionable of all faults with Scottish football might at last be effectually addressed.

The signing of Maurice Johnston may not have been the seminal moment that many were hoping for in regards to the wider problem of anti-Catholicism at Ibrox and in the wider culture, but over the ensuing years, once Rangers had officially abandoned its dogmatic, discriminatory policies, it was as if the floodgates had been opened and a raft of Catholic players eventually arrived at the club, most of them foreigners, at a time when British football was opening up its doors to the world. Rangers have now been captained by a Catholic, and managed by a Catholic, an unqualifiedly welcome development, which has rightly exposed all the old lies and excuses about outsiders supposedly not being able to fully commit to the team's cause.

The new Ibrox club of today has no compunction at all about signing footballers from all backgrounds, including even players from the Republic of Ireland, something that would have been unthinkable in Souness's day. And overall, it should be acknowledged that in spite of Neil Lennon's one-man quest to adjust the statistics, incidents of violent and anti-social behaviour at football in Scotland have fallen in recent years, as they have across the UK generally. Your modern bigot, it seems, often prefers to hide behind anonymous social media profiles, a keyboard warrior out there in cyberspace, spreading abuse and his warped view of the world, but ultimately causing less physical damage.

So, in the end, we got there with Rangers, even if at times it felt as though the old institution had to be dragged kicking and screaming into the 21st century. The extent of the club's denials and equivocation down the years has inevitably left many observers unconvinced about the nature of the progress within Ibrox, with the glaring lack of contrition or humility, coupled with the ongoing problems among the club's fans and even directors, suggesting that the changes at the club have been largely cosmetic and have been adopted chiefly for reasons of expediency. Regardless, what can be said with some certainty about the club is that Rangers lost the battle of ideas, in the present and in the past. From its very early years, the club seemed unable to grasp what sport, and football in particular, had the potential to achieve.

Once the game acquired widespread popularity, football became an enervating force for good, strengthening communities in an otherwise harsh and troubled society, bringing people from diverse backgrounds together and making them realise that, regardless of differences in geography and culture, ordinary working people had more in common with each other than perhaps they realised. Instead, Rangers looked to serve themselves, first and last, and being so blinkered, poisoned the otherwise inspiring story of Scottish football with a version of febrile religious bigotry which exists nowhere else in the global game.

Perhaps subsequent events off the field at Ibrox, as Rangers suffered a catastrophic financial collapse in 2012, would help to precipitate a re-evaluation, on the part of the club and its supporters, of what the famous old institution stands for in the modern age, and maybe, in the midst of

Rangers' greatest humiliation, a new perspective and greater humility might be sought.

Then again, perhaps not. As fans of Scottish football are wont to say, it's the hope that kills us.

PART TWO

FALL:
FINANCIAL
MALPRACTICE

8

THATCHER'S MAN

I N February 1986, Rangers' chief executive officer David Holmes
flew to Italy to finalise a deal that would bring the Sampdoria and
Scotland midfielder Graeme Souness, then 32 years old and with
an illustrious playing career already behind him, to Ibrox as the club's
new player-manager.

Holmes and his fellow directors had identified Souness as the man
to reinvigorate the ailing institution's fortunes on the field, while behind
the scenes, the board set about trying to implement their ambitious plans
to take the club forward and restore its dwindling reputation within the
Scottish game.

It may have looked like a seamless transition, but the eventual
appointment of the former Liverpool captain on 8 April, just a day
after the sacking of Jock Wallace, was the culmination of a long and
inevitably bitter process. Holmes himself had only been appointed
to the Rangers board in November 1985, a few days after the club
had suffered a demoralising 3-0 defeat at the hands of a resurgent
Hearts at Tynecastle. A man with no previous connection to Rangers,
Holmes was a joiner by trade, who had worked his way up through
the ranks of the Lawrence Building Group, eventually becoming
the firm's managing director. Described by journalist Jim Blair as 'a
builder from Falkirk who thought he was a carpenter from Nazareth',
his appointment was seen by many at the time as the prelude to a
boardroom power struggle.

Holmes's boss in Falkirk was Lawrence Marlborough, owner of the Lawrence Group, a tax exile who had based himself in Lake Tahoe, Nevada, since quitting the Rangers board in 1983. Marlborough was the grandson of the former Rangers chairman John Lawrence, who had joined the club's board at the end of the Struth era in the mid-1950s and had served as chairman for ten years until, in 1973, ill health forced his retirement. Lawrence's building firm had flourished during the slum clearances and the subsequent housing boom of the 1930s, and by the 1960s his company and its subsidiaries had built over 70,000 homes across Scotland, including 30,000 council houses.

When Lawrence died in 1977, he bequeathed a significant number of shares in Rangers to his grandson Marlborough, who, despite resigning from the board and moving abroad, appeared by the mid-1980s to be taking a renewed interest in his inheritance. Rangers' losses, season after season, were becoming a constant drain on the Lawrence Group and, clearly unimpressed with what had been going on at the club since his departure, Marlborough was now determined to step up and take a controlling interest in the company.

Marlborough's plan was simple; gain a majority shareholding in the club, turn the ship around and then, ideally, sell at a profit. As always with Rangers though, it was going to be an acrimonious process and Marlborough knew that his intended acquisition would be opposed by many of his former colleagues, who had maintained their positions on the board. The club was still under the control of a small group of amateur, old-style custodian-directors with Masonic connections, high priests of the old methodology at Rangers, who ran the business almost as a hobby and who were determined to resist what they saw as a hostile takeover bid from people whom they considered outsiders. In response to the eyebrow-raising in the media on his initial appointment to the board in November, Holmes had moved quickly to calm any suspicions about his immediate intentions. 'There is absolutely nothing sinister about what has happened. It's all very simple, above board and I'm sure will benefit Rangers greatly,' he announced at the time.

Despite such reassurances, however, what soon followed was described as, 'one of the most savage bloodlettings in the history of the Rangers board', and by early in the new year, Marlborough, dubbed 'the silent partner' by chairman John Paton, had acquired 52 per cent of the shares in the company. Orchestrated by Holmes, the key was persuading small-time businessman Jack Gillespie, the owner of a Vauxhall dealership in Lenzie, to sell a significant proportion of his stake to Marlborough. As a result, in February 1986, directors Tom Dawson and Jim Robinson, the proprietor of a scrap metal firm who had slowly been building up his stake in the club since 1960, were ousted and replaced by Hugh Adam and Freddie Fletcher, men who would bring acknowledged commercial expertise to their new roles. Former chairman Rae Simpson, a Kilmarnock surgeon who had inherited his shares from his grandfather, James Henderson, the first chairman of Rangers following the club's incorporation in 1899, also left his post, while Gillespie was reinstated as vice-chairman, following his removal in an earlier coup.

On Valentine's Day, Holmes was named the club's new chief executive, when he told the press, 'I'm no hatchet man. I did what I had to do, but I didn't flinch from it.' For the first time in its history, Rangers Football Club had a single majority shareholder and was now effectively under the control of one man, Lawrence Marlborough, the 'absentee landlord', who would act in Glasgow through his surrogate, Holmes.

The new CEO's immediate priority, once the dust had settled on the boardroom coup, was to deal with the situation regarding the position of team manager. Rangers at the time had been struggling for years, with the club's last title success coming as far back as 1978, and if anything, things were even worse for the club than the slump it had endured during Celtic's 'nine-in-a-row' years of the late '60s and early '70s. By 1986, Rangers, as a social institution as well as a football club, seemed to have reached the end of the road. The club was drifting with no sense of purpose or direction, going through the motions in terms of fulfilling its fixtures and meeting its obligations but with no apparent idea of how to extricate itself from the ever-deepening hole in which it was floundering. The popularity of the institution was at an all-time low, across many diverse sections of society, such as the Unions, once bastions of Protestant loyalty, and the Labour movement, where the club's name was mud, all the way through to the chattering classes of respectable Protestant society, and even the Kirk had been a forthright critic in recent years.

Needless to say, the exclusionary employment policy continued to be an albatross around the club's neck, while on the field the team was struggling to cope with the threat not just from Celtic, but from Aberdeen, Dundee United and now Hearts as well, as the Tynecastle side topped the league and were heading for the final of the Scottish Cup, having already eliminated Rangers from the competition by the time of Wallace's sacking.

After a 4-4 draw with Celtic at Ibrox on 22 March 1986, the Rangers squad appeared to celebrate as if they had won the game. With the home team already well out of the picture, the best outcome Rangers could expect from the fixture was to put a dent in Celtic's championship bid, which they had ultimately achieved by coming from behind to square the match. After the game, a clearly delighted Jock Wallace approached David Holmes in the boardroom, singing the Ulster loyalist anthem *The Sash*. Holmes, still a relative newcomer to the Rangers set-up and an outsider in terms of the club's more contentious traditions, couldn't understand either the joviality, after a home draw against a Celtic team reduced to ten men, or the sectarian singing.

In a subsequent conversation with Marlborough, the CEO was given the go-ahead to push the button on the anticipated changes, and using a journalist, Ken Gallacher, as the initial point of contact, Holmes and chairman John Paton had already received some early encouragement from Souness. Meetings were subsequently arranged with the club's putative new boss at the Mayfair Hotel in London and then in Milan to put the final touches to the agreement, all of which took place in secrecy and without the knowledge of Wallace, who was still the incumbent manager at the time.

Several people have since claimed the credit for suggesting the name of Graeme Souness as Wallace's replacement at Ibrox, with Holmes later maintaining that the idea to appoint the former Scotland international came to him in a dream. Souness himself had previously observed, in a television interview, that the man who turned Glasgow Rangers around would be made for life, and perhaps this inadvertent remark had struck a chord somewhere. Regardless, on Tuesday, 8 April, the new man-in-waiting was spirited into Ibrox via the back door, before he emerged into the Blue Room from the adjoining manager's office to face the media. It was an act of pure theatre, designed to impress and, despite the denouement being somewhat spoiled when the story was leaked the previous day. Nevertheless, the assembled gentlemen of the press were still astonished to see Graeme Souness, a genuine legend of the Scottish game, appearing in front of them.

Holmes had pulled off a masterstroke, albeit an expensive one. His new manager still had over a year left to run on his contract in Genoa so the deal to bring him to Glasgow cost Rangers £350,000, a record fee for the club at the time, although not one that would last. Souness was an untypical Scotsman in many ways; a chapter of his ghost-written autobiography, published while he was still in Italy, was entitled *Sometimes I wish I was English*. And despite the revulsion felt across Scotland at the time towards many of her policies, including the poll tax, introduced a year early north of the border as a political experiment, and the widespread dismantling of the country's industrial heartlands, he was very much a believer in Margaret Thatcher's economic policies and in her political philosophy. Arriving in Glasgow at the height of the late-1980s boom, Souness seemed to personify the direction that British football would take over the ensuing decades. In true Thatcherite manner, he came sweeping into Ibrox, riding roughshod over the admittedly shoddy practices of the past, and proceeded to set up his new order based on ego, money and self-aggrandisement.

Graeme James Souness was born in Edinburgh in May 1953. He grew up following his local team, Hibernian, but made occasional trips through to Glasgow to see Rangers, the dominant force in Scottish football at the time. His footballing talent was spotted by Celtic, who took him on trial, but he failed to impress at the Parkhead club and on one occasion, perhaps in anticipation of how he would later be viewed in that part of the city, he was confronted at a bus stop outside Celtic Park by a man wielding a sword.

His playing career began at Spurs, but he made little impact at the north London club. 'He was impatient, arrogant and tended to be flash,' youth team coach Pat Welton remembers, and at one point the youngster packed his bags and headed home to Edinburgh, apparently homesick, but also frustrated at a lack of first team opportunities. In more reflective mood years later, Souness recalled, 'Tottenham had Alan Mullery, England captain. They had Martin Peters, World Cup winner, ten years ahead of his time. They had Steve Perryman. And there was this little squirt from Carrickvale Secondary knocking on Bill Nic's [Nicolson's] door demanding to know why he wasn't getting a game.'

Spurs eventually gave up on their young prospect and sold the player to Middlesbrough, where he benefited from the down to earth, homespun wisdom of England World Cup hero Jack Charlton, helping the north-east club to promotion in 1974 after they won the Second Division by fully 15 points. On Teesside, he gained invaluable experience playing alongside European Cup winners Bobby Murdoch and Nobby Stiles, but a change of manager brought more frustration for Souness, and he was transferred to Liverpool in January 1978. The European champions were managed by soft-spoken Geordie Bob Paisley, whose strong north-east accent meant that even those who were close enough to hear him frequently couldn't understand what he was saying.

Yet Paisley, who had succeeded the legendary Bill Shankly at Anfield in 1974, became arguably the most successful English manager of all time, as over the course of the next five and a half years he added two further European Cups and four more league titles, thanks in no small part to his Scottish triumvirate of Souness, Alan Hansen and Kenny Dalglish. Describing the young Souness, Paisley observed, 'Most midfields are made up of a buzzer, a cruncher and a spreader. This boy is all three.' It was a worthy accolade for which Dalglish provided the layman's translation, 'There's no one I'd put in front of him when it comes to accurate and dangerous passing. He wins the ball then distributes it and dictates the pace of the game.'

Even in such illustrious company, Souness was known within the Anfield dressing room as 'Champagne Charlie' because of his lavish lifestyle and his rich boy affectations. Scotland team-mate Archie Gemmell dubbed him 'the chocolate soldier', not because he was no use in a fight, but in the belief that, had he been made of chocolate, he would have eaten himself. 'And he was dead right,' Souness later admitted.

He appeared in a cameo role as himself in the TV series *Boys from the Blackstuff*, a gritty drama written by Alan Bleasdale about a group of unemployed Liverpudlian tarmac layers struggling to find work in Thatcher's laissez-faire Britain. Souness didn't agree with the programme makers' politics, but he liked the idea of appearing on a television show nonetheless.

When Liverpool added a further European Cup to their array of trophies, under Paisley's successor Joe Fagan in 1984, beating Roma in the final at their own Olympic Stadium after a penalty shoot-out, Souness decided to quit Liverpool and try his luck in Italy at the Genoese club Sampdoria. Throughout his playing career and subsequently, Souness has candidly admitted, without any apparent sense of embarrassment, that he was a mercenary footballer who played primarily for money. Knowing the riches on offer in Italian football at the time, he decided to ask his new employer for double the wages that he was earning on Merseyside. When Sampdoria, with their initial offer, proposed instead to quadruple his basic salary, Souness quickly accepted, but later regretted that he didn't have the presence of mind to haggle for more. The Mediterranean lifestyle and culture suited Souness. He was a natural show-pony and the Italians, unlike the Scousers perhaps, loved him for it. He had a three-year contract in Genoa, but within barely half that time Rangers came calling.

The original plan had been to appoint Souness at the end of the season, but with Wallace's inept side lurching from one low to another, the move was brought forward to early April. Fortunately, his Genoese club proved very accommodating, but the new Ibrox manager still had to return to Italy to complete the season in advance of his transfer and Souness was forced to watch from a distance as his new team played out the remainder of the season in excruciating mediocrity. With newly appointed deputy Walter Smith in charge for the penultimate three matches, Rangers eventually limped over the line in fifth position, having lost more games than they won over the course of the season, including ten defeats and only three victories from 18 matches on the road.

But Souness had offered the players a bonus to qualify for the UEFA Cup, which they eventually achieved, meaning that over the summer he would be able to entice the big names to the club with the prospect of European football, something that was not available in England following the Heysel Stadium disaster. The new manager, only the second in Rangers' history to have no previous connection with the club on his appointment, took charge for the final game of the season and was surprised to note that, despite European football being secured the previous week when Celtic beat Dundee, the dressing room was apparently on a downer, because their city rivals had gone on to pip

Hearts for the title on the last day of the season. Souness was under no illusions that he would have to reshape his squad's priorities.

Rangers' new player-manager then flew off to Mexico as part of Scotland's squad for the World Cup, and while stopping off en route at the Scots' training camp in Santa Fe, Souness decided to make tentative enquiries to the accompanying media about the potential impact of signing a Catholic for Rangers. One journalist, Chick Young of the *Evening Times*, pointed to the gold cross, which was dangling immodestly around Souness's neck, and suggested that the quasi-religious symbol might arouse ill-feeling in certain quarters. The crucifix was a gift from Souness's first, Catholic wife, Danielle Wilson, a millionaire heiress whose father had founded the Army and Navy stores after World War One – not a working-class, west of Scotland Catholic to be sure, but a Catholic nonetheless. Souness wore the cross not for religious reasons but because he was a poser and, understandably, couldn't understand the aversion.

Bizarrely, Walter Smith was one of Souness's technical bosses in his role as assistant manager of the national team, while rival Alex Ferguson, still several months away from his appointment at Manchester United and in charge of Aberdeen, was the national coach. Ferguson had stepped into the role on a temporary basis the previous autumn following the untimely death of Jock Stein at Ninian Park in Cardiff at the end of a nervy World Cup qualifier against Wales, when the draw secured by Davie Cooper's late penalty allowed Scotland to progress to a play-off against Australia and ultimately ensured their participation in Mexico. Sadly the World Cup didn't go well for either Scotland or Souness. Drawn in the 'group of death', with Uruguay, West Germany and Denmark, the 'Holland of the 80s', Scotland failed to progress to the second stage and, after persistent squabbles between the pair, captain Souness was dropped by Ferguson for the final group game against the South Americans in favour of the Celtic youngster Paul McStay.

On his return to Ibrox, Souness wasted no time in getting to work on the huge task which lay ahead of him to reshape his squad of players into a force that could challenge for honours. One of the first changes to be implemented at the club by the new executive duo of Souness and Holmes was the abolition of the frugal salary structure, which was perceived to be holding the club back. When he arrived at Ibrox, the maximum wage at Rangers was £350 a week, but Holmes knew that in order to make the club appealing to the very best players, they would have to pay top dollar, so the limit was quietly done away with. Over the next few years, Rangers would pay some of the best salaries available in British football and attract to the club some of the most high-profile players in the country.

In many ways, Holmes's plan was sound economics; he borrowed money from the bank in order to fund the increased wages and the escalating transfer fees, and then hoped for a return over the short to medium term. Crowds had been down as low as 15,000 by the end of the Wallace era, and the intention and belief was that success would pay for itself through renewed interest and increased gate receipts. He also opened the club's first executive box, the Thornton Suite, situated in the heart of the Main Stand, which provided hospitality packages for the club's more well-heeled supporters. Combining football and fine dining, Rangers were one of the first clubs in Britain to appreciate the positive financial implications of this important new revenue stream. Holmes's strategy was a risk, something that would never have been countenanced under the sparing, puritanical stewardship of Willie Waddell, who had dogmatically refused to allow the club to fall into debt, but his time had passed and the new approach captured the Thatcherite mood of the day.

It didn't take long for the spending strategy to get under way, with the arrival from Watford in June of striker Colin West, who was allegedly 'tapped up' by Souness's international team-mate, David Speedie, in the players' lounge at Stamford Bridge after a game between Watford and Chelsea. The initial acquisition of West was quickly followed by the more eye-catching singings of England internationals Chris Woods, who cost £600,000 from Norwich City, and Terry Butcher, a £725,000 capture from relegated Ipswich Town, who arrived fresh from his own troubles at the World Cup after the infamous 'Hand of God' incident involving Diego Maradona, which saw England eliminated from the tournament at the quarter-final stage by Argentina. Tottenham Hotspur were left flabbergasted and disappointed when Butcher, the England captain, rejected a late move by manager David Pleat to bring him to White Hart Lane, with the player blazing a trail which others would soon follow by choosing instead to play his football north of the border.

Goalkeeper Woods was immediately asked about his religion when he was unveiled at Ibrox, but before he could reply Holmes intervened, 'We're not curious, he's a goalkeeper.' The CEO remonstrated with the media while Woods and his wife were left staring at their toes, 'He's 6ft 2in, four English caps, he's coming to Ibrox, that's all we want to know.'

The signings continued, with the manager often giving the English based players a personal tour of the spanking new stadium and selling the club to them; by the end of the year Souness had acquired Jimmy Nicholl, returning to the club from West Brom, Neil Woods from Doncaster and the English contingent was further augmented when no nonsense defender Graham Roberts joined the club in December from Spurs for a cool £500,000. Davie Kirkwood and goalkeeper Lindsay Hamilton, who between them managed just seven first team appearances for Rangers, completed Souness's signings in his first season, by the end of which he had spent over £2m of the club's money.

As for the players he inherited, Souness left them under no illusions about where he was intending to take the club. Winger Ted McMinn describes his first impression of meeting the new boss during those early days of pre-season training in the summer of 1986, 'There was a grit and determination in him, and a constant pent-up aggression. He told us that he was a born winner who wouldn't stand for second best and that our years of underachievement were now over.'

The manager accused many in his original squad of adopting bad habits and showing a lack of professionalism so it came as no surprise when, within two years, 23 players had left Rangers, many of them immediately, while others lingered on until they could be sold or their contracts expired, playing little more than a bit-part role in the Souness revolution. Another winger at the club, Bobby Russell, a stalwart of the team under Greig and Wallace, played just one league game for Souness at the start of the season, before eventually being transferred to Motherwell after kicking his heels in the reserves for almost a year. In a subsequent game against his former side, Russell nutmegged Souness and shouted 'Nuts!', to which Thatcher's man reportedly countered, 'How much money is in your bank account?'

Having been officially unveiled at the club back in April, Souness didn't make his playing debut for Rangers until the first match of the following season, when he was sent off at Easter Road, late in the first half, for an impetuous kick at Hibs' George McCluskey, another debutant on the day following his summer transfer from Leeds United. Souness later admitted that he had been warned by his assistant Smith about an opponent who was likely to go after him, but in trying to get his retaliation in first, he had unfortunately targeted the wrong man and subsequently sparked a mass brawl.

The most experienced player on the pitch, it was an inauspicious start for Souness, who would later describe being ordered off on his debut, against his home town club, just a few miles from where he grew up and in front of his watching father, as, 'the biggest low I ever had in football'. Afterwards in the dressing room, the player-manager was forced to apologise to his team-mates and admit, in a rare display of contrition, that he had been out of order. Rangers lost 2-1 in a game which saw eight yellow cards and one red, although the SFA later took retrospective action and issued cautions to all 21 players involved in the Souness-inspired mêlée, including Colin West who had thrown a punch at home defender Mark Fulton. Only Alan Rough, Hibs' keeper, who had stayed on his line during the incident, escaped censure.

CEO David Holmes was panicking. 'I could see all our good work disappearing,' he later admitted, and the slow start for Souness's Rangers continued the following week with a 3-2 home loss to Dundee United, in a game which Rangers had led 2-0. After scraping past East Fife in the Skol (League) Cup on penalties, the turning point seemed to come in the first meeting with champions Celtic at Ibrox. Form suggested that the visitors were favourites, but Rangers deservedly shaded the encounter, after Durrant scored the only goal. It was the first Glasgow derby in the league to be televised live and the match provided Rangers with a welcome financial windfall as well as a morale-boosting win. Victories over Celtic would prove crucial over the course of the season, as the August result signalled an end to the team's sluggish start under the new manager, while in late October, Rangers defeated their old rivals 2-1 in the Skol Cup Final to give Souness his first trophy in charge of the club.

A 1-1 draw between the teams in November at Celtic Park left the Parkhead club with a comfortable lead in the championship, which by the end of the month had stretched to nine points over their city rivals, but on New Year's Day, a 2-0 victory for the Ibrox men in the traditional derby fixture, with Souness strutting about like a peacock by the end, taunting Celtic with a display of flamboyant back-heels and step-overs, brought about such a surge in form that, by the time they headed up to Aberdeen for the penultimate match of the season, Rangers had overturned the deficit completely and required only a draw to secure the title.

During the six and a half years he enjoyed at Liverpool, Souness had not been sent off once, yet he was dismissed three times in what was a relatively brief playing career in Scotland, including on his debut at Easter Road and, framing the season nicely, on the day that Rangers clinched the title at Pittodrie. Despite the loss of the player-manager midway through the first half, after a second poor challenge on Aberdeen's Brian Irvine, who was clearly trying to wind him up, Terry Butcher opened the scoring with a header from Cooper's free kick. And although the home side equalised on the stroke of half-time, the ten men held on for the draw they needed to all but guarantee the title, which was confirmed mathematically when the result came through from Glasgow that Celtic had lost at home to Falkirk.

It was Rangers' first championship victory since 1978 and it immediately provoked a mass invasion of the Pittodrie field, involving many fans who had been locked out of the ground before the game. The stadium was utterly trashed in the ensuing mayhem; goals were dismantled, seats were ripped out and advertising boards smashed, leaving Rangers with a bill for damages that ran to many thousands of pounds. Amid the chaos, which threatened to get out of hand as the terrified Rangers players had their jerseys and boots ripped off them by over-exuberant fans, McCoist lost his gold chain and Butcher had to be rescued from the crowd by the police. Nevertheless, having made it back to the dressing room, the skipper joined in the celebrations, claiming, 'This is the happiest day of my life. It really was murder out there at the end, but I loved every minute of it.'

On his own misconduct, Souness admitted afterwards, 'On a personal note I have clouded the occasion by being sent off. I was not proud of that but it will never affect our style of play. Football is a physical game and we will continue to be a physical side.' Much later, the manager freely admitted that during his time in Scotland he allowed opponents to get under his skin far too easily, and that his big ego wouldn't allow him to walk away from situations, and instead he stupidly took the bait. Nevertheless, his first season had been a success, as Souness became the first manager, other than Jock Wallace, to win the league for Rangers since Scot Symon's Baxter-inspired domestic clean sweep of 1964. The chemistry in the dressing room seemed to be working, with level-headed assistant Walter Smith seemingly the perfect foil for the manager's more confrontational approach. The only blip came in January against Hamilton in the Scottish Cup, when Rangers suffered early elimination from the competition following a 1-0 defeat at Ibrox, after which Souness put his foot through the dressing room TV set.

Overall though, the impact of the manager's arrival had been positive for the club, with Scottish and indeed British football now forced to sit up and take notice. The mood music coming out of Ibrox was totally transformed, as in little over a year Rangers had gone from being a mediocre Scottish team to one of the best-placed clubs in Britain, challenging for further domestic honours and with almost unbroken access to European football. With a winning team on the park full of exotic new signings, the crowds rushed back to Ibrox, allowing the club to astutely exploit the law of supply and demand, as supporters were now asked to pay for their season tickets, on average, double what they had cost under Wallace.

Determined to build on his success, Souness continued spending over the close-season as he brought in ex-Liverpool man Avi Cohen for £100,000 from Maccabi Tel Aviv. Young Ian McCall came in from Dunfermline and more Englishmen arrived in the form of Trevor Francis and Mark Falco, from Atalanta and Watford respectively. The manager had experience of mixed dressing rooms from his time at Liverpool and he was keen to replicate in Scotland many of the successful training methods used by his former club. He added an intensity to the sessions, something which the coaching staff encouraged, although occasionally the cross-border banter and rivalry went too far, and for the practice matches on Friday mornings, with the squad divided along the lines of Scotland vs The Rest of the World or 'Scots' vs 'Anglos', with the manager siding with the English contingent, tempers would often flare up, and Walter Smith would have to intervene and take the ball away.

By now the media were so obsessed with finding Rangers' first Catholic signing of the modern era that they took to phoning up Mark

Falco's mother to inquire about his religion, on the grounds that Mark and Falco were a rather suspicious sounding combination of names. Mrs Falco disappointed the hacks when she informed them that they would have to carry on looking, because her son was no Catholic, and in the end, despite their assurances, Marlborough and Holmes would eventually leave Ibrox, like others before them, without delivering on their promise to sign a Catholic footballer for Rangers. In this case, however, serious attempts were made to end the policy, with Souness in particular genuinely determined to abandon the sectarian agendas and the old boys' networks in the west of Scotland, which he had never been party to. Nevertheless, a succession of suitable names, such as John Collins, Ray Houghton and Ian Rush all turned the club down.

The spending strategy continued however, although on the whole Scottish clubs were reluctant to do business with Souness, but he eventually picked up Richard Gough from Spurs for £1.1m. Dundee United had refused to sell the defender to Rangers a year earlier, but the manager eventually got his man as Gough, the Tottenham captain, became the country's first million pound player, doubling his wages on his return to Scotland. Another English veteran, Ray Wilkins, arrived from Paris Saint-Germain for the bargain price of £150,000 and by the end of the season Souness had signed John Brown from Dundee, Jan Bartram from Aarhus in Denmark and 'Rangers daft' youngster Ian Ferguson from St Mirren, possibly with an eye to eventually replacing the manager, for a whopping £850,000. When Mark Walters arrived from Aston Villa, it lifted Souness's spending in his two years at the club above the £6m mark.

At times it seemed hard to keep up with all the comings and goings, as another eight players left the club in 1987/88, some of whom Souness had only just signed. Described by Gough as a 'revolving door', and by others as 'permanent revolution', the turnover of the playing staff was remarkable. Francis lasted only four months, and exited without scoring a goal, Falco a little longer and there would be early departures for two other new arrivals in Mel Sterland and Kevin Drinkell, while Graham Roberts left the club under a cloud after telling the manager to 'fuck off'.

Clearly Souness was willing to discard those who didn't seem entirely at ease with his management style, but his dressing room psychopath reputation has to be qualified by the knowledge that it was often his players who would take the initiative in team disputes, particularly at half-time, if an individual was believed not to be pulling his weight. Souness describes how the verbal, and sometimes physical, dressing down by players such as Gough, Brown and Butcher would already be well under way by the time he arrived in the changing room, usually from his vantage point in the stand where he had been ordered to sit after a series of touchline bans, leaving the manager to merely observe while calmly drinking his half-time cup of tea, as the situation was resolved 'in-house'.

It was a dressing room culture and a style of management which wasn't to everyone's taste, even if it did prove effective at times, particularly when things were going well on the field, but it became more problematic during the difficult periods, when most of the arguments and fall-outs tended to occur. On the whole, however, these were few and far between during the Souness era; in 1987/88, an inspired Celtic team, under returning manager Billy McNeill, would win the league and cup Double in their centenary year, but in the grander scheme of things, it was only a temporary interruption to a period when Rangers held absolute dominance over the domestic game in Scotland.

It was a different story in Europe, however, as Rangers struggled to make an impact internationally over Souness's time in charge of the club. Not long after his appointment as Rangers' CEO, David Holmes had pledged that the club would do everything it could to bring the European Cup to Ibrox at some point in the near future. It was a tantalising promise, because no matter how many domestic honours Rangers won, the club's fans would always be envious of their rivals from across the city, who had secured the prestigious trophy, as well as Glasgow's European bragging rights, when Celtic famously defeated Inter Milan in the Lisbon final of the competition in 1967.

Souness was aware of the prestige and the importance to any big club of European football from his time at Liverpool and his heavily incentivised team had eventually qualified for the UEFA Cup for the start of the 1986/87 season. In the first European tie of the Souness era, in September 1986, Rangers were paired with the unknown Finnish side Ilves Tampere. A hat-trick from Robert Fleck at Ibrox helped the team to a 4-0 first leg victory and progress was assured despite a limp 2-0 defeat in front of barely 2,000 fans in Finland, meaning that Rangers would face Portuguese outfit Boavista in the next round.

Narrow home and away wins saw Rangers through to a third-round tie with Borussia Mönchengladbach, who held Rangers to a 1-1 draw at Ibrox, and then eliminated the Ibrox men on away goals following a tight, scoreless second leg in Germany. Their first foray into Europe under Souness had ended in November, but nevertheless Rangers were encouraged by what they considered to be an unlucky defeat against a strong German side. At Ibrox, a sloppy pass in midfield by Derek Ferguson, standing in for the injured manager, allowed Borussia to launch a counter-attack from which striker Rahn scored the crucial away goal, and in the return leg in the Bokelberg Stadium, Rangers had two players sent off, Cooper and Munro, and still managed not to concede, as the wily West Germans orchestrated their narrow win. The result came at a time when Scottish sides were still feared around Europe and Dundee United would show Rangers the way by reaching the final of the competition that season, with a run which included a 2-0 aggregate victory over Borussia in the semi-final, before the Taysiders were denied the trophy in the final by Gothenburg.

The following season, Souness's side won the league and qualified for the European Cup for the first time since the late 1970s. English clubs, who had dominated the tournament in Rangers' absence, were now banned from European competitions following the Heysel Stadium tragedy, for which Liverpool fans had been partially culpable. The subsequent ban had a deleterious effect on the strength of UEFA's flagship competition and many clubs including Rangers, in a particularly weak season for the tournament, sensed their opportunity to claim European football's ultimate prize.

Unfortunately, in the first round Rangers were drawn against the Soviet cracks Dynamo Kiev, one of the favourites for the competition, who had beaten Celtic with some ease the previous year on their way to the semi-final, where they had lost narrowly to the eventual champions, Porto. In the first leg in Kiev, in front of over 100,000 spectators, Souness played a containing game, with five men in midfield behind lone striker McCoist, and restricted the hosts to a 1-0 lead on the night, the game's only goal coming from the penalty spot, converted after 72 minutes by future Rangers player, Alexei Mikhailichenko. It had been a qualified success and Rangers had given themselves a chance for the return leg at Ibrox two weeks later. Perhaps in desperation, and in all probability sensing that if they could beat Kiev then the later rounds would hold no great fears for them, Souness resorted to the dubious tactic of narrowing the Ibrox pitch, from its customary width of 80 yards, to 70, the minimum allowed under the regulations.

Kiev were an eclectic, star-studded team, but Souness believed that their main threat came from their two wingers, both former European footballers of the year, the veteran Oleg Blokhin and his young apprentice Igor Belanov, who had excelled for the Soviet Union at the recent World Cup in Mexico. It may have been a questionable strategy, but it had the desired effect, and on a pulsating night at Ibrox, during which a frustrated Belanov had to be substituted, Rangers won 2-0 to progress to a second-round meeting with the Polish champions Gornik Zabrze. Strange as it may seem, certainly to modern fans of the convoluted Champions League, following a 4-2 aggregate win over the Poles, Rangers were through to the quarter-finals after only two rounds of the competition.

Their opponents in the spring would be Steaua Bucharest, who had won the European Cup in 1986, the first season following the English clubs' enforced absence, and the Romanians would reach the final again three years later in Barcelona, where ultimately they were handed a footballing lesson by Arrigo Sacchi's AC Milan, the first truly great European team to emerge since Heysel. Nevertheless, it was a time in the game's history when the talent pool in European football was spread more evenly across the continent, unlike today perhaps when it is concentrated in a few rich super-clubs, and Steaua were a team with some illustrious players, most notably winger Gheorghe Hagi and deep-lying striker Marius Lăcătuş.

Rangers lost the first leg 2-0 in Bucharest, and in the return at Ibrox, the home side were hampered by the ineligibility of four new signings, including winger Mark Walters. In addition, with the revolving door at Ibrox in full swing, Souness had sold two of his main attackers, Fleck and Falco, leaving McCoist as his only option in the striker's position for a game which Rangers needed to win by three clear goals. The manager's tendency to form impulsive, quick-tempered judgements on players had arguably cost his club on this occasion, as Rangers lost 3-2 on aggregate, and Souness's misery would be complete when an injury he aggravated in the second leg of the tie effectively ended his playing career.

Rangers' attempts on Europe subsequently petered out under Souness. In 1988/89 they were back in the UEFA Cup, suffering elimination in the second round at the hands of Cologne. The following year, they were knocked out of the European Cup in the first round by old foes Bayern Munich and in the season after that, Souness's final at the club, a 10-0 aggregate walkover against Valletta of Malta, by the end of which goalkeeper Chris Woods had been invited forward to take and subsequently miss a penalty, was followed by a second-round defeat, 4-1 on aggregate, at the hands of eventual champions Red Star Belgrade, after a 3-0 trouncing in Yugoslavia. 'How can I possibly win the European Cup with 11 Scots in the team?' Souness lamented after the defeat, an odd excuse given that less than half his team were Scottish. Despite the quarter-final appearance in 1988, by the time Souness left for pastures new in April 1991, Rangers were no closer to European glory than when he arrived at the club.

* * * *

By the start of 1988/89, Graeme Souness was beginning to gain the distinct impression from David Holmes that he was tiring of the continued spotlight on his joint roles as chief executive and now also chairman, and that his boss Lawrence Marlborough might be willing to sell his controlling interest in the club, particularly if Holmes was indeed close to packing it all in. When the manager eventually approached Holmes about the matter, his suspicions were confirmed and Souness immediately conveyed this information to his friend in Edinburgh, the businessman David Murray. In November 1988, after a series of meetings, Marlborough sold the club to a Murray-led consortium for £6m, with Murray himself taking a 70 per cent stake in the club and effectively becoming the new owner. The deal also involved taking on Rangers' overdraft, which, despite the vastly increased revenue generated over the previous two years, stood at an estimated £9m, chiefly as a result of the club's extravagant spending policy. The manager came in on the deal himself, investing enough of his personal wealth to make him the second largest shareholder at Rangers and putting him in the unique position of being player, manager, director and shareholder at the club.

Murray was another self-styled Thatcherite entrepreneur, the kind of which seemed to be popping up with increasing regularity in the late

1980s, with many going on to become involved in the football boom of the following decades, both north and south of the border. Despite hailing from Ayrshire, Murray was already an established part of the Edinburgh set and he had crossed paths with Souness almost as soon as the player returned to Scotland. Souness liked to use the Murray-owned Norton House Hotel near the city's airport to accommodate his squad and the pair soon became well acquainted.

Cultivating celebrity friendships would become an important part of the Murray mystique over the years ahead but, in this instance, he and Souness genuinely seemed to have plenty in common; contentious, egotistical, both men seemed to ooze belligerence from every pore, expressed in Souness through physical intimidation, while Murray's demeanour always smacked of the arrogance of money. True blue Tory boys, unlike David Holmes who had maintained his support for the Labour Party, it seemed like a marriage made in heaven when they embarked on the often risky venture of extending their established friendship into a business partnership.

Murray was born in Ayr in 1951, the son of a gambler and convicted fraudster. After his parents split up, he was forced to relinquish a private education at the exclusive Fettes College in Edinburgh, eventually leaving the nearby Broughton High School with five O Levels. At the age of 23, he formed a company, Murray International Metals, which traded in steel, and later, as his empire grew, his group of companies acquired the more corporate-friendly title of Murray International Holdings Ltd (MIH). Gradually over the years, the group's portfolio expanded into property, call centres, catering and even the media, although Murray's newspaper, the *Sunday Scot*, launched in partnership with Souness's old friend at *The Sun*, Jack Irvine, folded after only 18 weeks. In 1976, he lost both of his legs when he rolled his sports car, crashing into a tree at high speed after a tyre blowout on his way home from a rugby match. Using strips of cloth ripped from his jacket as tourniquets to staunch the bleeding, Murray's quick thinking saved his life, but his mangled legs were beyond repair and had to be amputated, leaving the young entrepreneur requiring the use of crutches for the rest of his life.

Around the same time, his father died and an early, unsuccessful business venture left him £100,000 out of pocket, but despite these setbacks, which he later admitted made him stronger and more determined, Murray was named Young Scottish Businessman of the Year in 1984. His interest in football had been piqued by Souness, and he had moved to acquire home town club Ayr United in early 1988, although his bid was rejected by the club's shareholders after manager Ally MacLeod, he of Argentina '78 fame, threatened to resign if the tycoon's offer was accepted. Murray had connections with the banking community in Edinburgh, and the Bank of Scotland, through its treasurer and managing director Gavin Masterton, had been lending money to Murray's companies as far back as 1981, when Murray became chairman of MIH.

The bank subsequently loaned the industrialist the necessary capital to acquire Rangers in November 1988, putting the club into the red right from the start of Murray's ownership. Throughout the 1990s and beyond, Bank of Scotland would lend Rangers ever more exorbitant sums of money, in an increasingly reckless and irresponsible manner, as the chairman's ambitions for the club seemed to grow exponentially with every trophy they acquired.

Souness was a hands-on manager, and after his joint acquisition of the club, he would now be running its affairs on a day to day basis, as initially, with David Holmes remaining chairman until the end of the season, Murray only came through to Glasgow when his presence was required, for matches and board meetings. Under the new regime at Rangers, the policy of speculate to accumulate continued, as the stadium underwent another facelift with a third tier added to the Main Stand, increasing the capacity to almost 50,000, and both the Govan and Main stands were furnished with a new array of executive boxes. In the same season, Souness signed a further three English players, including international right-back Gary Stevens from Everton for £1.25m, as Rangers regained the league title, notching up emphatic 5-1 and 4-1 wins over Celtic at Ibrox along the way.

However, with the Treble in sight, the Ibrox men lost the Scottish Cup Final to their old rivals, when Stevens's short back-pass let in Joe Miller to score the only goal of the game, as the famous old trophy continued to elude Souness. Undaunted, the spending increased the following season as the manager brought in Trevor Steven from Everton for £1.525m and Maurice Johnston from Nantes for £1.25m. Youngster Chris Vinnicombe arrived from Exeter and former Chelsea and Liverpool man Nigel Spackman came in from QPR, both for half a million pounds, with Rangers subsequently going on to retain the title for the first time since 1976.

On it went: in 1990/91, Rangers spent £500,000 to acquire England international Mark Hateley from Monaco. Unwanted back in his homeland, centre-forward Hateley had enjoyed spells in France and Italy at a time when a number of continental sides were experimenting with the idea of using a more physical and direct, British style of play on the back of successive English triumphs in the European Cup, before the post-Heysel ban allowed them to return to their traditional methods. Rangers, however, would be stung by criticism of their unsophisticated tactics, epitomised at this time by their strategy of playing long balls up to strongman Hateley and relying on his scurrying partner, initially Johnston then later McCoist, to win the second balls.

In response, the club started to add a more exotic mix around this period, with the signing of Oleg Kuznetsov from Dynamo Kiev for £1.2m and the spending policy continued with the capture of Peter Huistra from Twente Enschede in Holland and Brian Reid from Morton, while hammer-thrower Terry Hurlock arrived from Millwall. Rangers received some money from the sales of Terry Butcher, who had fallen out with the manager after giving an interview to the banned broadcaster STV, to Coventry for £500,000 and Derek Ferguson to Hearts for £750,000. In total, in just under five years at the club, Souness had spent £15.375m and recouped £6.375m in player sales. It's easy to be dismissive of such sums, given the eye-watering level of today's transfer fees, but the amount Souness was spending can be put into context when one considers that the club itself changed hands for a mere £6m in 1988. During roughly the same period, Souness and Rangers had spent more than Alex Ferguson at Manchester United and Kenny Dalglish at Liverpool, but it would just be the start of the journey for the ambitious Ibrox club.

For Souness, however, it was the end of the road; he left Rangers four weeks before the end of the 1991 season to take over as boss of his former team Liverpool. The Anfield board had identified Souness as the ideal candidate to take up the vacant manager's position at the Merseyside club, following the unexpected resignation of Kenny Dalglish in late February, but initially the Ibrox man turned down the approach, and re-emphasised publicly his long-term commitment to Rangers. Curiously however, Souness seemed to have undergone a change of heart in the six weeks since he was first offered the Liverpool job, and by early April he had accepted the position with his former club. The original intention had been for Souness to see out the remainder of the season with Rangers, but when news of his impending departure broke, David Murray insisted that he leave immediately and told him it was a decision he would come to regret.

Several theories have since been advanced as to why Souness eventually made up his mind to quit Ibrox. He arrived at Rangers looking to throw his weight about, but by the time he left, he was very much a marked man, complaining that he seemed to have a target on his back almost everywhere he went. During his time as a player, opponents, aware of his short fuse, would constantly try to wind him up, and Souness also claimed that he was targeted by referees, an idea which was publicly supported by his assistant Walter Smith. To be sure, the SFA offered no leniency for his repeated aberrations; by the end of his first year in Scotland, Souness had been hit with a total of three separate suspensions for his various on-field misdemeanours, and at the start of the following season he received his third red card as a Rangers player for a ridiculous lunge at Billy Stark in a match against Celtic at Celtic Park. Stark, who was attempting to retrieve a lost boot at the time of Souness's challenge, had earlier scored what proved to be the only goal of the game on his Old Firm debut, when he was upended by Souness, who had already been cautioned at the time.

The player-manager continued to argue with the referee, David Syme, after the game, calling him a 'big fucking poof', for which he was issued with a further two technical red cards, resulting in a five-match ban. Very much the author of his own misfortune on this occasion, Souness was apparently so upset by the whole incident that he was threatening to walk out of Scottish football there and then, until David Holmes intervened and talked him round.

If his disciplinary track record as a player in Scotland was poor, Souness found that his problems were about to get a whole lot worse once he hung up his boots. After a draw against Dundee United at Tannadice in February 1989, the Ibrox manager was called to appear before the SFA's Disciplinary and Referee Committee, where he was issued with a touchline ban through until the end of the season for abusive language towards a linesman. However, when Rangers met St Johnstone in the Scottish Cup semi-final at Celtic Park in April, Souness was spotted lurking in the dugout area, trying to communicate with his physiotherapist Phil Boersma, and consequently his suspension was extended until the end of the following season.

In effect, it was a year-long ban, but at times the manager seemed almost casually indifferent to his increasing raft of touchline exclusion orders, and he would often name himself as a substitute in an effort to circumvent the rules. There could be no chicanery however, when, during a televised game between Hearts and Rangers at Ibrox in February 1990, the cameras caught Souness loitering with intent in the tunnel area, while his ban was still very much in effect. Nobody seemed to have noticed the offence, but still images, lifted from the television coverage, of the manager defying his suspension were subsequently published in the *Daily Record*, and Souness found himself the subject of another ban, this time extending all the way until the end of 1991/92.

The SFA admitted that he was testing their disciplinary procedures to the limit and, in the event of any further misconduct, Souness was potentially looking at the prospect of the ultimate sanction, a lifetime ban. He was also copping increasingly hefty fines for his indiscretions, from zero, effectively a warning for a first offence, in December 1987, through to £100 for comments to the referee after a game against Aberdeen in January 1989. Subsequently the level of financial penalty increased to £1,000, then £2,000, for the Dundee United and St Johnstone breaches, and finally £5,000 for his transgression against Hearts.

Souness was furious about what had transpired at the Hearts game and he vented his anger in particular at Scottish Television, whom he accused of deliberately trying to set him up, after the incriminating shots were included in their edited highlights package on *Scotsport*. It was an irrational response on Souness's part, but the Rangers manager refused to cooperate with STV for the remainder of his stay in Scotland, often extending the veto to the entire ITV network in case any interviews or other material should be picked up and shown by the Scottish franchise.

The late 1980s were a time when the media were far less powerful than they are today, before the money ploughed into football by television companies ensured that they virtually ran the game in Britain, and Souness was able to continue his concerted campaigns against individuals and organisations in the industry with more or less complete impunity. It didn't take much to upset him, as he was always prickly and sensitive to criticism, and on one occasion he called James Traynor, a reporter who had questioned his tactics against Red Star Belgrade for an article in *The Herald*, a 'wee socialist shite'. The journalist later remarked that thereafter the socialism continued in his articles, as did, occasionally, the shite at Rangers. Traynor would later go on to serve as the Ibrox club's PR chief.

Souness's most famous fallout, however, was with a tea lady by the name of Aggie Moffat who worked for St Johnstone. After a dull, midweek draw in Perth in February 1991, so the story goes, the manager was smashing up the away dressing room at Muirton Park in his customary fashion, when in walked 'wee Aggie', who clearly wasn't best pleased to see, amid the mess, one of her favourite jugs in bits on the floor. It was fairly evident who the culprit was, and, in the eyes of Aggie, the Ibrox manager had form for such behaviour after an earlier confrontation between the pair on Rangers' previous visit to Perth.

On that occasion, Souness's mood was not helped by the fact that one of his new signings, Oleg Kuznetsov, had been seriously injured in only his second appearance for the club, ruling him out for the rest of the season and Aggie appeared, to Souness at least, to be somewhat unsympathetic as to the Ukrainian defender's condition. This time round, the animosity threatened to get physical, and when Aggie picked up the smashed crockery, intending to show it to her chairman Geoff Brown, Souness pursued her up the stairs. The incident ended with Souness, manager and also a director of Rangers Football Club, confronting the St Johnstone chairman and offering him outside.

Incredibly, Souness admitted in his subsequent autobiography that the incident in Perth, coming at a time when he had already been offered and declined the Liverpool job, played a role in changing his mind and hastening his departure from Ibrox. Fortunately, chairman Brown decided against taking the matter further, otherwise Souness would have been in more hot water, but the Rangers manager did make disparaging remarks about the referee in his post-match interviews, for which he received another summons to the SFA headquarters at Park Gardens. The media couldn't resist the Aggie story, but played it down as a 'storm in a teacup', and they ignored the coda incident with

Brown completely. Nevertheless, perhaps for the first time, Souness appeared to question his own conduct following the whole affair and it played a part in his subsequent decision to reconsider the offer from Anfield.

But there were other factors in his decision to leave Rangers. At the press conference confirming his departure, Souness cited personal reasons following the break-up of his marriage in 1988, after which his ex-wife had moved to Cheshire with their children. He also claimed, more enigmatically, that he believed he had taken Rangers as far as he would be allowed to go, a reference perhaps to Murray's recent decision to intervene more regularly in transfer-related business, after the chairman vetoed the signing of Andy Goram from Hibs. Souness then walked out of the press conference, claiming that he was too emotional to take further questions, and leaving Murray to tell the media, 'He's making the biggest mistake of his life.'

Once he was safely out of Scotland, Souness also revealed further clues to his decision-making process, when he admitted he was 'tired of all the politics and the bigotry associated with football in Scotland'. Whatever his reasons, having eventually made up his mind to join Liverpool, Souness was ushered towards the Ibrox exit door with four games of the season remaining.

Sadly, David Murray's prediction would be proved essentially correct and Souness's time back on Merseyside turned out to be something of a fiasco. At Liverpool, he went for the tried and trusted method of shelling out massive transfer fees for supposedly star players, but his signings didn't work out and overall opposing teams in England were far harder to bully and intimidate into submission and were less impressed by the publicity and hype surrounding his transfer dealings than had been the case in Scotland. In the process, Souness's iconoclastic tendencies, such an essential part of his success at Rangers, proved disastrous at Anfield, as his dictatorial approach and his drive to modernise effectively destroyed the culture of the Anfield boot room, the modest sanctuary where, since the days of Bill Shankly, the Liverpool coaching staff would retire to commune over pertinent issues, scheming and plotting the success behind the whole football operation at the club. Just to emphasise the point, the directors at Anfield had the boot room demolished to make way for a new media centre.

On the field, Souness's new team struggled, playing an unpopular brand of football that was not considered to be in the Liverpool tradition, but his gravest offence, which led to ruinous unpopularity in the eyes of the Anfield club's supporters, stemmed from his relationship with Margaret Thatcher's favourite newspaper, *The Sun*. The Rupert Murdoch-owned tabloid was despised on Merseyside, after the paper's biased and politically motivated coverage of the Hillsborough disaster, when it had wrongly blamed Liverpool supporters for being the main cause of the accident, falsely accusing the Scousers of being overwhelmingly drunk on the day, of fighting with the brave cops and of robbing and pissing on the dead. Subsequently, there had been campaigns on Merseyside to stop people from buying the paper and its circulation in the area soon plummeted. *The Sun* had always been a favourite of Souness's however, and he decided to give the paper the inside story of his triple heart by-pass operation, which was published, along with a picture of the manager in a flagrant embrace with his new girlfriend, the model Karen Levy, with appalling timing on the third anniversary of the disaster.

Souness was suffering from health problems, in all probability brought on by the stress and over-exertion which typified his lifestyle and his approach to his work, combined with his total inability to unwind. He had, his doctors reckoned, already suffered a heart attack without even realising and, still not yet 40 years of age, three of his main arteries were so clogged up that he required immediate surgery. The operation involved inserting tubes around the damaged arteries to do the job of taking the flow of blood away from the heart and circulating it to the main organs of the body, and, showing a remarkable degree of insensitivity, Souness had agreed to give the exclusive story of his condition to the proscribed right-wing tabloid, a decision which provoked a furious backlash from Liverpool supporters. Speaking recently of how he would describe his current relations with the city and with fans of the club he served with such distinction as a player, he lamented, 'Permanently damaged. I think I'll remain unpopular there and that's the price I'll have to pay. I made an error of judgement but I can only apologise so many times. I'm just going to have to live with that.'

Souness went on to manage other big clubs after three years of relative failure at Liverpool, but his obnoxious style had been found out and he was at best only a qualified success in his short spells at Galatasaray and Benfica. At Southampton, he kept the club in the Premier League, which was a considerable achievement, and later he had decent spells at Blackburn, leading them to promotion, and Newcastle, before quitting football management altogether. Souness's list of honours away from Rangers comprises three cups, one each at Liverpool, Blackburn and in Turkey with Galatasaray, where his confrontational tendencies were soon evident again. After defeating great rivals Fenerbahçe in the two-legged Turkish Cup Final, Souness ran on to the field and planted a huge Galatasaray flag in the centre circle of the away ground, almost provoking a riot in the stadium. He was soon fired.

David Murray's prediction about Souness coming to regret his decision to leave Ibrox was based on the owner's conceit that Rangers were the biggest club in Britain, rather than shrewd footballing analysis, something which remained beyond the businessman, despite the length of time he spent in the game. Souness later admitted, however, that his friend had been essentially correct, and Rangers remain the highlight of Graeme Souness's managerial career.

'Some say he is evil,' observed Ron Atkinson, while Jack Charlton suggested he had a 'nasty streak'. Even Murray admitted that Souness was an 'acquired taste' and 'not everyone's cup of tea', while Aggie Moffat, the St Johnstone tea lady, described him more succinctly as a 'plonker'.

In fairness, Souness has mellowed in recent years, perhaps as a result of his health scare – wisdom coming too late perhaps for Scottish football – and he can frequently be heard castigating himself in interviews for his naivety and arrogance during his spell at Rangers, while particular contrition is reserved for the upset caused on Merseyside by his *Sun* story.

Whatever view one takes of him, there is no doubt that Graeme Souness's five-year tenure of the Ibrox hotseat had wide-ranging and lasting repercussions for the whole of Scottish and even British football, which were still being felt many years later. The 'Souness revolution', as it became known, should have been a short, sharp injection to turn the club around and revitalise a struggling former giant of the Scottish game, but with a clear endgame in sight from the start. With interest regenerated, and the average attendance at Rangers soaring back up towards 40,000, and with sponsorship and sportswear deals pouring money into the club's coffers, the bank loans should have been paid back over time, and a level playing field restored, both on and off the park. Instead, in the years ahead, rather than return the club to proper governance, David Murray, drunk on success, ran Rangers as if he was on a one-man quest to indulge his ego, taking the club ever deeper into debt to its increasingly indulgent bankers, with no apparent regard for the long-term consequences.

Ultimately, Murray and Rangers inhaled too deeply, and, flying too close to the sun like Icarus, came subsequently crashing back to earth, almost bringing the whole of Scottish football down with them.

9

NINE! NINE! NINE!

THE immediate and most important task facing Walter Smith, following his appointment as Rangers manager on 19 April 1991, three days after the unexpected departure of Graeme Souness, was to maintain his team's position at the top of the Premier Division table and, with four games of the season remaining, to see the club over the line and ensure the retention of the league championship.

Rangers were involved in a tight title race with a resurgent Aberdeen team, which went down to the final day and a head-to-head, winner-takes-all meeting between the pair at Ibrox. At one point it had looked a certainty for the Glasgow side, but, ever since the infamous incident between Souness and the tea lady at St Johnstone, Rangers' form had been patchy and they were hampered by injuries and in particular suspensions, as the perennial issue of indiscipline, which Souness seemed to have finally brought under control, returned at the worst possible moment for the club.

In March, during a 2-0 Scottish Cup quarter-final defeat to Celtic at Celtic Park, three Rangers players were sent off; Englishmen Hurlock, Walters and Hateley were all red-carded for violent offences, as the match slipped away from Souness's men, after Celtic's Grant had initially been dismissed for encroachment. The two teams then met again a week later in a league encounter at the same venue, when another Rangers player, defender Scott Nisbet, received his marching orders, resulting this time in a 3-0 rout. Further points were dropped in early April after a goalless home draw with lowly Hibernian, in one of Souness's last games in charge of the club. Aberdeen, on the other hand, were flying. Since a defeat to Celtic on 18 January, they had embarked on an unbeaten run of 12 games, chalking up 11 wins and a draw, including a 1-0 victory over Souness's men at Pittodrie in early March. With just ten games of the season remaining, the gap between the teams extended to fully seven points, but the Dons had succeeded in gradually reducing the deficit and were now back in serious contention by the time of Smith's appointment.

The new Rangers manager won his first two games in charge of the club, as a nervy, error-strewn tussle with St Mirren in Paisley, settled by a late strike from youngster Sandy Robertson, was followed four days later by a close victory over Dundee United by the same scoreline, 1-0 at Ibrox. But with the finishing line in sight, Smith's side lost heavily, 3-0 away to Motherwell in the penultimate game of the season. The margin of defeat was potentially crucial as Aberdeen, managed by the astute Alex Smith, completed a narrow win over St Johnstone and, with the two sides now level on points and goal difference, the Dons moved to the top of the league due to their superior tally of goals scored and now only needed a draw in the final fixture to secure their first title of the post-Alex Ferguson era.

For the decider, Aberdeen would be without key defender Brian Irvine through injury as well as first-choice goalkeeper Theo Snelders, while Rangers were missing a number of important players such as Gough and Trevor Steven. With a lack of available alternatives, Smith was also forced to name both McCoist and Durrant as substitutes, despite neither being fully match fit, although sympathy for the Ibrox men was limited due to the amount of money they had spent on their team, with expensive imports such as Peter Huistra not even listed in the matchday squad.

Aberdeen started the game strongly, and were arguably the better side in the first half. They missed a clear chance to take the lead when Peter van de Ven shot straight at Woods after being put through on goal by McKimmie, and fellow Dutchman and top scorer Hans Gilhaus then headed Stephen Wright's cross over the bar from inside the six-yard box. Rangers grew into the game and five minutes before half-time, in front of a raucous Ibrox crowd, Hateley rose above McLeish to power a trademark header beyond Watt. The English striker had tried to unsettle Aberdeen's inexperienced young goalkeeper, targeting him for some rough treatment early in the game, as he later explained to the *Daily Record*, 'Top strikers try to identify the weakest link in a defence, whether it's a full-back, centre-half or a goalkeeper… Their keeper that day was a young lad and he was playing in the biggest day of his career in front of 52,000 [sic] screaming fans. I battered him that day. It was something which came about literally when we were in the tunnel before the game. I said to Gary Stevens that if he could put over one of his normal crosses, hang it up there, don't pick anyone out and just give me a chance to get in and make a challenge. I was up against the likes of Alex McLeish so their young keeper was the one to pinpoint.'

The home side extended their advantage early in the second half when a defensive mistake by substitute Scott Booth let in Hateley again, and he pounced from a suspiciously offside position on to a Johnston shot which had been spilled by Watt. Despite the capacity at Ibrox being reduced to 37,000, due to further renovations of the stadium, Booth describes the atmosphere on the day as the most hostile he has ever played in front of, 'I remember coming on at half-time and finding it hard to concentrate. It was just absolutely deafening. Guys like myself and Michael Watt, I think it's quite natural if we were slightly overawed by it all.' Booth went on to enjoy spells in Holland and Germany with Twente Enschede and Borussia Dortmund, and played 22 times for Scotland, but Michael Watt's career never fully recovered. He failed to live up to his early potential and, by the time he turned 30, he had left football altogether and was pursuing a career in financial services in Glasgow.

Two crucial goals in such a decisive game led to Hateley's belated acceptance by the Rangers supporters, after fans had initially been sceptical about the player, blaming him for keeping McCoist out of the team, although in reality it was Johnston who had relegated their favourite to the bench. The big English striker later admitted that his bulging eyes, fist-pumping celebrations that day were a 'get-it-right-up-you' gesture towards the old East Enclosure, a frightening bear pit under the Main Stand at Ibrox, where the most recalcitrant Rangers diehards were housed, in the only remaining standing area left inside the ground. Aberdeen's challenge flickered and died, and despite having to make readjustments when Cowan and Brown suffered serious injuries, Rangers saw the game out to take their third title in a row. Brian Irvine later admitted, 'It was pretty agonising to watch... if we'd got a goal early, it would have been a whole different game... When Rangers got their goal, it gave them confidence and it just drifted away from us.' It was the closest any team outside of Rangers and Celtic would come to winning the league in the modern era.

According to Hateley, the next four days were an alcoholic blur, with the striker describing the subsequent celebrations as 'carnage'. In particular, it was a triumph for the new manager, and the result led to his quick acceptance among the many who had doubted his suitability for the job. Despite the success that he would go on to enjoy, Smith was not an inevitable choice to succeed Souness, despite serving as his assistant for the previous five years. A self-effacing character, he was a relatively low-profile figure at the time, with plenty of coaching but no managerial experience, and he seemed to be shocked that he was even in contention for the vacant position. 'When the news broke, David Murray phoned me up and I went to see him the next day. He said that Graeme's departure had caught him unawares and that it would take him a few days to make up his mind,' Smith later recollected. 'That took me by surprise, because I realised that he was considering me for the job.'

Smith had, however, turned down the opportunity to join Souness and Phil Boersma at Liverpool, so he may have harboured hopes that he was at least in contention for a next-in-line promotion. In the end, Murray stuck to the promised timescale and Smith's appointment was confirmed within three days. Behind the scenes, the chairman had sought advice and considered the possibility of approaching a candidate with a better track record, but regardless of how much time he had to canvass opinion and complete a thorough due diligence on his new manager, Smith was the correct choice. An external appointment at such a late stage of the season could have been disruptive, whereas with Smith it was almost business as usual. Another option, delaying a final decision and installing Smith as caretaker manager until the end of the season, might have been the more prudent approach, but Murray was in no mood for equivocation and the advice he was receiving was that the assistant manager was ready to make the step up.

Smith was a popular appointment, particularly with the players, who welcomed some respite from all the head-banging and the shouting matches involved in Souness's more bellicose approach. Most were glad to see the back of the now former manager and the squad initially responded at least as much to Souness's absence as Smith's promotion, although the change of mindset involved in seeing a former assistant step out of the old boss's shadow and become the new gaffer was perhaps a factor in their struggle to hold on to the title. Gough also hinted at the relief that was felt elsewhere at Souness's departure. 'Walter's no soft touch but he's a bit different, and that will go a long way to helping our difficulties with the SFA and the press,' the captain admitted. Joining Smith at Ibrox as his assistant would be Archie Knox, the man who used to walk into the boot-room at Pittodrie carrying a baseball bat. Knox had been Ferguson's number two at both Aberdeen and Manchester United, and the Old Trafford supremo wasn't best pleased when Smith pinched his long-serving assistant on the eve of United's biggest game for many years, the Cup Winners' Cup Final against Barcelona in Rotterdam.

Smith was born in Lanark in 1948 and grew up in the Glasgow suburb of Carmyle, an isolated, almost rural enclave to the east of the city. He was taken to see Rangers as a boy by his grandfather and later admitted that he sang sectarian songs from the terraces of the old Ibrox. Like so many others from his background at that time, Smith had eschewed pop culture and Beatlemania while growing up during the Swinging Sixties in favour of an orthodox attachment to the old school Rangers traditions, and what his biographer, Neil Drysdale, euphemistically refers to as the club's 'cussed refusal to become trendy'.

As a teenager he signed for Dundee United from Junior side Ashfield in 1966, but failed to make the breakthrough to regular first team football. On the day of the Ibrox disaster, in January 1971, Smith was not named in United's squad and was consequently free to attend the match in Glasgow, missing the fatal crush at the end of the game along with his brother by only a few minutes. Even at a very early stage in his career, Smith had showed an interest in coaching, which was encouraged by Jerry Kerr, and by his long-serving successor in the Tannadice hotseat, Jim McLean, who invited Smith on to his staff in 1977, when a pelvic injury threatened to end the defender's playing days at the age of just 29. In the early 1980s, Smith combined his position as McLean's deputy with youth coaching roles, working under future Scotland manager Andy Roxburgh and leading the Scotland under-18 side to victory at the European Youth Championships in Finland in 1982, before moving on to the under-21s and then serving as Ferguson's assistant at the World Cup in Mexico in 1986.

McLean and Smith were a formidable combination at United, the manager's notorious dourness and inflexibility seeming to fit with his assistant's outlook as well. Smith wore the look of a man who would take no nonsense from anyone, but beneath his brooding, po-faced exterior, he nurtured a steely determination and a ferocious competitive instinct, another characteristic he shared with McLean. The pair were not averse to using physical intimidation and even violence towards their own squad in order to enforce discipline; one of Smith's favoured techniques was to lock himself in the dressing room with an errant player and offer him the first punch. Former United forward Kevin Gallacher remembers, 'Walter got me in the Tannadice boot-room and gave me what for. I was lucky because the room was small and he could only jab you there. If you were really unfortunate, Walter would get you in the gym and there was enough room for full-blooded punches to be thrown. He was absolutely ferocious when he was angry and the players feared him even more than they did McLean.'

With such an able enforcer at his side, McLean led Dundee United to League Cup success in December 1979 and, in 1983, with Smith now the assistant manager, to the Premier Division title, the first and only championship success in the club's history. The following year, United reached the European Cup semi-final, where, after beating Roma 2-0 at Tannadice, they were defeated 3-0 in the return leg at a hostile Olympic Stadium in somewhat mysterious circumstances – it was later revealed that Roma president, Giuseppe Viola, had attempted to bribe the referee – and consequently missed out on the opportunity to face Liverpool in a battle of Britain showdown in the final at the same venue.

By 1986, Smith was regarded as one of the better young coaches working in Scotland and, given his boyhood allegiances and his knowledge of the Scottish scene, he was an excellent and obvious choice to serve as assistant to Souness, who was not only unfamiliar with the local, domestic game, but he had, by his own admission, no clear idea of what he was letting himself in for when he agreed to become Rangers manager in April 1986.

Smith and Souness knew each other well from the Scotland set-up and the new assistant recognised that, as deputy to Souness, he would have to play a subtly different role from the bad cop/worse cop routine he had mastered under McLean; McLean had a notoriously short fuse, but Souness was like a smouldering volcano, which could blow its stack and erupt at any moment and Smith learned to complement his boss at Ibrox, picking up the loose ends, arbitrating the training sessions and expanding on the manager's notoriously short pre-match addresses with useful tactical advice. Inevitably, most of the credit for winning the league in 1991 went to the departed Souness, but the title-clinching victory over Aberdeen helped Smith establish himself in his new role and the following season, he set out from scratch to succeed on his own.

The manager began to reshape his squad with Trevor Steven, Chris Woods, Mark Walters, Terry Hurlock, Nigel Spackman and Maurice Johnston all leaving the club, while Rangers' penchant for exotic, expensive signings continued with the arrival of Soviet international midfielder Alexei Mikhailichenko, signed from Sampdoria for a tidy £2.2m, who joined his compatriot Oleg Kuznetsov at Ibrox. Smith realised, however, that UEFA's recently introduced 'three plus two' foreigner rule would be a hindrance to the club's European ambitions going forward and, with a squad bloated with non-Scots in the pre-Bosman era, he signed 'native' Scottish players Stuart McCall, David Robertson and goalkeeper Andy Goram, who immediately supplanted the discarded Woods. Rangers also continued to recruit from the English market, although there was concern that Smith would not be able to attract the same profile of player to Ibrox as his predecessor, as Dale Gordon and Paul Rideout arrived.

The departure of Maurice Johnston, after just two years at the club, paved the way for Hateley to be partnered in attack with McCoist, who was brought in from the cold by the new manager and given a new lease of life. Distrusted by Souness for his off-field misdemeanours, the Scottish striker had previously been dubbed 'the judge', because of the number of times he found himself sitting on the bench. Often known for his jovial Jack-the-lad image, which he liked to play up to, McCoist in reality was a tenacious, sometimes nasty competitor, with a tough winner's mentality. He went on to become an established part of the Rangers firmament and, benefitting greatly from Hateley's knock-downs, he won the European Golden Boot in 1992 and again in 1993, scoring an impressive 34 goals in each season.

Smith's Rangers swept all before them, with the club collecting a fourth consecutive title and, while there was disappointment in the League Cup after a semi-final defeat to Hibs, and in Europe with a low-key elimination to Sparta Prague on away goals, the Ibrox men recaptured the Scottish Cup for the first time in 11 years with a routine win over Airdrie in the Hampden final. The real struggle, however, had been in the semi-final against Celtic when a Rangers team reduced to ten men, after the early ordering off of David Robertson for a cynical challenge on his former Aberdeen team-mate Joe Miller, held on for a 1-0 win, despite a second-half pummelling from the Parkhead side.

Intriguingly, midfielder Stuart McCall later cited that win at a rain-soaked Hampden, rather than the title-clinching victory over Aberdeen the previous season, as the making of Walter Smith's team. It's a revealing admission; Celtic, struggling domestically at the time under Liam Brady, threw absolutely everything at their old rivals that night, leaving rope-a-dope Rangers hanging on defiantly after McCoist's counter-attacking strike just before half-time. Incredibly, years later, assistant manager Archie Knox admitted that he had paid the Rangers-supporting ball boys at half-time to counter the Celtic onslaught by delaying the retrieval of the ball when it went out of play. Grim determination, defensive bloody-mindedness and even bending the rules to their advantage would come to characterise Smith's teams in the years ahead, and the tone had been set.

The following year, in only his second full season in charge of the club, Rangers won the Treble under Smith, beating Aberdeen into second place in all three competitions, with the Ibrox side finishing nine points ahead of the Dons in the league and defeating them in both cup finals, 2-1 on each occasion. Extra time was required to separate the teams in an evenly fought League Cup Final in October, in the last match played at the old Hampden, before the destiny of the trophy was decided by a late own goal from the unfortunate Gary Smith, who had performed well in nullifying the threat from McCoist for the previous 114 minutes of the contest. Trevor Steven had returned from Marseille, in a good bit of business for the club, and he helped the team chalk up a 44 match unbeaten run over a seven-month period, including eight games unbeaten in Europe. Smith also signed Scotland international defender Dave McPherson, who was reacquired from Hearts after initially leaving Ibrox in 1987, and the home-grown contingent – players who were eligible in Europe – was augmented by the emergence of striker Gary McSwegan alongside defenders Neil Murray and Steven Pressley, as the club put in a serious challenge on the continent for the first time in many years.

Although the format of the competition had been altered the previous year to include group stages for the first time, 1992/93 saw the official introduction of the Champions League, rebranded from the old European Cup. In the first round, Rangers breezed past Danish outfit Lyngby, 3-0 on aggregate, to set up an intriguing second round play-off tie with Leeds United, the last English champions of the old First Division, recently abolished in favour of the money-spinning Premier League. With Scotsmen Gordon Strachan and Gary McAllister featuring in the English side, and Englishmen Steven, Gordon and Hateley all involved for the Scots, even by the expected standards of media cliché, the hype surrounding the 'Battle of Britain' clash was considerable, on both sides of the border. The Scottish press were firmly behind their Ibrox favourites, while their supercilious English counterparts, condescending to cover a Scottish side and coming across the lugubrious Smith for the first time, were moved to recall P.G. Wodehouse's unkind, but perhaps in this case merited aphorism, 'It is never difficult to distinguish between a Scotsman with a grievance and a ray of sunshine.'

With away fans banned from both matches, McAllister stunned a raucous Ibrox in the first minute of the tie, firing home a thunderous volley from the edge of the box, and Leeds should have increased their advantage shortly afterwards when Strachan's effort, following a neat one-two with Gary Speed, was wrongly disallowed for offside. Gradually Rangers grew into the game, and after a series of corners Leeds goalkeeper Lukic punched the ball into his own net, which, the local press boys noted with some amusement, put an end to the perennial English jibes about Scottish goalkeepers. A second shaky moment from Lukic at another corner allowed McCoist to pounce and the first leg finished 2-1 in Rangers' favour.

At Elland Road, Leeds believed that their away goal would prove decisive, and their confidence was once again shared by large sections of the English media, whose dismissal of his side's chances irritated Smith to such an extent that he marched into the away dressing room before the game, threw a pile of newspaper clippings on the floor, and, in lieu of a rousing pre-match address, simply told his players, 'If that doesn't motivate you, then nothing will.'

In a mirror image of the first leg, Hateley, who had been overlooked by English clubs as his contract ran down at Monaco and whose form in Scotland had failed to earn him a return to his country's national team, clipped in a spectacular volley from distance early in the game. The big striker then set up his partner McCoist for the crucial second goal on the counter-attack, which rendered Cantona's late consolation effectively meaningless.

With the gracious Elland Road crowd applauding them from the field, many of the Rangers players, in spite of the success the club would go on to enjoy over this period, later recalled the double header victory over Leeds as one of the highlights of their careers. They had beaten the English champions home and away in front of a UK-wide audience, most of whom had written them off before a ball had even been kicked as the champions of a Mickey Mouse league. It was a considerable achievement for the Scottish side, but not one they could afford to dwell on as the club progressed to the group stages, which were set to get under way later in November.

The eight qualified teams were divided into two groups of four, with Rangers drawn against Marseille, Bruges and CSKA Moscow, who had eliminated holders Barcelona in the previous round. It looked like a decent grouping from Rangers' point of view, but with only one team qualifying from the section, the Ibrox men's chances looked doomed when, in the first game at home to Marseille, they found themselves two goals down to arguably the most talented team in the tournament.

The French champions were considered one of the favourites for the competition, with renowned international performers such as Desailly, Deschamps and Barthez in their ranks, as well as foreign strikers Bokšić and Völler, whose goals shot the visitors into a half-time lead. With McCoist injured and having watched his team being outplayed for most of the match on a soggy Ibrox pitch, Smith threw on another tall striker in McSwegan, as Rangers began to bombard the Marseille penalty box. The ploy worked as late headed goals from McSwegan and Hateley brought Smith's side level and the match finished 2-2.

Rangers were well and truly back in contention when they defeated CSKA Moscow in the next game, with the former Soviet army team forced to play their 'home' fixture, due to the harsh conditions of the Russian winter, in Bochum, Germany. Then in the spring, Rangers faced a double header against Bruges, drawing the first game in Belgium and winning the return 2-1 at Ibrox, despite being reduced to ten men after Hateley was ordered off. The winner in the second half was an extraordinary fluke from defender Scott Nisbet, as the ball from his deflected cross-cum-shot flew up into the air, caught the breeze and looped down into the net after bouncing over the goalkeeper's head.

The only disappointment was the red card issued to Hateley, which meant that the striker would be suspended for the rest of the campaign. Having enjoyed a fruitful spell against Marseille when he was a player at Monaco, the Englishman maintains to this day that the referee, Ryszard Wójcik from Poland, was bribed by the French club's crooked president, Bernard Tapie, who was later found guilty of match-fixing and sent to prison for six months.

Without Hateley in the side for what Smith described as the club's biggest game in Europe for 30 years, Rangers managed a creditable draw in the Stade Velodrome, when a shot from Durrant equalised Franck Sauzée's opening strike, and the Ibrox side were still confident of reaching the final going into the concluding game. With Marseille top of the group on goal difference, Rangers needed Bruges to do them a favour against the leaders, and there was certainly no love lost between the Belgians and the French side, while the Ibrox men took care of CSKA in Glasgow. In the end though, a disappointing draw against the Russians, combined with Marseille's 1-0 victory in Belgium, saw Rangers eliminated and Marseille progress to a final meeting with AC Milan in Munich.

However, it was around this time that scandal began to engulf the French champions and in particular Bernard Tapie, the club's controversial owner and president. Tapie was later convicted of instigating the bribery of three players from lowly Valenciennes, including striker Jorge Burruchaga, who had netted the winning goal for Argentina in the World Cup Final in 1986. With the club closing in on their fifth consecutive French title and despite the fixture being brought forward to clear the weekend and allow his team more time to prepare for the Champions League Final, Tapie wanted to ensure that Valenciennes would 'take their foot off the gas' against his team, in their last domestic game before the meeting with Milan in Munich six days later.

The plot, however, was revealed the next day, when 250,000 French francs were found in an envelope at the house of the in-laws of Valenciennes player Christophe Robert, a former team-mate of Marseille's Jean-Jacques Eydelie, who was the alleged intermediary in Tapie's scam. In a season in which they both soared to new heights and plunged to unprecedented depths, Marseille went on to beat AC Milan 1-0 in the inaugural Champions League Final, the only goal coming from the head of defender Basile Boli just before half-time. Marseille consequently became the first French side to lift the European Cup, but it didn't spare them in their disgrace, as the club were stripped of the French title and demoted to Ligue 2, but despite these sanctions and the disrepute which was overwhelming the club, UEFA took no further action against Marseille and their title as European champions of 1993 was allowed to stand.

Rangers had made a name for themselves in the competition, as the Ibrox men came close to reaching the final, playing a minimum of eight players affiliated to Scotland under the new non-national rule. They had found a style of play, relying on team spirit and direct football, which Smith hoped would prove effective against European opposition in the years ahead, as midfielder Ian Durrant noted, 'The manager got us playing in a real British style. We were hard to beat and teams definitely didn't like playing against us. That was down to the way the manager organised us and the way he set up the team.'

But the revelations which were emerging surrounding rivals Marseille left a bitter taste in the mouth. In subsequent years, all sorts of conspiracy theories concerning other alleged irregularities during the European campaign surfaced and were lent credibility: CSKA's 6-0 capitulation in France, the way the Russians celebrated after drawing their last, supposedly meaningless match at Ibrox... had they been bought? Bruges's indifferent performance in their final game against a team they supposedly despised... had they too been got at? And what of Hateley's red card against Bruges? If the referee really had been bribed to send off the striker and trigger a suspension, as Hateley maintains, claiming that he had been warned in advance of the game about a potential situation by a mysterious telephone caller, then it was decidedly convenient of him to shove his elbow in the face of the Bruges defender as he went up for a challenge, and then raise his hands to the same opponent just a few seconds later. Hateley had committed two separate offences, either one of which could easily have seen him red-carded by an impartial official, but still the rumours of alleged impropriety persist to this day.

In the end, regardless of all the unsubstantiated allegations, it had been a tremendous effort from Rangers, despite winning only two of their six group games. They had, however, managed to remain unbeaten and, perhaps an even greater achievement, they had belatedly won some respect from the English press, who, having been so dismissive of their chances against Leeds earlier in the season, were treating the Glasgow side as one of their own by the end of the campaign.

It wasn't quite enough though, and ultimately the season represented a high-water mark for Smith's team in Europe. Chasing the dream of European glory and burning huge amounts of cash in order to achieve it, a series of subsequent embarrassing and painful failures on the Continent would eventually lead to the manager's downfall at Ibrox.

* * * *

Rangers knew that if they wished to continue to qualify for the revamped format of the Champions League they would have to maintain their dominance of the domestic game in Scotland, and to that end Smith splashed out a British record £4m in the summer of 1993 on Dundee United striker Duncan Ferguson. The Tannadice club had a long-standing policy of refusing to sell their best players to other Scottish sides, but Rangers' offer simply blew that idea out of the water, as chairman David Murray's extravagant spending continued at Ibrox.

The club's task at this time appeared to be made considerably easier by the declining challenge from their rivals, and in particular from their perennial adversaries Celtic, who found themselves engulfed by an extraordinary crisis in the early part of the decade. The Parkhead club was controlled by a trio of dynastic families, the Whites, Kellys and Grants, who had been stakeholders in Celtic and represented the club at boardroom level since the Victorian age. By the early 1990s, however, much like Rangers a decade before, the club had been allowed to wither on the vine and the board appeared ill-suited and unwilling to adapt to the transformations which were reshaping modern football.

Eventually, following a lengthy and often acrimonious tussle for control of the club, matters came to a head in March 1994 when the incumbent board were forced out and replaced by the Scots-born Canadian émigré, Fergus McCann. The new owner immediately paid off the old board's debts and set about recapitalising the club through a phenomenally successful share issue so that by the time of his departure from Celtic, on schedule at the end of his five-year plan in April 1999, McCann had increased the turnover of the company from £8.7m to £33.8m, rebuilt the old ground into a 60,000-capacity all-seater arena and won the league, preventing Rangers from attaining an unprecedented sequence of ten titles in a row.

Such a series of accomplishments must have seemed a long way off to Celtic's supporters back in 1994, but it was by no means just the Hoops who were feeling the squeeze at this time, as the challenge of Aberdeen by now was also wilting badly, and the team which had latterly done so well to compete with Rangers, on a fraction of the Ibrox club's budget, found that they could no longer keep up with Smith's cash-rich side.

It was a similar scenario for the other half of the 'New Firm' as Dundee United saw long-standing manager Jim McLean step down in the early 1990s to be replaced by the idiosyncratic Serb, Ivan Golac. In 1995, a time when Scottish football seemed to be diminishing in stature and prestige, ailing badly in comparison to the upsurge that was simultaneously taking place at the top of the English game, the two teams from the east coast, former rivals for European glory just a decade earlier, finished bottom of the league, with United sent down to the First Division, while Aberdeen, managed by former captain Willie Miller, only avoided a first-time relegation after overcoming Dunfermline in a two-legged play-off. Over in Edinburgh meanwhile, Hibs and Hearts, who avoided Aberdeen's fate only on the last day of the season, were squabbling with each other. Such was the perilous financial position at Hibernian, following an aborted takeover by a conman named David Duff, that Hearts chairman Wallace Mercer tried to merge the two clubs, effectively pursuing a hostile takeover which would spell the end of the Easter Road side.

With their rivals falling like flies, the task facing Rangers became increasingly clear; Celtic hadn't managed even a second-place finish since the centenary season Double of 1988, but having got their ducks in a row off the park under McCann's new regime, Rangers soon realised that if they could hold off the renewed threat from the east end of Glasgow, there was no other team in the league who would challenge them. Smith harboured no sentiment or illusions in regard to the guff spouted so often in more recent times about Scottish football needing a strong Celtic and Rangers. He viewed the potential rebirth and resurgence of Celtic, quite rightly, as a threat to his club's hegemony. Rangers responded to the Celtic renaissance in the only way that they knew how; they went out and bought players. Smith's spending at Ibrox, already excessive, was about to go through the roof.

Rangers had secured their fifth consecutive league title but at times, especially in the first half of the 1993/94 season, their form had been unconvincing both domestically, with the team acquiring the unfortunate habit of being unable to hold on to a lead, and in Europe, where an away goals defeat to Levski Sofia of Bulgaria sent them spinning out of the Champions League in the first qualifying round, ensuring that there would be no repeat of the previous season's heroics. Rangers won only five of their opening 14 league fixtures, a sequence which included home losses to Kilmarnock, Motherwell and Celtic as well as a 2-0 defeat to Aberdeen at Pittodrie, although the League Cup was won in October, with the winner against Hibs in the final at Celtic Park coming from substitute McCoist, returning to the team after breaking his leg on international duty in April, who settled the match with an acrobatic overhead kick.

The following week, however, Smith's side lost to Celtic, suffering a demoralising last-minute defeat, after a mistake from number two goalkeeper Ally Maxwell allowed Brian O'Neil to net the winner and give new Celtic manager Lou Macari victory in his first game in charge. With their indifferent start to the season continuing, Rangers spent £1.2m to acquire another striker, Gordon Durie, who was signed from Tottenham in November. The turning point in the season eventually arrived on New Year's Day at Celtic Park, when Hateley scored within the opening minute and Rangers soon raced into three-goal lead, a scoreline which provoked some Celtic fans in the main stand to start throwing chocolate bars at the directors' box, where the old board were still housed. The home team pulled it back to 3-2, leaving Rangers supporters worried that another established lead would be thrown away, but nerves were eventually settled by a decisive fourth strike from Oleg Kuznetsov. The Ibrox men subsequently notched up 17 games undefeated, taking them to the title, although they failed to land the Scottish Cup, which was lost in the Hampden final to Ivan Golac's first-time winners Dundee United, ending the dream of unprecedented back-to-back Trebles.

In April, the season was marred by an incident involving new signing Duncan Ferguson, making only his second start since September after spending most of his first year at Rangers on the treatment table. During a match at Ibrox, the volatile striker head-butted Raith Rovers' full-back Jock McStay, or 'nutted him a dull yin' in the Glasgow vernacular, following an innocuous challenge between the pair, after McStay, a relative of Celtic captain Paul, had allegedly questioned the excessive fee paid for Ferguson's services by the Ibrox club. It would lead to the striker's third conviction for assault, and a 44 day stint at Her Majesty's pleasure in the notorious Glasgow prison, Barlinnie.

Rangers' off-field problems continued when goalkeeper Andy Goram went on an unsanctioned bender in Tenerife, for which he was placed on the transfer list by Smith, but the goalkeeper was later reprieved due to a lack of interest from other parties. Goram would go on to play a key role in Rangers' success over the next four years; however, Ferguson's career at Ibrox proved to be short-lived, although the club did well to recoup over £4m for the forward when he joined Everton, as English clubs, enjoying their new found wealth in the lucrative breakaway Premier League, began to catch up with free-spending Rangers.

For some time there had been talk at Ibrox and in the media of the club matching Celtic's 'nine-in-a-row', the run of consecutive titles won by the Parkhead men under Jock Stein between 1966 and 1974. With six titles now in the bag, the chatter which Smith had been at pains to play down publicly was rising to a crescendo, with the Scottish players, in particular, aware of the significance of their target.

Goram recalled the mood among his team-mates at that time, 'When we got to that stage the pressure was really on us. We were beginning to edge closer to nine-in-a-row. We knew we had to try and win nine-in-a-row because the club might never get another chance to achieve it.' Defender David Robertson agreed, 'The first title win [in 1993] was special but the second one wasn't quite as enjoyable. The first time I remember the joy, but after that the pressure was on as we tried to go for nine-in-a-row. In the end each title became more of a relief than anything else.' Fellow rearguard man John Brown recollects how early the squad had their objective in mind as well as their confidence that they could ultimately achieve it, 'From our second or third title in a row we really believed that we were strong enough and good enough to make it nine-in-a-row.' Smith himself observed more cautiously, as his team closed in on their goal, 'You can't get ahead of yourself in these situations. When you have won two or three championship titles, nine seems an awfully long way off in the distance. Then when you have six or seven, you feel that it might be coming within touching distance. But ultimately, getting this close just makes you appreciate what a great feat it was by Celtic in the first place.'

Curiously, for a club with an acknowledged superiority complex, there was scant reference by anyone associated with Rangers – players, fans or management – to beating Celtic's record and extending their winning run of titles to ten. All the talk was of nine.

With six of those championships now under their belt, Rangers were hit with a serious setback before the new domestic campaign was even under way when they lost the opening leg of their Champions League qualifier, 2-0 to AEK Athens in Greece. Playing a sweeper behind two centre-halves with pushed-on full-backs, a defensive system which had been untested even in pre-season, Smith's men were undone at the back in the hostile atmosphere of AEK's Nikos Goumas Stadium with only goalkeeper Goram's heroics keeping the tie alive for the second leg. For the return two weeks later, in a similarly febrile environment at Ibrox, it was hoped that the Greek side could be put in their place, but instead it was Rangers who were brought down to earth as the underestimated Athenians, a team of relative unknowns in comparison to the Ibrox club's high-profile and expensive signings, out-thought and ultimately outplayed the Scottish champions, passing them to death at times, with tactically inept Rangers reduced to pumping hopeful long balls up to Hateley and Ferguson, surely one of the shortest-lived striking partnerships in the club's history.

After Savevski's goal in the 40th minute effectively killed the tie, the half-time analysis, in an STV studio decked out in Rangers colours, seemed more like an autopsy with pundit Maurice Johnston's perplexed and gloomy expression totally incongruent against a backdrop of images featuring rejoicing and celebrating Rangers players.

The 3-0 aggregate defeat amounted to a sobering lesson and a turning point in the manager's tenure at the club. In two of the previous three seasons, Rangers had exited the Champions League at the first qualifying stage, but the narrow losses were put down to circumstances and bad luck; against Sparta Prague a last-minute blunder by new goalkeeper Goram, deep into extra time, turned a relatively comfortable 2-0 lead at Ibrox on the night into an agonising defeat on away goals, while in Sofia two years later against Levski, another late goal, a wonder strike from Bulgarian international Nikolai Todorov, put Rangers out again, by the same narrow margin.

Against AEK however, there could be no doubt about who were the superior side, with even Smith admitting that his team had become predictable by the end. The defeat must have been particularly galling for new signing Basile Boli, who, if we were to believe the Scottish press, had turned down a more lucrative offer to play in Italy with Genoa for a shot at Champions League glory with Rangers. Explaining his hopes of recapturing the trophy he had won with Marseille, Boli told the media as he was unveiled at Ibrox, 'You need skill, experience, good tactics and good players to do that and I think Rangers are capable of it... I did not come to Glasgow just because I like the town. I want to play at the highest level and that is the Champions Cup.'

Following their elimination, Boli criticised Smith's tactics against AEK, in particular the strategy of lumping long balls up to the strikers, and complained about being played out of position. Published in a French magazine, the attack on the manager was downplayed publicly in Scotland, dismissed as a case of 'lost in translation', but ultimately the Ivorian-born defender's stay in Glasgow would be brief.

The early elimination plunged Ibrox into despair and worse was to follow for Rangers at the weekend when they lost badly to Celtic, the Parkhead men earning a deserved 2-0 win on the blue side of the city against a team containing Boli and the club's other high-profile summer acquisition, Brian Laudrup, the imperious Dane, who had arrived from

Fiorentina. Rangers on the day had to cope not only with a sprightly Celtic team, containing 11 Scots and led by new manager Tommy Burns, but also the scorn and derision of their own supporters, which cascaded down from the stands, much of it aimed in a very personal and spiteful way at both the chairman and manager. To compound the misery, another Ibrox defeat then followed when Rangers were knocked out of the League Cup, going down 2-1 to Falkirk, meaning that Smith's expensively assembled side had somehow contrived to lose three home games in a week.

Rangers ultimately rallied however, with Smith relying on the age-old tactic of ramping up the siege mentality, and motivating his players to rub their critics' noses in the dirt and prove the doubters wrong. In October, with a view to adapting their defensive strategy and playing the three at the back system in Europe more regularly, the manager recruited centre-half Alan McLaren from Hearts, raising the club's spending since the summer to more than £7m.

When asked if the signings would continue, chairman David Murray replied, 'We have done more in a couple of weeks than the rest of Scottish football in five years.'

With Celtic going through a laborious transitional season, ground-sharing at Hampden following Fergus McCann's takeover, the Ibrox men ran away with the league, eventually finishing 15 points ahead of second-placed Motherwell. They had relied heavily on the peerless Laudrup, voted Player of the Year in his first season in Scotland, who seemed to relish the freedom he was afforded by Smith, in contrast to the rigid tactical formations he was squeezed into in Italy, which stifled his running and creativity, and to a lesser extent on 33-year-old Mark Hateley, who quit the club at the end of the season to join QPR after five and a half years at Ibrox.

There was to be no mercy for Rangers' long-suffering opponents as the club once again ramped up the spending in the close season, bringing in the biggest star in British football at the time, maverick Geordie Paul Gascoigne, who signed from Lazio for £4.5m. Joining Gazza at Ibrox, with the club now bidding for eight titles in a row, would be World Cup Golden Boot winner Oleg Salenko (£2.5m from Valencia), Stephen Wright (£1.5m from Aberdeen) and Gordan Petrić (£1.2m from Dundee United), while over the course of the season Smith added

Derek McInnes, Peter van Vossen, Erik Bo Andersen and Theo Snelders to his squad.

Hope sprung eternal in the qualifying round for the Champions League, where Rangers had been eliminated in three of the previous four seasons, when the club were paired with Cypriot champions Anorthosis Famagusta, surely a more beatable opponent than their previous adversaries at this stage of the competition. A stilted performance in the first leg at Ibrox gave Rangers a 1-0 win thanks to a strike from Durie, which was followed by a more assured, but still tense and nervy, display in Cyprus, the goalless draw seeing Smith's side through to the tournament's group stages for only the second time.

Rangers were subsequently drawn in a tough section, which included Juventus and Borussia Dortmund, two teams who would contest the final of the competition only 18 months later. Abject humiliation followed; after losing their opening fixture in Bucharest against Steaua, with McLaren sent off in a 1-0 reverse, then drawing at home to Dortmund, Rangers were routed by Juventus in Turin, 4-1 the final score, although, at 3-0 after 23 minutes, the Italian custom of easing up and showing a reluctance to embarrass already beaten opponents spared Rangers, a team who still harboured delusions of grandeur at this level. The unfortunate patsy was journeyman full-back Alex Cleland, who was so bamboozled by the merciless skills of Alessandro del Piero that he ended up scything the Italian maestro to the ground and being ordered off. After the game, Smith appeared shell-shocked, with Goram reporting, 'He came into the dressing room and never really said much.' Later, according to the goalkeeper, the manager encouraged the players to get drunk on the flight home, 'Walter stood up and said, "If I see any of you are sober by the time we arrive back in Glasgow then you are getting fined." He just wiped the slate clean and it worked because we had a big game on the Saturday and we went out and battered Hearts in the league.'

If their experience in Turin wasn't enough, Juventus then arrived in Glasgow two weeks later and humbled Rangers again, extending the margin of victory this time to 4-0, with the visitors not flattered by late goals from Ravanelli and Marocchi. Despite these painful reverses, Rangers, theoretically, still had a chance to qualify, although they needed to win both their remaining group games. The club's perilous situation seemed to offer Gascoigne an opportunity to belatedly step into the limelight, but the player's performances in the final two fixtures, both drawn, seemed to sum up the mercurial Geordie – he scored a blinder against Steaua and was sent off against Dortmund. Despite, or perhaps because of the influence of their unknowable midfielder, Rangers finished bottom of the group.

Domestically, this was the season which saw the belated introduction of the three points for a win system in Scotland. A reinvigorated Celtic, rehoused back at their spiritual home in a partially rebuilt Parkhead, were playing the best football in the country under Tommy Burns, and lost only one league game all season, a 2-0 home defeat to Rangers in September. At half-time in the match, a furious Smith read the riot act to his players, who had been totally outplayed by the home team up to that point, despite Rangers' Cleland opening the scoring shortly before the interval, before Gascoigne sealed the win late on. The other three games between the title rivals finished even, including a rollicking 3-3 draw between the pair at Ibrox in November, but, in addition to their failure to beat Rangers, Celtic's inability to finish teams off and, when necessary, grind out important wins against dogged opponents meant that too many games were drawn, 11 in total, and they were beaten to the championship by Smith's more ruthless and efficient side, who collected their eighth title in a row.

The Ibrox men also eliminated Celtic from both cup competitions, meaning that, at a time when the Parkhead side were re-emerging from the club's worst slump in 30 years, Rangers were able to hold off their rivals' resurgence and keep them at arm's length. Smith's men eventually took the title in the penultimate game of the season at Ibrox, when Gascoigne scored a terrific hat-trick to beat Aberdeen 3-1, including two late goals which sealed the win with a virtuoso performance from the Englishman. A few weeks later, in the Scottish Cup Final, it was Laudrup's turn to dazzle as the Dane set up Durie for a hat-trick and then added two goals himself, Rangers rounding off the season with a 5-1 thrashing of Hearts at Hampden.

The Ibrox side's stranglehold over the Old Firm fixture would serve them well the following season as Rangers looked to match Celtic's record of nine consecutive titles. The pattern always seemed to be the same; Celtic attacks foundering on a strong defence, Rangers counter-attacking, relying on the strength of their defenders at set pieces and on the predatory instincts of McCoist, who would overtake legendary Celtic forward James McGrory and move into second place in the list of all-time leading scorers in Old Firm games. Rangers were particularly dependent on the heroics of goalkeeper Goram, who admitted, 'We were never gonna outplay Celtic at Parkhead, we all knew that. It's a hard place to go. The amount of times we came away from Parkhead winning 1-0 after getting a doing was ridiculous.'

Throw Gascoigne and Laudrup into the mix, and the result was clear – Rangers won all four of the league fixtures between the teams in 1996/97, a record which would prove decisive in the final tally. A frustrated Tommy Burns would be left to lament, 'Put on my tombstone, "Andy Goram broke my heart".' Celtic owner Fergus McCann had no time for such sentimentality, as he sacked his manager at the end of the season.

Smith's side geared up for the assault on the historic ninth championship with seven straight wins at the start of the campaign, culminating in a 2-0 success over Celtic at Ibrox, with Gascoigne's last-minute clincher handing the Parkhead men their first league defeat in almost a year. Rangers also negotiated their way past Russian champions Alania Vladikavkaz in the Champions League qualifiers, after a 3-1 win at Ibrox was followed by a remarkable 7-2 victory in the second leg in North Ossetia. The club's European ambitions at this time were aided by the legal dismantling of UEFA's notorious 'three plus two' foreigner rule, which had limited the availability of non-national players in European competitions. Based on the idealistic, old-fashioned premise that clubs should be encouraged to nurture their own talent, or at least source their players locally, instead of buying up and retaining a team full of foreign mercenaries, the directive ultimately fell foul of EU law and was abolished, following the landmark Bosman ruling by the European Supreme Court. Rangers vice-chairman Donald Findlay welcomed the court's decision, 'We are delighted with the verdict. It means that our foreign players are now just Rangers players, pure and simple, and are available for every game.'

Rangers had lost their last remaining excuse and were determined to make an impact on the continent for the first time in many years. With no restrictions now in place over non-Scots in the matchday squad and with nine domestic titles in their sights, Rangers had bolstered their options over the summer with the acquisitions of the Hamburg captain Jorg Albertz, who cost £4m, Swedish international defender Joachim Bjorklund, a £2.7m purchase from Vicenza, and in January they added Sebastian Rozental, the lesser-spotted Chilean striker, who cost £3.5m from Universidad Catolica, but seemed to be permanently injured. The newcomers to the set-up were immediately made aware of the importance of the season domestically, summed up by the supporter who told club captain Richard Gough that if Rangers didn't win the league this season, then all the other eight titles were effectively worthless.

For the group stages of the Champions League, Rangers were drawn in a seemingly more accommodating section, after the trauma of the previous season, when they were paired with Grasshoppers Zurich, Ajax and Auxerre. Maybe their minds were on nine-in-a-row, maybe it was something far more fundamental, but Rangers were awful; they lost all four of their opening fixtures, which included a particularly insipid 3-0 defeat to Grasshoppers on matchday one in Zurich, when their defensive frailties were once again exposed, and a 4-1 drubbing by Ajax in the new Amsterdam Arena stadium, in a game which saw the immature Gascoigne dismissed for an off-the-ball kick at Winston Bogarde.

Branded 'inexcusable' by team-mate McCoist, Gazza was shifting once again between genius and liability as Smith had to contend with the very public news of the player's abusive relationship with his wife, after the tabloid press were full of reports that the icon had assaulted Sheryl Gascoigne in a drunken rage at Gleneagles Hotel in Perthshire. In addition, there were rumours in the media about the Rangers players' indulgent lifestyles, with some of Smith's charges accused of excessive drinking and nightclubbing, leading to the issue of ill-discipline being raised at the club's AGM, where the manager was forced to defend his men.

Rangers eventually finished bottom of their group again, with one win and five defeats from their six matches. The club's persistent series of failures in Europe left everyone scratching their heads; how could such an expensively assembled team, containing acknowledged stars of the calibre of Gascoigne and Laudrup, alongside stalwarts such as Gough and McCoist, be so repeatedly found wanting on the European stage, even against equivalent or inferior sides? The most painful aspect was the raising of hopes, which were then dashed. After their dismantling of the Russian champions in the qualifiers, Rangers were considered by some in Scotland to be favourites for the group, but they had fallen flat on their faces once again. In reality, Smith's side were nothing more than Champions League cannon fodder.

Owner David Murray blamed all the talk surrounding the season's domestic significance for the club's dismal start to the European campaign. 'Nine-in-a-row is having a negative effect on us. Rangers will stand still until it disappears,' the chairman complained to the *Daily Record* in October. 'It's like a monkey on our backs. I've said before, I'd rather see success in Europe than nine-in-a-row and I stand by that now. Of course I'd take satisfaction out of nine-in-a-row – I'd love to see 19-in-a-row – but it is becoming a real strain on us.'

To be fair to the manager, he rarely allowed European failure to affect his team's domestic form and all the focus that season was on the league. Rangers even seemed half-hearted in their attitude towards the Scottish Cup, as they allowed themselves to go down to a rare defeat to Celtic in the quarter-finals, only their second loss to the Parkhead men in two and a half years. Rangers had won the opening league game between the rivals, 2-0 at Ibrox in September, and the return fixture was at Celtic Park just six weeks later, by which time the Parkhead men had moved to the top of the league. After a positive start from Celtic, Laudrup scored from his side's first attack, which left the home team desperately trying to press for an equaliser, but in the process leaving themselves glaringly exposed at the back.

On numerous occasions, Rangers failed to extend their lead with eye-opening chances on the counter-attack, most notably when van Vossen ran through and was teed up by Albertz, only for the Dutch winger to shoot over the bar instead of rolling the ball into the unguarded net, a miss which left Smith apoplectic in the stands. Rangers were then awarded a penalty when Kerr fouled Laudrup, but the young goalkeeper redeemed himself by saving Gascoigne's spot kick. With minutes remaining, Celtic won a penalty of their own after Gough's foul on Donnelly, but Goram saved from van Hooijdonk to keep Rangers in front. Almost unbelievably, the game had finished 1-0, and Smith's side moved back to the top of the league.

The crucial, defining fixture between the pair, however, came at Ibrox, on 2 January. In another titanic struggle, Albertz shot the home team into an early lead with a thunderous free kick, before Di Canio slotted home a deserved equaliser early in the second half. It seemed that the tide had turned in Celtic's favour, but Rangers regained the lead in the 83rd minute when a mix-up in the visitors' reorganised defence allowed substitute Erik Bo Andersen to score. At that point, a gripping battle between the two title rivals became mired in controversy; with just three minutes of normal time remaining, Celtic's Cadete struck an instinctive volley past Goram, but the goal was wrongly ruled out for offside by linesman Gordon McBride. It was a particularly baffling error by the official, as instantly available TV replays showed that at no point was the Portuguese striker in an offside position, with Petrić standing behind him when the ball was played, and even when it was received. Moments later, with Celtic still protesting the decision, the nimble Andersen clinched the game when he raced through to score again, a goal which sent Walter Smith racing down the touchline, his overcoat flapping in the breeze, celebrating with the fans as if nine-in-a-row had been clinched there and then.

It was, however, an unsatisfactory end to an engrossing contest. Referring to the disallowed goal, Smith's biographer, Neil Drysdale, wrote, 'The controversy sprang from the fact that this did not constitute an everyday cock-up by an official. Television pictures proved emphatically that Cadete had been comfortably onside when he had collected the ball, and that he had not strayed offside when he had polished off his shot. Even to the naked eye it looked an awful call, and yet Scotland's two main tabloid newspapers hardly mentioned the incident the following morning. What they did eventually reveal was that the linesman at the centre of the dispute was a Rangers season ticket holder, who drank in his local masonic club and was a self-confessed "loyal" fan of the Ibrox organisation.'

This is the murky end of Scottish football, which in the west of Scotland lurks never far from the surface, and where the red-tops love to stray whenever the opportunity presents itself. It was undoubtedly the case that Rangers' opponents, including Celtic, felt that they were too often on the wrong end of refereeing decisions around this period and there was particular bad blood between Celtic and the SFA at this time, with several ongoing disputes and disagreements rumbling along in the background, the most serious of which would eventually lead to the governing body's CEO, Jim Farry, being sacked for gross misconduct. Whether any of this played a part in McBride's appointment for the New Year fixture, or in his decision to disallow Cadete's 'goal', his involvement in such a high-profile and important game was a poor exercise of judgement by the SFA, which, at such a crucial stage of the season, exploded in their, or more accurately, in Celtic's faces. Of course Rangers were having none of this conspiracy theory nonsense. 'They were paranoid against us, they didny know how to beat us,' is Goram's more straightforward explanation of the hex that his side seemed to have over Celtic at this time.

Heading in to the latter stages of the season, and with the tension and importance of each Old Firm fixture increasing cumulatively, the final encounter between the pair was again at Celtic Park in March, with seven games remaining. The gap between the sides had been reduced from 14 points, after the Ne'erday match encounter in January, to just five, with Celtic hoping to emerge having shortened the deficit still further to a mere two. But, in a repeat of the meeting in November, the only goal was scored by Laudrup, the Dane latching on to Durrant's lob seconds before half-time, after another weak moment in the Celtic defence.

To say that the Rangers players were pumped up for the occasion would be an understatement, and almost inevitably, it was a scrappy, bad-tempered affair, with Mark Hateley, recalled from QPR on a short-term deal, sent off in the second half on his second debut for the club for a head-butt on Stewart Kerr. He was soon joined by Celtic's Mackay, who committed a second rash challenge while already on a yellow card, and Ian Ferguson was in trouble with the Celtic Park crowd, after the Rangers midfielder booted the ball into supporters in the North Stand from close range.

Ferguson then became involved in a running dispute towards the end of the game with Di Canio, which continued after the final whistle, when the Rangers players went into a huddle, mocking Celtic's customary pre-match ritual. Ten days earlier, the Parkhead men had celebrated their 2-0 win over their rivals in the Scottish Cup by regrouping en masse for a second huddle at the end of the match, and the cunning Smith, steeped in Scottish football's black arts, had used the Celtic players' reaction as extra motivation for his side, branding their behaviour disrespectful. Pumped up with a contrived sense of grievance, the Rangers players were now taunting their rivals on the Celtic Park pitch, with Goram later admitting that he and Ferguson had planned the gesture in advance, and that they had in fact intended to dance the conga all the way off the field and up the tunnel, but the fracas at the end of the game prevented them.

Despite winning all four of the head-to-heads against Celtic, their only title rival, Rangers stuttered badly in the run-in, losing at home to Kilmarnock and then, with the championship in sight, Motherwell, in front of a packed Ibrox expecting nine-in-a-row to be delivered. With nerves beginning to fray, the penultimate match of the season was away to Dundee United, who had already beaten Rangers twice that season. Top spot was secured following a 1-0 victory at Tannadice, thanks to a rare headed goal from Laudrup, with the victory immediately provoking a huge outpouring of celebration and relief among everyone concerned with the Ibrox club. The Rangers squad didn't arrive back in Glasgow until the small hours of the morning, but an estimated crowd of 6,000 fans had gathered around Ibrox, staying up to welcome and acknowledge their all-conquering heroes.

Captain Richard Gough, lifting the trophy at Tannadice, was moved to tears by the achievement, which provoked the indignation of his wife, who pointed out that he hadn't even cried when their children were born. Admitting there were times when he thought that Rangers would cave in under the intense pressure, the captain explained, 'Nine in a row was the big one for me. I think that everybody saw that from my reaction when I lifted the trophy. I think we all knew if we had failed that season then it would have been an absolute disaster for Rangers FC.' Laudrup summed up the sense of relief, 'I think, for a lot of the players, it would have been like they had failed. That was my impression.'

Overall, the sense was one of mission accomplished, even though Celtic's record had only been matched, not surpassed. In the close season, it was agreed that the bulk of the squad who had participated in the historic success would be allowed to stay on, to see if they could go one step further and achieve an unprecedented tenth title, but with their primary domestic objective now reached, Rangers refocused their attention on their other main aim, which had been temporarily put on the back-burner during nine-in-a-row, namely winning the Champions League.

To this end, and to counter the effects of age which were beginning to show in many of his players, Smith and Murray embarked on another huge spending spree over the summer, unprecedented even by the club's already enormous level of expenditure, acquiring Lorenzo Amoruso from Fiorentina, Champions League winner Sergio Porrini from Juventus, Marco Negri, top scorer with relegated Perugia, and his team-mate, future World Cup and Champions League winner Gennaro 'Rino' Gattuso. Staale Stensaas joined from Rosenberg, alongside experienced Swedish international Jonas Thern, who came from Roma. Around the same time Australian defender Tony Vidmar came from NAC Breda in Holland, Finnish forward Jonatan Johansson, signed from Estonian side FC Flora, while goalkeeper Antti Niemi also arrived at the club, from FC Copenhagen.

The cost in transfer fees alone to acquire these players, some of whom arrived for free under the Bosman rule, was approximately £14m, with the three experienced Italians alone costing around £4m each, pushing Smith's spending during his six-year spell past £50m. Rangers had spent more than any other club in Britain over the same period, but of course these figures didn't include the extravagant wages which were required to entice these superstars to Glasgow. The generous pay packages on offer at Ibrox, unsurprisingly, were a vital factor in attracting so many high-profile players from clubs in Italy's Serie A, a league which had been used to paying the highest salaries and consequently attracting the best players in the world only a few years earlier. Amoruso later admitted that Rangers had been determined to sign him after the club had apparently suffered the indignity of losing out on Gianluca Vialli, who had joined Chelsea the previous year. Rangers were consequently prepared to pay the Italian defender a fortune to secure his services, while Gattuso confessed that he was unconvinced about moving to Scotland until his father, with the dollar signs lighting up in his eyes at the prospect of his teenage son earning a basic wage of roughly £50,000 per week, 500 times more than what the old man had to make do with, persuaded young Rino that Rangers represented a 'good opportunity'.

Thern admitted when he arrived in Glasgow that the wages on offer were simply too good to turn down, with Rangers prepared to pay him more than his three previous clubs, Benfica, Napoli and Roma, could afford between them. Rangers also scorned the chance to recoup some revenue when the club turned down a bid from Ajax for Brian Laudrup, with the Amsterdam club prepared to pay £4m for a player with only one year left on his contract. They insisted that the Dane remain in Glasgow for another season and Laudrup subsequently left Glasgow the following summer on a free transfer, when he joined Chelsea.

These acquisitions and other expenses, such as servicing the club's spiralling debt, were partially funded by investment from ENIC, the company associated with the English businessman Joe Lewis, a tax exile based in the Bahamas, who put £40m into Rangers around this time, money that would ultimately be swallowed up by the financial black hole engulfing Ibrox. By contrast, at rivals Celtic, three of their best forwards, Cadete, Di Canio and van Hooijdonk, all left over the summer, with replacement Henrik Larsson coming in from Feyenoord for a paltry £650,000, prompting the *Daily Record*, at the start of the new season, to set out three Rangers teams it believed were capable of winning the league.

With so many quality new players in the squad complementing many of the old guard who had remained, or like Richard Gough, who returned after a few weeks in America, Rangers once again set out to make some sort of impression in the Champions League. Unfortunately, after routing a team from the Faroe Islands, they were eliminated at the second qualifying stage by the Swedish part-timers from Gothenburg, 4-1 on aggregate.

Englishman Peter Keeling, who had been coaching in Scandinavia for 16 years at the time, highlighted the cultural differences between the sides when he told *The Independent*, 'I think Swedish players are quite capable of changing the course of a match by themselves. That's the difference. Because players here are only part-time they are well aware of what goes on in the world outside football. They are used to making decisions for themselves in everyday life and they take that into their football. Players in Britain are cossetted. When they finish at 32 and 33 they may have plenty of experience of nightclubs, but no real experience of the outside world. Gothenburg have a framework in place, like many Swedish clubs, that has served them well over the years. They bring in boys at eight and the accent is on technique and teamwork with different coaches at different age levels. Rangers tend to buy players for their image, not what they can actually do. It is a policy that has proved their undoing in Europe and perhaps it is time they changed it.'

The defeat was a setback and a blow to Rangers' pride, but UEFA's newly introduced rule allowed teams eliminated in the Champions League qualifiers to have a go in the UEFA Cup instead. Dropping down into the secondary tournament, Smith's side duly lost home and away to lowly Strasbourg, a team who were struggling in the French league at the time, meaning that Rangers, for all their apparent wealth and ambition, became one of the first sides in history to be knocked out of two European competitions in one season.

It was the final straw; soon after their double elimination from Europe it was announced at the club's AGM in October that Smith would be leaving his post at the end of the season. A glance at the manager's record in Europe reveals how abysmally Rangers had failed in their stated objective over the course of Smith's tenure at the club. After the highs of 1992/93, which in retrospect seemed to have allowed a sense of false hope to pervade, Rangers only reached the group stages of the Champions League on two further occasions, finishing bottom of their section both times, with one win, three draws and eight defeats from their 12 matches. That was in the good years. In four seasons out of seven, Rangers failed to even qualify for a competition they had clear hopes of winning, provoking a prolonged series of inquests, in among all the navel-gazing and the exasperated self-immolation caused by the club's repeated disappointments in the European arena.

Many theories have been put forward regarding Rangers' failure to make an impact in Europe over this period, some inevitably more credible than others, but what seems unarguable is that the team's direct, bustling style of play, which was serving them so well domestically, was found to be an inadequate formula for consistent, top-level European success. Rangers were too dependent on the old British ideals of team spirit and aggressive intentions, which Liverpool had realised as far back as 1973 after a painful defeat in the European Cup at the hands of Red Star Belgrade, could only get you so far in Europe, where the stronger sides had the ability to frustrate and expose teams like Rangers by retaining the ball for long passages of play. The unsophisticated tactics were accompanied by a lack of professionalism at Ibrox, certainly by the standards of contemporary football, which were changing even in Britain, as exemplified at Arsenal under their French manager Arsène Wenger, who had introduced a more modern, continental approach at the north London club, with an emphasis on nutrition and sports science. By comparison, when Smith took charge at Rangers, he relaxed the rules on drinking, which had been much stricter under the Italian-trained Souness, in the hope of winning over his players and forging a team spirit, with captain Gough encapsulating the squad mantra when he claimed, 'the team that drinks together, wins together'.

It was sufficient in Scotland, where a majority of clubs operated under more or less the same principles, but in comparison to most of their European opponents, it was as if Rangers were operating in the dark ages. Too frequently, Rangers players, who seemed altogether too pleased with themselves for their domestic achievements, were caught boozing in nightclubs, which may have added to their aura in Scotland, but was nowhere near good enough among the abstemious professionals employed by top European clubs. Laudrup appeared to be in the wrong movie at times, admitting that he couldn't keep up with all the bevvying, 'I realised early on in my Rangers career that I just couldn't do it. I couldn't join the players every week, that's for sure, it was too tough on my body.'

Later Smith moved to counter this idea, claiming that the drinking culture at the club was exaggerated, while McCoist observed, 'If we had drunk as much as some people had made out, we would all have needed to book in to the Betty Ford Clinic.' Those 'some people' evidently included Andy Goram, who claimed that he and his team-mates couldn't remember half of their achievements during the 1990s, such was the alcoholic blur in which they were celebrated. The goalkeeper later admitted, 'We certainly went out for lunch... lasted three days... well documented. But then on a Saturday we'd come out and win three or four nil and play really well.' Unfortunately, this peculiar prescription for success failed to extend to a Tuesday or Wednesday, as Rangers' consistent series of embarrassments in Europe proved.

In addition to all the drinking and clubbing, there were further controversies for Smith's side, such as when Goram chose to wear a black armband on his Rangers jersey, allegedly in honour of the murdered UVF terrorist Billy Wright. The goalkeeper was later pictured holding up a flag bearing the name of the UVF and was subsequently accused by the *Sunday Mail* of building a 'chilling shrine to the infamous terrorists in his luxury home'. Then there were the usual, almost expected drink-driving convictions, while Durrant and Derek Ferguson were hauled in front of the courts after an incident in a kebab shop, and with Gazza playing the flute, egged on by his team-mates, in mock imitation of a loyalist marching band, and kicking the shit out of his wife, the overall impression is of a rather dislikeable bunch of players, arrogant, prone to fighting in training, revelling in the fame and fortune which accompanied their domestic success, while trying to take on the elite of Europe, sides such as Ajax and Juventus. With the benefit of hindsight, it was a recipe for the kind of sporting disaster which subsequently ensued.

Following the club's early, ignominious, double elimination from Europe, Rangers found themselves in the unwelcome position of being free to concentrate on their domestic form and the prospect of securing an unprecedented tenth consecutive title. However, their hearts didn't seem to be in it to quite the same extent. While Laudrup admits that there were times during the previous campaign when the team appeared to be too motivated, this season proved to be the opposite, despite all the new arrivals. The year started well, with Negri scoring in his first ten league games for the club, blasting 23 goals in the process, but the Italian striker soon faded and fell out of the picture at Ibrox. A three-way tussle began to develop between Rangers, Celtic and Hearts, as the Edinburgh club topped the league table for long periods over the course of the season and seemed to be in genuine contention for the title.

With Laudrup troubled by illness and loss of form in his final season at the club and with the new signings at Ibrox either injured or failing to settle, Rangers fell away in the second half of the season, winning only one game in six between the end of January and the middle of March, leaving the championship seemingly a straight fight between Celtic and Hearts. Both teams stuttered in the run-in however, allowing Rangers, minus the ineffective Gascoigne, who was sold to Middlesbrough in the spring, back into the race. After a 2-0 home win over Celtic, the Ibrox men once again topped the league on goal difference, but the following week at Pittodrie they lost to Aberdeen, after Amoruso was ordered off for violent conduct, while Celtic also dropped points after a home draw with lowly Hibernian. Hearts, meanwhile, eventually faded out of contention and with three games remaining, Rangers won 3-0 at Tynecastle, finally putting Jim Jefferies's side out of their misery.

Still trailing Celtic by a single point, the Ibrox men struggled in their penultimate fixture at home to Kilmarnock against an Ayrshire side still looking to qualify for the UEFA Cup. Refereed by Bobby Tait, another Rangers-supporting official who had requested, and received, one last game at Ibrox as a retirement present, Smith's side pushed desperately for a winner until deep into injury time when Kilmarnock broke away and scored the only goal of the game through Ally Mitchell. The loss meant that Celtic, managed by Dutch World Cup finalist Wim Jansen, now just had to win against Dunfermline at East End Park the following day to secure their first title in a decade, but after taking the lead, the Parkhead men became a bag of nerves, and conceded an equaliser as the race for the championship continued into the final week.

On the day, Rangers did all they could, winning 2-1 against Dundee United at Tannadice, while at Celtic Park the early tension was eased following a second-minute strike from Henrik Larsson against St Johnstone. But a draw would have been insufficient for Celtic, and as the game wore on into the second half, the Parkhead crowd were on tenterhooks as news of Rangers' lead on Tayside filtered through. A second goal, scored by Norwegian striker Harald Brattback midway through the second half, settled the nerves and the final minutes of the game were played out to scenes of near delirium in the rebuilt Celtic Park stands, with supporters seemingly overwhelmed by the end through a combination of relief and ecstasy.

The following week, Rangers faced Hearts in the Scottish Cup Final at Celtic Park. In Walter Smith's last game in charge, Rangers got off to the worst possible start when they conceded a penalty within 33 seconds after Hearts captain Steve Fulton was brought down by Ian Ferguson. Colin Cameron converted from the spot and the Edinburgh side then extended their lead in the second half, when a mistake from Amoruso allowed Frenchman Stéphane Adam in to score. Substitute McCoist pulled a goal back ten minutes from the end but Hearts, with a team put together for less than £1m, held on to secure their first trophy of any kind for 36 years, giving the men from Tynecastle some tangible reward for their efforts over the course of the season. But for Rangers there would only be tears of frustration and regret, and with so many players out of contract in the summer, many of the team finished the game slumped on the Parkhead pitch in despair. Smith himself admitted that his failure to bow out with a victory 'remains my biggest disappointment in football', explaining, 'This was their last game and I wanted them to go out on a high.'

Despite losing out on both the league and the cup in his final season, clearly Smith was bringing success to Rangers, and in that regard he can be seen as one of the great Ibrox managers. At times he was accused, and not without justification, of being a chequebook manager, but regardless of the arrangements that owner David Murray was enjoying with the club's bankers, Smith undoubtedly brought some great players to Rangers, although there were some expensive duds along the way too.

Overall, Smith is one of the more difficult Rangers managers to assess, because of the money he was allowed to spend, out of all proportion to the size of the club, and in comparison to their domestic opponents, who remained largely exasperated and bewildered by the financial power at Ibrox under the Smith/Murray regime. He was decent at Everton for a while, in a very different financial environment at Goodison Park, as Christmas hamper tycoon Peter Johnson sold out to Bill Kenwright, but he was eventually sacked after almost four years on Merseyside.

He improved things with Scotland, although again, Smith took over the national team at its lowest ebb after the debacle of the Bertie Vogts era, and the hype that accompanied his tenure at Hampden disguised some poor results and awful performances, with a 1-0 home loss to Belarus in an important qualifier springing painfully to mind.

He returned to Rangers in 2007, when, even with the club in a gathering financial maelstrom, he would continue to be wedded to the idea of the spending strategy, with disastrous consequences. The basics were his forte, motivating and nurturing a shared sense of purpose in his squad, and a hunger to stay in front and keep winning. In his first, seven-year spell at Ibrox, Smith fashioned a side that was very much in his own image – strong, steady, unspectacular, and ready to fight for the cause – but his belief in the pursuit of expensive and high-profile signings as the quickest and most effective route to success was storing up future problems for the club, which ultimately, they would be unable to solve.

In one of the final interviews he gave as Rangers boss, after his swansong was ruined following defeat to Hearts in the Scottish Cup

Final, the departing manager announced, 'The bad news for Scottish football is this is as bad as it gets for Glasgow Rangers.'

It was an assurance which epitomised Caledonian defiance at its best, yet Smith could hardly have been more painfully or catastrophically wrong in his prediction.

10

WORLD DOMINATION

I N the summer of 1998, a short time after Walter Smith's
departure from the club, Rangers chairman David Murray moved
to reassure colleagues, when he informed them, 'For every five
pounds Celtic spend, we will spend ten.' It was a statement which
summed up not only the strategy of the club at the time, but also the
hubris attached to it. After witnessing his team surrender the title to
their Glasgow rivals for the first time since his involvement at Ibrox,
Murray's expressed ambition was now to once again put as much
distance between his club and the team from the other side of the
city as possible, and, in the end, he achieved his goal, but only in the
manner of the unsuspecting Greek general, who consulted the Oracle
at Delphi before setting out to war and was told that if he embarked
on his risky, vainglorious expedition then he would destroy a great
army. It was a lesson which would ultimately be lost on Murray, as the
army which was eventually destroyed, like the Rangers chairman's,
turned out to be his own.

Talk of strategy as such at Murray's Rangers is in fact misleading;
there was no great plan or clear set of policies in place, no roadmap
to future success at the club. They may be overused words in modern
football, but there was no Ibrox 'project', no overarching 'philosophy' that
could be discerned, other than a belief in the power of the chequebook as
the quickest and surest route to success. Murray, hopelessly intoxicated

by the profile and prestige that his association with Rangers was bringing him, was the chief cultural architect of this flawed methodology, although it seems clear that he and Rangers, a club with an equally abrasive sense of self-importance seemingly written into its DNA, were the perfect fit for one other.

It may have looked like much of the money which was funding this vanity project was coming out of the chairman's own pocket, but, as we were later to learn, very little of it was, although the line which was being put out at the time could hardly have been less equivocal. It was generally assumed and indeed widely reported, in newspapers and books, that Murray's lavish spending on the club was being financed from his own largesse. Benevolent benefactor, entrepreneur, swashbuckling captain of industry, Murray had the media in the palm of his hand, dining on 'succulent lamb', another unsettling phrase which emerged at this time to describe the symbiotic relationship he enjoyed with the press, after he wined and dined an invited group of journalists at his holiday retreat in the Channel Islands.

Murray ran Rangers as if it was his own private fiefdom. He was in charge, so he considered, of 'the second most important institution in Scotland, after the Church of Scotland'. He gathered friendly reporters into his circle and for those who refused to get on message, or who dared to offer criticism, to which at times he seemed to display an almost hypersensitivity, there was excommunication.

On a certain level, it worked, just as, on a certain level, dictatorship works. If, for instance, Murray's manager wanted to sign a player, Rangers could, once the chairman had given his assent, move swiftly to negotiate a deal and conclude a transfer. By comparison, at Celtic, a club by now operating under a plc structure and therefore accountable to its shareholders, if the manager identified a player he thought might enhance his squad, he first had to wait for a board meeting to be convened, which might take up to a week, before the expenditure could be approved and the funds released. Rangers by contrast could snap up their targets at much shorter notice, but the Ibrox club, under the effective control of one man, were left exposed to the error and miscalculation of the individual; in this case an individual who was particularly vulnerable because he would brook no criticism nor pay heed to prudent advice, not that either of these were particularly forthcoming from the media or anyone else associated with the club, as the chairman surrounded himself with sycophants.

Murray believed that Rangers' obsession with nine-in-a-row was beneath their dignity; unlike the club's players and staff, he couldn't really give a stuff about Celtic, or their records, and he believed that the blinkered pursuit of the ninth title was holding up their ambitions in Europe. With the historic domestic achievement finally out of the way, the fact that his manager, Walter Smith, had again flopped in the Champions League was the final nail in his coffin. Murray's eye was again on Europe, and he proceeded to scan the continent looking for a suitable replacement, ideally northern European but certainly English-speaking, who would bring success and renown to the club in that arena. He also wanted his new head coach to be a disciplinarian, a man who would put an end to the drinking culture as well as the law-breaking and the poor professionalism at the club, which many Rangers partisans believed had cost their team the league in 1998.

Smith's notice of intended resignation had been tendered at the club's AGM at the end of October, prompting inevitable speculation about the identity of his successor. Amid a frenzy of conjecture, the intrepid reporters on the case would be on the phone to anyone they could possibly connect to the job, and as long as their enquiries weren't met with outright repudiation, the headlines would appear the next day, 'Gers swoop for so and so', or 'So and so issues "come and get me" plea'. Marcello Lippi, Fabio Capello and Sven-Goran Eriksson were all beating a path to Ibrox apparently, regardless of any quibbling concerns about their availability at the time. In the end, many Rangers fans were left distinctly underwhelmed with Murray's eventual choice, the Dutchman Dick Advocaat, who, it was announced in February, quashing the 'exclusive' red herrings, would take over at the start of the new season after working his notice at PSV Eindhoven.

Advocaat fitted the bill in terms of his track record, both as an enforcer of discipline – he once sent Ruud Gullit home from a training camp when manager of the Dutch national team, which he had led, without the dreadlocked talisman, to the quarter-finals of the 1994 World Cup – and as a winner of trophies, after he guided PSV to the Eredivisie title in 1997, toppling the domination of Ajax, whose Champions League-winning team of 1995 had begun to break up.

Despite the disappointment of some that Ottmar Hitzfeld or Arrigo Sacchi wouldn't be arriving at Ibrox, Murray was delighted to have landed his man. 'In Dick we have one of the biggest figures in world football,' the chairman announced. 'This shows that Rangers can attract the best in the world in terms of coaches and players.'

Advocaat admitted that he had to use the internet to research his new club, but he was certainly impressed with the almost unlimited budget that was being made available to him, as well as, once he arrived at Ibrox, the interesting décor. ''There is a sense of tradition and everyone who comes to visit me talks of it – the wood, the pictures, the paintings. I like all of that,' he pondered. Known as 'The Little General' from his time in Holland, after a period spent serving as assistant to Rinus Michels, the godfather of Dutch 'Totaalvoetball', and the original 'general', the nickname was eagerly adopted by the Scottish press, accustomed as they were to flattering Rangers managers at every suitable opportunity, although it was noticeable how quickly the moniker was dropped after rival fans began referring to Advocaat as 'the little genital'.

Murray considered Celtic's championship victory of 1998 to have been a mere interregnum. Determined to win back immediately what he referred to as 'our title', and with so many players to replace, Advocaat was given carte blanche to more or less sign whoever was required to bring the championship back to Ibrox and to make the longed-for impression in Europe. After clearing out a cabal of Smith's regulars over the summer, Advocaat's squad was depleted to such an extent that the new manager reckoned there were only three players left who were up to the task: Albertz, Amoruso, who was named the new club captain, and Porrini. 'There are some players here who in my opinion are not good enough,' the Dutchman admitted, adding, 'It has been difficult to move some on to other clubs, because they are on good salaries, but we had to build a new team.'

Arriving at the club over the summer were Arthur Numan, a Dutch international left-back and Advocaat's captain at PSV, for a fee of £5m, who was lured to Glasgow, the defender openly admitted, by 'ridiculous wages', his compatriot Giovanni van Bronkhorst, another £5m purchase from Feyenoord, the Ukrainian winger Andrei Kanchelskis, who signed from Fiorentina for a then Scottish record £5.5m despite being clearly past his best, Argentinian forward Gabriel Amato, £4.2m from Real

Mallorca, goalkeeper Lionel Charbonnier from Auxerre for £1.5m, while Romanian international Daniel Prodan was a £2.2m signing from Atletico Madrid, who joined up at Ibrox with an injured knee and failed to make a single appearance for the club. Accepting a share of the blame for the Prodan mistake, Murray later admitted that players 'were coming in by the hour' at that point and there wasn't enough time to put the defender through a proper medical.

Over the course of the season, Advocaat added Champions League winner Stefan Klos, who arrived from Borussia Dortmund for £700,000 on Christmas Eve and became one of the best-paid footballers in Europe at Ibrox, and Rod Wallace, who came from Leeds United on a free transfer. Stephane Guivarc'h (£3.5m from Newcastle) and USA captain Claudio Reyna, from Wolfsburg via parent club Bayer Leverkusen, with both German sides taking a share of the £2m transfer fee, were Rangers' other acquisitions, while Advocaat was even prepared to pay £2m to sign Neil McCann from Hearts.

With Durrant, Goram, Gough, Laudrup, McCall and McCoist all leaving, along with the departed manager Smith, there seemed little hope of the club retaining a Scottish identity or influence within the dressing room, although youngster Barry Ferguson, who had been stifled in his opportunities under the previous regime, was given a five-year contract and promoted to regular first-team action. In addition, national team captain and English Premier League winner Colin Hendry, who had led Scotland out at the Stade de France in the opening fixture of the World Cup over the summer, arrived from Blackburn Rovers for £3.5m shortly after the season commenced.

At a time when a new European approach was being adopted at Ibrox, it was alleged that Murray, a man who demonstrably knew nothing about the game of football, was heavily involved in bringing Hendry to Rangers, with the chairman apparently pulling rank on the manager in order to sign the Scottish defender in a practice that was not uncommon on the continent.

It wasn't a great success; Hendry, along with fellow newcomers Guivarc'h and Amato, would eventually depart after spending barely a full season in Glasgow, with Murray's club taking a £5m hit on the three under-performers, although the chairman generally considered such losses to be an occupational hazard.

A conservative estimate of the total expenditure on player acquisitions that season would be £32m, a British record for a single season at the time and by any regard a truly hideous sum of money in the context of Scottish football, with absolute fortunes also draining out of the club in agents' fees and players' pay. Rangers' spending, which had been risky but deliberate under Souness, reckless and extravagant under Smith, was now becoming irresponsible and unsustainable under Advocaat's regime, but the excessively high wages were the only way, the Dutchman candidly conceded, that the club could entice these superstars to come and play in Scotland.

The new manager's first game in charge was a UEFA Cup preliminary round tie against League of Ireland side Shelbourne, and it proved to be an inauspicious start, both on and off the field. Amid clashes between drunken Rangers fans and police, the Irish team bus was pelted with missiles as it approached Tranmere Rovers' Prenton Park ground in Birkenhead, where the game had been moved due to fears over potentially more serious crowd trouble in Dublin. Tranmere chairman Frank Corfe was so appalled by what he witnessed that he vowed never to allow Rangers to return to his club's ground again, branding the behaviour of the fans 'a disgrace to their club, their country and to the human race' and urging UEFA to take action 'by punishing these people where it really hurts – their football club'.

Perhaps in response to the treatment they had been afforded by their opponents' supporters, the semi-professional Irishmen soon raced into a two-goal lead, leaving Advocaat's aspiring Rangers galacticos staring at a potential embarrassment. The manager, to his credit, made adjustments at half-time and, despite the Irishmen adding a third goal shortly after the interval, his team recovered to win 5-3, with Amato, after being introduced from the bench, scoring two goals and Albertz converting twice from the penalty spot, before a routine 2-0 win at Ibrox in the second leg saw Rangers through.

The shaky start to the season continued when Rangers visited Tynecastle for the opening domestic fixture of the campaign and found themselves two goals down to Hearts after 20 minutes, eventually losing 2-1. In the aftermath, however, there was a rare outbreak of temperance in response to defeat at Ibrox, as the new manager's honeymoon period continued, and the loss was put down to the inevitable period of adjustment involved in converting the players, new and old, to the Dutchman's more nuanced tactical system.

The patient approach was rewarded as the season progressed, and with more of Advocaat's new signings being introduced into the team and settling into their surroundings, the league became plain sailing for Rangers. A last-minute penalty from Albertz gave Advocaat's side a 2-1 victory over Motherwell in their first home game, and if that seemed unconvincing to some, it was followed by 3-1 and 4-0 wins over Kilmarnock and St Johnstone before the end of August. By November the Ibrox men were sitting comfortably, six points ahead of Kilmarnock in second place and fully ten points clear of Celtic in third. A 5-1 defeat at Parkhead on 21 November brought Rangers back down to earth with a bump as two goals from recent signing Ľubomír Moravčik lit up Celtic Park, but the men from the east end of Glasgow were undergoing their own transitional season under yet another head coach, the cerebral Slovak Dr Jozef Vengloš, and the gap between the teams was merely reduced temporarily.

Meanwhile, on the European stage, Rangers made a positive impact for the first time in many years under their new coach. After eventually seeing off Shelbourne there were grounds for cautious optimism following well-orchestrated wins against PAOK Salonika and Beitar Jerusalem, before Advocaat's side were paired with Bayer Leverkusen, one of the leading sides of the day in Germany's Bundesliga. A classy performance, with Scottish youngster Barry Ferguson controlling the game from the base of midfield, saw Rangers come away from the first leg in Germany with a 2-1 advantage after goals from van Bronckhorst and Johansson. Two weeks later in Glasgow the sides drew 1-1, with the unheralded Johansson scoring again, a result which represented a terrific aggregate victory for the Ibrox men and probably the club's biggest scalp in Europe for 20 years.

A step up in class would be required again when Rangers were drawn to face Parma in the next round, the small-town Italian club whose ambitions were fuelled by the sponsorship and ownership of local multinational dairy firm Parmalat. Parma had a team full of genuine stars of the global game, such as World Cup winner Lilian Thuram, runner-up Dino Baggio, and future winners Gianluigi Buffon and Fabio Cannavaro, as well as Argentinian internationals Hernan Crespo and

Juan Veron. But it was Abel Balbo who gave the Italians the lead at Ibrox, in a match controlled by the visitors, before Rod Wallace's late equaliser gave Rangers hope. In the second leg in Emilia-Romagna, Albertz's strike put Rangers in charge, but they were let down by their own Italian contingent, after Porrini was sent off, and with the home side back in charge at 2-1, a typically obtuse mistake from Amoruso, swiping at the ball with his arm in the penalty box while under no pressure from an opponent, allowed Chiesa to convert from the spot and put Rangers out, ending their interest in European competition for another year.

Back home, the strongest challenge to Rangers and Celtic in the early part of the season had come from Kilmarnock, but the Ayrshire side were eventually overtaken by St Johnstone, who defeated the Ibrox men twice and their neighbours three times over the course of the season, although in between there was a scalding 5-0 reverse at Parkhead in late January and the Perth side also lost the League Cup Final to Rangers at the end of November.

The 1998/99 season had seen the introduction of the self-governing Scottish Premier League breakaway, modelled on the English version but on a far less lucrative scale, with a £45m deal secured with Sky over four years for the broadcast rights to SPL matches and a sponsorship agreement with Gavin Masterton's Bank of Scotland. New rules meant that teams now had to include two under-21 players in their 16-man matchday squads, and for the first time there would be a winter break in Scottish football as the season closed down for three weeks in January.

The time off seemed to serve Celtic particularly well as the Parkhead club's form, which had been patchy under Venglos earlier in the season, recovered notably after the resumption and they set out to reel Rangers in with a remarkable run of results all the way through to the end of April. However, the Ibrox men were also dropping very few points, until successive defeats in early spring, shortly after van Bronckhorst and Amoruso had stated in interviews that Scottish football was too easy, gave Celtic hope. But with four games remaining in an exhausting title chase, Rangers found themselves in a position where they could regain the league championship on the day of the final derby of the season, which was to take place at Celtic Park on Sunday, 2 May, with a kick-off time of 6.05pm on a bank holiday weekend. To the unwary, it may have seemed like a pleasant spring evening, but there was a storm brewing in the east end of Glasgow.

Advocaat had yet to record a victory over Celtic in three attempts, after two draws at Ibrox and a 5-1 humbling at Celtic Park in November, and the pre-match consensus suggested that Celtic would not allow their rivals to win the league at their ground. An early goal from Rangers' McCann certainly wasn't in the home team's script, and matters became worse for the Parkhead men when French full-back Stephane Mahé was ordered off by referee Hugh Dallas, receiving a second yellow card after taking exception to a foul by McCann. In the context of the white-hot atmosphere, Mahé's initial reaction was unremarkable and the referee, who behaved throughout as if he was the most important man on the field, could and should have done more to try and calm the player down and keep a lid on the situation. Instead, after his dismissal, the volatile Mahé totally lost the plot and had to be escorted from the field in tears by Celtic's assistant manager Eric Black. Already a goal down at the time after McCann's opener and now down to ten men, it was a setback from which Celtic were unable to recover.

But this was merely the prelude to a day of shame for the Parkhead club. As the game approached half-time, and with the Celtic Park crowd fizzing, referee Dallas awarded Rangers a free kick near the corner flag, then jogged over towards the byline and patted van Bronckhorst on the backside to encourage him to stop wasting time. As missiles rained down from the crowd, Dallas was struck by a coin and had to receive treatment on the field for a cut to his head; shortly after that, stewards and police hauled away a supporter who had invaded the field and was making an apparent beeline for the official. Then, seconds after getting back to his feet, as the free kick eventually came into the box, the referee, injured and angry, awarded Rangers a soft penalty for an apparent foul by Riseth on Vidmar, which Albertz, despite further insurgences on to the field by irate fans, calmly slotted away to extend the visitors' lead.

In the second half, McCann, playing through the middle and using his pace to good effect on the break, added a third goal allowing the Ibrox men, after two more red cards in the closing stages for Rangers' Wallace and Celtic's Riseth, who committed a shocking challenge on Reyna, to complete the win and regain the championship. It was the first title to have been decided on the day of the Old Firm fixture since May 1979, and only the fourth time in the history of the game.

In the aftermath, Celtic were fined £45,000 by the SFA, and in an atmosphere of general browbeating, the Rangers players were criticised for engaging in another post-match 'huddle' on the Celtic Park pitch, just as they had done two years earlier with an almost entirely different squad of players and staff, as they celebrated in front of their fans at the end of the game. This had provoked another torrent of improvised missiles to rain down from the crowd and the visiting delegation required a police escort just to get out of the ground.

The fall-out and repercussions continued as the fixture spelled the end for Sky TV's 6.05pm graveyard slot on a Sunday evening for their coverage of top-flight Scottish football, an experiment which had lasted all of one season. The match was the making of referee Hugh Dallas, the official from Bonkle, a village in North Lanarkshire, who had largely been a figure of fun in the media up to that point. On one occasion, after a particularly error-strewn performance, the press had christened him Hugh Bonkle, from Dallas. But he would go on to be a media darling, even earning his own slot on TV discussion shows.

Another consequence of the controversial derby was that referees' home towns would no longer be stipulated publicly, after a brick was thrown through Dallas's window by a neighbour who had been at the game, and in a final, bizarre episode, Celtic CEO Allan MacDonald, seemingly perturbed by the referee's bottom-patting gesture towards van Bronckhorst, hired a behavioural psychologist to analyse Dallas's conduct during the match. The idea inevitably backfired when the press got wind of it and mockingly used the affair as further evidence of Celtic's supposed 'paranoia' towards officials and the media at this time.

To compound the Parkhead men's misery, in a less controversial match between the two teams at the end of the month, Rangers lifted the Scottish Cup, winning 1-0 in a final which was once again refereed by Dallas. In the build-up, it was reported that even the corporate guests for the showpiece event at the newly rebuilt Hampden Park would have to be segregated and a police watch was stationed over the referee's house. But the game turned out to be a poor spectacle and passed almost without incident, with the only goal of the game scored by Wallace just after half-time to hand Advocaat's side the Treble in the manager's first season in charge of the club.

The following season Celtic imploded. Highlighting the sense of complacency and nepotism at the club, MacDonald appointed his friend Kenny Dalglish to the role of director of football; Dalglish then hired his former colleague John Barnes to coach the first team, following the departure over the summer of Jozef Vengloš, and Barnes then signed his mate Ian Wright to play centre-forward. It didn't work. All four men would be gone, or on the point of departure, by the end of the season, as Rangers romped to the title by a margin of 21 points.

The nadir for the Parkhead men came in early February, after a 3-1 home defeat to First Division Inverness Caledonian Thistle in the Scottish Cup, which prompted the memorable headline in *The Sun*, 'Super Caley go ballistic, Celtic are atrocious'. Following a row with the rookie manager and his assistant Eric Black, Australian striker Mark Viduka had taken his boots off in the dressing room at half-time and refused to take the field for the second half. The next morning Dalglish was recalled from the golfing resort of La Manga, Spain, where he had supposedly been on a scouting trip, and put in charge of first team affairs, after Barnes, with his side struggling in the league as well by this point, was removed from his post. Director Brian Quinn later admitted, 'Barnes just wasn't up to it... His tactical plans made a lot of sense, but it was one of those cases where he knew the words but didn't know the music.'

Much like Liam Brady at the start of the decade, another gifted winger who was handed the Celtic job as a chastening first experience in management, Barnes' career as a first team coach had ended almost before it had started.

Over at Rangers, by contrast, having delivered a domestic Treble and made a positive impression on Europe in his first season, Advocaat seemed to be fulfilling his remit.

The new season started with eight consecutive victories for the Ibrox club, as Rangers put four past Hearts, Motherwell and Dundee United in successive weeks, with recent arrivals Michael Mols, a £4m purchase from Utrecht, excelling in the striker's position, and Dariusz Adamczuk, signed from Dundee, slotting in as an occasional right-back. But Mols had played just nine league games for the club when he was injured on Champions League duty in a crucial group match against Bayern

Munich, and he would never again be the same player. Advocaat replaced his sidelined compatriot by purchasing Billy Dodds from Dundee United for £1.3m, and the later acquisition of Turkish international Tugay Kerimoğlu, signed for a similar amount from Galatasaray, completed the manager's more modest spending for season 1999/2000.

Money was instead being poured into the club's new training facility, which would eventually become Murray Park, and in addition, the Bank of Scotland, who had been bankrolling Murray's lavish borrowing for years, at last felt compelled to try and curb the chairman's excessive spending when, in February 1999, it acquired a so-called 'floating charge' over Rangers' income and assets, a security which could crystallise into a fixed charge should an insolvency event occur, with the bank also taking a seven per cent stake in the club. Throughout the decade, Rangers' level of debt had fluctuated between £20m and £40m, but despite the £40m share transfer from ENIC, all of which had been converted to revenue by the chairman just two years earlier, the club once again found itself heavily in the red by the turn of the century.

Rangers made further progress on the European front when they eliminated Finnish side FC Haka, then Parma, their conquerors of the previous season, from the Champions League qualifiers. Having gone on to win the UEFA Cup the previous season, Parma were now ranked among the top sides in Europe, but a terrific performance from Rangers, in a game which seemed to represent the template for the way Advocaat wanted his team to play against continental opposition, saw the Ibrox men earn a 2-0 home win. Rangers displayed pace and power throughout, following the red card shown to the Italians' captain, Fabio Cannavaro, after 26 minutes, and despite a 1-0 reverse in Italy in the second leg, Advocaat's side advanced to the group stages, where a tough section involving Valencia, PSV Eindhoven and Bayern Munich awaited.

Many within the Rangers camp wisely set their initial sights on achieving third position in the group and qualification for the UEFA Cup, and after a poor, lacklustre defeat to Valencia in their opening fixture, a team who would go on to finish runners-up in the competition that season, and a home draw with Bayern, who had agonisingly lost out to Manchester United in the final the previous year, Rangers knew that the double header against PSV would probably determine which team would secure the important third spot and continued participation in Europe. A 1-0 win in Eindhoven, thanks to a late goal from Albertz, set Rangers on their way and they completed the job three weeks later at Ibrox, defeating the Dutch side by the club's biggest ever margin of victory in the group stages, 4-1 on the night, including two goals against his fellow countrymen from the doomed Mols.

Rangers now needed just one more point to continue in the Champions League but hopes were dashed in the following two games, both of which were lost narrowly, 2-1 and 1-0, with an unlucky defeat in Munich made all the more painful by Mols's unfortunate, career-threatening injury, as the striker ruptured the cruciate ligaments in his knee following a challenge with Oliver Kahn.

Following that valiant effort, Rangers continued their European campaign in the UEFA Cup, where Borussia Dortmund awaited. A 2-0 win for the home team at Ibrox was reciprocated in the Westfalen Stadion, and with no further goals in extra time, the Germans displayed their customary efficiency in the subsequent penalty shoot-out as Advocaat's side, who had three spot kicks saved by Jens Lehmann, were eliminated in the most disappointing fashion. Rangers' misery was compounded when Amoruso was seen mouthing the words 'black bastard' in the direction of Dortmund's Nigerian striker Victor Ikpeba, and the Italian was lucky to escape with a slap on the wrist and a forced apology for his racist remark, after Ikpeba refused to complain about the incident.

Nevertheless it seemed that Advocaat, albeit backed by grotesque amounts of money, had achieved the seemingly impossible feat of turning Rangers into a genuinely credible force in Europe. Chairman David Murray was still not satisfied, however, and vowed to continue spending in order to improve the side. 'We are not talking here about players who only cost a million. Rangers are well down the road to huge signings and they will be of a much better standard than what we have now,' he boasted after the defeat in Germany.

On the domestic front, Advocaat's side were knocked out of the League Cup by Aberdeen, who lost to Celtic in the final, but they retained the Scottish Cup with a 4-0 victory over the same opponents at Hampden. Nothing went right for Aberdeen on the day of the final as goalkeeper Jim Leighton suffered an injury in only the second minute, meaning that diminutive forward Robbie Winters had to play in goal for almost the entire 90 minutes of the showpiece event. The game descended into farce and Rangers romped home with goals from van Bronckhorst, Vidmar, Dodds and Albertz to give Advocaat, after a first-season Treble, the Double in his second year.

Rangers fans attracted controversy at the final when, in a supposed tribute to the manager and the other Dutchmen at Ibrox, they decked themselves out en masse in the traditional colours of Advocaat's homeland, in what was dubbed 'the Oranje final'. Needless to say, large displays of orange regalia tend to carry sectarian connotations in the west of Scotland, particularly in a footballing context, and the fans had embraced the idea rather too gleefully for some. Not long afterwards, Rangers attracted further condemnation from anti-sectarian charities and campaigners when the club issued an orange away strip, although the Ibrox marketing department deflected some of the criticism by describing the shirt as 'tangerine'. The offending garment was eventually ditched 'for commercial rather than political reasons' after one full season, during which replica sales of the kit were estimated to have topped 300,000.

Success followed success and, on the field at least, it seemed that Rangers could barely put a foot wrong. The margin of victory in the league, 21 points over 36 games, which included a 4-0 rout of Celtic at Ibrox in March, provoked one radio pundit to suggest that it would take the Parkhead men 20 years to catch up with their all-conquering rivals. Up in the boardroom, however, chairman David Murray was scrambling around desperately trying to find finance for his debt-ridden club. The wage bill at Rangers had topped £23m in 1998/99, the equivalent one newspaper reported, without any apparent sense of irony, of employing 2,000 full-time manual workers at £11,500 per year.

The overall level of expenditure had only increased during Advocaat's second season in Glasgow, with players such as Rozental and Prodan picking up fortunes for next to nothing in return, while Marco Negri refused to leave Ibrox, running down his contract over the course of two years of almost complete inactivity. One might have assumed that the unhappy Italian would be yearning for home and the challenges of Serie A, a league which still offered some of the best wages available anywhere in the world at the time, but such were his earnings at Ibrox that Negri was determined to sit tight in Scotland, draining every penny that he was owed from Rangers, despite barely kicking a ball for the club. Advocaat admitted his frustration with the player, 'He just said, "I'm staying and you have to pay me my money." We tried so much to send him back to Italy, but he just didn't want to go.'

But with his minions in the media remaining on message and in full compliance mode, Murray sold them a fairytale about the future of his club and where he was intending to take it over the next few years, and the press duly obliged, faithfully reproducing the chairman's verbose assertions and the triumphalist tone which accompanied them, without stopping to scrutinise the feasibility of what they were so breathlessly reporting.

One particularly egregious example of uncritical, sycophantic reporting towards Murray and Rangers over this period came from *The Herald*'s veteran football correspondent, Ken Gallacher, and his piece on the chairman's future plans for the Ibrox club in anticipation of Advocaat's second championship victory in 2000, which was reproduced in both Rangers and Celtic fanzines in the years ahead as financial despair gripped the Govan institution, is worth quoting from at some length in order to give a feeling for the kind of brown-nosing servility which Murray was able to induce from sections of the mainstream media at this time:

31 March 2000
Murray's blueprint; £53m investment is only the beginning of a new era for Rangers.

By Ken Gallacher

> Just as promised, Rangers are moving on to another level from the rest of Scottish football, as chairman David Murray announced a new investment of £53m for the Ibrox club, with a further massive cash boost soon to follow.
>
> The eventual cash injection could soar as high as £80m as Murray guides the club into what he believes will be a new, golden era for the Scottish champions.
>
> The money involved, the biggest financial boost for any Scottish football club, will enable them to move into Europe's elite over the next few years.

It is clear from this latest move that the Glasgow giants are setting an agenda that no other Scottish club can match – and that appears to include their Old Firm rivals, Celtic, who are trailing by 15 points in the Premier League championship and are now looking at a financial gap which the Parkhead club might not be able to bridge.

The Ibrox chairman promised his shareholders good news and a more prudent financial strategy at the last annual meeting of the club.

He has now delivered this by taking on board several very heavy financial hitters, South African-based David King is worth around £300m – £20m of which he is investing in the club he followed as a young man in Glasgow.

Trevor Hemmings is worth even more – around £500m – and he is also on board. Tom Hunter, also worth several hundred million, is liable to join up soon and Murray himself is investing in excess of £9m, which is more than he spent when he took control of the club.

The Ibrox chairman has spent several months and many sleepless nights piecing together the plans which will eliminate Rangers' debt, currently sitting at around £40m, provide finance for the new training centre and the soccer academy which will be housed there, and still allow cash to invest in new players.

Yesterday, as he saw the months of delicate negotiation culminate in the announcement of a one-for-three rights issue of more than 15m shares being valued at £3.45p and the further news that he and King, as well as Alastair Johnston, a senior vice-president with IMG, the giant sports management group, were also taking up a number of shares, Murray was ready to talk about the new future for the club and his dreams for European success.

He said, 'I want to make it clear from the outset that while our small shareholders, our supporters who have an interest in the club, will have the opportunity to invest again if they want, there is no pressure on them to do so.

'The bulk of the rights issue is being taken up by myself and David King and some other smaller investors, including Alastair Johnston, who is a long-time Rangers supporter.

'We also have Trevor Hemmings coming in as an investor and Tom Hunter will join us some time in the future.

'Essentially, the investment we require is in place and we also have a major media deal in the pipeline which is very exciting and will bring in further serious investment to the club.

'I told you earlier this week that I had run the club up to now on a high-risk strategy which has involved carrying large debt.

'These days are over. The whole method of running the club is going to change, because we are in a situation right now where we do not need to take the risks we have had to take in the past.

'We don't have to spend the same money on players, for example, as we have had to do over the past two years when we were restructuring the team after the arrival of Dick Advocaat.

'At the moment, we have two new players set for next season, Allan Johnston and Fernando Ricksen, and Dick is looking for another quality striker. He is working hard on that right now.

'Dick and myself know what we are aiming for. We want to be in the Champions League every season. This is what we want for the club and this is what we have been working towards.

'However, we shall not be going on any wild spending sprees in the transfer market.

'We have a player or two to add to the squad – a top-class international front player, as I said, but we don't need to buy Numan, van Bronckhorst, Mols, Reyna, or McCann – because we have these lads in place already.

'Believe me when I tell you that we are going for it this time – we want to be successful in Europe, and the money we are raising now will take us there.

'This is the last part of the jigsaw for me, but we shall always be a part of Scottish football and we will take our domestic responsibilities seriously. We respect the other teams in the Premier League and we know this news will make them try even harder against us. But, so be it.'

However, the mega-deals Murray has been working on are sure to carry Rangers out of the reach of their rivals here at home and unless Celtic can somehow find the means to strengthen their own financial standing even the age-old rivalry between the Glasgow giants will be threatened as the Ibrox men grow even stronger.

Reading between the lines of this execrable guff, a more sceptical observer might have gleaned from Murray's unchallenged assertions something along the lines of: we're £40m in debt, I'm having to put the brakes on the spending (despite what I told you after the Dortmund defeat), hopefully some investment may be coming into the club soon but I don't really know... let's hope it does some good, because otherwise we're mullered.

That said, the most subversive and unsettling aspect of this piece is how effortlessly convincing it all sounds. Written in a supposedly respectable broadsheet newspaper by a veteran correspondent in the days before the criticism offered by social media and citizen journalism was widely available, there was very little comeback or right to reply in the face of all this hoopla. Without the benefit of hindsight, the reader of the day had little choice but to accept Gallacher's frenzied proclamations of imminent utopia at face value, especially as the message was being delivered across all platforms, with a parallel report appearing in the tabloid *Daily Record* a few days earlier.

It's certainly true that, following the rights issue, Dave King invested £20m through his Ben Nevis Holdings and became a non-executive director, remaining on the Rangers board until the club's liquidation in 2012, and Alistair Johnston, who introduced Murray to King, eventually joined up in February 2004 and succeeded Murray as chairman in 2009, but King's money soon disappeared down a financial black hole, while the other putative investors who Murray had name-dropped into the conversation must have gotten wise and headed for the hills over the months and years ahead, with a mere £3m eventually raised from private financiers, including Hemmings, the owner of Blackpool Tower.

Whatever the brave new world that Murray and his cronies were anticipating, it failed to materialise and in the summer, just a few months after this piece was published, Rangers signed Ronald de Boer from Barcelona and started cheating the taxman.

Even from the start, it seemed apparent that something wasn't quite right in all of this. Ducking and weaving among the rhetoric, Murray seemed to be stating quite categorically that there would be no need for vast fortunes to be spent on new players in the future because the Neil McCanns of this world were already in place at Ibrox. Yet over the close season and beyond, as well as the £4.5m to Barcelona for de Boer, Rangers spent a total on player acquisitions which again exceeded the £30m mark, securing the services of defender Bert Konterman from Feyenoord (£3.5m), who had apparently outshone Jaap Stam at Euro 2000, but in Scotland would acquire a reputation for not being able to tackle, head or pass the ball, right-back Fernando Ricksen from AZ Alkmaar (£4m), another target for the Ibrox boo-boys after a string of mistakes in big games, back-up goalkeeper Jesper Christiansen (£1.2m) from Odense, and Peter Lovenkrands from AB Copenhagen (£1.5m), who contributed some important goals but would later gain a reputation for only playing well when it suited him.

The manager also tried to augment the Scottish influence in the squad with the signatures of winger Allan Johnston from Sunderland (free), striker Kenny Miller from Hibs (£2m) and defender Paul Ritchie, a Bosman signing from Hearts who was sold to Manchester City a few weeks later for £500,000 before he could play a proper game for the first team. 'I felt sorry for him but I had a duty to the club so we sold him for a profit,' Advocaat said of the bizarre move, but his wheeling and dealing left the player inconsolable. 'Not to have played a competitive game for Rangers is something I'll find hard to deal with for the rest of my life,' Ritchie later lamented.

Then, on 30 August 2000, two days ahead of the Champions League transfer deadline, Ronald de Boer arrived in Glasgow and announced, 'I've agreed a four-year contract,' before adding enigmatically, 'Apparently there are a few minor issues to be sorted out between the clubs, but I fully expect to become a Rangers player.' Foreign footballers, wary of the various tax systems operating in different countries, often demand their wages to be paid net, leaving their agents along with the accountancy boffins to sort out the full structure of their remuneration. Whatever those 'minor issues' were, which de Boer had so fleetingly referred to, Rangers, having made a mockery of the concept of financial fair play since the early days of Souness, were now confirmed in their entry into the far murkier world of the tax wheeze.

And finally, in November, the *pièce de resistance*, as Rangers forked out £12m to sign Norwegian striker Tore André Flo from Chelsea. This was Murray's arrogance and recklessness at its most unforgivable – he was aware that Rangers' debt was out of control and had to be addressed. Even his allies in the media had recorded him admitting as much. He had talked unequivocally of the need for prudence, yet Murray, almost as if he was starting to believe his own press, went on to completely ignore his own advice.

The signings of Flo and de Boer would come back to haunt Rangers, not just because the players turned out to be expensive flops on the field, with Flo out of form and de Boer suffering a series of niggling injuries, but because of the nature of their contracts. Along with defender Craig Moore, who returned to the club from Crystal Palace in 1999, Flo and de Boer had agreed, through their representatives, to receive some of their pay through the 'discounted option scheme', which required part of a player's salary to be promised through side letters, in addition to the formal contract. These secret letters, guaranteeing tax-free income, would later alert HMRC and, in what became known colloquially as 'the wee tax case', the revenue and customs service eventually served Rangers with a bill of £2.8m in overdue tax and penalties on these contracts, an amount which would ultimately remain unpaid, despite the club admitting liability for the claim. The use of these side letters to sign and reward players such as Flo, de Boer, Moore and Stefan Klos would represent the start not only of Rangers' policy of tax avoidance, but also, *a fortiori*, of their acquiring and remunerating players whom they would otherwise have been unable to afford.

With the signing of Flo, Rangers were responding, in part at least, to the appointment of Martin O'Neill as Celtic manager, the Northern Irishman who galvanised his talented but underachieving squad and, over the course of the season, augmented it with the purchase of players who were experienced campaigners in the English Premier League, such as Neil Lennon (£5.75m from Leicester City), Alan Thompson (£2.75m from Aston Villa) and Chris Sutton (£6m from Chelsea), the English striker stating purposefully on his arrival that his team's job was to put Rangers in their place. Celtic, now free of Fergus McCann's scrupulous penny-pinching, had shown that they were prepared to flex their own financial muscles and, if not to match Rangers' exorbitant level of spending, at least to compete financially and use the transfer market to their advantage.

The impact was immediate and irrevocable. In the first Old Firm game of the season, played at Celtic Park on 27 August, Advocaat's side were trounced 6-2 by a rampant home team, who raced into a 3-0 lead after just 11 minutes with early goals from Sutton, Petrov and Lambert. Rangers' Dutch full-back Fernando Ricksen had to be hauled off by his manager midway through the first half after being tormented by his countryman, the previously ineffectual winger Bobby Petta, and, as one wag reported at the time, Ricksen left the Celtic Park pitch looking like he'd seen a ghost. Larsson, who had emerged as a converted world-class striker under Venglŏs, scored a further two goals; the first a sublime effort, chipping the ball over Klos after waltzing past the soft-tackling Bert Konterman, and the Swede would go on to surpass Jimmy McGrory's goalscoring record over the course of the season, netting 53 times for the Parkhead side. Celtic historian David Potter later observed of the game, 'It was the start of the modern Celtic.'

The defeat had knocked Rangers off their perch, but they didn't fully start to implode until October when they suffered consecutive defeats to Hibs, St Johnstone and then 3-0 at home to Kilmarnock, in a game which saw captain Lorenzo Amoruso barracked repeatedly by the Ibrox crowd. The result left Rangers, who had been top of the league before the Celtic Park debacle, fully 13 points off the pace in fourth position. Advocaat by now was furious with his players, accusing them of being 'fat-necks', a Dutch expression roughly equivalent to 'big-heads', and admitting that he could sense their complacency.

It was clear that the manager was aiming his criticism in particular at the Netherlands contingent, which by now numbered six players, all first team regulars, plus coaches and doctors, although there were also rumours of unrest within the dressing room caused by Advocaat's perceived favouritism towards his clique of compatriots. As a result of the in-fighting, and on the back of such a poor run of results, Amoruso was stripped of the captaincy, with the big defender's team-mates having long since lost confidence in the player. Amoruso, it seemed, with his long hair and shaved legs, was an Italian defender straight from central casting, whose vanity even extended to referring to himself in interviews in the third person. He irritated his team-mates with his inflated sense of self-importance, which manifested itself most visibly on the field with his insistence on taking long-range free kicks, most of which flew straight off the Italian's boot and into row Z.

Amoruso was resentful and unhappy at his public humiliation and he later claimed that the decision to replace him as captain was the turning point in the fortunes of Advocaat's Rangers, pointing out that the Dutchman, following a trophy-laden first couple of years at the club, subsequently won nothing in Scotland. The new skipper was 22-year-old Barry Ferguson, who led the team out at Ibrox three days after the Kilmarnock defeat for a League Cup tie against Dundee United. The disgruntled Amoruso, still smarting at his very public demotion, berated the young Scot from the start of the match, until Ferguson scored to give his team a 2-0 lead, which sealed the game and finally silenced the carping Italian.

The slump in domestic form occurred at the same time as Rangers were squandering a positive start to their Champions League group, having won the opening two games of their section against Sturm Graz and Monaco. The European campaign had started slowly as Rangers struggled to overcome Lithuanian non-entities Zalgiris Kaunas at Ibrox, with two late goals from substitute Dodds putting a gloss on the eventual 4-1 scoreline against a side reduced to nine men. Dodds in fact was in fine goalscoring form for the club, but was rated as 'not top quality' by Advocaat and underused by the manager, especially in Europe. Any complaints the striker may have had were dismissed by the Dutchman with typical brusqueness. 'He made a fortune in salary when he moved to Rangers, so he should be grateful to me,' Advocaat commented.

After a tedious second leg in the Baltic state, which finished goalless, Rangers dismissed Danish champions Herfolge 6-0 on aggregate to progress to the group stages, where a 5-0 win over Graz at Ibrox was followed by an equally impressive 1-0 defeat of Monaco in the Stade Louis II.

With the competition now formatted over two group stages, the games were coming thick and fast and Rangers' run of domestic defeats and the 'fat-necks' controversy couldn't have been more awkwardly timed, with a double-header looming against Galatasaray, the holders of the UEFA Cup following their tense victory over Arsenal on penalties in the Copenhagen final in May.

After a scoreless first half in Istanbul at the intimidating Ali Sami Yen stadium, there were five strikes in the second period, with the home team soon racing into a three-goal lead and although Rangers pulled it back to 3-2 in the dying stages, it was too little too late. Before the game, a spat developed between Advocaat and his counterpart with the Turkish champions, Mircea Lucescu, who claimed publicly that almost anyone who had access to the Dutchman's budget would be able to build a successful team. Advocaat's response was to call the 70-times capped Romanian an 'asshole', although he waited until he was on the point of departure in the foyer of Istanbul's Atatürk airport before delivering his rebuke.

The return leg, which finished goalless in Glasgow, was followed swiftly by a demoralising defeat in Austria, 2-0 to Sturm Graz. Rangers could still qualify from the group but another Ibrox draw, 2-2 against Monaco in the final game, with Amoruso once more copping flak from the home fans for defensive lapses at both goals, saw Rangers relegated into the UEFA Cup, where they were summarily dispatched by the unexceptional German side Kaiserslautern, meaning elimination yet again from Europe before Christmas.

It had looked like as easy a group as could be expected at this level, but for all their spending, increasing exponentially, on foreign talent, and despite a brief flirtation with respectability under the Dutchman, Rangers' best season in Europe in recent memory remained the class of '93, when they were led by a manager who was supposedly out of his depth at this level and the club was impeded by the three-foreigner rule, which limited his selection to a minimum of eight Scots. Only a repetition of the success of Walter Smith's Champions League trailblazers and participation in the latter stages of European competition, season after season, would have rendered Rangers' profligate spending policies financially viable, so defeat at any stage short of the quarter-finals had to be considered as a failure on the part of everyone at the club.

In November, Tore André Flo scored on his Rangers debut as the Ibrox men routed their Glasgow rivals 5-1 on home soil, with the club gaining a measure of revenge, if only fleetingly, for the 6-2 defeat at Parkhead in August. Advocaat's side subsequently embarked on a run of eight wins and a draw, until, facing Celtic once again in mid-February, they lost 1-0 at Celtic Park, with Fernando Ricksen sent off, four days after they had been eliminated from the League Cup, in the semi-final at Hampden, by the same opponents.

By now the manager's decision-making, for the first time, was starting to be called into question publicly and it almost seemed as if Rangers were willing to try anything when they signed Marcus Gayle from Wimbledon for £1m in early March, with Advocaat admitting that he had never seen the striker play live. Gayle, who managed a total of four appearances following his move to Ibrox, spoke vaguely at his initial press conference about Rangers being 'the only club up here', but within days his new team's season was effectively over after a deserved 1-0 defeat in the Scottish Cup at the hands of Dundee United. Following on from Ricksen's dismissal against Celtic in the league, this time it was the other Dutch enigma, the mercurial Konterman, who was ordered off.

A few days later, the Tannadice club's city rivals, Dundee, turned up at Ibrox and came away with a 2-0 win, and then United completed a successful month for the Tayside clubs when they also left Ibrox with a handsome 2-0 victory in the league. Celtic, having already wrapped up the title with six games to spare, were next to come calling to Ibrox, and the Parkhead men claimed a decisive 3-0 win, orchestrated by Larsson and Moravčik, leaving Advocaat to ponder the implications of three home defeats in a row.

For the first time under the Dutchman's stewardship, Rangers finished the season without a trophy, while Celtic, by contrast, completed their first Treble since 1969. The transformation at the top of the Scottish game, effected in under a year, was remarkable. As an outsider to the Scottish game, O'Neill had imported an infectious enthusiasm to his management of Celtic, often describing his team's performances, particularly in Europe, with repeated usage of words like 'extraordinary', 'immense' and even 'astonishingly brilliant', leaving Rangers' and Murray's cohorts in the media utterly flummoxed.

Having maintained a distant personal relationship with the press, Advocaat was now no longer invulnerable to criticism, as had appeared to be the case during his first two years in Scotland, and in fact, by the end of his tenure at Ibrox, his relationship with the media had broken down completely. Journalist Graham Spiers told *The Advocaat Years* authors, 'Dick has an arrogance about him and he thought he was impervious to criticism after the first two seasons because they went so well. At the beginning of their third season Rangers had disastrous injuries and he couldn't handle it – he began to rage against the world, flailing like a blind man.' Tabloid scribbler Bill Leckie agreed, 'Dick couldn't cope with it [Celtic's revival under O'Neill], he couldn't get his head round it. The 6-2 game was the turning point and that gave Celtic so much confidence that they went on a great run... Rangers didn't respond. Advocaat couldn't reverse it.'

Over the summer, Rangers unveiled their new Murray Park training complex, named with characteristic immodesty, after the club chairman. Advocaat had persuaded Murray that the facility, which cost £14m to complete, was the key to Rangers' future success, even threatening to resign at one point if the project didn't become the club's main off-field priority, with putative plans for a museum, the 'Blue Café' and an extra 1,200 seats inside the stadium having to be shelved at the Dutchman's insistence.

In the meantime, while their batch of intended young stars of the future were supposedly incubating at Murray Park, Rangers' spending had to continue and by the end of the summer the outlay under Advocaat's three-year regime was nearing the £80m mark, following the recruitment of Georgian forward Shota Arveladze, who cost £2m from Ajax, German midfielder Christian Nerlinger, £1.8m from Borussia Dortmund, English youngster Michael Ball from Everton for £6.5m, Russell Latapy on a free from Hibernian and Claudio Caniggia for £900,000 from spendthrifts Dundee, the long-haired Argentinian forward who had lit up the Italia '90 World Cup as a 23-year-old, but who now, 11 years later, was lured to Ibrox by the prospect of a crack at the Champions League.

Unfortunately for Caniggia and Rangers, after breezing past Maribor of Slovenia, 6-1 on aggregate, Rangers were eliminated in the final qualifying round by Fenerbahçe after a goalless draw at Ibrox was followed by a 2-1 defeat in Istanbul, with Advocaat's side subsequently relegated into the UEFA Cup. Rangers were, however, in the black over player sales, as van Bronckhorst, Albertz, Tugay and Reyna all left Ibrox during the course of the season, recouping the club over £13m.

Domestically, the new season picked up from where the previous one left off as Rangers, unbeaten but having already drawn three of their opening eight fixtures, welcomed Celtic to Ibrox at the end of September and suffered a 2-0 reverse. Advocaat's side subsequently won five successive games before the next scheduled meeting between the teams at Celtic Park in November, when the Parkhead men secured the points with a 2-1 win, consigning Rangers to a fifth consecutive defeat in the fixture. After Larsson scored from the penalty spot to give the home team a 2-0 lead, Advocaat substituted left-back Michael Ball and the young Englishman, clearly unhappy with the decision, publicly berated his manager as he left the field, much to the amusement of the home crowd. Ball's folly was compounded when his replacement, Lovenkrands, scored in the 77th minute to bring Rangers back into the game, but an equaliser ultimately eluded the Ibrox men. Responding to questions about the incident with Ball, Advocaat retorted, 'Maybe at a club like Everton you can do that but with a manager of my stature you can't,' before fining the player £10,000.

By now it seemed clear that the writing was on the wall for Advocaat and over the course of the next couple of weeks he effectively sacked himself. In another one of those uniquely Rangers arrangements, a reluctant Advocaat, who would have preferred a clean break, was persuaded by Murray to move upstairs and become the club's director of football, although his remit seemed unclear, with the Dutchman soon taking over once again as the coach of his country's national team. The tabloids reported the move, inevitably, as some sort of Murray masterstroke, but in reality it was a preposterous contrivance designed to save face and when he left the club altogether a few months later, to almost no publicity, the position which had been summarily created for Advocaat was quietly made redundant.

The timing of his departure left Advocaat vulnerable to criticism that, in the face of Celtic's resurgence, he was simply running away from the job, but with one of his last acts as manager, he engineered a goalless draw in Paris against PSG in the UEFA Cup and, after a similarly scoreless first leg at Ibrox, the tie went to penalties. Rangers eventually won the shoot-out 4-3 after PSG's Argentinian defender Mauricio Pochettino struck his sudden-death kick against the crossbar.

Against the odds, the Ibrox side had secured participation in European football beyond Christmas for the first time since 1993, and Advocaat was so overjoyed that the usually impassive manager ran on to the pitch, arms aloft, to embrace his relieved and celebrating players. The Dutchman had left Ibrox on a high.

11

AGENT McLEISH

I N March 2000, the dotcom bubble burst, leaving Rangers, in the words of Rowan Atkinson's *Blackadder,* 'up a certain creek, without a certain instrument'. To be fair, the Ibrox institution was already fairly deep in the brown stuff by the time the prevailing economic winds shifted and the bear market started becoming antsy over its tech stocks, but Rangers found themselves in a particularly vulnerable position because chairman David Murray, in a sanguine and misplaced belief that the boom years would never end, had recklessly allowed the club's financial position to become exposed to the slow-burning effects of an economic downturn and consequently the downsizing which they had been trying to avoid for years would now be forced upon them. One thing seemed certain, however; Rangers were not going to go quietly into the night.

The extraordinary story of the eventual loss of the Ibrox club's grip on financial reality can be dated back to 1998 when a pipe-smoking pornographer by the name of Paul Baxendale-Walker first suggested to Murray that the use of Employee Benefit Trusts (EBTs) might provide a convenient means of mitigating the considerable tax burden which a bloated squad full of extremely well-paid footballers was starting to place on his club. The difficulty for Rangers that summer, after seeing rivals Celtic walk off with the league title for the first time in ten years, was that the Parkhead institution, having finally got their ducks in a row off the field, now appeared to many impartial observers to be the better placed of the two clubs.

For all their misfortunes in the early '90s, Celtic, after the success of owner Fergus McCann's departing share offer, were now in an extremely sound financial position in comparison to Murray's improvident club, and with gate receipts proving such an important revenue stream in Scottish football due to the relatively meagre value of the broadcasting rights and sponsorship deals, the Parkhead side now had a new stadium which was 20 per cent larger and more modern than the once-revered Ibrox Park. Over the next few years, once their ground was fully rebuilt, Celtic enjoyed an average home attendance of over 58,000 paying spectators, including 53,000 season ticket holders, up from 7,500 in 1994.

During this period of growth in the game's global reach, which coincided with the proliferation of satellite and cable television coverage, it was Celtic who appeared to have the more recognisable and fondly regarded brand, with an extended community of supporters from the diaspora of Scottish and Irish expatriates, who could now pay to watch the club's matches in their homes, wherever they were in the world. In addition, the Parkhead club was a properly constituted plc, majority owned by supporters, with a cast list of financial heavyweights on its board of directors, including Brian Quinn, former deputy governor of the Bank of England, Sir Patrick Sheehy, former chairman of BAT Industries, and Frank O'Callaghan, former chairman of MacDonald Hotels, alongside moneybags Dermot Desmond, the company's new majority shareholder whose personal wealth dwarfed that of his Ibrox counterpart. By contrast, Rangers seemed relatively impoverished, even as part of the wider, increasingly debt-ridden Murray Group, with only Murray himself carrying any clout, as over the next few years, the Ibrox chairman found himself scurrying about desperately cutting corners in a bid to try and keep up.

Baxendale-Walker, at 34, seemed an unlikely saviour for Murray and Rangers. Brought up as an orphan in a Church of England home, he attended Hertford College, Oxford, and trained as a barrister, before switching to a solicitor and setting up his own practice in Mayfair, London. However, the erstwhile playboy and self-confessed sex addict later turned to producing and starring in his own pornographic movies, while reinventing himself as an 'adult entertainment magnate', after he was struck off as a lawyer in 2005. His original vocation though was as a tax adviser and Murray, in his desperation and his vulnerability, saw an opportunity in Baxendale-Walker's schemes for 'increased tax efficiency' and a potential advantage over rival clubs in the more challenging financial environment. Initially, the new fiscal arrangements were limited to a few key individuals, such as manager Dick Advocaat, who, in addition to his standard pay, benefited to the tune of £1.5m in tax-free income over the four and a half years of his involvement at Ibrox, and Champions League winner Stefan Klos, signed in late 1998, although the £2m the German goalkeeper received from his EBT trust between 1999 and 2003 represented only a fraction of his overall income, which totalled more than £8m in little over four years.

At first Murray's preference was for the more intricate and complex Discounted Option Scheme (DOS), which involved offering options on shares in a 'money-box' company to beneficiaries, who could then, once the share options had been exercised, extract cash from the company in the form of a dividend, an aggressive form of tax planning which was popular with bankers trying to avoid paying tax on their bonuses. It also particularly suited foreign and non-UK domiciled footballers, who could minimise their exposure to the taxman provided they didn't bring their earnings from the putative company, set up in an offshore tax haven, into the UK.

The arrival of Ronald de Boer, signed a few days after the pivotal 6-2 defeat at Celtic Park in August 2000 and paid substantially through the Discounted Option Scheme, signalled the first escalation in Rangers' policy of aggressive, and ultimately unlawful, tax avoidance. Over the next few years, Murray switched to a simpler form of EBT arrangement and, having initially dipped his toe in the water, the chairman now went all in for the scheme, as over the course of the next few years, the use of EBTs escalated and took hold of Rangers' entire recruitment strategy, with 40 per cent of all players eventually enrolling in the scheme, many of them receiving as much as half their income from the club in this way.

The idea of the EBT was simple; the employer, in this case Rangers' parent company Murray International Holdings (MIH), paid money into an offshore trust, called the Murray Group Management Ltd Remuneration Trust (MGMRT), and, in addition to his fully disclosed salary, a player or other employee would be able to take out loans from his individual sub-trust, of which he was the nominated 'protector', to an amount that was already agreed and stipulated in the secretive side letters. The nature of these loans seemed controversial, however; initially, they were supposed to be paid off after ten years, but the player could apply for an indefinite deferment, until in fact he eventually died, at which point the amount owed could be written off against inheritance tax. One journalist described the loans, ironically, as 'a bit like the ones you would offer a hard-up friend on a night out – here's £20, pay me back when you can but I'm not going to remember this so don't worry about it'.

Theoretically though, because they were loans, this extra remuneration was not subject to income tax and national insurance contributions, an arrangement which seemed to suit all parties, but here's the onion – if it could be proved that the money obtained from these sub-trusts was never intended to be repaid and was effectively contractual pay, or 'disguised remuneration', then the ruse would be exposed and Her Majesty's Revenue and Customs (HMRC) would be on the case. A lower tax bill at Ibrox would relieve some of the mounting pressure on Rangers' overall costs, meaning that the club could continue to sign better, more expensive players and afford to pay the wages that these top players demanded, and thus it was hoped that Rangers might be able to stay ahead of the pack and, most importantly of all, see off the threat from their rejuvenated rivals on the other side of the city.

The problem for Murray and Rangers, however, was that no self-respecting foreign mercenary was going to play for the club on the promise of a questionable loan, so the additional income had to be promised through side letters in order to guarantee to the player the non-standard element of his pay. These secretive letters were potentially the smoking gun, because they suggested that the trust was not being used properly, to provide discretionary loans, but was in fact shelling out contracted salary to footballers, who fully expected to receive a fixed amount from their MGMRT sub-trust along with their regular wage. The side letters were kept hidden and not revealed even to the SFA because to disclose them would alert HMRC. However, Rangers found themselves caught in a seemingly impossible position, between a legal Scylla and Charybdis, as not to disclose the letters to the proper sporting authorities was potentially even more serious for the club, with SFA rule 12.3 stating clearly that all payments for footballing activities must be stipulated when players are registered with the governing body and 'fully recorded within the relevant written agreement'.

This failure to disclose the full details of many of their players' remuneration called into question whether Rangers were taking to the field and fulfilling their fixtures with a team full of improperly registered footballers. The penalty for fielding just one ineligible player in any given match was a scratched game recorded as a 3-0 defeat against the offending team, a potential forfeit which held obvious implications for the validity of the numerous trophies won by the Ibrox club over this period. Rangers were playing with fire, walking the thin line between SFA rules and HMRC compliance, with the risk that in the end they would fall foul of both.

One of the main beneficiaries from the EBT scheme was the new Rangers manager, Alex McLeish, whose salary was topped up with an additional £1.7m from MGMRT over his four-and-a-half-year spell in charge of the club. With Dick Advocaat teetering on the brink, the Dutchman nominated the Hibernian manager as his successor in the Ibrox dugout and on 12 December, Murray made his approach to the Edinburgh club. 'I bet you never expected to get this phone call,' the chairman quipped to his prospective new head coach.

To many fans, who may not yet have been fully conversant with the new financial reality at Ibrox, it seemed that Rangers were going for the cheap option, and there was apprehension on McLeish's appointment about the prospect of a new era of austerity at Ibrox. Under Advocaat, the overspending at the club had reached epic proportions, and while it's certainly true that the new manager was made aware from the start that he wouldn't have access to the same level of resources which his predecessor had enjoyed, it would be wrong to think that Rangers were now suddenly broke. McLeish still had available to him full usage of Advocaat's expensively assembled squad, while the EBT tax avoidance ruse allowed him a great deal of flexibility and increased his options in the transfer market.

Besides, McLeish didn't care about the prospect of operating within a more restrictive financial environment, and he was delighted to accept the job. As a youngster, he had been taken to see Rangers by his father, but perhaps because his mother was a Catholic, and with a Celtic-supporting side to his family as well, McLeish lacked the hatred for all things concerning the Parkhead club which was so common among many of his peers. As a teenager, he was spotted by scouts from Aberdeen and taken to the Pittodrie club, then managed by future Scotland boss Ally MacLeod. He was given his debut by Billy McNeill in early 1978, before establishing himself and then flourishing under Alex Ferguson in the centre of defence alongside Willie Miller, another Glaswegian transported north to the Granite City, who had been playing for Aberdeen since 1973.

A redoubtable defender who won 77 caps for Scotland, McLeish was famously excused by Ferguson, along with his partner Miller, after a tame Aberdeen performance in the Scottish Cup Final against Rangers in 1983, which saw the Pittodrie men lift the trophy but only after Eric Black's extra-time winner against John Greig's struggling side. 'We're the luckiest team in the world. That was a disgraceful performance,' Ferguson fumed about his players on live TV minutes after their victory. 'Miller and McLeish won the cup for Aberdeen. Miller and McLeish played Rangers by themselves. I'm no caring, winning cups doesny matter. Our standards have been set long ago and I'm no gony accept that from any Aberdeen team. There's no way we can take any glory from this,' the grumpy manager moaned, ten days after his side had beaten Real Madrid and lifted the Cup Winners' Cup as well.

As a manager, McLeish had impressed in spells in charge of Motherwell, whom he led to a second-placed finish behind Walter Smith's Rangers in 1995, and, latterly, Hibernian, after guiding the Easter Road side out of the First Division and back into the Premier League. But there was little McLeish could realistically do to stop the Celtic juggernaut by the time he took charge of Rangers in December 2001 as the championship was already seemingly destined for Parkhead.

Following on from the Treble, won in Martin O'Neill's first season in charge, Celtic improved their domestic form in 2001/02, running up an astonishing tally of 103 points in the league, leading the title race from start to finish, although by the end of the season the Rangers fightback was seemingly on. McLeish had an immediate effect on the Ibrox club's morale and, after a 2-2 draw with Motherwell at Fir Park in his first game in charge, which left his team 16 points off the pace, Rangers won ten of their next 11 league matches under the new manager, until a 1-1 draw at

Ibrox against Celtic in March stopped the rot in terms of the Parkhead men's previous dominance of the fixture. This was underlined with another 1-1 draw between the sides at Celtic Park on 21 April, which punctured Celtic's 100 per cent record at Parkhead in their final home game of the season.

Admittedly Celtic, coasting towards the title and having won the first two meetings between the clubs, would probably have been content with two further draws in the league, but it was a different story in the cup competitions, as the sides met in the semi-final of the League Cup in early February. In an enthralling game, Rangers took the lead when Lovenkrands scored on the stroke of half-time, before Baldé scrambled an equaliser for Celtic in the second half. Almost immediately Rangers were awarded a penalty, which Arveladze struck against the crossbar, and with the tie heading into extra time there were further chances at both ends until Dutch defender Bert Konterman scored an absolute screamer, firing home an effort from distance that was still rising as it hit the back of the net, to send Rangers into the final and handing McLeish a victory in his first tussle with O'Neill.

In addition, there would be a sixth meeting of the season between the teams, in the Scottish Cup Final, which again looked to be heading for extra time at 2-2 until Lovenkrands, who by now had scored five goals in five games against Celtic, popped up again in the final minute to seal that trophy for Rangers too. Still working largely with Advocaat's players, McLeish had reinvigorated his squad and restored their fighting spirit, which despite the two cup wins, was perhaps most clearly illustrated by the award for Scottish PFA Player of the Year going to Lorenzo Amoruso, who had previously been a target for the boo-boys at Ibrox after a string of calamitous errors in high-profile games.

McLeish had salvaged a decent campaign for Rangers, but over the close season, David Murray decided that he could no longer continue as chairman and stepped down from the role, telling the club website, 'I feel a change of management style would be beneficial for the club, as the whole industry faces new challenges.'

It was an effective admission that keeping a tight ship and running a business properly were not in his skillset, and Murray's position had been further weakened by the Halifax/Bank of Scotland (HBOS) merger in June 2001, which saw the eventual retirement, on a £250,000 per annum pension, of the Bank of Scotland's treasurer and managing director Gavin Masterton, a long-term Murray ally. Masterton, despite his bank's refusal to lend Fergus McCann's Celtic more than £2.5m, which prompted the Canadian to immediately take his business elsewhere, had nevertheless squandered an estimated £200m in bad loans to Scottish football clubs during his time at the bank, most of it to Murray's Rangers, but also to his local team, Dunfermline Athletic, where he had been a director since 1990. Murray was replaced in July by his deputy, John McClelland, although the former chairman remained the largest shareholder and owner of the club, retaining the ill-defined title of honorary chairman.

As the media geared up to offer their departing eulogies, there was one man, former Ibrox director Hugh Adam, who had already delivered an ominous rebuke to the chairman, after selling his 59,000 shares in the Ibrox club, on the grounds that they would soon be worthless. Adam, who had operated the Rangers Pools since the early 1970s, raised an estimated £18m from the venture, which was popular even with Celtic fans, money which was put towards the reconstruction of Ibrox Park following the disaster of 1971. He was appointed a director at the start of the Souness era as part of the restructuring of the club which was taking place at the time, but his relationship with Murray, after the industrialist acquired Rangers in 1988, was fractious and twice he stepped down from the board only to be reappointed.

In an article which was published in *The Scotsman* in February 2002, Adam criticised Murray's chairmanship of the club, and, in one of the first open references to the possibility of an insolvency event at Ibrox, he suggested, 'That's the logical conclusion to a strategy that incurs serious loss year on year... The banks are well known for being a bit more tolerant of companies whose core business is a popular pursuit like football. But there is a limit to how far back they can bend to accommodate you.'

Speculating that he was unlikely to be the only stakeholder who was unhappy at the depleted value of Rangers' share price, with ENIC's £40m investment in 1997 now worth roughly £15m and falling, and the money itself having long since been squandered, Adam also contrasted the competent way in which rivals Celtic were being run, alleging, 'Rangers, with Murray, is a one-party state and the man in power has an allergy to any form of personal criticism. But he's not a businessman in the long-term sense of planning and prudence, he's more of an impresario.'

With Rangers now under new leadership, McLeish splashed out £4m in the summer of 2002 to bring Spanish midfielder Mikel Arteta to Ibrox from Barcelona, although the club's only other acquisition was Australian hard man Kevin Muscat, who arrived from Wolverhampton Wanderers. After a solid start in the Ibrox dugout the previous year, McLeish's first full term in charge would turn out to be Rangers' best domestic season since Advocaat's first year in Glasgow, with the Ibrox club eventually completing a clean sweep of the three available trophies, although it was a contrasting story in Europe, as Rangers suffered an away goals defeat to the uncelebrated Prague side Viktoria Žižkov in the first round of the UEFA Cup. The loss left McLeish with a record of two European defeats out of two, after Rangers had crashed out of the previous season's UEFA Cup in February following a fourth-round defeat to eventual champions Feyenoord.

Domestically, the first Old Firm game of the season was at Celtic Park in October and a thrilling match ended 3-3, with both sides at one time holding the advantage but being unable to shake off the other. The next encounter between the sides in December saw Celtic take the lead at Ibrox after just 19 seconds, the fastest recorded goal in the fixture, but Rangers came storming back to lead 3-1 by the interval with goals from Moore, de Boer and Mols, before the game finished 3-2 to the home side, a result which sent Rangers to the top of the league.

'It's very tight between the two of us,' McLeish admitted afterwards and with both sides dropping very few points against their other opponents, the season came to a head in March; Celtic beat Rangers in the league, Hartson's winner inflicting a first defeat in the fixture on McLeish at the seventh attempt, but the following week Rangers made amends, beating their old rivals 2-1 in the League Cup Final at Hampden after Hartson missed a last-minute penalty. Then, with Celtic continuing their run in Europe all the way to the UEFA Cup Final in Seville, Martin O'Neill's team took their eye off the ball in the Scottish Cup, with the Parkhead manager fielding a weakened side against First Division Inverness Caledonian Thistle and losing. Celtic's previous four fixtures had seen them play Rangers twice and Liverpool twice, so the resting of players was understandable, but the defeat left the Ibrox men as overwhelming favourites to collect the Treble.

The race for the title came down to the last day of the season; at one stage Rangers had been eight points clear but Celtic's win in March was followed by another victory at Ibrox in late April in a match which had been scheduled, following the announcement of the post-split fixtures, three days after the second leg of their UEFA Cup semi-final against Boavista, much to O'Neill's chagrin. When Rangers then dropped points in their next match, drawing 2-2 against Dundee in a game in which they were awarded three penalties, two of which were missed by Ferguson, the two rivals found themselves level on points. Even goal difference could not separate the sides going into the final fixture, although Rangers held the advantage by virtue of their greater number of goals scored. The season therefore came down to a final day shoot-out between the pair; Celtic, four days after losing a gruelling UEFA Cup Final 3-2 after extra time to Jose Mourinho's Porto, beat Kilmarnock 4-0 at Rugby Park, but that result was bettered by the 6-1 scoreline inflicted on Dunfermline at Ibrox, with a last-minute penalty from Arteta securing the title for Rangers.

After the defeat, Celtic striker Chris Sutton accused Dunfermline of 'lying down' in the game, claiming that the East End Park side, managed by the Rangers-affiliated duo of Jimmy Calderwood and Jimmy Nichol and with Gavin Masterton installed in the boardroom as the Fife club's majority shareholder, had not given their all in the Ibrox fixture. It later emerged that Calderwood believed he was being groomed for the Ibrox manager's job after being tempted back from Holland to Dunfermline on the back of a promise, ultimately never fulfilled, from David Murray. Regardless of the circumstantial evidence, however, Sutton's comments were without foundation and he later apologised. The following week, a tired-looking Rangers fell over the line to secure the Treble with a 1-0 victory over Dundee in the Scottish Cup Final, Amoruso marking his last game for the club by scoring with his head from a set piece.

Regardless of the on-field success, Rangers lost a staggering £30m in 2003, with debts at the spendthrift Ibrox institution rising to a mammoth £68m by the end of the financial year, despite the hidden benefits of the EBT scheme and the desperate efforts of chairman John McClelland to try and reduce the club's overheads. The message being put out by McClelland at the time was that there was no danger of an insolvency event at Ibrox due to the value of the club's assets, chiefly the playing squad, the stadium and the training ground at Auchenhowie, the combined worth equating to more than the net debt figure. The problem with the chairman's theory, however, was that it depended on Rangers' own preferred valuation of the tangible assets, with the stadium and training ground, by a neat accountancy trick, revalued in 2003 at £130m, up from £93m, and crucially, McClelland's calculations failed to factor in the ticking time-bomb of the EBT scheme and the huge potential tax bill that was being stored up which, if it crystallised and HMRC could make it stick, would call the chairman's safe assumptions into question.

After the highs of 2003, by the end of which Alex McLeish had secured all five of the domestic competitions realistically available to him, came the lows of 2004, when the Ibrox club finished the season without a trophy, in the process losing five times to Celtic with the Parkhead side, after an opening day draw with Dunfermline, reasserting their pre-eminence of the domestic game with a run of 25 consecutive league victories. It was a season in which Rangers, in reduced circumstances, were casting around desperately for players, after seeing such luminaries as Amoruso, Flo and McCann all leave. Numan also departed, the Dutchman choosing to retire rather than accept a new contract and suffer the indignity of playing for Rangers on reduced terms, as did Barry Ferguson, who decided that he fancied a crack at the English Premier League and joined Amoruso at Blackburn.

Ferguson would return with his tail between his legs 18 months later, but in the meantime the club, in the hope that they might find value for money in among the journeymen available in the Bosman market, had been experimenting with a whole troop of players, some of whose names even the most enthusiastic Rangers fans will struggle to remember, such was the minuscule significance of their contribution to the club. Following on from Norwegian international Dan Eggen (no league appearances, no goals for the club) and Frenchman Jérôme Bonnissel (three games, no goals) who arrived in January 2003, Rangers signed a whole host of lesser lights over the next year or so, including such instantly forgotten names as Federico Nieto (3/1), Bajram Fetai (1/0) and Dragan Mladenović (7/0), who cost £1.1m from Red Star Belgrade but failed to settle at the club. On it went; José-Karl Pierre-FanFan (7/1), Derek Carcary (0/0), Moses Ashikodi (1/0), Bojan Djordjic (5/0), Filippo Maniero (0/0), Dany N'Guessan (0/0) and Marc Kalenga (0/0).

It all seemed a far cry from the days when Rangers were signing players who were meant to win them the Champions League, although other arrivals were quite high-profile, such as Nuno Capucho (22/5), who cost £650,000 from Porto where he had won the UEFA Cup in 2003, Egil Ostenstadt (11/0), Henning Berg (20/0) and the Brazilian Emerson (14/0). Frank de Boer (15/2) even turned up at the end of the winter transfer window in early 2004, although poor Frank was on less than £5,000 per week, whereas his twin brother Ronald was still benefitting to the weekly tune of £35,000 from his pre-austerity era contract, but even the combination of the talented Dutch duo couldn't prevent Rangers, who had also ended the European campaign by finishing last in their Champions League group, from completing the season without a domestic trophy.

Results on the park were disappointing for everyone associated with Rangers in 2004 but, far more seriously, as the new season was set to get under way in earnest, the Ibrox institution faced its most grave financial crisis to date, as the burden of the club's continuing losses became too much for the company to bear. Rangers' spending in the transfer market had dropped from a sum in excess of £30m in 2000/01 to less than £11m in 2001/02, and the figure fell further, to roughly £6m in 2002/03, before bottoming out at under £1m in 2003/04, a year in which almost £10m was recouped from player sales. The club had also been transformed over the same period from one of the most prodigal spenders on players' salaries in Britain to a team hunting bargains at the basement end of the market, but these measures proved to be too little too late.

Behind the scenes, the chairman, the owner and the board of directors had utterly failed to grasp the urgency of the situation and, even while the club was suffering colossal losses year after year, the priority had always remained to keep a winning team on the park and to try not to lose face, rather than get to grips with the crippling debt, which stubbornly refused to come down, peaking at £73.9m in 2004. The financial predicament at Ibrox worsened further when, at the start of the new season, McLeish's side failed to qualify for the group stages of the Champions League, losing 3-2 on aggregate to CSKA Moscow, a result which cost Rangers an estimated £8m in prize money, gate receipts and television revenue.

It was at this point that owner David Murray made clear his intention to return to frontline business with the club, resuming the chairmanship of the Ibrox institution with immediate effect from 1 September. 'We do not like being second best, but we got it wrong,' the once and future chairman admitted, although he had previously tried to get at least one journalist sacked for trying to tell him as much. 'We obviously spent far too much money. We can't let it happen again because that would be total mismanagement,' he added.

Murray's reappearance was accompanied by the announcement of a £57m rights issue, which MIH, through a subsidiary company called Murray MHL, would underwrite to the tune of £50m, money which was intended to be used solely for the purpose of addressing the club's mountainous debt, with Murray confidently predicting that the business would be back in the black within a year. The rights issue, which invited existing shareholders to purchase new shares, valued at £1, on a one for one basis, as well as being open to fresh investment, faced an initial obstacle in the form of Murray's forgotten partners ENIC, who were unwilling to allow the dwindling value of their stock to be depleted further and who certainly weren't going to take up the offer to buy any more shares. Murray therefore had to first acquire their 20 per cent stake in the company, paying £8.7m for the shares which cost £40m in 1997, increasing his personal holding to over 90 per cent of the business.

In the end, £51.4m was raised from the rights issue, well short of the £57m target, and with £50.3m coming from the underwriters, MIH, the uptake from new and existing shareholders amounted to little more than £1m, a disappointing outcome. Nevertheless, the rights issue had addressed the immediate problem of the unsustainable level of debt and the club's effective insolvency, although with the uptake so low, Murray was merely moving vast amounts of debt around his group of companies, borrowing money with one hand and paying off Rangers' liabilities with the other. But with MIH showing a healthier overall balance sheet than its sporting subsidiary, despite its own debt burden increasing to £500m from £164m over the course of the next year, the bank held greater security over its claim now that the debt was off Rangers' books and transferred to the parent company.

The bank, HBOS, in full pre-credit crunch madness mode, also provided Rangers with a further £15m overdraft facility for 'ongoing working capital requirements' and agreed to restructure the remaining Ibrox debt, which now stood at £23.1m. Murray and Rangers had looked death in the face and the chairman, thanks to his friends at the bank and some powder puff coverage of his handling of the situation in the media, had come up smelling of roses.

Following the disappointment of missing out on the Champions League group stages, the month of August ended with Rangers losing another Old Firm game, Alan Thompson's late winner at Celtic Park condemning the Ibrox club to a record-breaking seventh consecutive defeat in the fixture. After six games unbeaten against the Parkhead side in the period immediately following his appointment as Rangers manager, McLeish had now chalked up an unprecedented series of losses against Celtic, with this latest setback handing their rivals an early five-point lead in the title race, an advantage which was extended further when Rangers could only draw their next game 0-0 against Hearts at Tynecastle.

After an insipid 1-0 defeat in Portugal against Maritimo in the UEFA Cup play-off round, a result which was only rectified following a penalty shoot-out at Ibrox in the second leg, Rangers fans were calling for McLeish's head on a stick. However, there was to be another dramatic end to the domestic league season in 2005, which rivalled the finish of two years earlier. Rangers had made productive use of the Bosman market over the summer, perhaps for the first time since the introduction of the landmark ruling almost a decade earlier, with the free transfer acquisitions of Dado Pršo, a Croatian forward, lured to Ibrox with the help of the owner's ostentatious use of his private jet, and Jean-Alain Boumsong, although the French defender was quickly sold on to Graeme Souness's Newcastle for £8m in January after turning out just 28 times in all competitions for the Ibrox club. With Rangers splashing the proceeds on new singings Sotirios Kyrgiakos, Thomas Buffel and Ronald Waterreus, the club had subsequently ended their run of bad luck in the Celtic fixture with wins at both venues, but in the final encounter in April, Celtic defeated McLeish's side at Ibrox to go five points clear at the top of the league with just four games of the season remaining.

The Parkhead club failed to consolidate their advantage however, losing the following week, 3-1 at home to Hibs, and with the other games after the match 33 league 'split' all resulting in wins for the Glasgow sides, Celtic still found themselves two points clear at the top going into the final fixture, but with Rangers holding a superior goal difference. The Parkhead men were well aware that only a win against Motherwell at Fir Park would be enough to guarantee them the title and things seemed to be going to plan for the visitors when Sutton fired home a loose ball on 29 minutes. Leading 1-0 as the clock ticked down on the season, and having spurned several opportunities to increase their advantage and put the title beyond doubt, Celtic conceded an equaliser to a strike from Australian forward Scott McDonald, who then netted a second goal on the counter-attack in the dying seconds of the game as the Parkhead men pushed to try and retake the lead.

Over at Easter Road, there was no question of nerves affecting the Rangers players, as many argued had happened with Celtic, because the game was being played out at walking pace. After Novo gave Rangers the lead with a deflected shot on the hour, the teams settled for the 1-0 result, which seemed to suit both parties as a heavier defeat would have jeopardised Hibs' hopes of finishing third and qualifying for the UEFA Cup. The only excitement at Easter Road came when news of Motherwell's two goals came through from Fir Park, both of which were greeted with huge roars from the Rangers end of the ground, and with the SPL trophy now en route to the presentation ceremony in Edinburgh, amid jubilant scenes, the commentator's announcement would be remembered by fans of the Ibrox club for many years, 'The helicopter is changing direction!'

Highlighting the rollercoaster nature of McLeish's tenure at the club, after the last-day title triumph of 2005 the extraordinary lows quickly returned the following season during a campaign which saw Rangers notch up a ten-game run without a victory over the autumn, a record-breaking winless streak for the Ibrox side. It was a remarkable display of mediocrity from McLeish's side, considering the colossal financial advantages which Rangers continued to enjoy over most of their domestic opponents, including the apex of the club's EBT usage, with a total of almost £10m plundered from MGMRT in tax-free earnings over the course of the year. After a goalless stalemate at Ibrox against the manager's former side Aberdeen in November 2005, Rangers' third successive league draw, which left them 12 points behind joint leaders Celtic and Hearts after just 14 games, a banner was unfurled by fans at the away end of the ground, directed at their former idol, which read: 'AGENT MCLEISH, MISSION ACCOMPLISHED, RETURN TO BASE'.

It was clear that the manager was living on borrowed time, as a few days later, Rangers were eliminated from the League Cup, losing 2-0 at Celtic Park. By early February the Ibrox men had also crashed out of the Scottish Cup, losing 3-0 at home to Hibs, a third victory of the season over Rangers for Tony Mowbray's young side, a result which saw hundreds of fans protesting outside the ground after the game. With Celtic, now managed by McLeish's former Aberdeen team-mate Gordon Strachan, running away with the league once again, their fourth wide-margin title success in six years, Rangers' domestic season was effectively over in midwinter. Even second place eventually eluded the club, with Hearts, despite using four managers over the course of the campaign, taking the runners-up spot and qualifying for the Champions League play-offs, the Edinburgh men becoming the first team outside of the Glasgow duopoly to break into the top two positions since 1995. Rangers' form had improved in the second half of the season, but McLeish's side still somehow contrived to finish third in what was generally considered to be a two-horse race.

There was some welcome respite for the beleaguered manager in Europe as Rangers made history by becoming the first Scottish side to reach the knockout stages of the Champions League, despite winning only one of their six group games. By the time of their narrow last-16 defeat on away goals to Villarreal, however, McLeish had already made known his intention to step down from the role at the end of the season. In another crafted managerial departure, Rangers had avoided any reference to their head coach being 'sacked', although by any loose definition – the club weren't happy with the results the manager was achieving and they believed they could get another guy in who could do a better job – not only was McLeish sacked, but his two predecessors were as well.

Adding to the suspicion that McLeish's decision was not entirely his own, by the time of the announcement, Murray and the club's chief executive Martin Bain were already some way down the line to appointing his replacement. Although an agreement had not yet been formally concluded, the coveted Frenchman Paul Le Guen, who had led Lyon to three consecutive titles in his homeland and twice to the quarter-finals of the Champions League, had already verbally consented to become the next Rangers manager. Forced to sit on his hands and wait while the contractual details were being negotiated, Murray, the great propagandist, announced to the club's in-house television channel that Rangers' troubles were coming to an end, and, unable to contain his excitement at the identity of McLeish's intended successor, the chairman proclaimed that it wasn't just light which he could see at the end of the proverbial tunnel, but moonbeams.

'There's a massive moonbeam of success awaiting us,' he blurted out on Rangers TV the day after McLeish's departure was made public, referring not only to Le Guen's expected appointment, but also to an imminent, multi-million-pound deal with the retailer JJB Sports. It seemed a typical piece of Murray hyperbole, but it backfired on him with neither Le Guen nor the retail partnership, which netted the club plenty of cash in the short term, but sacrificed an important revenue stream over the years ahead, living up to expectation. The expression 'moonbeams' has subsequently passed into shorthand, and been used by sceptics and rival fans to ridicule every pronouncement of expected good news to emanate from the Ibrox club, even amid its evidently degenerating circumstances.

Le Guen was one of the most sought-after managers in Europe, having been courted by a host of top clubs including Lazio, Dynamo Kiev and cash-rich Lokomotiv Moscow, all of whom he visited in person during the period of his sabbatical from the game. After quitting Lyon at the end of the 2005 season, the former French international defender, who earned 17 caps for his country between 1993 and 1997, had taken a year off from coaching and was working as a summariser and football analyst for the French TV station Canal Plus, so Le Guen was very much seen as available and, given his impressive track record at Rennes and Lyon, desirable by ambitious owners across the continent.

With his pick of leading European clubs to choose from, his eventual decision to join Rangers left many in France flummoxed, but Le Guen's single-mindedness meant that he had little time for the sceptics. 'I've not got a lot to say to people who think that I am making a mistake in going to Glasgow. To be honest I'm not interested in what other people might think. It doesn't bother me in the slightest,' he stated. What arguably delighted Murray most of all about his snaring of Le Guen was the Frenchman's acceptance of the budgetary restrictions which he would be working under at Ibrox. Now at last, the chairman could see a way forward for the club – they would navigate their way safely through troubled financial waters thanks to the sheer quality of the man at the tiller.

For his part, Le Guen had been impressed in particular by the Ibrox club's clarity of purpose and their determination to get their man, as he explained in an interview with Canal Plus's Darren Tulett, 'He [Murray] made me understand that I was going to be able to feel good at this club, that he was prepared to do everything necessary for that to be the case. And you know, he said all that with such force, such charisma and enthusiasm, that it gave it an extra dimension. He's the kind of guy who can't leave you indifferent.'

In May 2006, Le Guen finally confirmed the worst-kept secret in Scottish football when he announced that he was becoming the new manager of Rangers, and he and his family soon decamped en masse, along with a coterie of fellow Breton coaches, physios and translators, to Glasgow.

Le Guen's first game in charge, as the new season got under way, was against Motherwell at Fir Park. Goals from Pršo and new signing Libor Sionko gave Rangers a well-deserved 2-1 win, which was probably more comfortable than the scoreline suggested. Rangers had started the game strongly and scored early, and although the hosts came back into the game and equalised, Le Guen's side quickly restored their lead and held on to take the three points. Afterwards the manager seemed pleased with his team's performance. 'I am very happy,' he reflected. 'We made many chances but we weren't efficient enough, but it doesn't matter. There was a good rhythm and a good relationship between our players.'

It seemed like a positive start but from that opening-day victory, things began to unravel with startling alacrity for the Frenchman. In their first game at Ibrox, Rangers found themselves two goals down to Dundee United before a strike from substitute Chris Burke and an own goal rescued a 2-2 draw. By the end of August, Rangers, the pre-season favourites for the title with most, had dropped further points following draws with Dunfermline and Kilmarnock, as slowly but surely the hype and expectation following the manager's appointment began to dissipate.

Much of Le Guen's initial difficulties seemed to stem from the quality and calibre of his signings. Acting without a technical director and with sole responsibility for player acquisitions for the first time in his career, the new manager plundered Austria Vienna, downsizing at the time following the withdrawal of a long-standing sponsorship agreement with the vehicle component supplier Magna International, taking Filip Sebo, an awful Slovakian striker whom the incredulous Austrians managed to entice £1.8m from Rangers for, Saša Papac, a solid but unspectacular Bosnian left-back and the only one of Le Guen's 11 permanent signings, apart from the invisible Dean Furman, who would still be at the club the following season, as well as Sionko, the Czech winger, from the struggling Viennese side.

Other arrivals included Karl Svensson, an unremarkable Swedish defender, youngsters Furman, Antoine Ponroy and William Stanger, who between them managed only a single competitive appearance for the first team, Lionel Letizi, a blundering goalkeeper who was controversially reinstated after injury despite the impressive form of Allan McGregor, while Jérémy Clément looked like a decent player, but never fully settled into his surroundings and left after six months for the home comforts of Paris Saint-Germain.

If his signings were poor, Le Guen had even greater difficulty handling the players he inherited at the club. Even as early as pre-season, the Frenchman felt compelled to send Fernando Ricksen home from a training camp in South Africa after the Dutchman had got drunk on the flight and apparently offended a stewardess with his antics. To many of his team-mates, the defender's transgressions amounted to nothing more than simply 'Fernando being Fernando', but the new manager felt the need to act, and dispatched the player back to Glasgow on the next available flight. Within a few weeks, Ricksen had joined Dick Advocaat's Zenit St Petersburg on loan.

As the season progressed, the manager's stance regarding two other indigenous players, Boyd and McGregor, was also called into question.

Striker Boyd was constantly berated for not working hard enough outside the penalty box, despite the efficiency of his goalscoring when inside it, and used sparingly, while McGregor was dropped, even after the goalkeeper had been named Scotland's player of the month for September, in favour of the returning Letizi, who had missed several games with a calf strain and whose performances prior to injury had been anything but convincing.

The manager was left with egg on his face as a mistake from Letizi, parrying Dargo's long-range shot into the path of the grateful Bayne, allowed Inverness to record a famous 1-0 win at Ibrox in mid-October, the Highlanders' first ever victory over Rangers. 'I do not feel I put pressure on Lionel Letizi. I do not regret my decision. I am not used to discussing this in the press,' the Frenchman said, closing ranks when questioned about his selection after the game.

Having already lost successive matches to Hibernian and Celtic, Le Guen's side were now struggling badly, ten points behind the Parkhead men, and the situation only worsened in November. At the start of the month, Rangers lost a further league match, 2-1 away to Dundee United, leaving them 15 points off the pace and then, just a few days later, the Ibrox men were knocked out of the CIS League Cup, losing 2-0 at home to First Division St Johnstone. In a result which was similar to Celtic's epochal home loss to Inverness in 2000, although far less celebrated, Rangers were beaten by lower-league opposition at Ibrox for the first time in their history. It seemed that the bubble of Le Guen's reputation had well and truly burst.

Amid much speculation about the manager's position, chairman David Murray called a press conference days after the St Johnstone defeat with the intention of publicly backing the struggling Frenchman. 'Paul is here to do a long-term job,' Murray told the assembled media. 'Okay, our results have been bad, but if there's one thing I've learned in life, it comes from Captain Mainwaring: you don't panic... in life, in business, in anything,' the chairman expounded, presumably trying to apply an old adage from the 1970s BBC sitcom *Dad's Army* to the circumstances surrounding his flagging institution, but failing to remember that it was Clive Dunn's Lance Corporal Jones, the Walmington-on-Sea butcher, who had employed that particular catchphrase, not Arthur Lowe's Mainwaring. Perhaps an alert journalist might have suggested to Murray that Rangers' problems were due to the fact that they didn't 'like it up 'em', but no such notions were forthcoming.

Despite Murray's cack-handed intervention, which only served to further undermine the manager's position and his credibility with the media, Rangers' fortunes improved in the short term, with Le Guen's side winning their next three league games against Dunfermline, Hearts and Kilmarnock. But then, on a freezing, wet Sunday afternoon in early December, Rangers lost again, 1-0 away to a Falkirk side who had thoroughly outplayed the Ibrox men.

Within days Le Guen was on the phone to Murray, telling the chairman that the only way he could see the team progressing under his stewardship was if the club sold Barry Ferguson. The club captain had returned to the team in mid-September after a five-month lay-off with an injured ankle, but the new manager quickly grew frustrated by his apparent tactical indiscipline, with Ferguson seemingly incapable of following instructions and holding his position at the apex of the midfield.

But the animosity between captain and manager ran far deeper, with Le Guen later claiming that Ferguson had been trying to undermine him throughout his entire spell at the club. Ferguson was the leader of the Scottish clique within the dressing room, a recalcitrant group, sceptical of the manager's methods seemingly from the start, which even appeared to include club doctor Ian McGuinness, who was chastised and put aside by the manager for having too strong an influence over certain players and for frequently exceeding his remit.

Following a spirited 1-1 draw with Celtic at Ibrox on 17 December and a 2-1 win at Aberdeen, matters came to a head over the festive period as Rangers lost, once again, to Inverness, the Ibrox men suffering a 2-1 reverse in the Highland capital having initially led. Back in the dressing room, Le Guen applied his customary mantra of 'don't worry, let's stick together and move on', an approach to adversity which Ferguson decided he could stomach no longer. Quoting himself regarding the infamous mutiny, Ferguson subsequently related his own account of the incident: 'I said, "Aye, we must stick together, but it's not fucking okay that we've lost another three points. What part of that don't you get? This is Glasgow Rangers you are working for!" I admit I lost the head. I was just so angered by the lack of passion… Yes, maybe I was guilty of letting my emotions boil over... But I just couldn't take any more of it. But that was it. It wasn't as if I asked the guy outside for a square-go.'

Responding to suggestions that he failed to adhere to the manager's directives, Ferguson denied ever receiving any tactical instructions from the manager, but admitted, 'Yes, okay I might have eaten the occasional packet of Monster Munch which might have been against his nutritional rules, but come on... No one is going to tell me a packet of pickled onion now and again is going to take years off your career. It's nonsense.'

Clearly there was something of a clash of cultures going on behind the scenes at Le Guen's Rangers.

The club's next game was at home to St Mirren, a 1-1 draw with Ferguson again infuriating his manager by roaming all over the pitch instead of holding his position 'in the hole' behind the two strikers. With Celtic now disappearing into the distance at the top of the table, 16 points clear of second-placed Aberdeen and 17 ahead of Rangers in third, the exasperated Le Guen decided to act; he stripped Ferguson of the captaincy, dropped him from the side and informed the player that his days at the club were at an end. It was desperation stakes for the Frenchman; David Murray, who had sounded so bullish about Le Guen's long-term prospects at the club only a few weeks earlier flinched and refused to back his manager over the controversial decision.

The denouement finally came at Fir Park, Motherwell, the scene of such promise and optimism back in the heady days of late summer and Le Guen's first game in charge. Now in the cold of midwinter, the Rangers fans barracked the Frenchman as he stepped off the team coach and chanted Ferguson's name throughout the match, which was settled by a disputed Kris Boyd penalty midway through the second half. Having scored what turned out to be the game's only goal, Boyd melodramatically held up six fingers to the Rangers fans in support of Ferguson, who was so emotionally attached to his squad number that he was known simply as 'six' within the dressing room.

The end came quickly for the manager; bereft of the chairman's support, Le Guen was unable to definitively answer questions from the media, crammed into the incommodious Fir Park pressroom after the game, about his future. 'I don't know if Ferguson will be sold,' he shrugged. 'It remains to be seen.' The Frenchman seemed to appreciate that his days at the club were numbered, when he added, 'The situation of a manager in this case is precarious. I don't know if I'll be here in the months ahead. I am not here to protect myself... if I go, I go.' By the time his remarks were published in the press the next day, Le Guen had already spoken on the phone to Murray, now Sir David Murray, after the chairman was named in the New Year's Honours list for services to business. One of Sir David's first acts as a knight of the realm was to sanction Le Guen's departure from Ibrox, by mutual consent, after just 27 weeks and 31 games in the job, the shortest spell of any manager in the club's history.

Le Guen's brief tenure at Rangers was beset with problems from start to finish, some of which were of his own making: he was initially naïve with his choice of club and then made things more difficult for himself by failing to adapt to a foreign culture at an institution that was a cultural law unto itself. Le Guen was a quiet, understated, privately educated Catholic taking on a club known for its association with brash and triumphalist Protestantism, yet the Frenchman didn't seem to care, as he vainly tried to apply the methods at Ibrox which had worked for him in his homeland. The manager had a preference for light touch training sessions, with a ban on tackles and over-physical contact rigorously enforced, so that when Manchester United loanee Phil Bardsley, against explicit instructions, steamed into a challenge on team-mate Thomas Buffel, he was swiftly dispatched back to his parent club.

To the home-grown contingent, steeped in Rangers' customary methods, this was as bewildering as it was ineffective, and Le Guen maintains his belief that Barry Ferguson, with his sullen demeanour and his intractable ways, had been on a mission to destabilise his regime from the start, something the player has always denied. Far more plausibly, Ferguson was just acting normal and Le Guen had been in the wrong movie all along. In addition, his recruitment strategy was weak, albeit with limited financial resources, but despite the number of players who came into the club, the manager failed to unearth a single footballer who made more than a superficial contribution to the Ibrox cause.

Le Guen showed he was a man of honour when he quit the club and refused all forms of compensation from Rangers, asking only that Murray pay for his removal van, as the Frenchman left the country immediately, dragging his tearful daughters out of their local school. He deserves less sympathy, however, over his participation in the contentious EBT tax avoidance scheme; while footballers were generally able to plead ignorance over their involvement in the wheeze, citing their own ignorance and lack of intelligence in their defence against any perceived wrongdoing, it is harder to make that argument in the case of the urbane Le Guen, who along with several members of his staff, Yves Colleau (assistant manager), Joel Le Hir (physiotherapist) and Stephane Wiertelak (fitness coach) all signed up to the scheme, and who between them received £364,000 in untaxed income during their short stay in Glasgow.

It wouldn't be long, however, before the supposed secret of Rangers' success would come to light, as the club received a visit from the City of London Police.

12

THE PRODIGAL FATHER

BETWEEN 2006 and 2008 Celtic won three consecutive Scottish Premier League titles, a feat that was matched by Rangers, under returning father figure Walter Smith's management, between 2009 and 2011. These bare statistics conceal the more important story however, with even the seemingly eternal power struggle between the two old rivals at the top of the Scottish game becoming a secondary consideration at times over the course of this period as the ticking time bomb of tax evasion and maladministration at Rangers eventually went off, engulfing the Ibrox club in a legal and financial maelstrom which would ultimately only end with its insolvency.

Back in January 2008, however, over four years out from the spectre of liquidation and with matters still very much focused on football, the immediate priority of the newly knighted club chairman, Sir David Murray, was to find the man who could rescue Rangers from their on-field travails, after the failure of the Paul Le Guen experiment. For many older Rangers fans, the situation at the club bore a notable resemblance to events of almost 40 years earlier, when an attempt to introduce a more enlightened approach under Davie White ended with the young tracksuit manager being replaced by Willie Waddell, a man who knew the club inside out.

Now Rangers would revert to type once more, although the man Murray wanted to restore the club's fortunes was currently in employment within the game.

Walter Smith, after four years of, by his own admission, failure at Everton, was now in charge of the Scotland national team, and doing a fine job of repairing the country's battered credibility following the ineptitude and embarrassment of Berti Vogts's short tenure. Such inconveniences were of no concern to the Rangers chairman, however, and by the time Smith handed in his letter of resignation to the SFA on 10 January, he had already agreed a bumper three-year contract to become the next Rangers manager.

Needless to say, the governing body were none too pleased at having their most high-profile employee snatched from their grasp in such an audacious manner and the organisation's CEO, David Taylor, and president, John McBeth, immediately threatened legal action against Smith 'for breach of contract' and against Rangers 'for inducement to break the contract', although they soon backed down after compensation was agreed between the parties. Smith, dismissing the concerns of his former employers, observed, 'When I took over, these people [the president and the chief executive] had to be smuggled out of stadiums in the backs of cars with fans shouting that they should resign and that Scottish football was a shambles... When I came in it was a diabolical time, and this is how they act in the end.'

Having completed such an abrupt return to his spiritual home, Smith's first act in his second spell in charge of Rangers was to appoint Ally McCoist as his assistant, with the former striker having to relinquish his role as team captain on *A Question of Sport* in order to accept the position. He also brought in Kenny McDowall, who had been working without a contract as the boss of Celtic's youth and reserve sides, and promoted Ian Durrant from reserve team coach to first team coach, the former midfielder who, in his only game in charge after Le Guen's departure, had presided over Rangers' exit from the Scottish Cup at the hands of Dunfermline.

The new regime had an immediate impact as Smith's first game back in the Ibrox dugout ended in a 5-0 victory over Dundee United, a team who had beaten Le Guen's side as recently as November, with all the goals coming from Smith's Scottish contingent, including an 88th-minute strike from Barry Ferguson, restored to the captaincy and clearly back in his element after seeing off Le Guen's attempt to offload him.

Smith quickly identified that Rangers needed to shore up their defence and brought in centre-halves David Weir and Ugo Ehiogu during the January transfer window, with the latter scoring an unlikely winner at Celtic Park in March, as the revival under the new manager continued. Asked after the game if he thought the match would have a bearing on next season's championship race, Celtic boss Gordon Strachan replied, 'I hope so,' referring to his side's domination of the encounter, especially in the first half, but the defeat precipitated a wobble in their form as the Parkhead men lost to Falkirk and then drew with Dundee United, leaving Rangers, for a few hours at least, with a glimmer of hope of getting back into the title race.

Following their rivals' lunchtime stalemate at Tannadice, however, Rangers' chances finally seemed to evaporate later that afternoon, as Smith's side, after taking the lead, could only manage a home draw against ten-man Inverness, leaving Celtic to steer their way to the title, which was confirmed with four games to spare after a 2-1 win against Kilmarnock at Rugby Park. There was still time, however, for another morale-boosting victory over the champions, as Smith's charges recorded a late-season 2-0 success against Celtic at Ibrox, in a match which saw the otherwise prolific striker Kris Boyd score his only Old Firm goal.

With the scores reset to zero, the season of 2007/08 was much anticipated in Glasgow as it pitted the returning Smith, in charge of a seemingly revitalised Rangers, against Strachan's Celtic from the start; it would not disappoint. Having already spent £2m to acquire Kevin Thomson from Hibs in January, Smith demanded more money to strengthen his squad, bringing in a total of 15 players on permanent transfers over the summer, including DaMarcus Beasley, an American winger from PSV Eindhoven (£0.7m), right-back Steven Whittaker from Hibs (£2m), Daniel Cousin, a burly striker from the French side Lens (£1.1m), Carlos Cuellar, a Spanish centre-half from Osasuna who had helped knock Rangers out of the previous season's UEFA Cup (£2.37m), versatile Lee McCulloch from Wigan (£2.25m) and striker Steven Naismith in a last-minute, transfer deadline-busting deal from Kilmarnock (£2m), as well as Alan Gow, Roy Carroll, Kirk Broadfoot and Jean-Claude Darcheville on free transfers.

The season began in late July with Rangers seeing off FK Zeta and then Red Star Belgrade to qualify for the Champions League group stages. Already there were grumblings about the team's negative style of play, with the Ibrox men jeered from the park at half-time against the Montenegrins, while against the Serbs only Novo's last-minute strike silenced Smith's home-grown critics, a goal which eventually proved decisive after a scoreless encounter in the return leg in Belgrade. Rangers fans expected their team to be on the front foot against such sides, although, as Smith's biographer Neil Drysdale pointed out, 'Some of Rangers' fans have such a staggering superiority complex, which is untroubled by reality, that their displeasure was predictable.'

The fans suffered when their team was compared to rivals Celtic, with the Parkhead side generally adopting a more positive, aggressive approach but Smith, after experiencing such a series of traumatic nights at this level against the likes of Juventus and Ajax during his first spell at the club in the 1990s, had devised an ultra-defensive system, which involved deploying multiple men behind the ball and then hoping for the best up front, a mistake perhaps or a piece of luck which could lead to a potentially decisive goal. Against Barcelona at home, Rangers sat in, refusing even to counter-attack until the game's latter stages, and came away with a goalless draw, prompting Lionel Messi to observe, 'It's incredible, Rangers didn't want to play football. Right from the start they went for anti-football… It's a real pain playing against teams like them.' In the return leg at the Camp Nou, Rangers adopted the same tactics, refusing to come out and play even after finding themselves two goals down at the end of the first half, much to the bemusement of Barcelona head coach Frank Rijkaard, who couldn't believe that Smith's side would so obviously settle for a 2-0 defeat.

By then Rangers had already secured creditable wins at home to Stuttgart and then an eyebrow-raising result away to Lyon, Le Guen's former side, who Rangers picked off, showing admirable adherence to the game plan to come away with a 3-0 win, with goals from three of Smith's summer signings, McCulloch, Cousin and Beasley. A loss in the return game against Stuttgart meant that Rangers had to beat the French side again in the final fixture at Ibrox to finish in second place and progress to the knockout stages, and with such a crucial game looming, Rangers took the unprecedented step of seeking a postponement of their weekend fixture against the league's bottom side Gretna in order to give the team more time to prepare for the winner-takes-all encounter in the Champions League. The request caused bad blood, because it seemed gratuitous and unnecessary, with Rangers resorting to spurious arguments about the good of Scottish football and apparently using the pretext of the postponement of Celtic's and Rangers' fixtures the previous month, before Scotland's defining Euro 2008 qualifier against Italy at Hampden, to their advantage. The club also appeared to be claiming that Lyon had been granted a similar request and that the French side would have a full week to prepare for the game, but this was not in fact the case, despite what was being widely reported in the Scottish press, and Lyon's weekend game against Caen went ahead as scheduled. Many also felt that a busy schedule of fixtures was simply an occupational hazard for top players around Europe and that big clubs were generally just expected to get on with it, but Rangers appeared to be acting as if they should be considered a special case, especially after witnessing Celtic drop points against Hearts at Tynecastle the previous week, days before their equally vital game with AC Milan.

Presumably, it was a case of 'if you don't ask, you don't get' on Celtic's part, but when Aberdeen, once Rangers' wish for a postponement had been granted, made a similar request to the SPL the following week, asking for their trip to Motherwell, days before a crucial UEFA Cup group game against FC Copenhagen, to be postponed, permission was refused. In the end, Setanta Sports, the SPL's broadcast partner, reluctantly agreed to the rearrangement of a fixture it had scheduled to be shown live, but the company expressed concerns about the potential damage to the credibility of the league if such short-notice cancellations were to become the norm.

The decision eventually backfired on Rangers, however, as the postponement contributed to the fixture congestion which accumulated for the Ibrox club towards the end of the season and resulted in them having to play their final four games in just eight days. In addition, having opted for a free week of preparation instead of a potentially morale-boosting win on Sunday over a Gretna team sitting bottom of the league with just five points from their 15 games, Rangers lost 3-0 to Lyon with two late goals from 19-year-old striker Karim Benzema putting the seal on a deserved win for the French side. Substitute Jean-Claude Darchville endured a miserable cameo, spurning the chance of a vital equaliser when he missed the home side's best opportunity of the night, slicing the ball over the crossbar from inside the six-yard box, and the French striker compounded his error by getting himself sent off late on for a foul on Lyon's Kim Källström.

That defeat saw Rangers eventually finish third in the group, leaving them with the consolation of a place in the UEFA Cup knockout stages, meaning that Scottish football would see three teams playing in Europe after Christmas for the first time in many years. In addition to Rangers, Celtic had qualified for the last 16 of the Champions League for the second successive season and Aberdeen, despite the SPL's refusal to rearrange their game with Motherwell, went on to beat Copenhagen 4-0 at Pittodrie and qualify for the last 32 of the UEFA Cup. It was now that Smith, over the 180 minutes of the two-legged knockout ties, deployed his ultra-defensive tactics to full effect, and with jibes about anti-football and 'Wattienaccio' ringing in their ears, the Rangers fans were despairing of the strategy, particularly in games at Ibrox. The new mentality seemed to involve an acceptance that a goalless draw at home in the first leg wasn't such a bad result, and then if the team could keep its shape under pressure, defending diligently with men behind the ball, there would always be an opportunity at some point to score in the away leg.

This is exactly what happened in the last-32 tie with Panathinaikos and again in the quarter-final against Sporting Lisbon, when a 1-1 draw in Greece and a 2-0 win in Portugal followed scoreless first legs at Ibrox, allowing Rangers to advance on each occasion. In between Smith's men dispatched the formidable Werder Bremen, whose goalkeeper Tim Wiese seemed overawed by the occasion at Ibrox, coughing up a couple of soft goals either side of half-time, and then, in the return leg in Germany, the heroics of his opposite number Allan McGregor kept the score down to 1-0, a result which saw Rangers through despite what defender David Weir described as, 'The biggest doing I have played in. We hardly got out of our own half.'

In the semi-final against Fiorentina, a dull 90-minute tussle in Glasgow was followed by an equally stultifying 120-minute slog in Tuscany with neither side able to produce a goal over the two legs, an outcome which had even the traditionally overcautious Italians bleating about Rangers' crushingly negative tactics, after the Scots won the resulting penalty shoot-out and qualified for the final in Manchester.

Rangers' opponents at the City of Manchester Stadium would be Dick Advocaat's Zenit St Petersburg, who had dispatched Bayern Munich 5-1 on aggregate in the semi-final. The Ibrox men may not have attracted many plaudits for their style of play or won over many neutrals to their cause, but it was still a notable accomplishment to make the final, regardless of the crescendo of criticism surrounding their tactics, which was added to when former Rangers player Fernando Ricksen, still with Zenit after being sent into exile by Le Guen, described his old team as 'boring'. Yet Smith's side, spurred on by enormous mega-bonuses for reaching the latter stages and perhaps seeking to emulate Celtic's similar achievement in 2003, had somehow managed, on more than one occasion, to find a way past superior opposition. But having made it to Manchester and matched Celtic's exploits in the competition, the Ibrox men seemed to lose their mojo in the final against the Russians and went down to a tame 2-0 defeat, with a goal from Denisov and a last-minute clincher from Zyrianov giving Advocaat a famous victory over his former charges.

There would be no respite for Smith's men following the disappointment of the UEFA Cup Final as they had to switch their attention abruptly back to the domestic campaign and a title race which was heading for a dramatic conclusion. Once again the derby fixtures with Celtic had provided the most pivotal moments over the course of the season; in October, Rangers had earned a deserved 3-0 victory over their rivals at Ibrox, but the return game at Celtic Park, scheduled for the New Year, was called off in tragic circumstances after the untimely death of former Celtic midfielder Phil O'Donnell, who suffered heart failure while playing for Motherwell against Dundee United on 29 December. The next game between the sides, after further call-offs due to the weather, would therefore also be at Ibrox at the end of March and the match was settled by a Kevin Thomson goal just before half-time, giving Smith his fourth successive victory in the derby since his return to the club. A deflated Celtic then further handed the initiative to their rivals in their next match when they stumbled to an ignominious 1-0 home defeat to ten-man Motherwell, a result which left the Parkhead men six points behind Rangers, having played two games more. Of their eight remaining matches, however, two would be on home soil against Smith's side.

Rangers by now were accumulating a backlog of fixtures, which could not be easily accommodated into free midweek slots because of their continued progress in the UEFA Cup. The next derby game, held over from the New Year and squeezed in to an already crammed schedule on 16 April, saw Celtic take the lead through a brilliant swerving shot from Nakamura, before Novo equalised early in the second half. The influential Japanese then won a penalty for Celtic when his netbound shot was handled on the goal line by Cuellar, who was ordered off, but adding to the tension, McGregor then saved McDonald's spot kick, despite the Rangers goalkeeper sustaining an injured ankle which required him to be immediately substituted. With the home side piling on the pressure against Rangers' ten men, Vennegoor of Hesselink nodded in an injury-time winner, which ultimately saved Celtic's season.

The pair then met again at the end of April, the third encounter between the sides in four weeks. McDonald struck after just four minutes to give the home team an early lead, but the Ibrox men hit back and scored two almost identical goals, as first Weir, then Cousin headed in successive corners to turn the tables and give Rangers the advantage. Despite dominating the game, Celtic found themselves behind after conceding two soft goals from set pieces, although the Parkhead men managed to restore parity before half-time with another strike from McDonald. In the second half, the decisive moment came when the busy Australian striker was felled in the penalty box by Broadfoot and Barry Robson stepped up to settle the match from the spot. The title race, it seemed, was very much back on.

By this stage of the season, the matter of Rangers' remaining fixtures was becoming a source of controversy. On 22 April, as had been customary in the SPL since the introduction of the end of season league split in 2000, the fixture card for the remaining five games of the season was published. This year, however, there would be a notable difference, with the league announcing two alternatives schedules, dependent on whether or not Rangers won their pending semi-final against Fiorentina and reached the UEFA Cup Final. If Rangers went through, the season would be extended by four days to accommodate their backlog of postponed matches, which is ultimately what happened after they saw off the Italians on penalties in Florence. Rangers protested bitterly over the announcement however, because it meant that they would have to cram two midweek games into the final week of the season and they were also denied the opportunity to have some extra time off before the final, which put them at a perceived disadvantage compared to their well-rested opponents.

Conversely, some of the league's other clubs, most vocally Celtic, also complained that the integrity of the competition had been compromised by the extension to the season and argued against any leeway being given to Rangers at all. In a previous era, Rangers would simply have been asked to play their games in hand beyond the end of the season unilaterally, but the modern, internationally recognised practice was for the final round of league fixtures to kick off simultaneously, so all three matches on the last day of the season involving the top six sides were eventually moved back from the weekend to Thursday, 22 May.

In many ways, the League found themselves in the midst of a perfect storm and having to deal with a myriad of exceptional circumstances, including the tragic and unforeseeable death of Phil O'Donnell, the otherwise innocent postponement of Rangers' game with St Mirren prior to the Scotland versus Italy encounter in November, the rearrangement of the Gretna game, delayed before the Lyon defeat, further disruptive cancellations over the winter due to the weather, bad even by Scottish standards, as well as Rangers' run to the UEFA Cup Final, all of which contributed to what SPL secretary Ian Blair described as 'an exceptionally challenging season in terms of fixturing'. In the end, the League handled the situation as best they could with a compromise which inconvenienced both Rangers, by asking them to play four games in eight days, as well as the other five clubs in the section, by holding their final matches over until the following Thursday. As SPL chairman Lex Gold observed only partly in jest, they must have been doing something right if nobody was entirely happy with the outcome.

Almost as soon as Rangers had ensured their place in the UEFA Cup Final, however, and the league extension was confirmed, club chairman Sir David Murray was demanding the postponement of his team's game with Dundee United, which was scheduled to take place four days before the Manchester final, on 10 May. Murray's advocated solution was either to delay the final round of fixtures until 27 May, after the Scottish Cup Final, a proposal which would have required the other teams in the league to hang around for two and a half weeks after the penultimate round of matches in order to complete their seasons, or to move the date of that final, the traditional season-ending game, after which players usually either go on holiday or join up with their international squads.

With Scotland due to play the Czech Republic in Prague on 30 May and with other pre-Euro 2008 games arranged for some of Celtic's foreign players, the SPL turned down Murray's request, announcing that there was 'no viable alternative' to the published schedule and endorsing the decision to end the season on 22 May. The SFA also confirmed, through its chief executive Gordon Smith, a former Rangers player, that the Scottish Cup Final would not be moved and that the showpiece event would go ahead on the arranged date, with Rangers' opponents in the final, Queen of the South, already having to wait four weeks without a competitive game before taking on Smith's side in their first ever final.

Murray's response to the ruling bodies' inflexibility was to claim that the football world would 'laugh at this decision in disbelief'. Such was his indignation in fact that Murray, and his manager Smith, seemed to completely forget, in their subsequent criticism of the SPL, that the league season had already been extended on Rangers' behalf, an accommodation which was not afforded to Middlesbrough in 2006, when the Teessiders twice had to squeeze in two midweek games between their standard weekend fixtures while en route to the UEFA Cup Final that year, without any recorded complaints about the English Premier League being a source of global ridicule.

Rangers were, understandably perhaps, pursuing their own interests, but with a dogmatic disregard for the concerns and the potential impact on other affected parties including Aberdeen, Dundee United, Hibs and Motherwell, who were all still battling for a UEFA Cup spot. The fixture congestion was unfortunate for the Ibrox club, especially as Zenit St Petersburg, their opponents in Manchester, had not played a league game since 26 April and their last competitive match had been the 4-0 semi-final second-leg win over Bayern Munich on 1 May. With plenty of time to rearrange fixtures in a league still operating on a summer schedule, the Russian authorities had agreed to postpone Zenit's match away to Luch Energiya, meaning that Advocaat's side did not have to endure a 15,000km round trip across seven time zones to Vladivostok days before the final in Manchester.

However, as well as the unforeseen circumstances, Rangers had not helped their own cause by their failure to eliminate Hibernian and then First Division Partick Thistle at the first time of asking from the Scottish Cup, with both Ibrox ties requiring schedule-busting replays before they eventually progressed. The real folly, though, was the Gretna postponement in December, an unnecessary and unprecedented indulgence at the time, which now returned to bite the Ibrox club at the most inopportune moment, because despite all the cancellations and rearrangements and the unavailability of certain dates, there was only one outstanding fixture that could not be accommodated into the normal routine of two games per week once the league season had been extended, namely Rangers' visit to St Mirren, called off before the international break in November, a match which could have been played in January on the date which was allocated the rearranged Gretna game.

So Rangers, having lost the UEFA Cup Final on the Wednesday, now had to play Motherwell on the Saturday and St Mirren on the Monday before meeting Aberdeen in the final round of fixtures on the Thursday. It proved too much for them, with a draw at Fir Park handing the initiative to Celtic, due to their superior goal difference, although victory over St Mirren put Smith's side back level on points. The title therefore came down to the final game, with Rangers needing either to score half a dozen goals against Aberdeen at Pittodrie or better Celtic's result against Dundee United. With pubs across the west of Scotland betraying their allegiances by choosing which game to show, the tension continued to mount as both matches stood goalless at half-time. Early in the second period the pendulum swung Celtic's way when Lee Miller's goal for Aberdeen was followed by a red card for Rangers' Novo, with the errant Spaniard foolishly clapping the travelling fans, who he had just let down with his indiscipline, as he left the field.

The Celtic supporters at Tannadice were now increasingly confident that the night would end as they hoped, when Vennegoor of Hesselink scored what proved to be the only goal of the game, heading in Hartley's corner with 20 minutes remaining. A second goal for Aberdeen at Pittodrie only confirmed Celtic's third title in as many years, as the Parkhead men celebrated at the end of what had been a gruelling season for all concerned. At one stage Smith's side had been on course for an unlikely quadruple, after beating Dundee United on penalties in the League Cup Final in March, but now Rangers had to settle for the two domestic cups, following a 3-2 victory over Queen of the South in the Scottish Cup Final at the weekend, less than 48 hours after losing the league.

There would be revenge for Smith's Rangers the following year, as the Ibrox side finally regained the championship after yet another final-fixture denouement, a result which saw Celtic manager Gordon Strachan leave Parkhead after four years in charge. The season started alarmingly for Rangers, however, as they were knocked out of Europe at the first hurdle, losing 2-1 on aggregate to Lithuanian minnows FBK Kaunas after conceding a late, decisive goal deep into the second leg, a dreadful anti-climax after the drama and elation of the previous year's run to the UEFA Cup Final.

The defeat reinforced Smith's view that there was a general lack of flair and overall quality in his squad and his response to adversity was to spend big once again as Rangers signed nine players over the summer, most of them after the Kaunas reverse, including Kenny Miller, the striker returning to the club in a £2m deal from Derby after a short, largely unsuccessful spell at Celtic, Andrius Velička, another striker, formerly of Hearts, but now with Viking Stavanger of Norway, who received £1m from Rangers for the player, Madjid Bougherra, an Algerian defender from Charlton Athletic for £2.5m, Kyle Lafferty, once coveted by Celtic, who came in from Burnley at a cost of £3.25m, the Portuguese midfielder Pedro Mendes, a £3m capture from Portsmouth, and Maurice Edu, an American midfielder, £2.6m from Toronto FC, while the loan signings of Andy Webster and Steven Davis were converted to permanent transfers, at a combined cost of £3.5m.

In addition to the transfer fees, the wage bill at Ibrox had trebled since Smith's return, but chief executive Martin Bain defended the budget that was being made available to the manager, even in such uncertain economic times. 'We know what our supporters demand and we know the quality that they like to see on the pitch,' he explained, summing up the source of Rangers' difficulties rather neatly, it seemed. It wouldn't be long before such blithe statements about the club's spending power would be a thing of the past at Ibrox.

Rangers received transfer fees from the sales of Cuellar and Cousin, just as they had the previous season with Alan Hutton, who had to be almost frog-marched to Glasgow airport when a £9m bid was received from Tottenham in January, after the full-back appeared initially reluctant to leave Ibrox. But this income, along with the money earned from their European adventures, was making little or no impact on Rangers' net debt, and the downsizing which might have saved the club if it had been implemented properly and opportunely was not taking place.

Murray's confident prediction in 2004 that the club would be back in the black within a year turned out to be another moonbeam, and although the debt stood at a manageable £6m in 2006, vastly reduced from two years earlier, Smith's extravagant expenditure on his playing squad in the 18 months since his return to the club had helped to push the total level back up to around £30m. Part of the problem seemed to lie in Smith's initial reluctance, having been in charge of Rangers during such a successful era in the 1990s, to preside over a period of managed decline in the club's affairs and to work within a more limited budget, something which his predecessor, Paul Le Guen, had been far more sanguine about. The ability to make and enforce such decisions, however, would now be taken out of the Ibrox club's hands.

Rangers, it seemed, were already well down the road to ruin when, in September 2008, the club lost the ability to independently govern its own affairs following the crisis in the international banking system. The credit crunch, as it became known, an economic earthquake which had been rumbling away in the background for some 12 months or so, had already claimed its first victim in the UK, when fears about a liquidity crisis and potential bankruptcy the previous September had caused a run on the Northern Rock bank, which was eventually taken into public ownership in February after customers queued up round the block to withdraw their savings at the bank's branches.

Just as with the dotcom bubble crisis a few years earlier, from which lessons had clearly not been learnt, Rangers and the Murray Group found themselves at the sharp end of the crisis due to their high levels of debt, which they were unable to effectively service. This time, however, the financial meltdown was far deeper and more serious, with the victims including not just debtors, but creditors too. Further bailouts followed for the collapsed banks, funded at eye-watering levels of cost to the taxpayer, with the most reckless lenders the worst affected, such as Rangers' bankers HBOS, who were left in a hopeless position due to their near suicidal policies in the retail banking sector and their penchant for 'rolling over' and repackaging troublesome corporate debts.

In September, two days after the collapse of American investment firm Lehman Brothers and with HBOS now heading for a liquidity crisis similar to that of Northern Rock, but on a far larger scale, only a government-approved merger with former competitors Lloyds TSB, effectively a takeover by a smaller, but more stable and better capitalised bank, allowed HBOS to continue trading.

Having acquired Rangers' debt as part of the merger, it's fair to say that Lloyds were utterly appalled by what they found once they peered under the bonnet and took an unflinching look at the club's financial position and the indulgent relationship which had existed between HBOS and the Murray Group. New rules applied, as Rangers' entire squad of players were made available for sale in the January transfer window, as Lloyds attempted to implement the cutbacks which should have been put in place years earlier. Having gorged themselves on a diet of expensive signings for the best part of a generation, Rangers fans were now apoplectic at the club's suddenly diminished position, with Ewing Grahame noting in the *Telegraph*, 'The fear is that Rangers' self-styled status as Scotland's premier sporting institution (which they consider themselves to be) may be heading the way of other national totems such as the Bank of Scotland, which funded much of the borrowing which saw Rangers outperform the domestic opposition during the 1990s.'

However, with Smith doing his best to shield his squad from the financial bad news, and showing admirable defiance in the face of adversity, many players were reluctant to leave Rangers. Kris Boyd was linked heavily with Birmingham City, the Midlands club who were then managed by former Ibrox boss Alex McLeish, but the striker could not be persuaded to join the Championship side on the terms that were being offered, with the bulk of Birmingham's financial package for the player dependent on promotion to the Premier League. Others who were brought to Ibrox by Smith were on inflated, Rangers-style wages, which buying clubs were generally unwilling to match, regardless of the football industry's apparent immunity to the global economic crisis. In the end, despite all the hype about a potential fire-sale during the transfer window, only Jean-Claude Darcheville and Chris Burke were offloaded in January, with both fringe players leaving on free transfers. Lloyds had tried to impose austerity on the club, but with so few players leaving, very little seemed to have changed at Ibrox. There had been little or no impact on the club's expensive lifestyle – the squad were still staying at the same hotels, there would be a pre-season trip to Australia the following summer – and as a result the business was continuing to haemorrhage cash at an alarming rate.

On the field, Rangers lost the League Cup Final to Celtic in mid-March, going down 2-0 after extra time in what was, perhaps surprisingly, Smith's first final as Rangers manager against their old adversaries. The Ibrox men made up for that defeat in early May, however, with a 1-0 home win over the Parkhead side sending them two points clear at top of the league with only three games of the season remaining. But with another tense end to the campaign looming, Rangers then stumbled, handing the advantage back to their title rivals by drawing their next game against Hibernian, a result which left Celtic ahead on goal difference. The Edinburgh club then claimed a noted double, however, when they held the Parkhead men to a draw the following week and Rangers made no mistake on the final day, winning 3-0 at Tannadice against Dundee United to claim their first title in four years. Smith's men also added the Scottish Cup the following week with a fortunate 1-0 win over a brave Falkirk side; Rangers had been so thoroughly outplayed in the first half by John Hughes's relegation-threatened team that Smith was forced into a substitution at half-time, bringing on Novo for the ineffective Boyd. The diminutive Spaniard made an immediate impact, lashing home a volley from the edge of the box with his first touch to score what proved to be the only goal of the game.

One player who Rangers finally managed to get off their books at the end of the season was club captain Barry Ferguson, who departed Ibrox in disgrace over the summer. While on international duty in late March, Ferguson, along with team-mate Allan McGregor, had indulged in an all-night drinking session at Cameron House, the Scotland team hotel, after the squad flew back from a World Cup qualifier in the Netherlands, which the Scots lost 3-0. McGregor's personal bender had apparently extended all the way through until the following morning when the goalkeeper should have been at training, and he was reportedly still in the bar as lunchtime approached, before eventually being carried to his room. The Rangers duo were subsequently dropped for Scotland's next fixture a few days later against Iceland at Hampden, but while sitting on the bench, under the gaze of the photographers' lenses, both players were seen to make sly V-signs at the cameras, giving them the Vickies as it were, surreptitiously placing two fingers between nose and ear in an unmistakable attempt to try and ruin the snappers' pictures.

The stunt inevitably backfired as the offending images appeared all over the tabloids the next day, and in the aftermath of what became known as 'booze-gate' or 'bevvy-gate', it was announced that both players would not be considered for selection for Scotland again, although McGregor was later reprieved. Having staged such a passable audition for *Dumb and Dumber*, Rangers also took action against the pair, suspending them for two weeks without pay after Smith had phoned the players once stories about the drinking session had become public and issued instructions not to attract any further attention. Both men looked set to be sold at the end of the season, although, again, McGregor was later accorded an amnesty and reinstated as the club's first-choice goalkeeper; Ferguson, however, had transgressed once too often and he was eventually offloaded to McLeish's Birmingham City.

Rangers were also able to sell Charlie Adam to Blackpool during the close season and Pedro Mendes to Sporting Lisbon in January, although, with the purse strings now securely tightened, the only new face at Ibrox over the summer was winger Jérôme Rothen, who arrived on loan from PSG and made no impact at the club. A more significant departure at the same time was Sir David Murray, who stepped down as chairman in August and was succeeded by director Alastair Johnston. Denying that he was being ushered towards the exit door by the bank and claiming that it was his decision to leave, Murray, who remained the club's owner and majority shareholder, stated that he felt it was 'an appropriate time to go', adding, 'We are about to go into the draw for the Champions League, we won the league and the Scottish Cup, we've kept our best players and things are better than people would like to perceive.'

His replacement, Johnston, an accountant by trade, had joined the Rangers board as a non-executive director in February 2004 having previously enjoyed a long association with IMG, the sports management company, where he had risen to become the firm's vice-chairman. On succeeding to the role of Rangers chairman, Johnston confirmed that the days of showy expenditure at Ibrox were over, when he announced bluntly, 'My mercurial friend and predecessor had a way of operating that was unique and it is not one I will be following.'

Rangers fans seemed equivocal on Murray's tenure, with one spokesman noting the divide between the early years of spending and success and the latter period, apparently marked by the arrival of Martin O'Neill at Celtic, which was more troubled both on and off the park. Nevertheless, it seemed that the great and the good, both from the world of Scottish football and beyond, were lining up to pay tribute to Murray, with First Minister Alex Salmond declaring, 'David Murray has made an astonishing impact for the better at Rangers and introduced new attitudes and a new professionalism. He departs from his active role as a hugely respected figure in Scottish football.'

Rangers' title win in 2009 had kept the wolves from the door, albeit temporarily, allowing the club direct entry into the group stages of the Champions League and providing a much-needed financial boost. Having qualified for the lucrative competition, however, and banked the money, a clearly relieved Rangers almost seemed to forget about the football, with the team collecting only two points in a relatively easy section with Sevilla, Stuttgart and Unirea Urziceni, the unheralded Romanian champions, who went on to inflict a 4-1 defeat on Rangers at Ibrox. Coming so soon on the back of another 4-1 home loss to Sevilla, when the manager tried, unsuccessfully, to play a more expansive brand of football, many believed that Smith's anti-football strategy of two years earlier had been belatedly vindicated, as the Ibrox men eventually finished bottom of the group.

Fortunately, things appeared better for the club on the domestic scene, with Celtic, their only major rival, struggling under new manager Tony Mowbray. Rangers started the season slowly and found themselves four points behind the Parkhead men after going through the entire month of September without winning a game or even scoring a goal. But Mowbray's Celtic, after a promising start, appeared to lose their way alarmingly quickly and it wasn't long before the Parkhead manager was attracting scorn from the club's fans for his repeated use of the post-match interview mantra, 'We'll take it on the chin and move on.'

Sadly, there would be no moving on from a 4-0 defeat to St Mirren in March, as Mowbray was sacked in the aftermath and replaced, initially on an interim basis, by the former club captain Neil Lennon. The Northern Irishman, if he was auditioning for a permanent appointment to the role, impressed by winning all eight of Celtic's remaining league fixtures, although he blotted his copybook in April with an agonising defeat to First Division Ross County in the semi-final of the Scottish Cup, depriving his club of their last realistic chance of a trophy. By then Rangers were already within touching distance of the title, which was eventually secured after a 1-0 win at Easter Road at the end of the month, the Ibrox men's only title triumph by more than a single point since the profligate days of Dick Advocaat in 1999/2000.

Smith's side had earlier regained the League Cup in an extraordinary final against St Mirren, during which Rangers were reduced to nine men. The Paisley side had looked the stronger team when both sides had a full complement of players, but seemed unable to handle the pressure once they were expected to win, after Rangers' Thomson and Wilson were sent off by referee Craig Thomson, and the cup was settled late on by Kenny Miller's counter-attacking strike.

During the season, in October, banker Donald Muir, viewed as a 'company doctor' after a series of successful business turnarounds, was placed on the club's board by Lloyds Bank, with instructions to keep a watchful eye on efforts to reduce the debt at Ibrox. The move prompted Smith, in the aftermath of his side's 1-1 draw with Hibernian at the end of the month, to concede publicly, 'As far as I am concerned, the bank is running Rangers.' Clearly pining for the good old days of front-loaded Murray extravagance and indulgent corporate loans, Smith complained, 'Sir David has stepped down now and a representative of the bank has been placed on the board. It's not a situation anyone wants the club to be in… It was a bad thing when Sir David stepped down as chairman as he always tried to invest.'

The manager's assertion was in direct contradiction to his chairman Alastair Johnston, who had previously stressed that he, and not Lloyds, was in day to day charge of the Rangers operation and Smith's claim also produced a swift statement of rebuttal from the bank itself, who insisted, 'We do not run or manage the companies that we bank – that is, quite properly, the responsibility of the management. Given the recent press coverage, we would therefore like to be clear that Rangers FC is neither operated nor run by Lloyds Banking Group. We would also like to be clear that Sir David Murray's decision to step down as chairman was a personal decision and not at the behest of Lloyds Banking Group.'

David Murray Jnr, son of the owner and managing director of Murray Capital, the investment arm of MIH, also expressed his belief that 'a little bit of frustration' had got the better of Smith, and repeated the position that the club and the bank would continue to work together to reduce the debt until a buyer could be found. Smith's statement was an expression of annoyance and disappointment brought about by the lack of new signings, which he felt was contributing to a 'stagnation' at the club, and perhaps by Lloyd's refusal to offer him and his staff a renewal of their contracts, which were due to expire in January. The bank were unwilling to discourage any potential new owners, who might want to bring in their own coaching staff, with the unwelcome prospect of having to first pay off the incumbent management team, although Smith was at pains to point out that he appreciated this point and was comfortable with his contractual situation.

Despite all the refutations about who was running the club, there was no doubt about where the fans' loyalties lay, especially as they could see that the club wasn't signing any players and that the team was struggling on the park, particularly in Europe. Smith, the popular manager, and chief executive Martin Bain were insisting that any new business model must leave Rangers capable of competing with Celtic for the SPL title, whereas the bank were more concerned with their twin objectives of recovering the £30m which they were owed and of finding a way forward which might save the business, ideally under new ownership.

Smith's expressions of unease about the bank provoked various fans' groups to come together and issue a joint statement, which threatened an organised boycott of the Lloyds Group and its products and facilities, if the situation at the club should deteriorate further, and it wasn't long before Muir, the bank's man on the board, was being branded as 'the enemy within' by the Ibrox clientele. While Lloyds's position seemed logical to many outside of the football community, it appeared that there was a general lack of appreciation among fans, the media and not least Smith himself about the nature of Rangers' financial plight and of the self-inflicted mess in which the club now found itself. Another aspect which was regularly overlooked was that, despite the embargo on new signings, Smith's current squad had still cost more to assemble than any other team in the league, and quite possibly more than all the club's rivals put together, and that was without taking into consideration the continuing benefits to the club from its as yet unreported use of the EBT tax wheeze, which allowed Rangers to recruit and retain players who they would otherwise have been unable to afford.

Tellingly, during this period, Smith was being continuously lauded by the mainstream media for apparently fending off the challenge of rival teams 'on a shoestring budget' and 'with one hand tied behind his back', a complete misrepresentation of the reality of the situation, but the press's failure to fully appreciate the nature of what was happening behind the scenes at Ibrox and their inability to get to grips with the enormity of the whole unfolding crisis at Rangers would soon be brutally exposed.

In April 2010, it finally emerged that Rangers were facing a colossal tax bill from HMRC over the club's use of the controversial EBT and DOS tax avoidance schemes. The revenue and customs service were demanding an astonishing total of roughly £50m, broken down as £24m in unpaid taxes, known as the 'core amount', plus £12m in backdated interest, as well as non-payment fines, which were a negotiable sum but precedent suggested that penalties of 50 per cent to 75 per cent of the underpayment would also be applied. Rangers were disputing the assessment and the case was set to go to court, to the first tier tax tribunal in Edinburgh, starting in October 2010, but coming on top of all the other financial woes at Ibrox, including the £30m still owed to Lloyds Bank, this new liability was potentially a killer blow to the club.

Things had started to unravel for Rangers behind the scenes when, in July 2007, the City of London Police, who operate in the UK capital's 'square mile' financial district, raided Ibrox in connection with the former Metropolitan Police Commissioner Lord John Stevens's inquiry into under-the-table transfer 'bungs' in football. The Stevens report ultimately found 'unresolved issues' in the case of the transfer from Rangers to Newcastle of Jean-Alain Boumsong in January 2005, although the matter, along with 16 other deals involving British clubs between 1 January 2004 and 31 January 2006 which Stevens had been unable to sign off in his report, was ultimately not pursued by either the FA or FIFA.

However, Stevens's team of forensic accountants uncovered evidence of the use of EBTs at Ibrox, and in particular the shoddy way in which the scheme was being administered through secretive side-letters, and passed on the information they had acquired to HMRC, an unfortunate consequence from Rangers' point of view. The revenue service had been investigating Rangers since as far back as 2004, but had been blocked at every turn by the club's denials, obfuscations and even the destruction of evidence, after CEO Martin Bain was found to have issued instructions that his own letter requesting a £100,000 tax-free bonus was to be shredded. Finally, it now seemed, HMRC had the smoking gun they needed to pursue their case against Rangers.

Perhaps not unexpectedly, the media in Scotland were slow to pick up on HMRC's investigation of Rangers, and even seemed to be ignoring the story altogether at times, until in May 2010, Phil Mac Giolla Bháin, a blogger and freelance journalist with unabashed Celtic sympathies, managed to get his scoop about the Ibrox tax case on to the cover of the *News of the World*'s Scotland edition. On the inside pages, Mac Giolla Bháin's exclusive elaborated on the extent of HMRC's claim against the Ibrox club. Under the headline 'Simply the bust' – not, as it may have appeared at first glance, a typical Sunday tabloid exposé, but a play on Ibrox stadium's adopted signature tune, the Tina Turner classic 'Simply the Best' – Mac Giolla Bháin reported, 'Officials are worried the hammer blow from Her Majesty's Revenue and Customs could make the club **UNSELLABLE** – and could even push them towards **ADMINISTRATION**.'

It was the first public reference to the possibility that Rangers' financial difficulties might pose a potentially terminal threat to the club, and of course the full use of HMRC's official, acronym-free title in the piece was no accident. Rangers were being investigated at the behest of Her Majesty, an ironic and uncomfortable position for a club with not one, but two portraits of the young Queen Elizabeth adorning the home dressing room. The article also claimed that a host of Rangers players were poised for imminent transfers, with members of the youth team squad at the club apparently being briefed to prepare for first team action the following season, and that the manager and his coaching team were also considering their positions. In the end though, Smith decided to tough it out for another season, and rather than sell a number of players over the summer to bring in some much-needed revenue, Rangers instead bought Nikica Jelavić from Rapid Vienna for £4m.

Even after the *News of the World* revelations, there was disbelief. One Glasgow radio station claimed the next day that Rangers were consulting their lawyers over the Sunday tabloid's allegations of a potentially ruinous tax bill at Ibrox, but Mac Giolla Bháin had done his homework and had an impeccable source for his story, none other than the club's chief executive Martin Bain, who had admitted the details of the case to the journalist in a series of phone calls. Still there seemed to be a sanguine belief that all would be well in the end, with Graham Spiers, a much respected journalist for *The Times*, expressing his opinion that David Murray would be 'morally compelled' to pick up the tab from Hector the Taxman out of his own pocket.

What Spiers and many of his colleagues had failed to appreciate, however, was that the Murray Group, or MIH as it was still known, Rangers' parent company, had itself been absolutely clobbered by the credit crunch and was now in debt to Lloyds Bank to the tune of around £900m, far more than the value of its assets, leaving the group technically insolvent. Murray's personal fortune, meanwhile, had collapsed from £500m to a mere £110m over the previous year, and was down 85 per cent over the previous two years, rendering the Ibrox tycoon the single biggest faller on the 2010 *Sunday Times* 'rich list'.

Spiers's view that Rangers would ultimately be able to rely on Murray's casual philanthropy was based on the general perception of the Ibrox owner as a 'benevolent benefactor', who had funded Rangers' profligate spending down the years at his own expense. But the club's track record of historical debt and MIH's eye-watering levels of exposure to the bank revealed the stark reality that it was largely other people's money which had subsidised Murray's vanity project at Rangers, whether that was down to the former chairman's talent for persuading people such as Dave King and ENIC's Joe Lewis, both of whom lost fortunes, to invest, or his ability to convince friendly bankers to lend him the vast sums of money which were required to continue the club's pursuit of domestic and international success.

Moreover, as details of the EBT scheme slowly emerged, it became clear that Murray himself was the single biggest beneficiary from the trust payment system, with the Rangers owner trousering a total of £6.3m in tax-free income from MGMRT, more than the combined totals received by Dick Advocaat, Stefan Klos and Barry Ferguson. All that was required was a carefully worded letter to the trustees, acknowledging their notional discretion, and sums of up to £1m would be transferred to Murray's personal disposal, no questions asked. So much for never taking a penny out of the club. Murray later bragged that if he wanted any extra tickets for matches, he paid for them himself, but in reality, he was very far from the benefactor figure which he was often portrayed to be by his friends in the media, and with no 'white knight' on the horizon thanks to the toxic liabilities at Ibrox, which by now were in the public domain, it soon became obvious, especially if the tax tribunal should rule in HMRC's favour, that Rangers were a dying club.

The most successful team in the history of Scottish football and the self-styled 'establishment club' was facing the prospect of bankruptcy and disgrace and still very few people seemed interested, until in January 2011 Mac Giolla Bháin came back with further revelations about Rangers offering HMRC £10m to settle the case. He appeared on a radio phone-in show and explained the details of the court action for a mass audience, after which the penny seemed to finally drop and the story went viral.

If the first Gulf War of 1991 was the making of the cable news network CNN, with their reporters on the ground and in Baghdad hotels as the cruise missiles flew over the Iraqi capital, and the second Gulf War of 2003 brought to prominence the Qatari station Al Jazeera, the Rangers liquidation story would be owned by the internet bloggers and social media newshounds of the west of Scotland, who prodded away online and, despite the acknowledged rival affiliations of some, nevertheless examined the story more accurately and in far more forensic detail than their counterparts in the mainstream press ever displayed. As well as Mac Giolla Bháin, there was Paul Brennan's *Celticquicknews*, which provided business expertise, an area where the floundering sports hacks were regularly out of their depth, and *Rangerstaxcase*, an anonymous blogger, who went on to win the Orwell

Prize for online journalism shortly before the Ibrox club was liquidated, as well as many others.

The bloggers were dubbed the 'internet bampots' by their mainstream media equivalents, who in turn came to be branded 'churnalists' by the online community, or 'stenographers', after an article appeared in *The Guardian* in which Professor Roy Greenslade, the paper's media commentator, lambasted the willingness of newspapers, and the *Daily Record* in particular, to regurgitate Ibrox press releases unexamined, as if they were news. 'The mainstream media,' wrote Greenslade in reference to the coverage of Rangers' collapse, 'whether by commission or omission, failed to do its job. Rather than hold the people in charge [of Rangers] to account, it acted as a spin doctor.' *Rangerstaxcase*, who started blogging in March 2011, cited the lack of proper coverage in the press as his (or her) reason for taking an interest in the case, 'In their hurry to publish, they shamelessly rush from fax-machine (or whatever PR firms use these days) to the press without editing or critical thought. In short, readers are paying to read PR-fluff written and produced by people with agendas... Rangers fans are fed this diet of regurgitated lamb and foolishly lap it up like it is a kebab at closing time.'

In the end, the press in Scotland had been beaten to the story of the scandal engulfing Ibrox by a bunch of amateurs who, despite their professed allegiances, reported the facts of the case with far more accuracy and objectivity than their compromised mainstream counterparts could ever manage, many of whom had largely ignored one of the biggest stories in the history of British sport until it slowly and inevitably unfolded in front of them.

With the details of the tax case now public, David Murray took the club he had been vainly trying to sell since 2006 off the market because, surely, only a complete fool would want to buy a club that was cripplingly indebted to the bank and facing a potentially ruinous tax bill. Far better, one assumed, for interested parties to wait until the administration process had cleared the business of its debts and then, with the creditors having received no more than a few meagre pence in the pound, pick up the assets at a bargain price. That would certainly have been the logical way for events to unfold but, by the end of 2010/11, this story was about to become a lot stranger.

In the meantime, however, on the field the two duelling Glasgow sides played each other a total of seven times during the season, with Celtic emerging as victors after a Scottish Cup fifth round replay, and Rangers gaining revenge with a 2-1 win after extra time in the League Cup Final, during which Smith's team demonstrated what could be achieved with a more attacking brand of football than they were typically used to showing on these occasions. After the Scottish Cup tie, which had ended with three Ibrox men being ordered off, Rangers assistant manager Ally McCoist and Celtic boss Neil Lennon became involved in a brief, but highly visible confrontation, which had to be broken up by surrounding stewards and personnel from both clubs. Lennon had been angered by a remark McCoist made to him while the pair shook hands as the benches came together at the end of the match. Lennon has since been coy about revealing details of the scuffle and claimed later that the two men were enjoying a glass of wine in his office moments after the incident, but whatever McCoist said, it clearly wasn't along the lines of 'congratulations, well played', which is what his comments should have been restricted to at that particular time.

In the aftermath of the incident, it seemed that all hell broke loose; the media had a field day with the fallout, as the implications even reached the BBC's *Question Time* programme, with reactive First Minister Alex Salmond subsequently calling a Holyrood summit to tackle the issue of sectarianism.

The season had begun well for Rangers on the field with wins in the first nine fixtures, including a 3-1 victory at Celtic Park at the end of October, which ended the Hoops' similarly perfect start to the campaign under Lennon. In the Champions League, Rangers' dreary, ultra-defensive approach continued when they earned a goalless draw at Old Trafford against a weakened Manchester United side, and with one win and three draws from the section, Rangers ultimately finished third in the group and progressed into the UEFA Cup.

In the secondary competition, Smith's team beat Sporting Lisbon on away goals after two drawn matches, but the run ultimately ended with a defeat to PSV Eindhoven in the last 16, after which UEFA took action against Rangers fans' sectarian singing by fining the club £36,000 and banning supporters from travelling to their team's next away game, with a further one match ban suspended.

Then, in November, Rangers supporters were given hope that the club's financial woes might be coming to an end, as the longed-for 'Whyte knight' finally appeared on the landscape of Scottish football in the form of the hitherto unheralded businessman, Craig Whyte, who, it was revealed, was in negotiations with David Murray to buy the club. According to a report in the *Daily Record*, Whyte was a 'financial whizzkid from Motherwell' and a 'self-made billionaire', whose 'wealth is off the radar' and who now stood 'on the brink of pulling off the biggest deal of his life' by completing a takeover of his beloved Glasgow Rangers, the club he had supported since he was a boy.

With the ruinous tax case still hanging over Ibrox, Rangers fans were overjoyed at the imminent prospect of an end to their worst fears, but the main problem with the *Record* story was that it was bollocks. Whyte was interested in buying the club all right, but he was very far from being a billionaire, as any quick Google search of his record would have revealed. He seemed in fact to be a complete nobody, a spiv with a portfolio of collapsed businesses and a history of specialising in breaking up liquidated and financially stricken firms. He had even been disqualified from being a company director for seven years in June 2000, after two of his companies failed to deliver their annual accounts, at which point the prospective new Rangers owner had decamped to Monaco and become an international man of mystery.

It seems that Whyte had simply told his PR people, when journalists enquired about the extent of his wealth, to 'tell them I'm a billionaire' and the *Record* had grasped the line only too eagerly, before adding its own embellishments. The November report in the tabloid had also claimed that Whyte may have been in a position to tie up a deal with Murray in time to fund a massive spending spree in the January transfer window, but the negotiations dragged on, with Whyte's lawyers frustrated by Rangers' apparent reluctance to reveal the full extent of the club's tax liabilities, and other financial issues, to the prospective buyer's due diligence process.

Similarly, Rangers chairman Alastair Johnston, as head of the takeover approval board, the club's vetting committee, was sceptical about Whyte's alleged resources after engaging the services of a firm of private investigators to scrutinise the potential new owner's distinctly unimpressive business background. Johnston eventually urged Murray to walk away from the Whyte deal, but, with the tax case looming, the former chairman was by now desperate to offload the club and he had been incentivised to do so by Lloyds, who promised to allow Murray to buy back his metals business, the original trading function of MIH, at a discounted rate if he could sell his 85 per cent shareholding in Rangers and recoup the money which the bank were still owed.

Johnston and the vetting committee lacked the power to block the takeover, and ultimately it was Murray's decision to sell, with the owner eventually informing Johnston that it was too late to stop the deal going ahead. In the end, Murray sold the club, of which he had been the owner, custodian and majority shareholder for over 22 years, and chairman for most of that time, to Whyte's Wavetower Limited, a company registered in the British Virgin Islands and soon to be renamed The Rangers Football Club Group Ltd, for a token £1, on 6 May 2011.

Of course, Whyte, in addition to the £1, still had to find the money to pay off Lloyds, and with the downsizing measures put in place by the bank finally taking effect, and thanks largely to two consecutive seasons of Champions League participation, the club's debts had been significantly reduced, from £30m in 2008 to £18m by the time of Whyte's purchase. But, not being a billionaire, the new owner didn't have a spare £18m in loose change lying about in his Granton-on-Spey castle, so he mortgaged the club's future season ticket sales with a company called Ticketus in London and secured the money for his takeover that way.

By paying off Lloyds, Whyte also made sure that he inherited the 'floating charge' which the Bank of Scotland had secured over the club in the late 1990s, allowing the new owner to become the only secured creditor of the teetering company and ensuring that, if it all went south rather rapidly, Whyte, in theory at least, would not lose out. David Murray had once bragged that he would take great satisfaction from turning Rangers into a family dynasty by bequeathing control of the club to his son, but when young David Junior showed no interest for the fray, his dad later claimed, 'If and when I leave the club, I will make sure that it's left with people of a similar mind and a similar nature. We're not talking about Russians and people coming in, if I move on from Rangers, I will leave it in the hands of people that I think have got the best interests of the club.' (sic)

It was imperative for Murray's tarnished legacy at Ibrox that he should at least pass the club on to a competent successor, but instead he had now handed Rangers over to a man who appeared to be a liquidation specialist.

13

THE
LIQUIDATION GAME

C RAIG Whyte's takeover of Rangers was completed just in time for the new owner to witness his club clinching the SPL championship with a 5-1 victory over Kilmarnock at Rugby Park. Celtic had held the initiative in the title race after a draw at Ibrox in April, but manager Neil Lennon's inexperience showed as his team blew up at Inverness, losing 3-2 to Terry Butcher's side and Rangers cruised home, winning all four of their remaining fixtures.

Walter Smith bowed out from the Ibrox hot-seat on a high, soaking up the accolades before handing over the reins to his assistant Ally McCoist, his contractually designated successor, although the departing manager's elation was difficult to detect in some of his subsequent remarks. Even as Lennon was congratulating his opposite number and offering the view that he couldn't have lost to a better bloke, the increasingly dour and tetchy Smith was haranguing Celtic for supposedly putting pressure on referees over the course of the season.

It was unquestionably the case that peripheral issues surrounding match officials, often directly or indirectly involving Celtic, had been an unwelcome diversion over the course of the campaign, but it was hard to see how Smith's criticisms, especially at the end of a successful season, could be justified, with even his eulogising biographer, Neil Drysdale, admitting, 'With hindsight, this was one outburst too many.'

Perhaps the gloomy mood was understandable, even as Smith vacated his position at Ibrox with the plaudits ringing in his ears. An intelligent man, he was almost certainly aware that he was leaving the club he loved, and which he had arguably helped bring to its knees, in a decrepit, dying condition.

Smith continued to insist, even on the day he stepped down, that investment was needed from the new owner; not in order to pay the club's bills, the immediate priority if insolvency was to be averted, but to keep a competitive team on the park and to stay ahead of Celtic. Admitting that the club had struggled on the park when compelled to operate within a more stabilised financial environment, Smith urged Whyte to immediately release funds to strengthen the playing squad, 'Historically, if you look at Rangers over the last 20 years, they have needed a fairly large investment in the team to boost them. When the team has not had that, it has not been successful. The team now needs this boost. I think [Whyte] would be blind if he didn't realise that.'

The pressure on Whyte to start spreading it around was immense, from departing legend Smith, from new manager McCoist and of course from the fans, whose expectation levels had been raised after reports of his 'off the radar' wealth in the tabloids. Whyte immediately announced his intention to make £25m available to the manager over a five-year period, a promise which turned out to be a David Murray-style moonbeam, but to his credit, the new owner also made some measured remarks about managing expectations and running the club properly. 'We want to get the best players that we can, but in terms of paying English Premiership salaries of £100,000 or £200,000 per week, it is not financial reality for Rangers or any other club in Scotland,' Whyte cautioned. 'We are in the Scottish league, we don't have television income to speak of, and so to bring the top players up here is pretty difficult... There will be investment but the club has to pay its way.'

Nevertheless, over the summer, Whyte, at the insistence of McCoist, agreed lucrative five- and six-year contract extensions for key players Davis, Whittaker and McGregor, none of which the club could afford. In addition, over the close season, Rangers signed seven new players on permanent transfers, including American internationals Carlos Bocanegra and Alejandro Bedoya, Romanian international defender Dorin Goian and left-back Lee Wallace from Hearts, at a total cost of almost £4m, while in November, Sone Aluko bought out his own contract at Aberdeen in order to put himself in the shop window at Ibrox.

Rangers' recent domestic title successes had guaranteed direct entry into the Champions League over the previous two seasons and now it was imperative that the new manager, having spent so much money to retain his key players and to strengthen his squad with reinforcements, guided the team into the group stages of the competition, where a welcome £17m in prize money potentially awaited the club. Without Champions League income, Rangers were running at a £10m annual deficit, and with 60 per cent of the season ticket sales now mortgaged through Ticketus for the next three years, it was vital for the club that revenue from European football was maximised.

Unfortunately, due to Scottish football's diminishing UEFA co-efficient, McCoist's side first had to negotiate their way through two potentially tricky qualifying rounds before they could reach the group stages and claim the pot of gold. In the first game, Rangers were paired with Malmö, and lost 1-0 at Ibrox in the first leg, after a mistake from Steven Whittaker allowed Daniel Larsson to score the game's only goal. The return match in Sweden saw the implementation of UEFA's ban on travelling Rangers fans, after the club was sanctioned following incidents of sectarian singing during the club's elimination from the UEFA Cup at the hands of PSV Eindhoven the previous season. It turned out to be a bad-tempered affair, with Whittaker, unforgivably in such a crucial qualifier, and then Bougherra, who was later sold, both getting themselves stupidly ordered off, as the match finished 1-1, sending Rangers out of the Champions League at the first hurdle.

The Ibrox club was subsequently relegated to the Europa League, where they faced a play-off against Slovenian champions Maribor with the winner guaranteed a place in the secondary tournament's group stages, a respectable consolation after missing out on the Champions League, while for the loser, in this case Rangers after a 3-2 aggregate defeat, there would be no further participation in European football at all that season. The club's record in Europe since reaching the UEFA Cup Final in Manchester in 2008 now extended to just one win in 22 matches.

Disaster had struck, but no sooner had McCoist's side been eliminated from Europe than questions began to arise, almost exclusively among the online community, about whether Rangers should have been permitted to play in European competition at all that season. It turned out that HMRC were pursuing the Ibrox club over two separate tax issues; the first an assessment of £2.8m over payments to a small number of players, including Ronald de Boer and Tore André Flo, made through the Discounted Option Scheme (DOS) between 1999 and 2003, which became known as the 'wee tax case', and the second, far larger EBT bill through which numerous employees, including dozens of players, were being paid until 2010. Rangers were contesting in court HMRC's £49m claim for the latter, the so-called 'big tax case', but the club had already admitted liability for the DOS bill of £2.8m, which was now outstanding and would ultimately remain unpaid. In order to gain a UEFA licence to participate in European competitions, rules state that an applicant club must not be owing to a tax authority by a deadline of 31 March before the season commences.

Clearly Rangers, having admitted liability for the wee tax case, and with interest continuing to accrue, had failed to meet the required criteria by the stipulated date, yet the club's application for a European licence was waved through by the SFA. On 1 April, the day after the deadline had passed, Rangers finally produced their delayed mid-term accounts and admitted openly for the first time that two separate tax cases were hanging over the club. When asked if Rangers could go bust as a result of HMRC's claims against them, chairman Alastair Johnston appeared to agree but initially, rather than provide a verbal answer, he cleverly assented with a nod of the head, a reaction which provoked an unseemly row among rivals in the media as to how the gesture should be interpreted and reported, and whether the prospect of insolvency had actually been admitted by the chairman or not. It was all very unnecessary, with Johnston going on to concede, 'The reality is there is a possibility that there could be a judgment that the club can't pay... It's like a gorilla in the room and you don't know what its appetite is.' On the wee tax case, Johnston acknowledged, 'There are two HMRC situations. One has been ongoing and another one, which is noted in the accounts, has just arisen in the last couple of months. It's £2.8m... It relates to no more than two or three players and an issue ten or 11 years ago.'

Still the SFA refused to probe Rangers' eligibility for a European licence, and it wasn't until September 2017 that the governing body finally issued instructions to its compliance officer to investigate whether Rangers had lied over the club's application to play in Europe in 2011. By then, former finance director Donald McIntyre had admitted in court, during the Craig Whyte fraud trial in April 2017, that Rangers had 'no choice but to accept liability' for the wee tax case, after HMRC produced copies of the side-letters which the club had been using to guarantee supposedly discretionary payments to players, evidence which had been gained from the raid on Ibrox in 2007 in connection with the Stevens inquiry. It seems that with European income considered vital to Rangers' continuing existence, the club had tried to maintain during the licence application process that they were in discussions with HMRC about structuring the repayment, when in reality the revenue service had refused all offers to parley with the Ibrox club and were demanding repayment in full.

Despite the trauma of their European misadventures, the domestic season began positively for McCoist and at one point, over the first weekend in November, Rangers were 15 points clear of Celtic after a laborious start to the campaign by Lennon's side. The Parkhead men slowly reeled them in however, as Rangers began to drop points towards the end of the year, culminating in a 1-0 defeat at St Mirren on Christmas Eve, which reduced the gap at the top of the table to just a single point. Celtic then hit the front after a 1-0 win in the derby on 28 December and from there they never looked back, enjoying a run of 17 consecutive league victories to put themselves within touching distance of their first title since the dramatic Thursday-night finale at the end of the season in 2008.

The only blip came after a 3-2 defeat at Ibrox in March on a day when the championship could have been clinched, but revenge came the following month for Celtic with a 3-0 home victory over a Rangers side making what turned out to be a valedictory appearance in the famous fixture.

By then the Ibrox institution was heading for oblivion. Many experts feel that administration would have inevitably hit the club as early as October, but after McCoist's failure in the European qualifiers had deprived Rangers of the elixir of Champions League revenue, owner Craig Whyte took to using money which should have been collected as tax, through PAYE and VAT, as working capital to fund the club's day-to-day overheads. In the circumstances, such an egregious display of short-term thinking was always going to end in tears, as the club ran up yet another tax bill over the first half of the season, increasing the total liabilities to HMRC by a further £9m. Despite selling their best player, Nikica Jelavić, to Everton for £5m at the end of January, the striker whose goals had been instrumental in the club retaining the championship and who finished the year as the team's top scorer even after his mid-season departure, Rangers entered administration just two weeks later on 14 February 2012, 26 years to the day since David Holmes was named the club's CEO, ushering in the Souness revolution and a new era of spending at Ibrox.

Despite HMRC's successful petition to trigger the insolvency event, Whyte managed to persuade the Court of Session in Edinburgh to allow him to appoint his preferred administrators, the London-based firm Duff and Phelps, who had advised and assisted the owner with his takeover less than a year earlier. A statement on the company's website claimed that the financial services partnership were, 'renowned for saving businesses, reputations and livelihoods, even in the most difficult of situations'.

It sounded like exactly what the famous old institution in Govan needed, but anyone, seemingly, who had any connection with Rangers around this time was liable to have their reputation absolutely trashed through their association with the club and Duff and Phelps, or 'Duff and Duffer' as they became known during a chaotic period of trying to stave off liquidation, were no exception. Had HMRC been allowed to appoint their own firm, the administration of Rangers FC would in all likelihood have proceeded along very different lines, with the beleaguered Scottish game already well-acquainted with the normal practice of what happens during the bankruptcy process after similar events at clubs such as Dundee, Motherwell and Livingston. The customary procedure was for the insolvency practitioners to call a meeting with all employees, including the players, where the highest earners would invariably be informed of the unhappy news that their contracts were being ripped up in an effort to drastically reduce costs.

Yet almost unfathomably, immediately after entering administration, Paul Clark and David Whitehouse, Duff and Phelps's appointed joint administrators and the men who were supposedly now running the club, allowed Rangers to proceed with their attempt to bring in a new striker, the out-of-contract Gabon international Daniel Cousin, who had previously played at Ibrox under Walter Smith. Scottish football was almost as stunned by the attempted signing as it was by witnessing the country's most successful football club suffering the indignity of having to appoint administrators in the first place. Quite properly, the SPL refused to sanction the recruitment of Cousin, with the League's rules stating clearly that, barring exceptional circumstances, clubs in administration cannot sign players.

It all smacked of a failure to appreciate the reality of what was happening, particularly on the part of the manager McCoist, who was heralded by supporters for his use of the trite maxim 'We don't do walking away' to describe the reaction to the testing circumstances in which the club now found itself. Joint administrator Paul Clark was also sounding sanguine about the club's immediate prospects when he announced, 'We are wholly confident that Rangers will continue as a football club. We do not think that liquidation and the closure of the club is a likely outcome at all.'

In addition, administration had triggered an automatic ten-point deduction by the SPL, but despite the gap to Celtic being extended from four to 14 points, McCoist still seemed bullish about his team's prospects of making up the deficit and winning the league. Reality bit, however, after Rangers' first game under the administrators' regime, with a 1-0 home loss to Kilmarnock leaving them 17 points off the pace and all but out of contention. Finally, the focus at Ibrox shifted from the pursuit of Celtic to a new priority, namely seeing out the season. To this end, following exhaustive negotiations and with McCoist heavily influential behind the scenes, the Rangers players agreed to take a temporary, tiered wage cut of up to 75 per cent for the top earners, saving the club £1m per month, in the hope that further redundancies and failure to complete the season could be avoided. In exchange, the players insisted on minimum release clauses being inserted into their contracts, which would allow them to speak to other clubs and leave Rangers for discounted transfer fees, once they reverted to full salary at the end of May.

With Craig Whyte having fled the scene after the *Daily Record* finally turned on the former billionaire and exposed his takeover arrangement with Ticketus, the administrators' immediate priority was to try and find a new owner for the business, ideally in time to avert liquidation. Various consortia appeared and were named in the media, four of which were confirmed by Duff and Phelps, including the 'Blue Knights' group, a brazenly populist syndicate of ex-directors and prominent supporters whose credibility was hampered not only by their silly name, but also by their lack of funds.

In the absence of any other viable contenders, the American Bill Miller, a truck and tow magnate from Tennessee who had dreams of owning a sports club, was given 'preferred bidder' status by Clark and Whitehouse in early May. But Miller's plan involved the formation of a 'Newco', a new company which would allow Rangers to continue as a going concern but only after the existing institution, formed in 1872 and incorporated in 1899, had been set aside. Liquidation, and the subsequent loss of Rangers' heritage and history, was the biggest fear of everyone associated with the club, so Miller came up with an intriguing plan to try and save the day, which he attempted to explain in a lengthy written statement.

'In order to preserve the club's history, records, championships and assets,' Miller expounded, 'I will put the "heart" of the club into an "incubator" company [his quotation marks] while Duff and Phelps works to make the "sick patient" healthy through a CVA process that effectively works to "radiate" the toxicity of past administrations' sins out of the patient while the "healthy heart" is preserved and moves forward. Once the CVA process has been completed and the patient is on the mend, the administrators will return Rangers Football Club to me for a nominal sum. The healthy heart and the healthy patient (The Rangers Football Club plc) will then be reunited through merger. In this scenario, the club can continue with all of its business assets, including its history, protected from the present illness. Thus a new corporate entity will own the club's assets during the incubation period including all of its history. Any suggestion that Rangers' history is lost by such a process is preposterous.'

Rangers fans were seemingly unimpressed with all of this jargon, when they held up placards at Ibrox advising Miller to 'truck off' and bombarded the businessman with scores of abusive e-mails. After a short delay during which he claimed to have taken another look at the books, and with his plans for the club producing so much invective, Miller decided to make a tactical retreat and withdrew his offer to buy the club, with his spokesman, Jon Pritchitt, explaining to viewers of *Newsnight Scotland*, 'The hole is maybe a little deeper and the length of time is a little farther than originally expected.'

With Duff and Phelps confirming in April that the club's total liabilities could reach £134m, liquidation seemed unavoidable. The only alternative was a Company Voluntary Arrangement (CVA), referred to in Miller's statement, which would allow the business to continue in its present guise if creditors agreed to receive a percentage of what they were owed through a 'pence in the pound' deal. For this to happen 75 per cent of the creditors, by value, had to agree to the proposal, which meant that even with the 'big tax case' still pending, HMRC could unilaterally pull the plug on the idea of a CVA and force the club into liquidation.

Time was now the enemy for Rangers, with the club in danger of simply running out of cash, when Duff and Phelps announced on 13 May, the same day that the Ibrox men recorded a 4-0 victory over St Johnstone in the their final match of a troubled season, that a new, previously unrecognised consortium led by the Yorkshire businessman Charles Green had come forward and entered into a binding contract with the administrators to buy the club. It was already a done deal; Whyte had signed over his shares to Green's consortium in a lawyer's office in London for the sum of £1, prompting Green to announce at a Murray Park media conference that he had happily given Whyte another £1 from his own pocket, allowing the former owner to make a 100 per cent profit on his sale of the club. Green and Whyte had reached an agreement to save Rangers and it wasn't just Celtic fans who picked up on the colour-coded irony involved in the transaction.

Green, a former non-league footballer, had previously been chief executive of Sheffield United, the club he played for as a schoolboy, where he had been dogged by allegations of interference in team affairs. Always an unpopular figure with the club's supporters, particularly after the acrimonious departure of long-serving manager Dave Bassett in December 1995, Green was eventually forced out in 1998 by demonstrating fans after selling the South Yorkshire club's best players and provoking the resignation of boss Nigel Spackman.

On his arrival in Glasgow, fans of the Blades bombarded Rangers message boards, urging them not to have anything to do with Green, with one contributor noting, 'As if things couldn't get any worse [at Rangers], up pops Charles Green.' Not much else was known in Scotland about Green's business history, although *The Herald* informed its readers, 'Records held by Companies House reveal that nine of the companies Mr Green has been involved with in the past have been dissolved, while he has a track record of moving very quickly between posts, having resigned a total of 31 different appointments during his career.'

Green's bid vehicle for Rangers was the London-registered company Sevco 5088 Ltd, an operation which had only been formed at the end of March, with a search of business directories revealing only, 'This company has not yet filed a description of their activities.' Nevertheless, Green claimed to be the head of a 'global consortium' with the financial backing of up to 20 individuals and families from as far afield as Singapore and Mongolia, although he steadfastly refused to identify his partners until his CVA proposal was carried through.

Meanwhile, as soon as administration was triggered, the SFA launched an independent inquiry into whether Craig Whyte had been a 'fit and proper' person to own and operate Rangers. The subsequent report found that SFA rules had been breached by Whyte, by now the undisputed villain of the piece, over his failure to disclose his previous disqualification as a director and his decision, while in charge of Rangers, to withhold over £9m which had been deducted as PAYE and VAT, and using the taxman's money to cover the club's overheads. The club itself was also charged with 'bringing the game into disrepute' for becoming insolvent, and faced sanctions over the failure to pay Dundee United their share of the gate receipts from a recent cup tie at Ibrox, totalling £61,000.

As the case went forward to an SFA judicial panel to determine punishment, joint administrator David Whitehouse urged the SFA not to confuse Rangers, the institution, with the actions of the renegade Whyte. 'We look forward to stating the club's case to the judicial panel,' a statement from the administrators read. 'We believe there are mitigating factors and we hope to demonstrate the distinction between the club and the actions of any individuals.'

On 23 April the SFA panel rejected this defence on the grounds of corporate liability and imposed a 12-month transfer embargo and fines totalling £160,000 on Rangers in relation to the club's financial transgressions, including the appointment of Whyte as chairman, while the owner himself was banned for life from holding a position within Scottish football and fined a total of £200,000. Whyte, however, didn't give the impression that he was about to pay up, telling the SFA, 'Good luck collecting the money.'

Branding the decision of the tribunal 'a complete joke', the Rangers owner claimed, '[Chief executive] Stewart Regan and [president] Campbell Ogilvie had dinner with me in November and they told me it wouldn't be a problem. Now they're just reacting to all the publicity since February... They are playing to the media.' In the circumstances, it was perhaps unsurprising that Whyte had remained hopeful that there would be little, if any, interference from the SFA over his activities at Ibrox, as Campbell Ogilvie, now president of the governing body, was the same former Rangers director who had administered the EBT scheme at the club, and received a total of £95,000 from the Trust himself, although Regan defended his colleague's integrity over the issue, despite the apparent conflict of interests.

At the same time, a statement from Duff and Phelps in response to the verdict declared that they were 'utterly shocked and dismayed' at the 'draconian' punishment handed down to the club and, requesting 'an immediate, expedited appeals process over the sanctions', called for 'pragmatic and commercially sensible penalties' to be imposed instead. But McCoist went further, accusing the SFA of trying to kill off Rangers and targeting in particular the governing body's three-man judicial panel. 'I found out the decision last night and I was shocked and absolutely appalled by the way this supposedly independent judicial panel was coming down on us in this form,' the Rangers manager fumed on the club's in-house television channel. 'Who are these people? I want to know who these people are. I'm a Rangers supporter and the Rangers supporters and the Scottish public deserve to know who these people are, people who are working for the SFA. Make no mistake about it, this is an SFA decision. They have appointed the panel so therefore they are working for the SFA, but who are they? I think we have a right to know who is handing out this punishment to us, I really do. This decision could kill our football club, simple as that. Make no mistake about it.'

McCoist's ranting indignation seemed curious, because he knew fine well who the tribunal members were. Rangers' head of football administration, Andrew Dickson, had attended the hearing and sat across the room from the three-man board, so if McCoist was really concerned about SFA transparency and the names of the panel members, Dickson could easily have provided him with the information. It wouldn't be long before Strathclyde Police were investigating 'abusive and threatening communications' made against the trio, including Raith Rovers director Eric Drysdale, after their identities had been 'compromised' on the internet.

A defiant McCoist later emphasised that he had no regrets over his call for the SFA panel members, who had been randomly selected from a 'cab-rank' system of 100 or so names, to be publicly identified, despite his belated admission that he knew their names all along, and he claimed that the 'lunatic fringe' who had been responsible for the threats and intimidation against the board was not his concern. It was arguably the case that the sanctions imposed on the club may have had a discouraging effect on some of the more airy-fairy parties interested in acquiring Rangers, but it seemed that McCoist's real fear was that a Newco Rangers, hampered by a signing embargo and possibly playing out of the Scottish Football League's Third Division, might not be able to flex its muscles in the transfer market and deal with its opponents in the traditional manner.

The case inevitably went forward to a hastily convened appeal, where a new three-man judicial board, who were openly named, found that there were no grounds for reversing the original decision and ruled that the transfer embargo should be upheld. Suggesting that the potential impact on the club of the ban on new signings had been exaggerated, given that Rangers still had over 40 professional footballers on their books, the appellate panel noted, 'This sanction was proportionate to the breach, dissuasive to others and effective in the context of serious misconduct.'

In addition, the SFA published a 167-page document, which outlined the findings of the original panel, allowing the deliberations and the rationale of the tribunal to be made public. In consideration of Rangers' failure to withhold PAYE and VAT payments in the first half of the season, the three-man board felt that 'only match fixing in its various forms might be a more serious breach', and contemplated suspending or ending the Ibrox club's SFA membership. The reason stated for the imposition of a transfer embargo on Rangers was that 'the punishment should relate in some meaningful way to the unpaid taxes arising from high wages and salaries among certain players', while the panel also rejected the idea that Craig Whyte alone was at fault with regard to the non-payment, finding instead that 'directors and employees must have known that what was happening within Rangers FC was entirely wrong and illegitimate but they chose to do nothing to bring it to the attention of the public', a verdict which scuppered the notion that one individual alone was responsible for all of Rangers' crimes and misdemeanours.

Channel 4's Alex Thomson, one of the few English journalists to retain an interest in the Rangers saga, noted on his blog, 'That [verdict] strikes a blow to the heart of Rangers' notorious culture of passing the buck whilst winning glory with money it did not have and potentially millions which should have gone to the taxman... People knew it was happening and did nothing about it. All of which makes the simple and childish scapegoating of Craig Whyte wrong in principle, wrong in fact and wrong in law.'

The embargo was, however, later overturned at the Court of Session, as Rangers continued the appeals process through the legal system, before it was eventually accepted by the club as part of a compromise deal prior to the start of the new season, which allowed Newco Rangers to receive a licence to play football, after a transfer of membership from the liquidated club was approved by the governing bodies.

Charles Green's stated objective was for Rangers to exit administration via a CVA and to that end he offered the club's creditors a total of £8.5m, a fraction of the total £55.4m debt and considerably less than the £11.2m Bill Miller had put on the table. The alternative to accepting Green's CVA proposal, however, was liquidation, which, according to the Yorkshireman, would result in, 'the history, the tradition, everything that's great about this club [being] swept aside'. On 12 June, at a meeting of Rangers' creditors, Green's CVA offer was formally rejected, and the club founded in 1872 and incorporated in 1899 was consigned to liquidation.

HMRC had been offered roughly £1.9m of their established £14.4m liability, which consisted of the 'wee tax case', now with interest accruing standing at £4m, plus the withheld PAYE and VAT contributions, a total which marginally exceeded the 25 per cent threshold, confirming that with HMRC's rejection, the possibility of an agreement was precluded. Even just a few days before the vote, Green had remained optimistic, publicly at least, about his offer being accepted, when he stated, 'HMRC have had the documentation for over a week, so with each day that passes we have to assume that they are on board. It would be awful if they were to announce on the day that they were turning it down.'

All of this was wishful thinking; HMRC had given no encouragement to the idea that they would vote to accept a CVA, with their website making clear the official policy in such cases, 'We are likely to reject a voluntary arrangement where there is evidence of evasion of statutory liabilities.' There was simply no motivation on the part of HMRC to agree to a settlement which may have incentivised other companies, including other football clubs, to disregard their financial responsibilities and obligations in the hope that they might ultimately be able to barter with the agency to accept a few pence in the pound of what they were owed, once liquidation was looming.

Explaining their decision to reject Green's offer, HMRC announced, 'A liquidation provides the best opportunity to protect taxpayers, by allowing the potential investigation and pursuit of possible claims against those responsible for the company's financial affairs in recent years.' At the time of writing, the inquiry of the liquidating firm, Binder Dijker Otte (BDO), into what happened at Rangers in the years prior to insolvency, including the conduct of the club's directors, has yet to be published.

The club's other substantial creditor was the finance firm Ticketus, who were still owed £26.7m of £30.5m borrowed, after Whyte mortgaged a fourth year's worth of season ticket sales when he couldn't pay back the first instalment on the other three. There were also outstanding bills to other football clubs, including Celtic, Dunfermline and Dundee United, and further afield Arsenal, Chelsea and St Etienne, as well as Rapid Vienna, who were still due more than £1m over the purchase of Nikica Jelavić. The Scottish Ambulance Service, Strathclyde Police and Glasgow City Council were all owed tens of thousands of pounds, while others who lost out as the Rangers edifice crumbled included taxi firms and catering companies, as well as face painters and local garages.

In fact, a glance through the list of creditors confirmed the impression that Rangers owed money all over town: there were a total of 276 unsecured creditors, including Bhutta's Newsagents, Glasgow (£567.45); Joe Lennon Picture Framing, Bearsden (£840); Posh Deli, Glasgow (£260) and, intriguingly, given former chief executive Martin Bain's history of destroying evidence of the club's use of EBTs, Shred-It, Glasgow (£444).

Rangers had died, and the media buried them. 'Rangers Football Club Born 1872, Died 2012', lamented *The Herald* over its entire front page; the tabloid *Scottish Sun* carried a picture of a coffin, tastefully adorned with a Rangers wreath, being lowered into a grave; the *Daily Record*'s page one spread featured a photo of Tom Vallance's Gallant Pioneers, the Rangers team who had taken on Vale of Leven in the Scottish Cup Final of 1877, under the headline R.I.P. RFC, with the paper declaring, 'Rangers football club were plunged into liquidation yesterday by the taxman – bringing the curtain down on 140 years of history'; while the headline story in the *Glasgow Evening Times* focused on how short the creditors' meeting had lasted, '140 years of Rangers ends in eight minutes'.

Of course, there was still a viable football club in Govan, with a stadium and a state-of-the-art training facility, provided the punters could be persuaded to come out and support it, and following the decision to liquidate, the sale of Rangers' 'basket of assets' to Charles Green's Sevco Scotland consortium now proceeded as expected. Green complained about HMRC's decision to turn down his CVA offer, but he was playing to the gallery. In the end, HMRC spared Rangers by not contesting Green's stripped-down asset purchase, despite debts to the taxman which were now predicted to reach, depending on the verdict in the 'big tax case', an epic £75m. Precluding the possibility of selling off Ibrox and Murray Park, a statement from the revenue and customs service explained, 'The intention is not to wipe Rangers off the face of the map.'

Sevco 5088, now renamed Sevco Scotland Ltd, acquired the bones of Rangers for £5.5m, an amount which barely covered the administrators' fees. Green paid £1.5m for the 'heritable properties', namely Murray Park and Ibrox Park, which had been valued at £119m in 2005 when the club was trying to fight off insolvency by overstating the value of its assets. Half of the purchase price, a total of £2.75m, was for 'player registrations', which, given that the club would soon be liquidated and the players' contracts would be null and void, didn't augur well for those concerned about Green's competence.

The new owner insisted that all contracts held by Oldco Rangers had been automatically transferred to his Newco, but several high-earning squad members, including Allan McGregor, Kyle Lafferty and the three Stevens – Whittaker, Davis and Naismith – all disagreed and declined to join Green's new entity, citing their right to have their contracts cancelled under the Transfer of Undertakings (Protection of Employment), or TUPE, code of practice. TUPE regulations were designed to allow employees in such circumstances to join a new company on the same terms as they had previously enjoyed, but there was no obligation to do so. Refusing to accept that Green's club was the same Rangers and instead referring repeatedly to the new entity as 'Sevco', Naismith insisted, 'I am disappointed and angry that Rangers Football Club no longer exists in its original form... My loyalty is with Rangers, not with Sevco, who I don't know anything about,' while Whittaker concurred, 'We owe no loyalty to the new club. There is no history there for us.'

Green's company, which later changed its name from 'Sevco Scotland Ltd' to 'The Rangers Football Club Ltd', a subtle but important difference from the original 'The Rangers Football Club plc', eventually received a small fee from Southampton for the expedited transfer of Steven Davis, while the two Lees, Wallace and McCulloch, agreed to stay on, despite not yet knowing what division the new club would be playing in.

The initial proposal was for Green's Newco, despite the failure of the CVA, to be allowed to assume the liquidated club's position in the SPL through a transfer of membership, which would see a new 'Rangers' parachute directly into Scottish football's top flight ahead of the new season. The Ibrox institution had provided a valuable source of income for cash-strapped SPL clubs, who were used to benefitting from up to four home games per year against the Old Firm sides, fixtures which brought increased gate receipts, thanks to the Glasgow clubs' large travelling support, and broadcasting revenues, with the games against Celtic and Rangers regularly selected for live transmission by the television companies. With Rangers now gone, there was concern among many about further reduced circumstances in Scottish football and the potential impact of yet another financial blow to the national game, so the proposal to retain the Ibrox franchise within the top division was widely assumed to be a *fait accompli*.

However, before the vote, supporters of the other SPL clubs, who for months had been gaming out such a scenario on websites and on social media, began making clear their objection to the plan, with fans mobilised through a campaign to say 'No to Newco', and bombarding chairmen and directors with messages expressing their opposition, on the grounds of sporting integrity, to the idea of a liquidated Rangers being treated as a special case and permitted to play in the country's top division. A spokesman for Aberdeen FC confided to the BBC, 'The consequences of not voting no would be overwhelming from a supporters' perspective. There is now an avalanche in terms of fans' feelings here,' while Motherwell, whose supporters had gained an influence over the Lanarkshire club's board after their own painful administration in 2002, balloted their fans directly on the proposal, with 82 per cent of respondents opposed to the idea.

Suddenly, 'sporting integrity' became the new catchphrase of Scottish football, and with an 8-4 majority required for the motion to be accepted, the outcome was already known in advance, as one by one, almost every club in the division lined up to publicly state their voting intentions ahead of the meeting at Hampden on 4 July, with only Celtic choosing to keep their counsel on the matter. Faced with the prospect of isolating their own customers, the SPL clubs voted overwhelmingly to reject the application to transfer Rangers' SPL membership to Newco, by a margin of ten to one, with only Kilmarnock abstaining and Rangers voting in favour.

The eventual decision to deny Newco Rangers immediate access to the SPL offered a timely reminder of where the real power in football lay; not with the media, not with the moneymen or the directors of clubs, but with the fans themselves, so often the forgotten constituency in modern football, who in the end had reminded those running the game, in the face of much sneering commentary in the popular press, of the importance of fair competition and integrity in sport, over short-term financial considerations.

Almost inevitably, however, the vote to reject Newco's application to join the SPL only increased the pandemonium in the Scottish game caused by Rangers' disintegration. The immediate problem of where

Green's club would be playing next season had only been kicked into the long grass for a week, with the 30 clubs in the lower divisions of the Scottish Football League now finding themselves obliged, somewhat reluctantly in the case of many, to decide on the new club's immediate future. As Green and his people made a tactical withdrawal, SFA chief executive Stewart Regan, and his counterpart at the SPL, Neil Doncaster, went into bat for Newco, taking on the responsibility of persuading the lower-league clubs that a relaunched Rangers should be allowed to start out in the SFL's First Division, with either Dundee, who finished second behind promoted Ross County, or Dunfermline, the 12th-placed team in the SPL, taking the available place in the top flight for the start of the new season. Despite there being no precedent for a new club to be elected to the First Division, and no apparent mechanism within the existing rules for such an arrangement, Regan and Doncaster went to town on the lower-tier clubs, leaving them in no doubt about the consequences if they should ignore the executives' entreaties and consign Newco, still a vacuous entity of a football club with no SFA membership, to the relative wilderness of the Third Division.

On top of exaggerated warnings about 'Armageddon' and a 'slow lingering death' for Scottish football, threats were issued about invalidated sponsorship and television deals, which would reportedly see the total revenue of the SPL drop from £17m per annum to as low as £1.5m, with the trickle-down effect resulting in the likelihood of as many as ten of the smaller clubs in Scotland going out of business. Regan even suggested that there might be an outbreak of 'social unrest' if Rangers fans were left without a viable team to support, an odd argument which seemed to make the case for giving in to mob rule and public intimidation, rather than standing up against such forces in society.

In fact over at Ibrox, by contrast, there seemed to be an acceptance that Newco would be starting off the new season on the bottom rung of the Scottish game, with manager Ally McCoist telling the club's website, 'We have to rebuild, so SFL3 would give us a better chance to rebuild,' while even the fans seemed to be embracing the idea of Division Three, rather than offer the prospect of financial succour to the clubs which had rejected them. But the game's executives were insistent, with Doncaster maintaining publicly that SFL3 'would inflict massive damage on the whole of the game in Scotland and effectively punish 41 innocent clubs for the misdeeds of one', while Regan seemed to be suggesting that the ideal scenario was for Newco Rangers to spend only a year in SFL1 before being promoted, allowing a resumption of the status quo after an interval of only one season.

Doncaster's position was perhaps excusable, given his remit as a bottom-line moneyman employed by the SPL, whose clubs were clearly desperate for a hasty return of the Ibrox cash-cow, but Regan was head of the SFA, the organisation charged with safeguarding the whole of the Scottish game, and yet he had apparently expressed a preference, on financial grounds, for which club should win one of the country's four senior divisions and gain the only available promotion slot to the SPL. 'Notwithstanding the moral and ethical arguments,' Regan maintained, 'holistically the alternatives to [Newco] playing in any division other than the First will not help the game. The game cannot survive without it… It's fair to say that the broadcasters would live with a year, because it could be a fantastic story for them, which is why I think First Division rights will be an interest as people will want to see how this club is going to bounce back… If Rangers don't get promoted, then the game has got another year to suffer with the financial consequences that brings.'

Despite offering incentives to counterbalance the dire warnings of financial meltdown, such as play-offs, parachute payments and the purchase for £1m of Newco Rangers' television rights by the SPL, Regan and Doncaster had overplayed their hand and underestimated the resolve and anger of the SFL club chairmen, the majority of whom refused to submit to such tactics. The executives found that with their tough talk they had managed to isolate the very people they would come to depend on, with a statement from Clyde FC making the obvious point, 'A proposal to allow a newco to enter the First Division… is contrary to the rules of the SFL.' Instead the Cumbernauld club, who had faced their own financial difficulties in the 1980s when they were forced to leave their original Glasgow home of Shawfield Park, insisted that any changes to the rules and procedures should not come through 'threat or inducement'.

The game's administrators also had to get their plans past Raith Rovers chairman Turnbull Hutton, who was in no mood to forget how his club had been treated by Rangers as recently as April, when Stark's Park director Eric Drysdale, one of the volunteers who had served on the SFA's three-man judicial panel that dealt with the charges against Rangers over their insolvency, had his anonymity compromised by a ranting Ally McCoist. Hutton insisted, 'This is the same Rangers whose supporters threatened to torch our stadium and whose manager demanded one of our directors was named over his involvement with the SFA judicial panel. That resulted in TV cameras camping outside his door and threats being made by various outlandish factions. We also had [former Rangers player] Sandy Jardine publicly calling for repercussions for those clubs who have not supported Rangers. Given that, how could I be expected to roll over and have my tummy tickled by some inducement to allow Rangers to come into the First Division?'

Hutton also revealed some of the methods that were being used by the game's hierarchy in order to get their way for the re-formed Ibrox club, 'If we are at the stage of bending rules and accommodating, threatening or blackmailing, we want to give it up. There is a lot of pressure being applied on various people. There has been an abdication of duty from the SPL. Now the Scottish FA wade in and it's being punted to the SFL to let them try and sort it out. And, just to help the process along, why don't we blackmail and frighten them? It's bizarre.'

Enticed to elaborate on his position by a series of questions from reporters on the steps of Hampden before a preliminary meeting on 3 July, Hutton repeated his claim that the SFL clubs had been put in an impossible position and they were now being 'bullied, railroaded and lied to' by the SFA and the SPL.

This was fairly astonishing stuff, albeit refreshing in its honesty. Modern Scottish football had been modelled on an anglicised version of the game, where money was king, even if, as in the case of the game north of the border, money was the one thing which was in conspicuously short supply. In the end, however, Regan and Doncaster discovered that they were talking a different language from the owners and directors of the small, provincial, community clubs, who for the most part were more than willing to reject all the big-time talk of marketing and revenue, and instead firmly but politely point the administrators of the game in the direction of their own rules.

The result on 13 July saw 29 of the 30 clubs vote to grant Newco associate membership of the SFL, with 25 rejecting the appeal by Regan and Doncaster to admit Green's club directly into the First Division, and obliging the new Rangers to start again in Scottish football's fourth tier instead. The feelings of the SFL members had been made clear, with clubs from all across the country choosing to do the right thing and apply the rules rather than think only of the financial implications. Tiny Albion Rovers, for example, voted Newco into the Third Division, despite knowing that as a consequence they would miss out on two full houses against local rivals Airdrie United, who were now promoted to the First Division, with the Monklands club left instead to consider the prospect of gates of around 400 for their matches against Stranraer, who were moved up from the fourth tier.

Even Cowdenbeath chairman Donald Findlay voted against the Newco proposal, with the disgraced former Ibrox director expressing his disapproval of the methods used by the game's administrators in no uncertain terms. 'I won't forget the way they [Regan and Doncaster] have tried to bend me and this club to their will,' Findlay harrumphed. The result was announced by SFL chief executive David Longmuir in a statement which explained, 'The member clubs have voted willingly to accept Rangers into the SFL. The only acceptable position was to accept the Newco in Division Three from the start of 2012/13.'

The eventual outcome was, on the face of it, gracefully accepted by Green and McCoist, although the manager went on to accuse the league of pursuing 'as hostile an agenda as possible' towards Newco, and grudges over the summer's events would be harboured at Ibrox for many years to come, especially towards some of the SPL clubs, with particular *Schadenfreude* reserved for Dundee United's demise and relegation in 2016, when no less a figure than Walter Smith waded in to kick the club, which gave him his first opportunity in the game, when it was down.

A motion of no confidence in Stewart Regan was called by Livingston chairman Gordon McDougall and seconded by Cowdenbeath secretary Alex Anderson, after an e-mail leaked to Alex Thomson of *Channel 4 News* suggested that the SFA had been attempting to carve up a deal with Green's club behind the scenes, but SFL president Jim Ballantyne intervened and blocked the vote. Regan lasted a further five and a half years in his position as head of the SFA, eventually stepping down in 2018 in the wake of his failed attempt to recruit Michael O'Neill to the post of national team manager, while Neil Doncaster has since assumed the chief executive post at the amalgamated SPFL.

In the end there was no Armageddon for Scottish football, with clubs such as St Mirren, St Johnstone, Aberdeen, Inverness, Ross County and Hibernian all winning major trophies after the decision was taken to place Newco Rangers in the Third Division, and although Hearts and Dunfermline both subsequently suffered their own insolvency events, their issues and problems pre-dated the demise of Rangers and, in some ways at least, were arguably associated with the flawed policies and agendas of the stricken Ibrox club, whose downfall served as a salutary warning to others about the potentially catastrophic consequences for even the biggest football clubs of reckless overspending and chasing fairytales.

By contrast, while nobody was claiming that a golden era was dawning for Scottish football, the solidarity which had been demonstrated among fans, the disregard shown to the trumpeting of causes and the vested interests of the media and the game's moneymen, as well as the continuing popularity and passion for football across the community in Scotland, all offered hope for the future.

In the meantime, however, Charles Green was still struggling to get his new Ibrox entity up and running. The hapless owner was finding it difficult to win the confidence of the club's supporters, with estimates of only 250 season tickets being sold ahead of the new campaign, which was scheduled to start as early as 29 July with a Ramsdens Cup tie against Brechin City at Glebe Park. Almost as soon as his asset purchase was completed, Green was offered a quick profit on his acquisition when another consortium, led by former manager Walter Smith and sponsored by wealthy local businessmen Jim McColl and Douglas Park, came forward and offered the Yorkshireman £6m for the club, £500,000 more than he had just paid. Smith claimed that his group had originally made its offer to Duff and Phelps, but the '11th-hour bid', as it was dubbed by the press, came too late, with Green already assured of 'preferred bidder' status after entering into a binding agreement with the administrators.

Instead, with more of a 13th-hour bid, Smith now approached Green directly once the club's liquidation was confirmed. Claiming that the best way forward was for 'Rangers people who know the club inside and out to control its destiny', Smith and his consortium were backed by the Rangers Supporters' Trust, who issued a statement urging fans not to buy season tickets in an effort to force Green into agreeing to a quick sale. Smith's bid was hastily declined, however, but Green, aware of the former manager's standing among his putative customers, made a counteroffer to the legendary figure and tried to recruit him into his new venture, chiefly in a cheerleading capacity. Rejecting the job offer, and announcing the withdrawal of his bid after apparently receiving certain assurances from Green, Smith could only offer the new club the best of luck for the future. 'We wish the new Rangers football club every good fortune,' he stated.

Further doubts about Green's credibility and trustworthiness among the Ibrox clientele were alleged by former Ibrox defender John Brown, another 'real Rangers man' who claimed to have put together an international consortium of investors to buy Green out. Brown had been alarmed by Green's apparent unwillingness to provide proof of ownership, with the suggestion remaining that the new owner was still somehow involved with the disgraced Craig Whyte, an arrangement which, if true, seemed to preclude the possibility of an immediate sale. Demanding that Green 'show us the title deeds', Brown spoke before a large gathering of fans outside Ibrox. 'You come into my house and I'll show you the title deeds in my name. Now get tae... [gesture], this is my house. Why is Charles Green not coming out and just showing us that bit of paper?' Brown asked on the steps of Ibrox in front of supporters who hung effigies of former owners David Murray and Craig Whyte.

It all seemed very confusing for the club's beleaguered supporters, who had witnessed their team go from the Champions League to the Ramsdens Cup in the space of little more than a year. Bewildered by administration, liquidation, TUPE regulations, Green and Whyte, and the indignity of being shafted by Her Majesty, now fans were even unsure if they should come out and offer their support to the relaunched Ibrox entity. In the end, it was club legend and manager Ally McCoist who played a key role in getting the supporters back on board, despite their ongoing reservations about Green.

Ahead of their opening Third Division fixture against Peterhead at the Balmoor Stadium in Aberdeenshire, McCoist declared, 'I'm a firm believer that the most important relationship at a club is between manager and chief executive. We are in the very early days of ours but it is growing day by day and we each have a good appreciation of the other's situation within the club... Our fans deserve to see top-class players at

Ibrox and this is just the start of the rebuilding process. We have already added top quality to the squad – Ian Black, Fran Sandaza, Dean Shiels, Emilson Cribari and Kevin Kyle – and I can assure fans more players will follow before the transfer deadline. We need to add to the squad to prepare for the next two seasons in the SFL and season ticket money is a major source of income for the club.'

It worked, and tens of thousands of supporters came forward and bought season tickets ahead of the new campaign, with the deadline for 'renewals' extended following the manager's call to arms. The only outstanding issue was the club's membership of the SFA, which still had not been settled in the days leading up to Newco's opening fixture of the season against Brechin City at the end of July, a match scheduled for live transmission on BBC Alba. Charles Green had paid a nominal £1 for Rangers' membership of the SFA as part of his asset purchase, but with the Ibrox club heading for liquidation a transfer of membership to the Newco had yet to be approved by the governing body. The stumbling block appeared to be the sanctions which were hanging over the stricken club, imposed by the SFA's independent judicial panel in April, most of which Green and McCoist were still belligerently contesting.

The SFA had the power to insist on the penalties against Rangers being applied to Newco under clause 14.1 of the governing body's Articles of Association, which stated, 'Transfer of membership will be reviewed by the Board, which will have the complete discretion to reject or to grant such application on such terms and conditions as the Board may think fit.' The matter was only resolved at the last minute by the now infamous 'five-way agreement' between the three regulatory bodies, the SFA, the SPL and the SFL, as well as the two Rangers clubs, 'Oldco', consigned to liquidation and represented by Duff and Phelps, and Green's 'Newco', still at this point officially known as Sevco Scotland Limited. According to the secretive agreement, which has never been fully published, in return for the transfer of SFA membership, Newco agreed to pay the football debts of the old Rangers, including the £160,000 fine for bringing the game into disrepute, and to accept the transfer embargo which had been imposed by the judicial panel but sent back to the SFA by the Court of Session in Edinburgh.

Prior to the eventual agreement, McCoist had continued to complain about the transfer embargo, stating, 'It is important to remember we have already had a ten-point deduction from the SPL, lost our Champions League place for finishing second last season, had a £160,000 fine, been refused entry to the SPL, been relegated to Division Three and lost the majority of our first team squad – yet still the governing body has chosen to impose further sanctions.'

The manager, however, seemed to be confusing punishments, imposed by external bodies, with the mere consequences of the club's own actions; of the list of sanctions mentioned, only the paltry £160,000 fine was a genuine punishment for Rangers' transgressions, the rest simply constituted what followed under the normal course of events as a result of the club's erroneous behaviour. Like the convicted fraudster pleading for clemency after being caught embezzling from the firm – 'I've lost my job and my wife's left me, so please don't send me to jail' – McCoist's disingenuous appeals cut little ice and the transfer embargo was eventually accepted by the club, although not with immediate effect.

The ban would not be applied until 1 September, allowing the manager to stockpile players for the challenges of the Third Division before the transfer window closed. Green had also been insisting that the SPL should drop its inquiry into the club's use of side-letters and undisclosed payments in the implementation of the controversial EBT scheme between 1998 and 2010, after an initial investigation by the league's solicitors, Harper Macleod, found 'prima facie' evidence of a case to answer against the Ibrox club. The logical conclusion of a decision going against Rangers and the club being found guilty of fielding improperly registered players in over 700 matches would have seen results being overturned on an unprecedented scale and the numerous trophies amassed over the relevant period being declared void and stricken from the records.

McCoist had already stated defiantly that he would 'never accept' the club being stripped of titles it had won during the EBT years, but with time running out before the start of the season, Newco were not in a strong position, and the inquiry chaired by Lord Nimmo Smith went ahead, but with a restricted remit. With the five-way agreement signed by all the respective parties, a transfer of membership between Rangers FC (In Administration) and Sevco Scotland Ltd was approved, although as Rangers were still officially an SPL club at the time, an unprecedented 'conditional membership', for which there was no proviso in the SFA's

Articles of Association, had to be granted in order that the Ramsdens Cup tie at Brechin could go ahead on time, a contrivance which failed to weaken the perception that the game's administrators were making things up as they went along.

When full membership was confirmed the following week, the final encumbrance to Newco's participation in officially organised league and cup matches was removed; the good ship Sevco was about to set sail. And it would prove to be an eventful journey, with the response of the supporters producing world record attendances at Ibrox for a fourth-tier club, as fans also enjoyed following the team to some of the more remote and overlooked outposts of the Scottish game, a testament to Glasgow footballing passions and confounding those who assumed that few people would come out and support a disgraced institution playing out of the Third Division; players were brought in on extortionate wages, including Brazilians, Spaniards and Scotland internationals, provoking all the old clichés about sledgehammers and cracking nuts, and leaving many people wondering where all the money was coming from; there was a share issue in December 2012 which raised an estimated £22m, but the out-of-control club burnt through the cash at such a rate that by February 2014 the new Rangers entity was running out of funds once more and had to be bailed out by loans from Laxey Partners, an Isle of Man-based hedge fund and the club's biggest single shareholder, and director Sandy Easdale, who between them put up £1.5m to see the club through to the end of the season.

Meanwhile, suggestions remained that Charles Green was still in cahoots with fall guy Craig Whyte, with Green's defence against the accusation, after Whyte revealed taped conversations of the pair discussing their takeover strategy, seeming to suggest that the Yorkshireman had, instead of colluding with Whyte by agreeing to be his frontman, tricked the former owner and obtained the sole ownership of Sevco from him by deception. The SFA immediately wrote to Green seeking clarification and answers, but instead of proceeding with an investigation into whether the banned Whyte was still involved with Newco Rangers, the governing body allowed the Ibrox club to commission their own inquiry into the matter instead.

To the astonishment of no one, the investigation, led by legal firm Pinsent Masons, refuted the idea of a close link with Whyte, but Green was eventually hounded out of town and details of the report were not published. The problems and the turmoil at the phoenix club were perhaps best illustrated when McCoist announced over the summer of 2013 that he was delighted with the permanent appointment of CEO Craig Mather, who had replaced the hastily departed Green on an interim basis in April. 'I'm on the same wavelength as Craig. We can go for a beer and he likes a bit of Bruce Springsteen, just like me,' the manager confided. 'I've been working with Craig over players and pre-season and him and I are getting on really, really well,' McCoist claimed, in a rare instance of a manager giving the chief executive his vote of confidence.

Gradually, however, over the next few years, the internecine squabbling at Ibrox swelled to reach epic proportions. Matters came to a head at an Extraordinary General Meeting in March 2015 when a group of 'requisitioners', led by former Oldco directors Dave King and Paul Murray, finally gained control of the club and ousted members of the sitting board including James Easdale and chairman David Sommers as well as chief executive Derek Llambias, a business associate of the Sports Direct magnate Mike Ashley, who had bought shares in the club following Green's acquisition and whose loans were now helping to keep the struggling company afloat.

What stood out for many was the tax-fiddling past of some of those involved in the squabble over the Ibrox brand, leading Alex Thomson of *Channel 4 News* to observe that Rangers were 'probably the most tax-toxic sporting institution in Britain'; football board chairman Sandy Easdale, brother of ousted director James, had been jailed in the 1990s for VAT fraud, while King, their intended usurper, had accrued a remarkable 41 criminal convictions in South Africa relating to income tax breaches and been branded a 'glib and shameless liar' and a 'mendacious witness whose evidence should not be accepted on any issue' by a judge in that country. Such was King's toxicity that, following his coup, no bank would lend money or offer overdraft facilities to the Ibrox entity and the club's nominated advisor, or NOMAD, WH Ireland, the firm which ran their listing on the stock exchange, resigned, causing shares in the company to be suspended and ultimately delisted, after King was subsequently unable to secure a replacement. To anyone who was familiar with this story, however, it came as no surprise when King found himself free to assume the chairmanship of Newco after the SFA ruled that he was a 'fit and proper person' to take charge of the club.

By this time, a very strange thing seemed to have happened with regards to the new Ibrox entity; certain media outlets, who had confirmed the demise and death of Rangers, and all its history, when the club was consigned to liquidation, now instead started talking in mysterious terms of 'a traumatic summer for the club' following the events of June and July 2012, while others began referring retrospectively to 'some initial confusion' at the time over the universal response to HMRC's decision to vote down Charles Green's CVA offer. Everyone had naturally assumed that bankruptcy and liquidation spelled the end of the club which had dominated Scottish football for 140 years, but Newco Rangers, on their website and elsewhere, had always maintained that they were still the same club. For the most part, this was largely seen as defiance and an attempt to sell season tickets, but it now seemed that the Ibrox club really had risen from the grave, and liquidation, the terminal end which had to be avoided at all costs, was now viewed as merely something that had happened to somebody else.

It was the company, Scottish football was latterly informed, namely The Rangers Football Club plc, Company Number SC004276 and incorporated in May 1899, which had died, while the ethereal 'club', along with all its history and heritage, had in fact survived the insolvency process and been bought up by Green as part of his acquisition. References to Green's purchase of the 'business and assets' of Rangers were amended to the 'business, history and assets' and anyone who suggested otherwise, or used references to Rangers being a 'new club' or a 'relaunched club' would face public intimidation and be flooded with abusive communications.

Nobody in their right mind was claiming that the Ibrox supporters shouldn't continue to follow the new entity as if it were the old Rangers, and carry the club with them in their hearts, but that was not what was happening, with everyone from Rangers fans and directors to the media who had buried the club, to SPL chief executive Neil Doncaster now claiming that the old and the new Rangers were legally one and the same thing, and woe betide anyone who should suggest otherwise. It wasn't long before the 'same club' contention became the almost universally accepted position in Scottish football, except among fans of other clubs, needless to say, who, despite being the only group not to have performed an Orwellian volte-face on the issue, were once again marginalised and denigrated for alleged narrow-mindedness by the more powerful mainstream narrative.

'Rangers' seemed to be having their cake and eating it, keeping the parts of the old club which they liked, such as its history and honours, but conveniently shedding its debts and responsibilities, including any potential sanctions as a result of the SPL inquiry into the alleged use of undisclosed payments to players at Ibrox, as Ewan Murray observed in *The Guardian*, 'The Rangers public relations stance is that the club remain the same as ever, history intact, despite the fresh corporate identity created by liquidation. It would be an obvious stance were it not contradicted by insistence from within Ibrox that the club should not be retrospectively punished if found guilty of illegally registering players during use of the now infamous employee benefit trust scheme.'

And what of the said infamous, tax-dodging scheme? To general astonishment, not least among those associated with Rangers, the First Tier Tribunal returned a verdict which found in the Ibrox club's favour, by a margin of two to one, in November 2012. HMRC immediately launched an appeal against the decision that the EBTs were for the most part used lawfully by the Ibrox club, sparking off another legal merry-go-round in the various courts and producing a delay which benefited Rangers in the long run in two important ways: firstly, it allowed the SPL inquiry into the matter of undisclosed payments to players, chaired by Lord William Nimmo Smith, to proceed on the basis that the EBTs were perfectly legal. The inquiry subsequently found that the use of EBTs conferred no sporting advantage on Rangers, presumably because such a perfectly lawful scheme was open to every other club, if only they'd had the gumption to use it, and the dreaded 'title-stripping' of trophies won between 2001 and 2010 did not take place.

Nimmo Smith's findings hung on the evidence of Sandy Bryson, the SFA's head of registrations, who maintained in his submission to the inquiry that a player's registration is valid once it is logged with the governing body, and remains so for the duration of his contract, regardless of whether there are subsequent breaches of the rules, such as failure to disclose the player's full salary. Rangers, it seemed, had escaped title-stripping on a technicality, but in other regards Nimmo Smith was scathing of the club's conduct during the period in question, particularly over its persistent reluctance to disclose information and to co-operate with the regulatory bodies.

This did not seem to matter, however, because the humiliating prospect of seeing trophies struck from the record books had been avoided, much to Green's elation. The Newco owner appeared on Sky Sports News, once the judge had published his report in February 2013, talking of Rangers' 'innocence', despite Nimmo Smith imposing a £250,000 fine on the liquidated club, while former chairman Sir David Murray, under whose ownership the scheme had been introduced, was equally relieved. 'The imposition of an irrecoverable fine on an entity which is now in liquidation is futile… It is saddening that so much time, effort and money has been expended in pursuing a retrospective witch hunt against an entity in crisis,' Murray crowed.

Secondly, the length of time taken by the judicial process to eventually reach a final, binding verdict on Rangers' use of EBTs allowed enough of an interval to pass for the regulatory bodies to attempt to put the whole matter behind them. The SPL and the SFL were no longer in existence, having been amalgamated into the Scottish Professional Football League (SPFL) by the time of the verdict from the Supreme Court in July 2017, which upheld an earlier decision to overturn the original judgment and ruled in HMRC's favour.

In the light of the new evidence, now confirmed some seven years after the case became public, that Rangers had effectively cheated both Scottish football and the British taxpayer for ten years or more, the league's senior counsel, Gerry Moynihan QC, nevertheless advised the SPFL that it had 'no power in law' to revisit the Nimmo Smith commission and in particular the finding that Rangers 'did not gain any unfair competitive advantage' during the EBT years. Instead, SPFL chairman Ralph Topping proposed an independent review into 'Scottish football's actions and processes' over the affair and invited the SFA to agree terms of reference for such a review. But to the astonishment of no one, the governing body issued a statement declaring that the image of the game in Scotland would only be damaged further by 'raking over the coals' of the whole Rangers fiasco and declined the offer to participate in the review, claiming that it would serve no meaningful purpose, with former SFA vice-president Rod Petrie and others urging people to 'move on' from the whole debacle. It is perhaps not surprising, for those involved in Scottish football at least, that when Shakespeare's Hamlet spoke of 'the law's delay' in his famous 'to be or not to be' soliloquy, he was contemplating suicide at the time.

Nevertheless, Rangers' disgrace was ultimately confirmed by the verdict of the Supreme Court in London, meaning that everything achieved by the club over the relevant period would be tainted by the industrial scale use of an illegitimate tax avoidance scheme, which, in a wage meritocracy such as professional football, gave Rangers a clear and obvious competitive advantage over opponents who were meeting their obligations to the tax authorities in full and registering their players in accordance with the SFA's Articles of Association.

The Ibrox club won five league titles this century, by an aggregate total of just 12 points, with four of those triumphs not settled until the final day of the season. Rivals Celtic, meanwhile, lifted the championship trophy seven times over the same period, winning by huge margins on most occasions, so there was no doubt which club was dominating and what the EBTs, and the subsequent advantages conferred by small margins, allowed Rangers to achieve in those tight seasons. Celtic were cheated the most; they were involved in a direct, head-to-head rivalry and they lost leagues by the narrowest of margins, and cup finals and semi-finals to last-minute goals and extra-time winners scored by the Ibrox club.

It was by no means just they who lost out though; it could certainly be argued that the real victims of Rangers' malpractices were the smaller, provincial clubs, the ones who were working within their means, once administration had cleared out most of the chancers, and often trying to meekly live off slices from the Old Firm's banquet. Week in, week out and in very much straitened circumstances, these teams were facing a financially doped monster, which was not playing by the same rules as everyone else, and particular sympathy must go to those sides who lost to Rangers in cup finals – the Queen of the Souths and Ayr Uniteds of this world – who were denied a once-in-a-generation or a once-in-a-lifetime opportunity for sporting glory and missed out on adding a special bit of history to their often lean existences.

'Rangers' eventually made their way through the lower leagues, but failed to gain promotion from the second-tier Scottish Championship at the first attempt, beaten to the title by Hearts' team of talented youngsters before being crushed 6-1 on aggregate by Motherwell in a Premiership play-off.

The recast club had spent not three but four years out of the top flight and still 'Armageddon' failed to materialise for Scottish football. In fact, despite everything, and notwithstanding the appalling lack of finance which continues to hinder the game's progress at club level, Scottish football remains in a remarkably vibrant condition, all things considered, with the evident affinity and widespread support which still exists for the game of football in Scotland seemingly undiminished by the off-field trauma which has often been inflicted upon it down the years.

The future for Scottish football remains bright, it seems, but that, assuredly, is no thanks to Rangers.

SELECTED
BIBLIOGRAPHY

Barclay, Patrick – *Football - Bloody Hell!: The Biography of Alex Ferguson* Yellow Jersey, London, 2010

Burns, Scott – *Walter Smith, The Ibrox Gaffer, A Tribute to a Rangers Legend* Black and White, Edinburgh, 2011

Butcher, Terry – *Butcher, My Autobiography* Highdown, Newbury, 2005

Campbell, Tom – *Celtic's Paranoia, All in the Mind?* Fort, Ayr, 2012 (revised edition)

Campbell, Tom (ed.) – *Ten Days That Shook Celtic* Fort, Ayr, 2005

Campbell, Tom and Woods, Pat – *Dreams and Songs to Sing, A New History of Celtic* Mainstream, Edinburgh, 1996

Collier, Paul and Taylor, Donald S. – *Stairway 13, The Story of the 1971 Ibrox Disaster* Bluecoat Press, Liverpool, 2007

Crick, Michael – *The Boss, The Many Sides of Alex Ferguson* Pocket Books, London, 2003 (revised edition)

Devine, Tom (ed.) – *Scotland's Shame? Bigotry and Sectarianism in Modern Scotland* Mainstream, Edinburgh, 2000

Duff, Iain – *Temple of Dreams, The Changing Face of Ibrox* Breedon Books, Derby, 2008

Drysdale, Neil – *SilverSmith, The Biography of Walter Smith* Birlinn, Edinburgh, 2011 (revised edition)

Esplin, Ronnie (ed.) – *Ten Days That Shook Rangers* Fort, Ayr, 2005

Esplin, Ronnie and Anderson, Alex – *The Advocaat Years* Argyll Publishing, Glendaruel, 2004

Esplin, Ronnie and Walker, Graham – *The Official Biography of Rangers* Hachette Scotland, Glasgow, 2011

Ferguson, Alex – *Managing My Life, My Autobiography* Hodder & Stoughton, London, 2009

Ferguson, Barry (with Iain King) – *Blue; The Life and Times of Barry Ferguson* Mainstream, Edinburgh, 2006

Ferrier, Bob and McElroy, Robert – *Rangers: The Complete Record* Breedon Books, Derby, 2005

Flint, John & Kelly, John (eds.) – *Bigotry, Football and Scotland* Edinburgh University Press, Edinburgh, 2013

Gallagher, Tom – *Glasgow, The Uneasy Peace* Manchester University Press, Manchester, 1987

Gordon, Alex – *Celtic: The Awakening* Mainstream, Edinburgh, 2013

Gordon, Alex – *Jinx Dogs Burns Now Flu* Ringwood, Glasgow, 2015

Grant, Michael and Robertson, Rob – *The Management, Scotland's Great Football Bosses* Birlinn, Edinburgh, 2010

Greig, John (with Jim Black) – *My Story* Headline, London, 2005

Halliday, Stephen – *Rangers, The Waddell Years 1938–1984* André Deutsch, London, 1999

Herron, Lindsay – *The Official Rangers Hall of Fame* Hachette Scotland, Glasgow, 2009

Holmes, Jeff – *Blue Thunder, The Jock Wallace Story* Pitch, Worthing, 2014

Holmes, Jeff – *1986: Rangers Revolution: The Year Which Changed the Club Forever* Pitch, Worthing, 2016

Jamieson, Sandy – *Graeme Souness, The Rangers Revolution and the Legacy of the Iron Lady's Man* Mainstream, Edinburgh, 1997

Kelly, Stephen F. – *Graeme Souness, A Soccer Revolutionary* Headline, London, 1994

Leggat, David – *Great Scot: The James Scotland Symon Story* Black and White, Edinburgh, 2012

Leggat, David – *Struth: Story of an Ibrox Legend* Black and White, Edinburgh, 2013

Leggat, David – *Big Jock, The Real Jock Wallace* Black and White, Edinburgh, 2014

McElroy, Robert – *The Enduring Dream, 50 Years of Rangers in Europe* Stadia, Stroud, 2007

Mac Giolla Bháin, Phil – *Downfall: How Rangers FC Self-destructed* Frontline Noir, Edinburgh, 2012

McMinn, Ted (with Robin Hutchison) – *The Tin Man, The Ted McMinn Story* Black and White, Edinburgh, 2008

Macpherson, Archie – *Flower of Scotland? A Scottish Football Odyssey* Highdown, Newbury, 2005

Mason, David – *Rangers: The Managers* Mainstream, Edinburgh, 2000

Mason, David and Stewart, Ian – *Mr Struth, The Boss* Headline, London, 2013

Miller, Tom – *Slim Jim, Simply the Best* Black and White, Edinburgh, 2014

Murray, Bill – *The Old Firm: Sectarianism, Sport and Society in Scotland* John Donald, Edinburgh, 2000 (revised edition)

Murray, Bill – *Glasgow's Giants, 100 Years of the Old Firm* Mainstream, Edinburgh, 1988

Potter, David – *Walk On: Celtic since McCann* Fort, Ayr, 2003

Ralston, Gary – *The Gallant Pioneers, Rangers 1872* Breedon Books, Derby, 2010

Romanos, Joseph – *Great Sporting Rivals* Hurricane Press, Cambridge NZ, 2012

Smith, Paul – *To Barcelona and Beyond, The Men who Lived Rangers' European Dream* Birlinn, Edinburgh, 2011

Smith, Paul – *For Richer, For Poorer. Rangers: The Fight for Survival* Mainstream, Edinburgh, 2012

Soar, Phil and Tyler, Martin – *The Illustrated Encyclopaedia of British Football* Marshall Cavendish, London, 1977 and 1989

Souness, Graeme (with Mike Ellis) – *Souness, The Management Years* André Deutsch, London, 1999

Spiers, Graham – *Paul Le Guen: Enigma; A Chronicle of Trauma and Turmoil at Rangers* Mainstream, Edinburgh, 2007

Tempany, Adrian – *And the Sun Shines Now, How Hillsborough and the Premier League Changed Britain* Faber and Faber, London, 2016

Walker, Graham and Gallagher, Tom (eds.) – *Sermons and Battle Hymns: Protestant Popular Culture in Modern Scotland* Edinburgh University Press, Edinburgh, 1991

Weir, David – *Extra Time, My Autobiography* Hodder and Stoughton, London, 2011

Young, Chick – *Rebirth of the Blues, The Story of a Rangers Revolution* Mainstream, Edinburgh, 1987